Personality and Temperament

Personality
and
Temperament

SOLOMON DIAMOND

Professor of Psychology, Los Angeles State College

HARPER & BROTHERS, PUBLISHERS, NEW YORK

Contents

v

Contents

Foreword

As I have worked on the manuscript of this book, I have thought many times of my debt to three fine teachers of psychology. Lawrence E. Cole awakened an enthusiasm for behavioral research which gave the first purpose to my intellectual development. Presley D. Stout inspired in all his students a deep respect for thorough scholarship and scrupulous honesty in criticism. Gardner Murphy exemplified the possibility of a fructifying synthesis of scientific method and warm humanism. I hope that I have sometimes been able to transmit a part of their inspiration to my own students.

Among my students, I am in debt especially to those who have patiently endured the dittoed notes which preceded the finished manuscript, and who often revealed to me, in lively discussions, shortcomings which I hope I have overcome.

What I owe to countless authors and their publishers is mostly evident in the following pages. Because its help is not evident, I wish here to express my appreciation for the courtesies extended by a friendly neighbor, the Library of the University of Southern California.

S. D.

April, 1957

Personality and Temperament

CHAPTER 1

On Purpose and Method

*T*he problem of personality presents itself to us in the evident fact that to different men, in the same situation, different modes of response appear natural and even inevitable. Where one man runs, another will fight; where one finds lively enjoyment, another grows drowsy with boredom. Even casual experience teaches us that from the observation of how a given person responds in one situation, we may be able to infer something about how he will probably respond in another situation. To explore such consistencies, and to uncover their determinants, is the study of personality.

Our initial interest in this study is quite spontaneous. The intent stare which every normal infant turns upon the faces that move about him show how deep are the roots for the fascination which, as adults, we continue to feel in coming closer to an understanding of why people act in the ways they do. As children and as adults, we continue our lifelong study of personality, and most of us believe that we have become pretty good "practical psychologists," competent at least to recognize a friendly disposition or an angry one, a man to be trusted or one to be watched with suspicion. Most of us also enjoy an esthetic satisfaction in the observation of our fellow men, and we have probably learned to deepen this by sharing the sharper

insights of great writers. Allport's (1950) advice to students of
psychology, to study the writings of the masters of the novel
and the drama, reminds us that a great deal may be learned
by intelligent and sensitive observation even when it lacks the
controls of science.

However, as we read the works of those masters—the great
Menschenkenner or true seers of personality, like Tolstoy or
Shakespeare—we also become aware that we are interested in
personality as self-actualization, and that we often evaluate it
by some philosophic, ethical, or esthetic standard of "the
good life." Each of us imputes to human behavior, and seeks
in the panorama of human individuation, meanings beyond
those of survival and gratification. We are prone, therefore,
when we wish to describe people or to explain their behavior,
to think in terms of those aspects of cultural living which give
personality its richest meanings, and to neglect the relatively
simple beginnings of individual differences. As a result, we are
often in danger of confusing effects and causes, explaining the
child in terms of the man. The need for scientific method in the
study of personality is largely to avoid errors of this kind. Let
us illustrate. In Wilder's beautiful novelette, *The Bridge of San
Luis Rey,* an accident snuffs out the lives of a group of trav-
elers who, quite by chance, were crossing the bridge at the same
time. Reading on, we learn that at this moment each life was
at such a point of completion that a continuance of living would
have been without meaning. We allow ourselves to be captured for the nonce by the author's doctrine of fatalism, and
do not concern ourselves with the necessary physical reasons for
the collapse of a bridge. In the work of art, the "meaning" of life
is reason enough. In the same way, we may uncritically look
for the moving principles of our lives in the things which, in
our refined and civilized judgment, give life its meaning: the
appreciation of beauty, the scientific achievements of intellect,
the virtues of courage and generosity, or whatever we may
personally regard as the crowning achievements of human

personality. A psychology of personality which did not help us to achieve a better understanding of these things would indeed be an empty discipline, but to focus our attention upon them at the outset might lead us to underrate the importance of more primitive influences upon our behavior. Perhaps the great difference between the psychology which we meet in literature and the psychology which presents itself as science is the patient, rigorous procedure by which the scientist tries to defend himself from the ever-present danger of self-deception.

To guard against such self-deception, we shall take certain precautions, which must now be explained. It is no part of the purpose of this book to discourse on scientific method, or even to present in detail the specific methods that have been found useful in the study of personality. (These methods will be described only as need arises, when we have specific interest in their products.) From the outset, however, we shall try to make our study scientific in the sense that we shall fit it into the framework of the general study of behavior. In this way we hope to gain a solid foundation of fact before we enter, as finally we must, into the construction of hypotheses concerning matters which are as yet imperfectly understood. Everyone will agree that it is reasonable to give fact priority over fancy, but not everyone will agree with the method we have chosen to achieve this. We must anticipate that many readers will be not only surprised but annoyed at the prominence which is given in the early chapters of this book to the experimental study of temperament in animals. We must take a few paragraphs, therefore, to justify our use of the comparative approach to a study of human personality.

A crucial problem in the study of personality is to determine what are the most fundamental respects in which individuals differ from each other. All attempts to do this on the basis of observation of adult human behavior, no matter how sophisticated in either a statistical or a clinical sense, have the common failing that they are unable to distinguish between the essential foundations of individuality and its cultural elaborations. Developmental methods, which give a longitudinal account of behavior starting with infancy and early childhood, do not escape this difficulty, for they can offer no sure criterion of distinction between the early effects of cultural influences and the gradual appearance of behavioral elements which are as much a part of growth as, for example, beards and baldness, neither of which appears until relatively late in life. It is of great advantage, therefore, to be able to study the temperamental foundations of personality as they appear in the culture-free behavior of animals.

The human being, whatever else he may be, is first of all an animal, and must be understood as such. We must all agree with Freud's observation (**1932, 1950 b**)[1] that there are some things which are "true of the whole animal kingdom, from which men have no business to exclude themselves." Human behavior is the expression of a physical organism which is basically similar to that of other mammals. It is true that there are certain very important respects in which our bodies differ from those of our animal cousins and forebears, in ways that make new forms of behavior possible. A better hand, better vocal organs, and above all a better brain, constitute the foundations for human culture, within which personality flourishes. Nevertheless, we must recognize that much of human individuality rests upon foundations of temperament and emotion which we share with other mammals, and which can be more readily discerned in them. Furthermore, many individual characteristics of the behavior of persons result from factors of experience which operate upon us in just the same way that they operate upon other animals, producing modifications of temperament in them just as in us. It is good to have an understanding of these elementary dimensions and processes before proceeding to any discussion of the

---

[1] Boldface numerals indicate the date of a publication that is not listed among the references, or one that is listed in a translation of much later date.

more complex phenomena of human personality. If we are to attain a scientific, as distinguished from an empathic, understanding of personality, we must adopt that same rule which Morgan (1901) first stated for animal psychology: that nothing shall be explained as the outcome of a higher mental process, which can be understood as the outcome of a lower process. Hence, nothing may be attributed to specifically human qualities, which can be found in the behavior of animals. Along these lines, it will be a thesis of this book that the most useful system of basic categories for the description of behavior is one which applies equally to all forms of mammaliam life. They all exhibit the primitive manifestations of fear, rage, and love, and it is these dispositions which give rise to focal problems with which each person must deal in his progress toward maturity.

We hope that no reader will see in this argument an attempt to equate human and animal behavior, or to belittle the role of culture in shaping personality. Admittedly, human behavior is qualitatively different from animal behavior. When we say this, we mean that an adequate description of human behavior must make use of terms which are unnecessary for the description of animal behavior, and which would usually be meaningless and irrelevant if applied to animals. Each new "quality" of description is in fact a new dimension of measurement. The operational meaning of the statement that human behavior is "qualitatively more complex" than animal behavior is that new dimensions for measurement have appeared, which did not exist in animal behavior. However, there is no dimension which is relevant to the description of animal behavior which does not continue to be relevant to the description of human behavior, since all such dimensions have their basis in physiological characteristics which men and animals have in common. Therefore, wherever our study may lead us, its proper beginning is an appreciation of the biological foundations of behavior.

As a consequence of this viewpoint, constitutional influences on behavior will be given somewhat greater recognition in this book than is generally the case in contemporary discussions of personality theory. This will be done in the conviction that *we shall thereby be better able to understand the effects of environment*. It is not our intention to argue that hereditary influences are "more important" than environmental influences. Indeed, it seems clear enough that if one were forced to make a choice between a purely genetic and a purely environmentalist approach, in the effort to understand the kinds of differences among persons that engage our interest, it is the latter that would be much the more fruitful. Fortunately, there is no such compulsion. We are permitted to study constitution and environment in their interaction, and we shall see that a reasonable amount of attention to hereditary influences on behavior will be richly repaid by an increased understanding of how environmental influences operate to modify them. It is a truism to state, as we did in our very first sentence of this chapter, that two individuals may respond very differently to the same set of environmental circumstances. Before we can use our knowledge of environment effectively, for the prediction and control of behavior, we shall have to make this something more than a platitude, and undertake to learn something about the constitutional factors which determine that different individuals do respond in different ways.

This program cannot be carried out if we confine ourselves to the observation of what has been called a "hollow organism," one that is defined solely in terms of its responses to external stimulation. Lewin (1935), Skinner (1938, 1953), and Tolman (1932) have been prominent among those who have felt that psychology has little to gain from looking inside the organism, in a physiological sense. In defense of their position, it is possible to point to a history of many mistaken hypotheses that were founded on the errors of neurologists. It is not possible to say with assurance that similar errors will not mislead us in the future. The lesson of history should teach us caution, but it should not cause us to become scientific isolationists. Physiologists have taught us a great deal that is already indispensable

CHAPTER 2

The Basic Pattern

*T*his chapter will summarize a few important principles which govern the adaptive behavior of animals generally. Only a summary statement of these principles can be given, because it would take a long book to present the facts upon which they are based. It should be emphasized, however, that these are not questionable hypotheses, such as may be found aplenty in later chapters, but theoretical formulations which have extensive experimental support. It would be convenient to be able to say that they also enjoy universal acceptance, but this is unfortunately not possible. For the most part, differences in expert opinion relate to matters of terminology or of relative emphasis, and not to the essentials, but in one area—regarding the characteristics of natively organized or unlearned behavior— a good deal of controversy remains. We can only acknowledge this as a fact, and hope that in the course of our later discussions the reader will concede, if he is not now prepared to do so, the value and the necessity of the position which we take on this question.

Taken together, the principles which we are about to state define the basic pattern of behavior of all higher animals. The distinctive values of human cultural existence are outgrowths of this basic pattern, but they do not displace it.

PRIMACY OF BASIC NEEDS

The primary needs of the living organism are those that are related to the basic processes of metabolism. The assimilation of nutrients, and the elimination of waste products, go on ceaselessly in the cells. To permit this, the internal fluids of the body must carry a steady and adequate supply of the needed substances and must remove those whose excessive accumulation would be harmful. These ends are directly served by the so-called *vegetative* processes, which include respiration, digestion, circulation, elimination, temperature regulation, and the functions of reproduction. They are indirectly served by the *animal* processes, such as locomotion and feeding, which relate the organism to its environment, including other individuals of the species.

The terms *animal* and *vegetative* also carry the connotations *active* and *passive*. The plant exposes its feeding surfaces, its leaves and roots, to the environment, from which it passively receives its needs. Light, air, water, food, and warmth must impinge upon these surfaces from without. Wind, or visiting insects, must carry the pollen that fertilizes the plant's seeds. The plant prospers if it meets favorable conditions, withers if it does not. It can do very little to influence the outcome.

Animals, on the other hand, have turned their feeding surfaces inward, forming them into protected bags, and have thus committed themselves to an active quest for food. At the same time, they have developed the apparatus of behavior, which includes receptor organs that are sensitive to various forms of energy change in the environment, and motor organs that enable them to pursue, to bite and grasp, to attack and defend. The animal actively seeks and even creates the conditions for its own existence. However, this animal apparatus has come into being and is organized primarily in the service of the vegetative organs (Kempf, 1918).

These two systems of organs, which are so differently specialized to serve the needs of living, do not function independently. There are multiple "feedback" processes, by which the condition of one system, or some part of it, influences the operation of the other. There are at least three categories of such feedback controls which it is important for us to distinguish. (1) In the normal and uneventful flow of life's activities, some of the vegetative processes have a cyclical character which finds indirect expression in periodic activity of the whole organism, motivated by drives that arise in these processes. Thus hunger, sex need, and the need for elimination make their periodic appearance, and each initiates a characteristic pattern of activity in the animal apparatus. (2) When unfavorable circumstances have upset the smooth operation of the vegetative processes, the resulting disequilibrium likewise creates a drive state which expresses itself in behavior. Unfavorable temperature conditions, lack of oxygen, toxic conditions, or the lack of some essential nutrient may serve as examples. (3) When the organization is confronted by an external threat which requires a quick mobilization of energy, the vegetative processes so modify their functions as to provide this assistance to the striped musculature, along with many other adjustments that might be helpful at such a time. This complex of adaptive adjustments was called the "emergency response" by Cannon (1927). It fits into the larger context of homeostatic controls which maintain the constancy of the internal environment (Cannon, 1932). Selye's (1950) recent work on physiological stress, or the "general adaptation syndrome" by which the body responds to any prolonged or repeated stimulation of a threatening nature, is essentially a reinterpretation of these relationships, and one which gives them a place of central importance in the modern theory of psychosomatic illness. It should be noted that the first two types of feedback represent influences of the vegetative on the animal system, while the third represents a modification of vegetative function which is initiated by the animal apparatus. Thus neither system can be said to maintain a general dominance over the other.

The concept of homeostasis can be extended to include the entire range of economic and cultural activities by means of which men feed and shelter themselves and otherwise foster their metabolic processes. With respect to architecture, for example, "man's solution to the problem of external climate, so severe as to overpower his physiological mechanisms for heat regulation, is to construct an artificial intermediary environment in which his homeostatic capacity is adequate" (Dempsey, 1951). There is no more important concept in psychology than this, that the ultimate regulatory control over bodily activity is not exercised by mind or brain, but by visceral organs, by the basic needs of life. The relevance of these needs to problems of social psychology has been stressed by such authors as Klineberg (1940), who includes them among his "dependable motives," and Sherif (1948), who refers to them as "biogenic needs" and emphasizes the far-reaching effects of deprivation regarding them. Nevertheless, the attempt to extend this into a universal principle which governs every instance of behavior (e.g., Stagner and Karwoski, 1952) is unduly forced. Life can have meanings beyond the satisfaction of basic needs. Claude Bernard (1859), the father of the concept of homeostasis, recognized that the maintenance of constancy in the internal environment of the cells is the necessary foundation for a high degree of specialization in cell function, and hence for the development of "freedom of action." In his general theory of motivation, Maslow (1943a) places homeostatic needs at the most fundamental level, and he states that other forms of motivation become prominent in behavior only when these needs are adequately met. When homeostatic controls are adequate to the stresses placed upon them, they do not draw our attention. When they prove inadequate, either because of unusual stress or because of some basic defect or weakness in the apparatus of control, the resulting agitation may seem to be the most central characteristic of the individual's temperament!

NATIVELY ORGANIZED BEHAVIOR

When we study the adaptive behavior of any animal species, we are first impressed by its consistency rather than its variability. Each animal species has its characteristic way of coping with problems of survival, and within the species there is a striking degree of uniformity, especially in meeting situations which recur in the lives of each generation. These species-characteristic modes of response are the behavioral expression of structural uniformities. No matter how marvelously adaptive they may be, there is no reason to think of them as anything more than the direct expression of physiological determinants of behavior that are ultimately accessible to our full understanding. Unfortunately, the concept of instinct has sometimes been invoked in the effort to throw doubt upon the adequacy of a completely materialistic approach to the study of animal behavior. Such an attitude would be alien to the whole spirit of our presentation, but we must not slip into the error of refusing to acknowledge the existence and importance of natively organized behavior patterns, because we do not like the word that has been used to designate them (i.e., *instinct*), or the theories which have formerly been associated with an emphasis upon them. Neither is it useful to debate such straw men as the outmoded concepts that "instincts" are immutable, or absolutely uniform in their appearance. If we do this, we will only block our understanding of how a great deal of individuality arises out of the relatively slight modifications of unlearned response patterns which result partly from the inevitable variations inherent in all aspects of structure and function and partly from the effects of experience, to which they are by no means immune.

Since the viewpoint which is being presented here is contrary to that which many readers have accepted "on good authority," and because we cannot take the space for a full discussion of the instinct controversy, we shall quote the testimony of two eminent experimentalists who were both long identified with the antinativist movement. The first of these is Leonard Carmichael, who is at present the director of the Smithsonian Institute. His distinguished reputation as a scientific worker is based in part on a careful series of investigations of the prenatal organization of behavior in guinea pigs. Looking back on these and other studies, he has said (1941): "Every experiment that I have done in the field of early growth of behavior has forced me to retreat from the environmentalist hypothesis. Now, literally nothing seems to me to be left of this hypothesis so far as the very early development of behavior is concerned." The second is K. S. Lashley, who is known to every student of psychology for his experimental studies of discrimination behavior in the rat. These studies gave rise to the important concept of mass action of the brain, and hence they seemed to refute the possibility of existence at the cortical level of specific, sharply defined nerve paths, which might seem to be a necessary basis for inheritance of involved behavior patterns. However, on the basis of subsequent researches, including his anatomical studies of the brains of spider monkeys, he was led to declare (1947): "We are compelled to recognize that the genetic determination of behavior may extend to very intricate and precise coördinative processes." These outstanding scientific workers have added to their greatness by these open-minded admissions that the convictions which had inspired much of their early work were mistaken. We must try to be equally flexible in our opinions.

In *The Study of Instinct* (1951), Tinbergen has summarized the present knowledge of the mechanism of instinctive behavior in animals. From his discussion, four major principles emerge, each of which has some importance for our subject. They deal, respectively, with the sensory, the motor, the motivational, and the maturational aspects of unlearned behavior. Tinbergen's best known experimental work is concerned with the behavior of fish, but the principles which he enunciates have very broad application.

1. *The sensory aspect.* Every organism has special sensitivity to certain kinds of stimulation, which Tinbergen calls "sign stimuli" or "releasers." It has been demonstrated experimentally that these releasers often have a configurational character, that is, they may consist of moderately complex perceptual patterns. A strikingly dramatic example of this exists in the work of

Lorenz (1937). He showed that inexperienced goslings will react differently to the flight profile of a hawk, which has a short neck and a long tail, and that of a goose, which has a long neck and a short tail. The surprising aptness of many instances of natively organized behavior is based upon the genetically determined prepotency of the sign stimuli, and the instances which astound us most are those which are evoked by stimuli to which we are relatively insensitive. For example, some of the mating behavior of insects is oriented by minute quantities of chemical substances to which their very highly specialized receptors are sharply attuned. Also, it has recently been shown that the homing behavior of some simple seashore creatures depends on their special sensitivity to polarized light. The mystery of such behavior disappears when this special sensitivity, which often amounts to a virtual enslavement to a certain kind of stimulus, is recognized.

2. *The motor aspect.* The sign stimulus only triggers, and to some degree orients, the response pattern. The latter may consist of a stereotyped reflex chain, or of relatively variable unit responses, like the elements of fighting behavior. In either case, the sign stimulus must not be thought of as initiating the response, according to the conventional S-R formulation. It is more profitable to think of the response as a self-contained mechanism that is constantly primed for action, ready to come into play as soon as some block is removed. The effect of the releaser is therefore a trigger action, which Tinbergen calls an "internal release mechanism" (IRM). The importance of this principle will appear when we discuss the role of inhibition, and interference with inhibition or disinhibition, in behavior. Although we have called this the motor aspect of response, it should be understood to include all the effector aspects, including visceral response. It would be more accurate to call it the neuro-efferent aspect.

3. *The motivational aspect.* It is often necessary to distinguish between the appetitive and consummatory phases in a

total pattern of natively organized behavior. The appetitive phase consists of responses to inwardly determined sources of stimulation. It is characterized by increasing drive tension which may express itself in varied behavior, from apparent restlessness to rather systematic hunting. The consummatory phase is initiated by the external sign stimulus, and leads to tension reduction. Antinativists have usually concentrated their attention on the random character of the appetitive behavior, while instinctivists have emphasized the high degree of uniformity in the consummatory act. Neither phase can be fully understood except in conjunction with the other.

4. *The maturational aspect.* For each instinctive response, there is a critical period in the life of the organism during which it can be activated most readily. If the appropriate releaser is absent during the critical period, so that the expected behavior is not evoked, it may never appear under otherwise normal conditions. In other words, sensitivity to the sign stimulus will decline if it has not been reinforced by practice. This obviously implies that the later performance of instinctive acts is greatly influenced by learning.

These four principles can be illustrated in the behavior of humans as well as in that of animals. There are many typical human ways of behaving which seem so obvious, on the one hand, or so completely socialized, on the other, that we commonly overlook their essential similarity to parallel instances of natively organized behavior in animals. We readily acknowledge as instinctive that the ear of the fledgling bird is attuned to the warning call of its species, so that at the first experience of this call it may instantly take to flight. On the other hand, it does not occur to us that a child's startle in response to a shriek of terror (whose imperative quality is so obvious *to us*) needs any special explanation. Yet both are equally examples of specialized response to a particular kind of stimulation. We acknowledge as instinctive the behavior of courtship, mating, and parental care by animals generally, but when we turn to the study of human beings, we may regard the great variety of conventional formalizations of marriage customs and family structure as evidence that biological elements have been completely submerged. It is clear, however, that these different customs are but so many different ways of disciplining unlearned biological dispositions which may show themselves in any corner of the globe, in defiance of unpermissive mores. Through such customs, each society adjusts itself to the human animal, as truly as the human individual adjusts himself to society.

The fact that the conditions of living in cultural communities lead to widespread modification of innate response patterns should not cause us to overlook the importance of the unlearned dispositions which provide the basis for learning the mores. A child's biting, scratching, and kicking may seem like an ineffective method of fighting, but it is obviously an unlearned response pattern, in the same sense that the fighting pattern of the cat or the dog is unlearned. The child has a good deal to learn before he can become a pugilist or a wrestler, but he would probably be quite untrainable in these directions if he did not have a basic fighting pattern from which to start.

DEVELOPMENTAL PATTERN

The mention of "critical periods" brings us to another very important principle of all animal life, which is that each organism possesses not only a spatial, but also a temporal pattern. That is, each animal has not only a characteristic physical organization, which permits certain kinds of action and excludes other kinds— as a horse's legs determine that he shall run and a bird's wings that he shall fly—but also a characteristic history, which is likewise fixed by genetic factors. Each individual member of a species passes through the same developmental stages to reach maturity, then declines in vigor and dies, after its characteristic span of life. Favorable or unfavorable circumstances influence the details of this process, but they do not alter its basic characteristics, nor greatly modify the time relationships, except by the total interruption of death. The endocrine glands play a leading part in the control of development, for the onset of each developmental stage is initiated by a sharp rise or decline in the output of one or more hormones. In the rare case where an individual's developmental history differs markedly from the expected pattern, endocrine pathology is almost certainly the cause. The intraspecies consistency of the maturational pattern is an interesting parallel to the homeostatic principle. Where the latter insures the *status quo,* the former assures the *status nascendi,* so that even major environmental differences are permitted to produce only minor changes in the pattern of growth.

The recognition of this temporal pattern helps us in at least two ways. First, it makes us aware that behavioral predispositions, unlearned forms of response, may make their first appearance rather late in life. Such response mechanisms are often functional considerably before the time when they show themselves in action. That is, the muscular and neural components of the response seem to be ready for action, but some sensitizing element is absent. Thus Beach, in his authoritative survey of *Hormones and Behavior* (1948), reaches the following very important conclusion:

Neuromuscular elements responsible for such hormonally conditioned behavior as courtship, mating, and care of the young are fully organized and ready to function relatively early in life, well in advance of the time that they will normally be activated. They may be completely developed at birth or attain this condition at some time thereafter, but their organization is complete prior to the time that the hormones which will sensitize them to stimulation are secreted in sufficient quantities to become effective.

An excellent illustration of this is provided by an experimental study of the factors which influence the posture of the male dog in the act of micturition. With sexual maturity, the characteristic three-legged stance of the adult male replaces the juvenile posture, which is like that of the female dog. It can be shown that this change does not result from the maturing of the nervous or muscular components of the act, but from the presence of the male hormone. Its appearance may be greatly accelerated by administration of the hormone, and in castrates this posture may be made to come and go at the will of the experimenter, who can regulate it by the administration and withdrawal of the hormone. (Martins and Valle, 1948.)

Secondly, the recognition of the temporal pattern of development also calls our attention to a very important source of individual differences, namely, individual differences in the tempo of development. Although such a difference may be a very transient thing in itself, it may indirectly lead to long-range results of considerable importance, through causing the individual to regard himself as an oddity, or through some form of interaction with the social environment. In Chapter 4, we shall see that a puppy which takes a subordinate position in its litter during the first weeks of postnatal life, perhaps because of a slower rate of early growth, may continue to play the role of an underdog even after he has caught up to the others in size and weight. In human societies, the child and the youth judge themselves and are judged by others against a certain standard tempo of development. Since this standard varies from one culture to another, the optimal tempo for healthy individual maturation also varies (Mead, 1947). Many young people in the California Growth Study faced difficult adjustment problems because their adolescence came too early or too late (Jones, 1943). With changing patterns of dating among early teen-agers in America, young girls may be envied for what would have been an embarrassingly precocious development a generation ago, and others are unhappy because they do not mature any faster than what seemed a comfortable pace to their mothers.

Nonprimary Drives

In current psychological usage, the *drive* is based upon some physiological tension which arises from a basic life process. A *motive,* on the other hand, is a result of learning, and represents the attachment of motivational force to some act or thing, because of its association with the relief of a drive. Thus the drive is primary and the motive is secondary, while *motivation* embraces both. There is much merit in this unambiguous terminology, to which we shall adhere.

It is difficult to find appropriate designation for another important type of motivation, which occupies an intermediate position. We have in mind motivation that is primary, in the sense that it is independent of learning, but which nevertheless has no basis in the primary needs, as we discussed them a few pages back. Those needs, and the drives that arise out of them, are related to the vegetative functions of the organism, while the motivation with which we are now concerned arises out of the animal functions. We cannot use the term *animal drive,* as we might like to do, because of the confusion that would result due to Holt's use of that phrase in a different sense (1931). We shall therefore call them *nonprimary drives,* understanding this to mean drives that are not based on the primary life needs, but which do nevertheless have a definite physiological basis, prior to experience. The following discussion of the nonprimary drives is based on an earlier article (Diamond, 1939).

Not all the motivated behavior of the organism can be regarded as serving the vegetative or primary drives, even indirectly. The sensorimotor apparatus of adjustment is an independent source of motivation. In common speech, we often refer to a motivating state as an "itch." Like the itch, every effective stimulus demands our response, which, like scratching the itch, must be relevant to the stimulus itself. A great deal of our behavior consists in "scratching our itches," restlessly exploiting the possibilities of experience which are offered by the sensorimotor apparatus. Not all this behavior serves any purpose, but like the flight of a moth into the light, every response of the integrated organism tends inevitably to regulate the intensity with which the dominant stimulus of the moment acts on the sense organs.

Such control over the course of behavior by the relevancy or

effect of the response is, after all, precisely what is meant by motivation. A source of motivation is a physiological mechanism whose activity does not merely determine that the rest of the organism shall be active, but that this activity shall modify the conditions under which this particular mechanism operates. Hunger and sex drive are the expression of such mechanisms, but virtually every type of external sensory stimulation can play a similar role.

Motivational theory has suffered from a too exclusive emphasis on the visceral drives. A more satisfactory approach to many problems of motivation is to recognize that the sensorimotor apparatus does not merely function to satisfy vital needs, to adjust to the environment in the sense of securing what is needed for life and growth, but that it also demands stimulation, demands the opportunity to react in ways that force the environment to stimulate it more effectively, and that this demand is an expression of its physiological organization. As a consequence of the evolutionary process by which the animal apparatus has been developed to serve the vegetative needs, self-stimulation takes its place alongside of self-preservation as a motivating principle.

The "itch" that demands our attention need not arise from any sense organ, but may have its source within the brain. The increasing complexity of the nervous system leads to an increase in intraneural activity, and thus provides a physiological basis for the appearance of what may legitimately be called native intellectual motivation—not in the sense of a set of motivating ideas, but as a need for manipulation of the content of awareness, which is comparable to the child's need for physical manipulation of objects and to the play of both animals and humans. Murphy (1947) has restated this viewpoint with greater eloquence:

. . . Needs for intellectual, esthetic, and other individual and social activities may arise, simply and naturally, from the way in which the human nervous system is constructed and from its inter-relations with the rest of the body. From this point of view the music of songbirds, the curiosity and playfulness of chipmunks and kittens,

the self-decoration of primates find a phylogenetic place, with science, invention, and art as the natural and necessary products of the sheer process by which complicated functions have led into still more and more complicated functions. . . . The more complex behavior patterns of complex organisms are genuinely functions of their complexity, not merely new revelations of the simpler energies.

The recognition of nonprimary drives will therefore help us to understand the motivation behind many of the more complex forms of human individuality.

<h2 style="text-align:center">FLEXIBILITY IN BEHAVIOR</h2>

All animals, even protozoa, exhibit variability in response, which is one of the conditions that favor successful adaptation. When we cannot specify the reasons for variability we describe the behavior as "random." Let us briefly review a few of the known causes for variability of response by the same individual, giving some examples of each.

1. The internal drive state of the organism may change. An insect may be phototropic before it has eaten, leading it to climb stems to the tender leaves which are its natural food, and photophobic immediately after, leading it to descend the same stems and burrow into the ground. A female rat will behave differently toward a male when she is in heat and when she is not, and differently toward a litter before she has mated and just after she has given birth. To us, a steak smells better before we have eaten our dinner than after the dessert.

2. Maturation may have taken place. We may recall the example, given above, of the male dog which urinates in a squatting posture when it is a juvenile but changes to a three-legged stance when it is an adult. The child who would not have feared a snake when he was 3, does so spontaneously at 5 (Jones and Jones, 1928).

3. The continued action of a drive or a motive after initial responses have brought no relief may lead to a different form of response. In Pflüger's classical demonstration of the spread of reflex excitation, the decerebrate frog, when it had failed to

remove an irritant on its side by the scratching movements of one leg, brought the opposite leg also into play. The child who is not noticed for being good attracts attention by being naughty.

4. Perceptual shift may cause a restructuring of figure-ground relationships, leading to different behavior. Köhler's (1925) chimpanzee Sultan, after having vainly tried to reach a banana with a single stick, and having abandoned the attempt, returned to his task with a new plan when he perceived that two sticks can be fitted together to make a longer one. This "aha!" experience is an important element of intellectual achievement even at the highest scientific levels.

5. The recurrence of a stimulus may evoke a response that was formerly given to another stimulus, as a result of one or more paired presentations of the two together. This is the classical type of conditioning (Pavlov, 1927), which is sometimes called stimulus substitution, and has been designated by Skinner (1938) as Type S conditioning. Watson used it to condition the infant Albert to give fear response to a rabbit, by presenting the rabbit several times in combination with a loud noise (Watson and Rayner, 1920). Although it seems probable that this type of conditioning is not so general as was once thought to be the case (cf. page 191), it does certainly play an important part in emotional learning, as in the famous example which we have just cited. The redintegration of characteristic personal patterns of emotional and motor response, made up of elements which were originally only loosely tied together, may be a consequence of such conditioning, by which the part responses become linked to kinesthetic and other stimuli arising out of the activity itself.

6. Closely related to Type S conditioning is the phenomenon of stimulus generalization. After Albert had been taught to fear a rabbit, he also exhibited fear of a white rat and of inanimate, white, fluffy objects. Some generalization is necessary, if we are to apply our learning to new situations, but too much generalization can be a source of difficulties.

7. When the performance of a response has been followed closely by the satisfaction of a need, this response will be more likely to recur in a similar situation. This constitutes learning by what has been variously termed the "law of effect" (Thorndike, 1932), the principle of reinforcement by need reduction (Hull, 1943), and Type R conditioning (Skinner, 1938). This is the classical paradigm of learning *per se,* which it would be superfluous to illustrate. As such, it is also the principal target for Tolman's reminder, that, "There is more than one kind of learning" (1949).

8. Paradoxically, this list is not complete without some mention of loss of flexibility as one way in which behavior can be modified. This has been best illustrated by Maier's (1949) demonstration that under certain conditions of frustration, the normal flexibility which rats exhibit in a problem situation can give way to a nonadaptive stereotypy of response. He also points to the parallelism between this and some forms of neurotic behavior in humans, who may go on behaving in ways which they know to be profitless.

These many different kinds of flexibility fall naturally into two groups. In the first group we find those characteristics of the adaptive organism which result in variable response even to constant stimulus conditions. Included in this group is the phenomenon of perceptual restructuring, which is a basis for intelligent learning, but in itself is still a direct expression of the organism's capacity for variable response. The second group includes those kinds of behavioral change which, although they are based on an underlying capacity for "trial and error," represent in themselves so many ways of reducing variation in behavior, by substituting the tried and tested response for the random trial. It is not surprising, therefore, that the mechanisms which underlie them should sometimes get out of hand, to produce the rigidity of abnormal fixation.

Since there are so many different sources of flexibility in behavior, we must recognize the likelihood that individual

variation in the relative importance of different kinds of learning is an important aspect of individuality. When the attempt is made to explain all instances of behavioral change as the results of some one process of learning, such as need reduction, a potential source of individuality is being overlooked.

Anterior Dominance

One of the earliest generalizations which we make about the organization of adaptive behavior is that it is directed by or from the "head" of the animal. The commonplace observations on which this conclusion is placed are as sound as the scientific data which give rise to the more imposing phrase, anterior dominance. However, anterior dominance has the advantage of embracing a good many related phenomena, and it thus offers a valuable theoretical framework for their understanding. It includes, for example, the fact that if an earthworm is chopped into shorter lengths, any piece that contains several segments is capable of coördinated locomotion. This is because any segment is capable of assuming dominance in establishing the rhythm of locomotion, over relatively posterior segments, although all the segments are anatomically identical. In this example, anterior dominance is presumably the result of a relatively simple physiological gradient, a quantitative differentiation in the strength of an excitatory process. Child (1924) pointed out the importance of such gradients, both in determining the axes along which the structure of the organism is laid down and as a continuing factor in the regulation of behavior.

At the other extreme, anterior dominance also embraces the fact that each higher, or later addition to the vertebrate brain exerts some modifying control over the lower or older parts. Some of the instances of such control are called cortical inhibition, and later we shall place great stress on the importance of this phenomenon for personality organization. It will help us then to remember that it is only a late variant on the old theme of anterior dominance.

SUMMARY

Those organic processes that are most directly involved in the maintenance of life are classified as vegetative, while the actions that in some way modify the relationship between the organism and the environment, other than by metabolic change, are called animal activity, or behavior. The organism's basic needs arise from the vegetative functions, in whose service the animal apparatus has been developed. However, the latter apparatus gives rise independently to nonprimary drives, which attain increasing importance as this apparatus grows in complexity. The repertoire of behavior includes many natively organized modes of response, which are adapted to serve the organism under many specific circumstances. Each animal also exhibits a characteristic developmental pattern, and some provision for flexibility in behavior. The behavior apparatus is characterized—except in some of the simpler animal forms—by a hierarchic type of organization which may be described in terms of anterior dominance.

These principles may be regarded as a concise statement of the master plan of animal behavior. They apply to human life with the same force as to any other living form. It is true that human behavior is characterized by much greater flexibility than that of other animals, and that the phenomena of human individuality are therefore more complex. But humans also differ from each other in the strength of their basic drives, in their nonprimary needs, in their developmental patterns, etc. Every aspect of this universal pattern of animal behavior makes its contribution to the full picture of human individuality. However, although this constitutes the background against which individuality appears, the essential dimensions of temperament cannot be read directly from it. In search of these, and mindful of the fact that being human is just one variant of being animal, we turn to the more detailed observation of certain mammals, which will occupy us for the next three chapters.

CHAPTER 3

The Emotional Problems of Rats and Mice

*I*f a child psychologist were asked to discuss the varieties of behavior disorders, before a lay audience, he might well describe four different problem children, somewhat as follows. One is exceptionally fearful, always apprehensive and readily thrown into a state of terror. Another is resistant to authority, picks quarrels with his playmates, and is cruel to small animals. A third is constantly getting into trouble because he acts on impulse, seemingly without thought of the consequences to himself or to others. Finally, there is one who is apathetic, or generally disinterested. The apathy extends to all personal relationships, and, indeed, has its basis in the lack of any warm bond of affection with other persons. The psychologist will explain that these are simplified pictures, which present four kinds of emotional disturbance which are never found in such pure or unmixed forms. Nevertheless, one or another of these four types of response is likely to be prominent in any individual case of emotional disorder in childhood.

If the psychologist is asked to explain how these different kinds of disturbance originate, he will probably say that in every case there is a complex interaction of constitutional and environmental factors. He will acknowledge the difficulty of disentangling these two sets of determinants, and then, if he is a typical psychologist, he will proceed to deal almost exclusively

with the influences of early family environment. A good deal
may be said in defense of this course, as a practical way of
acquitting himself of his professional responsibility to his audience. Perhaps, though the point is debatable, this is the kind of
information which will be most useful to them.

We cannot acquit ourselves so simply of the scientific responsibility for explanation. We cannot say, in effect, "Let us dismiss
the constitutional influences as unimportant, since we would
rather have them that way, and in the present state of our
knowledge it would be hard to prove otherwise." Any of us
would be ashamed to make such a blunt statement of prejudice,
yet this kind of denial of reality is implicit in many discussions
of this general problem. We must look at the available evidence.
If it is difficult to disentangle the influences of constitution and
environment in the behavior of children, because we cannot
prearrange their parenthood and ruthlessly disrupt their family
living, there is nevertheless available a considerable body of
evidence from experimental work with animals, with whom it is
less difficult to assess the role of genetic factors in behavior. We
shall try to keep this discussion to a minimum, because our
major interest is in the personalities of human children and
adults, but we cannot afford to skip carelessly over it.

In this chapter, we shall survey some of the evidence which
has been provided by experimental work with rodents. We shall
concentrate our attention on those findings which are most
directly related to the question that has been posed, as to how
it happens that in the symptomatology of emotional illness there
are distinctive syndromes which may be described as abnormal
states of fearfulness, aggressiveness, impulsiveness, and apathetic
aloofness. As it happens, the observation of rodents throws a
good deal of light on the first two parts of this multiple question.
In the next chapter, dealing with the behavior of dogs and cats,
we shall find clearer indications regarding the other two parts.

FEARFULNESS

One of the characteristics of rats is that they commonly manifest fear in strange places, and that they show their upset by

urinating or defecating, and by partial or complete inhibition of eating. This behavior is obviously similar to the display of fear by humans under conditions of extreme danger, and it constitutes a maladaptive disturbance of the normal process of energy mobilization which was described by Cannon (1927) as the emergency response. With rats, as with men, such lack of adequate control over autonomic functions may interfere with adjustment, especially under the conditions imposed by civilization. The fearful rat takes longer to learn to run a maze to food, because it takes him longer to accustom himself to working in the maze. Slinking along the walls, he has a greater tendency to enter blind alleys, because learning the true path requires that he abandon this seeming protection. He is less docile in the problem situation of the laboratory, and doubtless also less fit for survival in the grain field and the sewer.

Hall (1934) established an objective measure of fearfulness in rats, which he called the "open field" situation. The rat is placed alone in a brightly lit, enclosed area, 8 feet in diameter, in which food is available, and is left there for two minutes. A record is taken of eating, and of any eliminative behavior. This is repeated once daily for 12 days. Most rats will show their emotional upset when they are first exposed to this situation by urinating and by refraining from eating, but after a few days they will become accustomed to it, to the extent that they will eat freely. In an unselected population—that is, one that has not been selectively bred with respect to this characteristic— there will be considerable variation in the number of trials needed before this adaptation takes place. Hall showed that the non-feeding score and the eliminative behavior score showed good agreement with each other, but the latter has generally been adopted as standard for the situation. Following Hall's own unfortunate usage in his first publication regarding the test, the trait measured is usually designated as emotionality rather than fearfulness. However, it should be clear that we are dealing here with only one important aspect of emotional behavior.

By selective breeding, Hall established two strains, called

emotional and nonemotional. In the parent generation from which both stocks originated, the mean open field score (that is, the number of days on which defecation or urination was observed) was about four. The emotional strain, which was produced by continuous inbreeding of high-scoring animals, showed a fairly steady rise in mean score. It reached an average of 10 in the ninth generation of offspring, after which the score became stabilized at that level. At the same time, the intra-strain variability declined. The establishment of the nonemotional strain followed a different course. In the very first generation of offspring, the mean score was below 0.5, showing that most of the animals did not have a single "accident." However, this low level could not be maintained even with continuous inbreeding. The average score of the ninth to twelfth generations was 1.4, due primarily to the occasional occurrence of high-scoring individuals (Hall, 1951). The history of either strain demonstrates that we are dealing with a complexly determined phenomenon, that is, one which is influenced by many genes rather than a single pair, but it is nonetheless obvious that some rats are constitutionally more disposed than others to the kind of emotionality that is measured by the open field test.

It is likely that the difference between the two strains has a glandular basis. This hypothesis is supported by the findings of Yeakel and Rhoades (1941), who compared the glandular weights of animals from the two strains. They found that the thyroids were heavier in both male and female rats of the emotional strain; in addition, the emotional males had heavier adrenals, and the emotional females had heavier pituitaries.

AGGRESSIVITY

Another important respect in which individual rats differ from each other is the readiness with which they engage in fighting behavior, and the fierceness with which they continue a fight once begun. Aggressiveness in behavior is influenced by factors of experience, as well as by genetic factors. To avoid confusion, it is well to use the distinctive word form *aggressivity* to denote the native disposition to such behavior.

There is considerable interest in the question whether animals have a tendency to aggressive behavior, and a widespread reluctance to accept such a possibility, because of possible implications for social psychology and sociology, and for the theoretical understanding of behavior disorders in children or various forms of antisocial behavior in adults. We have such profound reasons to *wish* we could disprove the existence of native aggressivity, which we dread as a sort of biological sanction for war, that we appeal to every remote possibility to explain it otherwise. Therefore we may wilfully misread the evidence even with respect to rats and mice. Among them, however, the differences between sexes and between different breeds is so striking that there can be no reasonable doubt about the physiological foundations of their aggressive behavior.

Perhaps, it is sometimes argued, we do not sufficiently recognize the force of social circumstance even among these lowly creatures. How much of the aggressivity of their young results from the manner in which they have been handled and the example they have been shown by their mothers? With gentler handling, might not any infant rodent grow to be a nonaggressive adult? With some such thought as this, Ginsburg and Allee (1942) split the litters of black and albino mice, born on the same day, so that each mother reared both black and albino offspring. The black strain used (identified as C57, and serving as subjects in quite a few of the experiments we shall consider in this chapter) was known to be markedly more aggressive. Alas! the black mice reared by the albino mother grew to be more aggressive than the albino mice reared by the black foster mother. It is a pity that we cannot judge the relative pleasure which each of the mothers took in watching the development of their more belligerent and less belligerent charges.

Fredericson (1952a) repeated this experiment on a more extensive scale, and confirmed the results. In this case, entire litters were transferred to foster mothers. The natively aggressive mice, far from being subdued by the influence of their gentler foster mothers, were observed to challenge the latter in the competitive feeding situation which was used as the test of aggressiveness, forcing the milder parents to adopt the fighting pattern of their foster children.

In another study, Fredericson (1950) observed the spontaneous appearance of aggressive behavior among mice, when no external incentive to competitive behavior was introduced. He used a litter of six male mice of the C57 strain, grouped in three pairs for the purposes of the experiment. They were all weaned and isolated at the age of 21 days, and starting with the twenty-third day the mice of each pair were given an opportunity to explore a common space between their cages, as well as to visit in each other's cages. For 10 days or more, this daily social interlude (which lasted for 20 minutes) was the occasion for much friendly behavior, which included "huddling, nosing, and mutual grooming." The mice of one pair fought on the thirty-fourth day, and those of the other two pairs fought on the thirty-sixth day. Fighting also took place on every subsequent day, as long as the observations were continued. These animals were supplied with abundant food and water at all times. Thus it appears that aggressive behavior arises as a result of maturation, even between mice that have been trained to accept one another. Elsewhere, Fredericson (1952b) has reported that this type of spontaneous aggression does not appear among females of the same strain, although they do show competitive fighting when hungry. This difference between the sexes is consistent with Beeman's (1947) finding, which was based on a comparison of male mice of this same strain and those of the less aggressive albino variety, that the intensity of aggressive behavior is directly related to the size of the seminal vescicles and the prostate glands. She also found that castration removed practically all the aggressivity in either strain, regardless of the age at operation. Then, by administering male hormone in the form of testosterone propionate pellets, implanted subcutaneously, she succeeded in restoring the characteristic aggressive behavior. Taken together, this series of investigations gives strong support to the view that aggressivity must be regarded as an important component of the pattern of masculine behavior.

Tests, Ranks, and Rating Scales

We may take this opportunity to distinguish between three different techniques which are frequently used in the appraisal of behavior: the psychological test, the procedure of ranking, and the rating scale. We shall meet with each of these methods repeatedly in our study of human personality, but we can already see why one or another of these methods may be more appropriate in dealing with a given problem.

Hall's method of assessing fearfulness, or emotionality, in rats is an example of a psychological test. Hall focused his attention on one of the symptoms of fearfulness, because it was more expedient to observe and to quantify than others that might have been chosen. Respiration rate, heart rate, or blood pressure might be observed in the rat as they have been in humans and in other animals, but not with the same ease. Postural attitude, or some other distinctive response, might also have been selected. Hall's choice of eliminative behavior was directed by his judgment that this function would be adequately representative of disturbed autonomic function generally. He then designed a standardized situation in which to observe this behavior, which he must already have observed many times under less precisely controlled conditions. These are the essentials of a test: a defined segment of behavior, which is assumed to be typical of a broader area, to be observed in a standardized situation, which is fairly representative of other life situations. Thus, how a rat behaves in the open field tells us something of what to expect from the same animal in a strange maze, on the jumping platform, or in a goal chamber where he had experienced electric shock. We should not expect perfect agreement between prediction and occurrence in such other situations, but unless there is better than chance prediction the initial test was

without value. By such criteria, the validity of the open field test
has been demonstrated many times.

No one has devised an equally satisfactory test for aggressiveness. Since aggressive behavior always involves the interaction
of two animals, it is necessary for the investigator to enlist the
services of one animal, as it were, to administer the test to
another. Some investigators have done this, either by the use
of trained fighters who can be relied upon to be maximally
aggressive, or, at the other extreme, by dangling helpless animals
by their tails, and swinging them against the animal under
observation as an act of provocation. More often, the animals
are simply observed in pairs, and after every possible pairing in
a small group of animals has been studied in this way, it is
usually possible for the observer to rank the individual animals,
from the most aggressive to the least aggressive. However, such
a ranking would tell us nothing about whether the animals as
a group were aggressive or nonaggressive. To make such a judgment, each animal must have not a rank but a score or rating.
We must be able to distinguish between weak aggression and
strong aggression. However, the judgment of an observer who
is guided by so vague a criterion will usually be very unreliable.
Rating scales are useful under these conditions. A rating scale
consists of a series of concrete, descriptive statements about the
kind of behavior that is to be observed, arranged in steps that
are assumed to correspond to successive positions along the
dimension that is being defined. In theory, it is desirable that
these successive steps should represent equal units of measurement on that dimension, but in practice it is found that a rating
scale gives good results as long as it has a fair number of steps
that stand in an unambiguous ordinal relationship. To construct
such a scale requires an intimate knowledge of the kind of behavior that is being observed. An example of a rating scale
applied to human behavior, whose validity will be immediately
evident to any reader, is one which Redlich, Levine, and Sohler
(1951) devised for use in a study of humor. The responses of
their subjects to cartoons were rated as negative, no response,

half-smile, smile, chuckle, laugh. This may be compared with the following seven-step scale which Hall and Klein (1942) devised for the study of aggressiveness in rats.

0. No interest in each other except occasional slight nosing.
1. Frequent vigorous nosing. No blocking, shoving, crowding, or any other display of hostility.
2. Occasional blocking, shoving, or crowding.
3. Frequent blocking, shoving, or crowding of opponent. The aggressor keeps after the other animal throughout the period.
4. Slight wrestling and/or assuming a dancing position in which the rats clasp each other while standing nose to nose.
5. Fierce wrestling. They jump, roll, and turn over the cage very rapidly.
6. Fierce wrestling. A rat bites the other hard enough to draw blood.

The use of rating scales makes it possible to assign a quantitative score for behavior which cannot be counted or directly measured, but which can be judged according to some appropriate system of classification. The application of a rating scale may call for considerable training on the part of the rater, whereas it is often possible to obtain useful rankings even from untrained observers.

In general, ranking procedures, which rely upon a global estimate of behavior, are the most feasible when we are first exploring a supposed dimension of behavior. The use of a rating scale presupposes enough knowledge so that we are able to define distinguishable steps along the dimension. Finally, the development of a test depends upon our ability to isolate representative elements of the behavior that we are studying, and to devise appropriate situations in which to observe them.

DOMINANCE RELATIONSHIPS

For reasons that we have already mentioned, a good deal of attention has been given to the question whether the native aggressivity of rodents can be modified by training. However, repeated observations of this sort in any group of animals become, in fact, observations of developing dominance-submission relationships. A system of such relationships, which usually has a hierarchic arrangement, appears in any group of animals living together, and shows itself in the exercise and acknowledgement of priorities with respect to food, sex objects, and the like. This social hierarchy is frequently called a pecking order, because it is commonly observed as a barnyard phenomenon, and the first theoretical formulations were based by Schjelderup-Ebbe (1935) on his work with domestic fowl. Although the development of dominance is influenced by the relative aggressivity of the animals, it is by no means the same thing as aggressiveness, for it involves an acceptance of the submissive role by the other individual in the pair. The same individual may be dominant toward one of his peers, and submissive toward another. Indeed, it is only at the extremes of the hierarchic order that one can find consistently submissive or consistently dominant behavior.

It will be recalled that Ginsburg and Allee (1942) demonstrated the hereditary basis of aggressivity, in strains of mice with which they had been working. They went on to observe the later development of fighting behavior within each strain. For 200 days, they observed their mice in paired encounters, paying particular attention to the question whether the experience of defeat would make an animal less aggressive, or the experience of success make him more so. They found that a stable order of dominance relationships in a group of animals emerged only after many battles. A very important finding is that "it is far easier to condition a socially superior mouse downward in the scale by a series of defeats than it is to condition a socially inferior mouse upward." Thus, for example, among five albino mice that were observed in paired encounters with each other, the two who had shared the top of the order at the start declined to middle positions. The mouse that had originally been in fourth position rose fairly rapidly to be top man. But *the mouse that started at the bottom of the order stayed there,* never being able to challenge any of the others. We shall find repeated parallels to this case.

Scott (1947), pursuing the same problem, devised a method

by which he could impose severe defeats even on very aggressive animals. He used eight pairs of the very aggressive C57 mice. Four of the experimental animals, and their four controls, were raised in isolation, while the others were mated, each with a single female. None had any opportunity for fighting experience, except as planned in the experiment, since male mice do not attack females. Each of the experimental animals was exposed for 30 minutes to a trained "fighter," who administered a severe and painful defeat, and forced him to retreat to cover repeatedly. On later days, the experimental and control animals were tested for aggressiveness, by having helpless males dangled before them. The experimental animals made more attacks, indicating greater aggressiveness. Thus the defeat experience had not reduced their aggressiveness, but apparently increased it. This is a good demonstration of the difference between aggressiveness and dominance, for these highly aggressive animals would doubtless assume submissive attitudes toward the fighters, if they were to meet them several times.

Kahn (1951) investigated the question whether the animal's age, at the time of the defeat, would influence the result. He used Scott's technique of trained fighters, and later tests with helpless danglers. Some of his experimental animals were 21 days old (just weaned) at the time of their defeat experience, others 35 days old (entering adolescence), and others were sexually mature. The animals of the first group became "significantly [1] more defensive and significantly less aggressive" than their controls. The same relationship appeared among the 35-day groups, but it was less pronounced, while the difference between the experimental and control animals of the oldest group was very

---

[1] Wherever the word *significant* appears in this book, in relation to the results of an experimental investigation, it should be understood in the technical statistical sense. That is, it is not meant to underline the importance of a finding, but to assure the reader that the finding is, within certain limits, trustworthy. According to this technical usage, it is conventional to state that a finding is "significant" if any suitable statistical test indicates that there is not more than 1 chance in 20 that a replication of the experiment would fail to reach an outcome that is similar in tendency

slight. The implication is that the experience of severe defeat tends to reduce aggression, when it takes place early in life. Presumably, the contrary result in Scott's experiment must be explained by the fact that he used somewhat older animals, although it is possible that strain differences were also in part responsible.

Miller (1948) has used rats in an experiment designed to show that "displacement of aggression" can be explained as the generalization of a learned response. He put rats in pairs into a compartment in which electric shock could be administered through the floor. Each time the current was turned on, it would continue until the rats started to fight. He also placed a rat-size baby doll, of white rubber, in the same compartment. The doll was ignored by the rats when they were in pairs, but if a rat were alone, and subjected to punishment, it would strike at the doll in order to win an abatement. In this case it is clear that the "aggression" is a learned response, with definite adaptive value, and that it can be "displaced" by generalization to another object than that toward which it was originally directed. However, this does not prove that aggression is always or even usually a learned response. On the contrary, we should recall that there is much evidence in the literature on learning to show that the ease with which an act can be "conditioned," or integrated with a given stimulus situation, depends on the readiness with which it is performed in the first place. Some acts are more available for learning than others. Therefore, while recognizing that an animal can be taught to be aggressive, we have good reason to believe that the naturally more aggressive animal will take such instruction more readily, and generalize it more broadly.

(though not necessarily equal in magnitude) to that which is being reported. The statement that a result is "very significant" is reserved for those instances in which this chance is not more than 1 in 100. Of course, the reader has the right to assume that any experimental results which are cited are in fact "significant," whenever there is no specific statement to the contrary. Therefore the need to mention this fact arises only when special comparisons are made, or when the test of significance was not reported in the original publication.

Mowrer (1941) studied the development of dominance hierarchies among rats that were made to compete, in groups of three, for single pellets of food. He observed that the behavior of the subordinate rats was influenced in other situations as well. They became fearful of eating even when no other animal was present, and they became shy and restrained even in their home cages. "More significant still," he concluded, "is the fact that their problem-solving capacities are likely to be considerably impaired. 'Intelligence' thus appears to be capable of being depressed by social experience."

Similar observations were made by Gordon (1943), in a very different setting. He observed chipmunks and squirrels in their normal forest habitat, and set learning problems for them. The animals showed a dominance order in their competitive feeding, and those that were low in the dominance hierarchy did not participate in the learning problems.

Finally, Riess (1946) made observations of "freezing" behavior in rats that had been reared in isolation, as compared with others who had been reared in cages housing six rats to a cage. "Freezing" is a term which describes the refusal of an animal to become active in a problem situation, because of fear, just as a frightened gunner may freeze and become powerless to pull the trigger in a combat situation. Of 80 rats that were reared in isolation, and who were therefore never exposed to the competitive stress of communal housing, only two exhibited freezing when they were placed in a maze-learning situation. Of 124 that had been raised socially, 18 froze. Of these 18, fifteen were identified as having been "almost consistently the dominated or submissive rats in their respective cages." This very significant difference demonstrates that the inhibition developed in the competitive social situation is very often carried over into other stress situations, and is, in these animals, the principal source of failures to adapt to problem-solving situations. It is also interesting to note that the proportion of freezing of nonsubmissive animals among those raised socially, three in 124, is the same as that among animals raised in isolation, two in 80. Thus there is a small proportion of animals in whom the freezing response is apparently independent of their social experience.

EFFECTS OF INFANT STRESS

It is quite evident, from these examples, that in the usual course of development of social relationships among rodents the native dispositions to fearfulness and to aggression both play a part. Also, the lowest position in the social hierarchy, within any group, is often accompanied by an excessive fearfulness which extends even into nonsocial situations, and which must be regarded as a form of emotional pathology. Apparently early experiences are more potent than later experiences as determinants of such behavior. This last conclusion is consistent with the hypothesis which has been developed from the observation of humans, that infants who experience extreme deprivation or fear-provoking stimulation grow up to be emotionally less stable as adults. Although the clinical evidence for this hypothesis seems quite convincing, it is difficult to put it to a direct experimental test, because we cannot ethically subject human infants to controlled stress situations of great severity. A number of experimenters have therefore turned to rats and mice, in the effort to demonstrate the neat relationships that have been assumed to exist.

Hunt (1941) investigated the influence of an early period of food deprivation on the later hoarding behavior of rats.[2] One

---

[2] I resist the temptation to enter into a fuller discussion of hoarding, but take this opportunity to mention that Licklider and Licklider (1950) have shown that when food deprivation is *not* a factor, what we may call esthetic determinants appear. When well-fed rats were given a choice between hoarding naked food pellets and others that were wrapped in bright aluminum foil, four out of six animals showed a very pronounced preference for the wrapped pellets, while only one showed the opposite preference. The Lickliders concluded that the motivation of hoarding is quite complex, and that "sensory and perceptual factors, rather than blood chemistry, hold the key." This finding and conclusion are consistent with well-substantiated reports about the behavior of the so-called trade rat, which torments campers in the West by leaving pebbles or bits of wood in place of the bright metal objects which he loves to carry away to his nest. This is an instance of the operation of nonprimary drives even in rodent behavior.

group of experimental animals was subjected to an irregular feeding schedule, with enforced periods of hunger, soon after they had been weaned. When mature, these animals hoarded no more than controls during periods when they were freely fed, but after a period of enforced hunger, the experimental group hoarded significantly more than those who had not experienced such deprivation before. However, a shadow of doubt was thrown on this dramatic result by the fact that in a parallel experiment, in which the preliminary deprivation started on the thirty-second instead of the twenty-fourth day, the result was negative. The contrast suggested the *ad hoc* explanation that only *infant* deprivation would give rise to the effect. However, later experiments (Hunt et al., 1947; McKelvey and Marx, 1951) have indicated that the effect is, in any event, not very pronounced. The principal importance of Hunt's work is in opening up a fertile field of experiment.

Hall and Whiteman (1951) subjected infant mice to the emotional trauma of a loud ringing bell in a metal tub, for two minutes daily, on four successive days, starting on the fourth day after birth. The open field test was administered to these mice and their controls, starting on the thirtieth day. At that time, the experimental animals appeared to be more fearful. The test was repeated when the animals were 100 days old, and at that time the difference still conformed in direction to the hypothesis, but it was no longer significant. In the later tests, both groups showed increased variability, which must be regarded as a result of uncontrolled experience factors. Taking this circumstance into account, there seems no reason to discount the significance of the earlier open field test. The trauma inflicted repeatedly during the first week of life did lead to an increased emotionality about one month later; the persistence of this effect into adulthood was not so pronounced as to yield a significant result at that time. Apparently, rats can outgrow some of their early problems.

Griffiths and Stringer (1952) reported negative results from an experiment of similar plan, using rats as the subjects. These animals were given the open field test in advance of the experiment, but the scores are not reported in detail. It is interesting to note, however, that the only rat which did have a moderately high score on this initial open field test was one of the few who showed any signs of being traumatized by the stress experience to which the experimental animals were later subjected. It seems likely, therefore, that the overall results might be different if the population were one which showed a greater initial susceptibility to fear. We introduce this speculation because it is in line with a general thesis which we shall emphasize: that environment can only foster what is already latent as disposition.

Another investigation which is relevant to this general question, although it is not concerned specifically with the effects of infant experience, is a medically oriented experiment by Farris, Yeakel, and Medoff (1945) on the causes of hypertension (high blood pressure). Experimental and control groups of rats were first matched on the basis of open field scores. In each group, the range of scores was fairly wide. The experimental animals were then subjected, once daily for 167 days, to the sound of an air blast—a highly disturbing stimulus to a rat. At the end of that time, 10 of the 12 rats in the experimental group were suffering from hypertension, while only one of the 11 controls was hypertensive. Of great interest is the fact that the two experimental animals that escaped the disease were at the lower end of the distribution for emotionality in the original open field test. They provide an example of relative immunity from the adverse effects of harsh environmental conditions, due to an originally sound constitution.

The uncertainty of the results obtained by Hunt, by Hall, and others, makes all the more striking the successful outcome of an ingenious experiment by Wolf (1943). Wolf used 44 rats, coming from seven litters. Two animals from each litter had their ears sealed with cotton and paraffin, 10 days after birth; two others had their eyes sealed with paraffin helmets a few days later, one day after the eyes had begun to function. The timing was intended to insure a genuine deprivation experience, rather than simple absence of function. All the seals were removed on the twenty-fifth day, and the rats were then weaned and placed in isolation. Starting two weeks later, and continuing for 10 days, each of these 28 animals and their 16 litter mates who were, to serve as controls was trained to wait at one end of a detention chamber until a signal light was shown, and then run to the other end to receive a piece of food. All the animals learned this readily, and performed with equal promptness in the situation. During the next 20 days, for 10 trials daily, they were placed *in pairs* in the same situation, which thus became competitive. Each animal that had been deprived in infancy of the use of its eyes was paired with one that had been deprived of the use of its ears. In every one of these 14 pairs, the visually deprived animal was the "loser" in such competition. There followed 10 days of individual training in a similar problem, using a buzzer as the cue, and then 20 more days of competition between the same pairs. In this situation, the auditory-deprived animals, who had been regularly the winners in the visual-cue problem, became almost as regularly the losers (12 out of 14). Among the eight pairs of control animals, the animal that excelled in the first situation always excelled in the second.

All the animals were capable of making full use of both visual and auditory cues, when not under stress. This was shown by the fact that they could respond rapidly to either type of stimulus during noncompetitive trials. In the competitive situation, however, those animals which had a history of infant deprivation in the use of the particular sense organ to which the cue was directed "would always assume a rigid, tense position in the reception chamber and then hesitatingly follow the other animal to the feeding chamber." This experiment is an unusually forceful demonstration of how adult behavior can be influenced by infant experience. It is hardly possible to overemphasize the importance of the circumstance that the influence does not show itself directly, but takes the form of a disposition which becomes evident in adulthood only under conditions of stress. Among the control animals, the outcome of the auditory competition was evidently determined in each pair by the dominance-submission relationship which had been developed during the visual competition. It is remarkable that this dominance relationship was able to assert itself in only 2 of the 14 experimental pairs.

Experimental Frustration

We wish now to consider several experiments in which rats have been led to behave in maladaptive ways, which have some of the characteristics of neurotic behavior in humans, as a result of punishment or frustration systematically inflicted upon them. Maier (1949) has summarized a series of experiments which he and his co-workers have done on this problem, and has drawn theoretical conclusions of far-reaching importance. He has challenged the generally accepted view that neurotic symptoms which are themselves maladaptive, in the sense that they interfere with satisfactions rather than helping to obtain them, are to be understood as purposeful though misdirected defensive devices, or that they necessarily have any meaning with respect to the conflict that gives rise to them. He contends instead that they are fixations, or stereotyped responses such as those which he observed in rats, who would endlessly repeat a single alternative in a problem situation, despite the fact that this would involve invariable punishment and thwarting.

An unfortunate feature of Maier's experiments is his use of the air blast as a method of forcing his rats to respond. The rat, placed on a jumping-stool, must jump to one of two windows, in each of which a distinctive card stands as a kind of shutter. If he makes the correct choice, the card falls back easily, he has a comfortable landing and obtains his food reward. The other card is locked in place, and if he makes this choice he not only fails to obtain the morsel of food, but he also makes the uncomfortable drop into a net below. Under these conditions, rats learn discriminations of moderate difficulty much more quickly than in the ordinary choice box. But when the problem has been made frustratingly difficult, the rat prefers not to jump at all. As Mowrer (1950) has stated in his critique of Maier's work, the rat now is motivated by a fear of jumping, rather than by a desire for food. It is then that the air blast is brought into play, in order to compel him to leave the stool. Since the air blast has the effect of producing audiogenic seizure, a type of violent convulsive behavior, in many rats, some of the behavior which Maier has described has been attributed by others to the effect of the air blast, rather than the frustration. This has served to distract attention from the essential facts.

The writer may be excused, therefore, if he recalls his earlier description of stereotyped or abnormally fixated behavior (Diamond, 1934). When rats were given a choice of two paths by which to enter a goal chamber in which they would receive food, and *either* path involved crossing a charged punishment grid, they formed position habits more quickly, and held to them more consistently, than control animals that were not subjected to punishment. Indeed, several of the punished animals, having experienced punishment on their first trial while traversing one of the alleys, never once attempted the other alley. If this had been an ordinary learning problem, with right and wrong choices, they would never have discovered that there was a path to the food which did not involve punishment. This stereotypy of response persisted despite the fact that

. . . entrance into the goal compartment occurred after hesitant approach to each of the paths. A typical trial might run thus: approach to R, turning away to look into L, then retreat to the rear of the choice compartment and very likely to the entrance, approach to L, slight turn facing toward R, looking again into L, sudden turn and dash through R. Such a trial might last between one and two minutes, and a longer chain of similar activity might fill five minutes. The same rat might behave thus day after day . . . and yet always finally enter by the same path.

Physical punishment is not essential to produce such stereotypy. To check on this fact, rats were trained to jump across a small gap to a single window, and later given a choice of two open windows, with a somewhat wider gap to be crossed. Neither choice involved punishment,· and food was visible at both windows. However, the situation provoked hesitant "choosing" behavior on the first choice trial. On the second and all later trials, every rat used in this phase of the experiment jumped to the same window that he had chosen the first time. On each of these trials the rats would "approach the edge of the stool, sidle to right and left along it, and glance uneasily at each of the windows before jumping to one." Maier described the same sort of hesitant choosing behavior, in which the invariable performance of the fixated response was preceded by tentative movements in the direction of the other window. In fact, he was able to show by his analysis of the time spent in these different postural attitudes that the rats often continued performing the wrong response, after they knew what the correct response was.

We have described these experiments at some length, because we believe it is important to establish the fact that abnormal fixation may take place in situations in which there is no problem, no punishment, and no forcing of response. The only thing that seems necessary to produce rapid fixation of a compulsive response is that the animal shall make a choice while experiencing fear. Such loss of response flexibility represents an alteration of behavior which is so profoundly maladaptive as surely to justify Maier's term, "abnormal fixation." It is significant that an animal as simple as the rat can be driven to such fixations by emotional stress which does not involve any painful stimulation.

Cook (1939) has described the production of "experimental neurosis" in rats, under conditions more like those used classically by Pavlov with dogs, and by Liddell with sheep. He made several attempts to induce maladaptive behavior in rats, by subjecting them to the stress of a too difficult discrimination, but he had success only when he placed them in a harness which was so restrictive that the rat had virtually no freedom of movement except to flex or unflex the right leg, to which shock was being applied as the unconditioned stimulus. Even under these conditions, only three of six rats showed behavior which Cook was willing to call neurotic in the sense of being genuinely maladaptive. The other rats sometimes became jumpy, and occasionally could not inhibit the flexing response at moments when it was not called for, but their behavior included no bizarre elements. We are interested in the detailed account which Cook gives of the behavior of his three "neurotic" rats, because the differences are related to an important variable in temperament, the contrast of excitability and inhibition.

Cook's rat No. 1 at first showed excessive jumpiness, and then a tendency to stiffen and remain motionless when touched (catatonic behavior). This developed "to the point where the animal could be made to hold any sort of pose almost indefinitely." In the experimental harness, the animal lost all ability to inhibit the flexing response, giving an unbroken series of flexions. Rat No. 2, in contrast, slept for longer periods than normal, and would even sleep up to the time of the experiment, a period when most experimental animals tend to become restlessly active, in anticipation of their daily feeding period. He also had inactive periods in the experimental harness, when he failed to respond to either stimulus used in the discrimination problem. The behavior of Rat No. 3 presented some of the characteristics of both of the other rats described. Like No. 1, he lost the capacity to inhibit flexions; like No. 2, he took to sleeping excessively in his cage.

Cook's principal observations may be summarized in three points: (1) bizarre behavior did not appear until the element of restraint was introduced, as one of the frustrating factors; (2) even then, some of the animals seemed almost immune to the methods employed, even though "from the standpoint of an observer, the environmental conditions imposed on these animals were far more severe" than those which had produced breakdown in others; (3) when maladaptive behavior did occur, it took on distinctive individual characteristics, which may be described as different pathologies of inhibition, varying between the extremes of hyperexcitability and marked loss of responsiveness, with one animal showing a medley of both types of symptoms.

Mating and Parental Behavior

Although we cannot attempt to give a comprehensive account of rodent behavior in all its aspects, we should give at least a brief summary of an area which gives rise to such important determinants of human individuality.

The female rat has an estrous cycle of about four to five days. At what may be called the height of this cycle, for a brief period of only six hours, she is highly motivated, very active, and receptive to the attention of males. At this time she is simultaneously exciting to males, who need only a minimum amount of opportunity for practice to become effective masters of the art of copulation, which includes mounting the crouching female from behind and performing a quick series of pelvic thrusts. If he has not been raised in isolation, the normally aggressive young male has had this practice in juvenile play long before he is sexually mature. Submissive males, on the contrary, will be very backward in their sexual experience. The marital relationships of male and female do not extend beyond the brief experience of intercourse, which may, however, be repeated several times in a short space of time. From this point forward, it is the female who carries all the responsibilities. At the approach of parturition she builds a nest; she cleans her offspring, presumably because she has a strong appetite for the afterbirth, and during the nursing period she displays great skill and amazing persistence in caring for her infants and in retrieving them from all sorts of fiendish dangers contrived by experimentalists. After three weeks, lactation stops, and her interest in the litter disappears.

We shall not attempt to review the extensive literature of

investigation into the determinants of this elaborate complex of behavior. The interested reader may turn to Beach (1948, 1951) or, for a briefer summary, to Morgan and Stellar (1950). It is scarcely necessary to state that individual differences appear in the strength of motivation, and that these, as well as the vagaries induced by experimental interventions, provide striking illustrations of hormonal influences on behavior. It is important to recognize that the complex of reproductive behavior, broadly defined, includes far more than the immediate sexual act and the act of parturition, both of which may be defined as consummatory. It includes courtship on the one hand, which is at a minimum in the case of the rat, and parental care on the other. The male and female roles are distinctive at every point, although it should always be borne in mind that ambiguities are possible, because both masculinizing and feminizing hormones are present in the individuals of both sexes, though in different proportions (Koster, 1943). Nor is there a simple relationship between one hormone and all the behavioral dispositions which are characteristic of one sex. For example, the presence of prolactin, a pituitary secretion, is known to be conducive to the display of parental behavior, which is characteristically feminine, but ovarian secretion actually tends to suppress such behavior! Moreover, different aspects of mating and parental behavior are cued in complex ways by different forms of external stimulation, which ordinarily summate their effects, but also serve to insure that these overwhelmingly important functions will not readily be disrupted by the loss of a single sensory avenue.

SOME MAJOR DIMENSIONS OF TEMPERAMENT

In this chapter, we have seen many striking analogies between the behavior of rats and men, which encourage us in the view that there are variables of temperament which are common to both, and that discovering these in rats may help us to discern them in men. It is clear that all rats and mice have innate dispositions to fearful and aggressive behavior. In the life history of each rat, these original dispositions to fearful withdrawal from danger and to aggressive attack against victims or competitors are often in conflict, and undergo many modifying experiences. These tendencies correspond to two principal modes of adjustive behavior, two ways in which the animal apparatus serves the vegetative. At this point, we shall not try to name other dimensions, although the reader is free to speculate about them. Instead, we shall try to define the problem of temperament in very general terms, basing ourselves on a consideration of just these two dimensions.

Neither fearfulness nor aggressiveness can be created by environmental circumstance. Each must exist as an innate disposition, which may then be fostered or in a measure suppressed. The innate strength of each disposition, absolutely and relative to that of rival dispositions, is one factor which helps to determine the part that it will play in behavior. We shall define temperament, therefore, as including *those aspects of individuality which depend on the ease of arousal of innate patterns of response*—always remembering that this ease of arousal is itself subject to modification by experience. It follows from this definition that temperament cannot be reduced in its entirety to any small number of dimensions, because innate response organization is itself quite complex. However, we shall continue the search for a few major dimensions of temperament, which are related to the principal patterns of emotional disturbance in children, and hence to the core problems of personality development.

CHAPTER 4

Dogs and Cats

*F*or most of us, rats are untouchable, and we may even read about them with distaste and reluctance. But dogs are our friends, and stories about them rival love stories and mysteries in popular appeal. The dog, more than any other animal, is the companion of man, his friend as well as his servant. Cats, too, are our familiars, and we all have a wealth of experiences which have impressed us with the differences between canine and feline behavior. The rapidly growing literature of the experimental study of the behavior of these animals only serves to give definition to what we already know, in a general way, about their temperaments. In this chapter, we shall first review some of the findings with respect to breed and individual differences among dogs, and we shall then discuss how cats differ from dogs in the inhibitory control of their behavior.

Breed Differences

Dogs are specialized to serve us in many ways: as watchdogs, bird dogs, trackers, sled dogs, and herders. Each breed is fitted for a certain type of service, not only by its physique, but also by its characteristic ways of responding to certain situations. The dog trainer takes advantage of these innate dispositions, but does not create them. For example, an experienced dog breeder describes the contrasting dispositions of two common breeds of hunting dogs as follows:

A setter dog is interested in birds, hunts with head high, retrieves, mouths his prey, and enjoys water. In contrast, a hound is interested in animal tracks, does not point, hunts with head to the ground, is a poor retriever, crushes his prey. (Whitney, 1947.)

The geneticist Stockard recognized that the behavioral differences among dogs, no less than their structural differences, should be made the objects of scientific study. Here is one of his most striking observations, based on an ingenious experiment in the genetics of temperament:

> When the short-legged basset hound is crossed with the normal, wild-type, long-legged German shepherd, often in error called police dog, the hybrid offspring are all very closely alike in form, coat texture, color, and behavior; progeny are all short-legged like the basset parent and none have the long legs of the shepherd. . . . (They) all have the long drooping ears of the hound and never the erect ears of the shepherd, and the voice or bark is also more hound-like than shepherd-like. When these hybrid pups are reared by a shepherd mother and have never seen a basset hound, they will, when put on the field for the first time, scent with their noses down and bark as they run, behaving as their hound father would do, acting in a manner entirely unlike their shepherd mother with whom they have always associated. Thus their hunting instincts are as truly inherited as leg-lengths or hair-color, being probably associated with acuteness of smell, and are not, in this case at least, developed as a conditioned reflex. (*The Physical Basis of Personality,* 1931.)

When such hybrids are bred among each other, their offspring are no longer homogeneous, but show every sort of mixture and blend of the physical characteristics of the grandparents. Their behavioral characteristics are similarly unpredictable, and, what is of the greatest importance, they stand in no consistent relationship to physique. However, it is quite possible that they are associated with special sensitivities, such as the acuteness of smell to which Stockard refers above. This would be in keeping with the fact, which we mentioned in Chapter 2, that special sensitivities to certain kinds of stimulation are a very important aspect of all unlearned response patterns.

Stockard advanced the theory that many of the marked structural variations among dogs, and the concomitant behavioral differences, were the results of differences in glandular development, especially of the thyroid gland. The great variety of such differences results from the fact that the effect of a glandular hypertrophy or hypotrophy depends on the developmental stage at which it occurs. One embryonic stage may be particularly critical for the development of limbs, another for the development of eyes, or ears, or vocal structures. Thus, differences in glandular heredity may produce a variety of structural peculiarities, in addition to modifying the temperament of the grown animal. Stockard may be credited with having made out a very good case for his general theory. His exclusive emphasis on the thyroid gland may be attributed to the state of endocrinology at the time.

James (1941), in collaboration with Stockard, observed the behavior of basset hounds, German shepherds, and their hybrids in the course of conditioning experiments. He had in mind the assertion by Pavlov (1927) that dogs could be classified into two types, as excitable or inhibited, according to whether the inhibitory or excitatory nervous function was more prominent in their behavior. Pavlov also stated that the differentiation appeared most clearly in the type of neurotic or maladaptive behavior which the dog displayed when it was confronted by the frustrating demand for a discrimination which was beyond its capacity. James did not attempt to precipitate experimental neuroses, but he observed the behavior of his dogs during the acquisition and performance of both conditioned feeding and conditioned avoidance responses. In both situations, he found that most of his dogs could be classified as either Active or Lethargic. (He prefers these behavior-oriented terms to Pavlov's neurologically derived terms, Excitable and Inhibited.) In reading his description of these contrasting types, we must keep in mind a picture of the laboratory conditions under which such conditioning experiments are conducted. The dog is alone in a small room, so that he shall not try to take cues from the movements of the experimenter, nor be disturbed by other extraneous stimuli. He is on a table, tied in an experimental harness.

In the behavior of the lethargic animals, "there is a gradual elimination of bodily movements not absolutely essential for food taking. The adjustment is directed toward an economical performance, and the animals soon cease to orient to the signals or even to the food pan. . . . At times the animals may even go to sleep." Yet, when these same animals are removed from the monotony of the laboratory and tested with the conditioned stimuli out of doors, where there are enough distracting stimuli present to maintain an adequate level of excitement, the conditioned reactions reappear. The active animals are more difficult to train, and after training they are overactive. They often respond to the negative stimulus, more from their uncontained excitement than from a failure to discriminate. They also fail to inhibit their response during the delay period which follows the conditioned stimulus.

Pure-bred basset hounds are lethargic, while German shepherds are active. Their first-generation hybrids show intermediate characteristics, and hence adjust better to the laboratory situation than either parent. The later generation hybrids are variable in both structure and behavior, and, as has already been indicated above, it is not possible to predict the type of behavior they will show on the basis of their greater physical resemblance to one or another of the parent breeds.

James found that a few of his dogs could not be classified as belonging to either type, or as simply intermediate between them. These dogs exhibited behavioral peculiarities which made them unamenable to training. He classified two dogs as belonging to a "withdrawal type," and two others as showing a "hysterical syndrome" or "total pattern of escape." We are particularly interested in the fact that the two dogs of "withdrawal type" are stated as being each at the bottom of the dominance hierarchy in its litter. This is another instance (comparable to some we have seen among rats, and some others we shall see among dogs) of such complete subordination of a single animal in a small social group, arising out of intragroup competition, that the victimized animal becomes incapable of making a satisfactory adjustment in any situation that requires a modicum of aggressiveness, even though no social element is present. The frequency of such observations in small groups of animals should alert us to the similar danger which exists for children in human families and in play groups.

Cocker spaniels and fox terriers present a contrast in excitability which is somewhat similar to that between basset hounds and German shepherds. Fuller and Gillum (1950) compared the performance of these two breeds in a delayed-response learning experiment. The animals were also given standardized tests for activity, timidity, and dominance. The learning trials started when the animals were 7 or 8 months old. The problem required the dogs to choose one of two doors, after attention had been called to the correct door by having it opened and vigorously slammed shut four times. While this was going on, and for some seconds thereafter, the subject was restrained in the starting box. Only one of the four terriers was able to master this problem, with a delay of 10 seconds. He was the least active of the terriers, whose activity score fell within the range for the spaniels. Three of the spaniels were successful, reaching delays of 10 seconds, 20 seconds, and 60 seconds. The one that failed to learn had the highest score for timidity, and is described as extremely inhibited in his relations with his handler. Although the delayed response problem has often been called the best device for comparative intelligence ratings, it is obvious from these results that it is not a simple measure of intelligence, but is greatly influenced by temperamental factors. Most dog lovers would agree that the fox terrier is a "more intelligent" breed than the cocker spaniel. However, the impetuous terrier cannot meet the requirements of this problem nearly so well as the relatively placid cocker spaniel.

Finally, we must take note of the extraordinary readiness of dogs to attach themselves to human masters. This devotion is so strong that it leads Stockard (1941) to conjecture that perhaps the dog domesticated man, rather than the other way around! Lorenz (1952) points out that breeds of dogs differ considerably in the age at which they form irrevocable attachments to their human masters. He approaches this problem from the background of his extensive experimental work on the phenomenon which he has called "imprinting." We all remember the little lines of goslings and ducklings that we have seen parading after their mothers. Lorenz showed that the graylag gosling would follow any large moving object during the first hours after it was hatched, and that during this period the Gestalt of the particular object becomes "imprinted," so that no substitute is later acceptable. Normally it is Mother Goose that plays the leader, but if she is removed a man may play the part, and the goslings remain thereafter his devoted followers. By a correct combination of gymnastic and phonetic exercises, Lorenz and others have similarly seduced other young birds, such as Mallard ducks, and Jaynes (1956) has even developed in newborn chicks a touching devotion to green cubes and red cylinders. Something of the same sort evidently takes place in the establishment of every affectional relationship. With respect to dogs, Lorenz states that those breeds which are descended from the wolf form their attachments early, and that chows, for example, should be trained by their future masters from the age of 4 or 5 months. These are "one-man dogs," who are incapable of transferring their loyalty to new masters. On the other hand, those breeds that are descended from the jackal, such as the airedale, can switch their allegiance to new masters after they are grown. Less intensely loyal, they impress us as friendlier animals. Commenting on this, the psychoanalyst Bowlby (1953) has remarked: "If domestic breeds of dogs can differ so greatly in the rigidity of their object relationships, and in the age limits within which the critical phase for their development occurs, may it not also be so of humans?"

INDIVIDUAL DIFFERENCES

Although we have been discussing primarily the temperamental differences between breeds, our attention has been drawn several times to the special characteristics of individuals. Indeed, the study of breeds only interests us here because it brings into sharper relief the kinds of variation that are found among individuals. Within each breed, we find the same kinds of variation, over a more limited range. It would be tedious and without point to amass evidence of this obvious fact. However, we wish now to report briefly several studies which have been made with moderately large populations of dogs, in the attempt to discern the principal variables of canine temperament, by observing the reactions of many different dogs under similar test conditions.

Fuller (1946) subjected 34 dogs of different breeds to a variety of stimulating conditions, such as the presence of another dog, the ringing of a bell, handling by a person, etc. From a study of the reactions he classified his dogs as belonging to four types:

(1) An impassive type showing little external or internal response; (2) repressed type showing slight external response but increased heart rate and irregular respiration; (3) nervous type with marked internal response and visible trembling becoming convulsive in extreme cases; (4) excited type with rapid breathing and only moderate heart increases.

Types (1) and (4) probably correspond to the Lethargic and Active types described by James, while types (2) and (3) may be related to his "withdrawn" type and the "hysterical syndrome" which he described. The description used here also draws attention to the fact that there is an apparent independence of the external, motor reactions and the internal, visceral reactions. The picture suggested is a complex one, which permits not only of intermediate stages between types, but also of mixed types of reaction in the same individual, with some reaction systems manifesting one type of response and some another. Cook's rat No. 3, which lost the capacity to inhibit flexions but also took to sleeping excessively in his cage, was apparently an instance of such a mixed reaction type.

Fuller returned to this problem in another study (1948), in which he rated 40 dogs from various breeds with respect to level of overt activity in response to a standardized handling routine. He used a five-point rating scale, extending from "submissive or hypoactive" to "struggling and aggressive." Heart rate changes were simultaneously recorded. Although he found consistent individual variations in both sets of measures, there was no significant correlation between them, such as would be expected if they were the expressions of the same dimension of temperament.

DEVELOPMENT OF DOMINANCE RELATIONSHIPS

Temperamental factors and specific individual experience combine to influence the development of the characteristic reaction patterns of the mature dog. One of the most interesting aspects of this process is the growth and modification of social behavior, and especially of the dominance-submission relationships between each individual animal and his peers. When the puppies of a litter are permitted to grow up together, a dominance hierarchy always develops. The position which the individual dog holds in this hierarchy is a factor that influences many other areas of his behavior, even in adulthood.

Scott and Marston (1950) have described the development of the dog as falling into five periods, which, they state, are meaningful also with respect to other mammals, including man. From their account of these periods, we take only what is relevant to our immediate topic. Their description is based on the close observation of 73 puppies of seven breeds, raised under uniform conditions, which included the periodic systematic testing of social relationships within the litters and toward handlers.

In the neonatal period, which lasts for about two weeks, there is no aggressive fighting, but there is escape behavior and yelping as a response to pain. Social relationships are of course limited by the fact that the eyes are not yet open. That event marks the beginning of the transition period, which occupies approximately the next two weeks. During this time puppies begin to walk unsteadily, and to chew on each other, behavior which seems to be correlated with the eruption of teeth. Whining becomes less frequent. Toward the end of this period fighting play appears, "and includes clumsy pawing and biting of the litter mates or portions of the mother's body. Growling is occasionally present but not barking." There is also a startle reaction to loud sounds. The third period is called the period of socialization, a designation which indicates the crucial importance which Scott and Marston attribute to it. The puppies now come into extensive contact with people, and with animals other than their litter mates and their mother. They begin to approach other dogs and humans with wagging tails, and will lick and paw the other animal, apparently in a gesture of food begging. Playful fighting increases. In the course of such play, a posture of subordination may be assumed by the underpup. Dominance relationships begin to develop, but no marked dominance postures appear until the end of this period. Barking develops. Toward the end of the period, two or three puppies may surround and playfully attack another. When the fight appears to become more serious, the losing pup assumes a subordinate attitude. The fourth period extends from weaning until maturity, and is called the juvenile period. Early in this period, by 15 weeks, "the playful fighting has been pretty well organized into a dominance system and there is, therefore, less bodily contact." "The definite bodily postures of dominance (tail erect, growling, and placing fore feet on the other animal), and subordination (crouching with tail between legs or rolling on back with paws outstretched) have been developed." Severe fighting is rare. "In free living, this is the period which would be spent in learning to hunt and become self-supporting."

With respect to the consistency of dominance relationships, the authors state that at the age of five weeks, "31 percent of the relationships between puppies can be recognized as dominance, whereas by 11 weeks this percentage has risen to 95 percent. . . . However, about one-third of the dominance relationships observed at 11 weeks are changed by 15 weeks."

Except for changes due to mating behavior, the dominance order at one year is likely to be just as it was at 15 weeks. This is one reason why the "period of socialization" is of such crucial importance.

The influence of temperament on dominance is clearly demonstrated in a study by James (1951). He split litters of wire-haired terriers and beagles, so that three beagles and two terriers were raised by a terrier, and three of each breed by a beagle mother. Dominance tests were conducted within each group when they were a year old. In each group, all the terriers were dominant over all the beagles, despite the greater weight of the latter, a factor which tends to promote dominance in normal, homogeneous litters. The reason is apparent in their typical behavior.

> The terriers are highly active and excitable animals. They would invariably come forward as the experimenter entered the runs and begin to jump up as if trying to get attention. The beagles, on the other hand, would remain in the background. . . . When cornered, they would take the passive, defensive attitude. They are definitely of a more inhibited type than the terriers.

From this description, it appears likely that the initial temperamental difference between terriers and beagles was not only responsible for causing the former to occupy the top places in the dominance hierarchy, but that this in turn has caused the beagles to be more fearful of human contacts than they would otherwise have been.

The animals in each group were given an opportunity, in a specially constructed apparatus, to indicate their preference for companionship among those with whom they had been raised. Each animal made its choice between every possible pair among the puppies with whom it had been raised. In every case, both beagles and terriers showed preference for the company of beagles. Thus even the terriers did not approve of their own hyperactive, go-getter personalities, in other dogs. (It may be assumed that the outcome of this sociometric experiment is quite different from what would occur in groups of children, comprising a roughly similar social structure. In that case, the prestige factor would often lead a submissive child to prefer the companionship of a dominant playmate, indicating the greater complexity of human interactions.)

In still another study, James (1949) observed the development of dominance relationships in a litter of four Dalmatian-setter hybrids, which included three males and one female. His observations started when they were about 12 weeks old. At that time one of the males was definitely submissive to all its litter-mates, and the others had approximately equal status. At 17 weeks, the female suddenly shifted to the dominant position. It was observed that when conflict over food arose among the dominant animals in the group, "it did not necessarily result in actual combat between them. In most cases, this frustration was transferred to the submissive animal." Thus the underdog also became the scapegoat. Two attempts were made to free him from this unenviable position. The first was by "alcohol therapy." On nine occasions he was given a small dose of alcohol about 10 minutes before feeding began. On these occasions he ventured closer to the feeding pan, suggesting that his inhibitions had been somewhat reduced, and there was some increase in his food intake, but the difference was not significant. He was then favored with special feeding periods, which brought his weight up to that of the other males. However, he retained his submissive attitudes, and was still unable to get enough food under competitive conditions. Once again, we see how difficult it is to overcome the harmful effects of unfavorable early experience.

It is evident from what has been said that in the development of dominance relationships the interplay of temperamental factors is important. Thus the behavior of the mature dog is not simply an expression of his own temperament, but indirectly also of the temperament of his litter mates, and of other environmental circumstances. There is evidence that such circumstances have especially forceful impact in the crucial period between 10 weeks and 15 weeks of age. When attitudes of submission are fixed at this time, it is extremely difficult to eradicate them later, and they seem to exercise an inhibiting influence on the behavior of the animal generally. The reader may ponder, if he wishes, whether similar generalizations might not be made about human behavior, but we shall not take space for discussion of this problem until later chapters.

CATS AND DOGS: A CONTRAST IN TEMPERAMENT

Everyone has observed that the behaviors of cats and dogs are strikingly different in many ways. Common cats are considered less docile and less affectionate than dogs. They become housebroken more readily, but only because they are cleaner by nature, and it often seems impossible to make them conform in other ways to the routine of the household, which must rather accept their schedule. They are more fastidious eaters, and even when hungry may reject food that is not what they think it should be, whereas it is not rare for a dog to gorge himself with garbage. They show greater control in hunting, as exemplified particularly in the game of "cat and mouse," or in their cautious stalking of a bird. They are less impulsive in their actions, less stimulus-bound, seeming to follow their own intent while ignoring distractions that would redirect the activity of a dog. Gates (1928) states that a cat will characteristically give undivided attention to what it is doing, while the dog will repeatedly glance at his master, as if for hints or approval. This anecdotal evidence receives support from the laboratory, for Dworkin (1939) points out that it is relatively easy to inhibit the performance of a conditioned response in a dog by introducing an extraneous stimulus, but it is difficult to do this with cats.[1] Like many children, they have the ability to "close their ears" to what they do not wish

---

[1] Dworkin concludes that the inhibitory functions are relatively weak in the cat. We would prefer to interpret this as a failure on the part of the dog to inhibit response to the distracting stimulus. Greater distractibility signifies less effective inhibition, internally, even though it results in what the Pavlov school calls "external inhibition" of the conditioned response.

to hear. It is probably this independence of chance stimuli which results in the extraordinary stereotypy of movement which is characteristic of their performance of learned motor acts, and which has been noticed by everyone who has used cats as subjects in learning experiments. Masserman (1943) tells how cats that had learned to depress a control switch by accidentally rubbing against it, continued to operate it in the same manner thereafter; those that had been taught by having their paws pressed against it, continued to use their paws; while those that had been enticed to the switch by a dish of salmon juice, would generally use their snouts to depress it. Guthrie and Horton (1946), in their monograph on *Cats in a Problem Box,* make a special point of demonstrating this extraordinary stereotypy of movement, which they regard as evidence in favor of Guthrie's theory that all learning is by contiguous association. However, we may feel confident that if they had used dogs as their subjects in the same problem boxes, they would have had very different results.

The cat is commonly considered to be "proud," in contrast to the dog, because it does not beg for affection in the same manner, although it does exhibit its skill to its master in an apparent bid for approval. I can offer an anecdotal illustration of feline pride, from the behavior of our own household pets of several years back. The cat and the dog—a cocker spaniel—tolerated each other's presence rather well, with the cat more dominant in play situations. Either one, if it entered a room in which my wife sat reading, would ask to be taken into her lap. If the cat were already there, the dog would be especially urgent in his appeal. If the dog were anywhere near, the cat would stalk quietly away, as if he were unwilling to share the affections of his mistress. Another illustration of the extraordinary "dignity" which cats sometimes display in situations which involve emotional conflict is given by Masserman (1943). He describes how several of his cats, who were supposed to learn how to escape from a cage in order to avoid the punishment of an electric shock, "even after successful escapes from the grid, abandoned further attempts at adaptation to the experimental conditions, showed only transient restlessness at the preliminary signals, and then squatted with paws folded under to endure the grid shocks with martyred mien."

Thorndike (1911), who used cats as subjects in many of his pioneering experiments on animal learning, remarked that it is easier to teach a cat to do something, than to teach it not to do something, that is, to refrain from an act. Housewives who have tried to teach cats not to scratch the furniture, or not to kill birds in the garden, will readily agree. We must accept cats into our homes pretty much on their own terms, be pleased that their habits are not too objectionable, admire the cleverness with which they discover things for themselves, but despair of persuading them to change their ways. They are arch conservatives.

Of course, it may be objected, such generalizations do not hold for *all* dogs and *all* cats. Indeed, they do not; if they did, the distinction would be of less importance to us. What we have described is a difference *between* species, which certainly has a physiological basis, even though we do not fully understand the factors involved. In lesser degree, differences of the same kind exist *within* the species, among different breeds, and within the breeds, among individuals. For example, it is true that the Siamese cat solicits affection from its master (and is therefore often described as being, in this respect, "just like a dog"), and that some dogs may be fastidious eaters. It would seem reasonable to suppose that in so far as such differences are characteristic of breeds they are based on variations of the same physiological factors—sensory, glandular, nervous, or whatever— that cause the overall differences between the behavior of cats and dogs. When they appear as individual peculiarities within the breed, although we cannot exclude the possibility of genetic variation, we must look to the effects of experience as the more likely cause.

Our interest in presenting this temperamental contrast between canine and feline behavior arises from the circumstance that it can be used to highlight one very important determinant of human individuality, which apparently has its basis in nervous structure. We are referring to the importance of excitation—inhibition as a temperamental variable. Although this dimension of behavior is imperfectly understood, it deserves great emphasis, and no discussion of temperament can afford to neglect it.

Excitation-Inhibition

The concepts of excitation and inhibition have already been mentioned several times. We have used them as descriptive terms applied to behavior, on a macroscopic level, but they also designate nervous processes, on a microscopic level. We must try now to clarify them.

The nervous system is an organ which is specialized in conduction. Its primary function is to conduct excitatory impulses, which instigate reactions in other organs. It serves as the middle member in stimulus response, receptor-effector relationships. However, the impulses it transmits do not always have a peripheral origin; that is, they do not all originate in sensory nerve endings. Metabolic processes, whether of the neurons themselves or of the tissues closely associated with them in the supporting structure of the brain, must be the source of the electrical activity that can be detected in the resting brain. The brain is therefore not merely a passive conductor, but to some extent also an independent source of excitations, which must have some influence on the final outcome of behavior. Equally important is the fact that some nervous impulses, which are in themselves not distinguishable in so far as their electrochemical characteristics are detectable, serve not to excite but to inhibit or depress the activity of the effector organ in which they terminate. This fact has been well established. The classic examples are the kinesthetic control of antagonistic muscles in locomotion, as demonstrated by Sherrington (1906), and the depressing effect of vagus nerve stimulation on heart activity. It is not yet definitely known how these inhibitory effects are achieved, although the trend of evidence would seem to favor the view that they are mediated by special end plates of the effector neurons, which secrete inhibitory hormones. Whatever the explanation, the fact is clear, and the implication for us is that we cannot continue to think of nervous impulses as always excitatory in their effects.

Even more important for our immediate topic, it is also well established that nervous activity can depress other nervous activity, or, to state it otherwise, that the activity of one part of the nervous system can negate or counteract or depress the activity of another part. A great many illustrations of such effects might be given. We shall select three, each of which has a particular relevance to some phase of our problem.

Our first illustration is taken from the experimental investigation of the nervous control of emotional expression. Goltz (1892) first observed that decorticate animals may give a violent display of emotional behavior, which has been called "sham rage" in recognition of the fact that it lacks some of the characteristics of genuine emotional response. Since then, many workers have studied this phenomenon, striving to define with all possible precision the exact brain areas that are involved. Bard (1950) summarizes his own definitive work and that of others. The critical area is found to lie within the hypothalamus. What we wish to stress at this point is not that a given structure is involved in the performance of the gestural components of the rage pattern, but that it is the removal of other structures which releases the mechanisms involved, so that quite trivial stimulation may then suffice to provoke a manifestation of extreme rage. It is evident, as Bard had stated earlier (1934), that

inhibitory cortical influences normally prevent the primitive activities from dominating behavior. The subcortical processes are at all times ready to seize control of the motor reactions and when the cortical check is released they do so promptly and with elemental vigor.

Bard and Mountcastle (1947) carried the analysis of this phenomenon further. They demonstrated that it is possible to remove a good deal of the cerebral cortex without releasing sham rage, as long as certain areas, designated as the amygdaloid complex and the transitional cortex, are left intact. Indeed, under these conditions cats become especially placid, so that it is virtually impossible to provoke them to angry behavior. Thus that area of the cat's brain that exercises inhibitory control over the hypothalamic rage-provoking mechanisms is rather closely defined. This is a special case of the general principle that all instinctive responses are, as Tinbergen (1951) put it, constantly primed, awaiting only the removal of inhibitory blocks.

Our second illustration of internal inhibition—the inhibition of one part of the nervous system by another part, without the participation of an external distraction—is the fact that recent studies of the localization of brain functions have led to the discovery of certain "suppressor areas." Morgan and Stellar (1950) give the following brief statement of the technique used in these studies, and of the results which interest us here.

Strychnine, a convulsive drug, is applied locally to a region of the cortex while electrodes placed in other areas pick up any resulting change in activity. Strychnine always strongly excites or "fires" the region to which it is applied, and if some other area is affected by the use of the drug we know that there is a connection between the two areas. . . . With the technique of strychninization, it has been possible to tell that certain areas of the cortex facilitate or even fire other areas concerned in motor function. . . . Now we come to another interesting aspect of intercortical motor functions. This is the existence, and the connections, of suppressor areas of the cortex. Such areas are called suppressor areas because, when they are fired with strychnine, they suppress rather than augment electrical activity in other areas of the brain. . . . Sometimes the suppression can be seen in behavior—it prevents or stops movements that otherwise can be elicited by stimulating one of the cortical motor areas. . . . Altogether there are five suppressor areas that we know about so far.

Stanley and Jaynes (1949) have discussed the implications of this phenomenon for psychological theory. They point out that the ability to perform successfully in a delayed reaction problem—such as that which Fuller and Gillum used in their comparative study of fox terriers and cocker spaniels—depends upon a function of "cortical act-inhibition." The reality of such motor inhibition within the cortex has now been demonstrated.

A third illustration of internal inhibition is the experimental demonstration that removal of the frontal poles of the cerebrum causes a marked increase in the general rate of activity. This has been demonstrated in the behavior of rats, cats, and monkeys. (See Morgan and Stellar, 1950, for a general review of this material.) Removal of one pole results in a marked increase in activity, while removal of both may cause such unremitting activity that the animal very nearly runs itself to death. Clinical experience provides human examples of similar restless behavior following frontal lesions of the brain. It is evident that the frontal poles normally exercise an inhibitory control over the nervous mechanisms that are involved in the locomotor pattern, in very much the same way that other cortical areas inhibit the mechanisms that are involved in emotional expression.

These illustrations will suffice to demonstrate that when we use the term "inhibition," we are speaking of a physiological process, and not simply of an external aspect of behavior. Within the brain, there is a constant rivalry of potential behaviors, a constant interplay of their neural antecedents. This rivalry does not lead to a compromising or summative outcome, but to a choice, which results from the fact that all but one of the possible responses are, for the moment at least, inhibited. Furthermore, the smooth performance of this one response implies a constant regulatory process which is itself inhibitory. Morgan and Stellar go so far as to say that "probably the most important of all factors in coordinated movement is restraint or inhibition." Without continuous inhibitory control of motor response, every act would overshoot its mark, as occurs in some forms of motor disturbance. Finally, we should take note of the fact that many of the instances of inhibitory control can be subsumed under the single great principle of anterior dominance. However, the widespread effects of the suppressor areas, and particularly their reciprocal effects upon one another, are enough to show that the hierarchic organization of the cortex is not so strict that it is possible to apply this principle to every instance of inhibition.

These generalizations are based on experiments which deal exclusively with overt behavior, but it is clear that they must apply equally to the rivalry of intracortical processes which do not immediately issue into action. "Sometimes (again quoting Morgan and Stellar) the suppression is simply of the spontaneous activity that normally goes on in various areas of the cortex. Sometimes the suppression can be seen in behavior." Sometimes, surely, it affects the processes of thought. We are here reminded of the statement by Sechenov (1863), the teacher of Pavlov, that a thought is a reflex whose motor component has been inhibited.

From time to time, we shall have to add new emphasis to the subject of inhibition. Without laboring the point, we ask the reader now to take judicial notice of the fact that all learning involves inhibition of inappropriate wrong responses, just as much as it involves establishing relationships between cues and right responses. A rather good case can be made out, also, for the hypothesis that all voluntary movement is primarily a phenomenon of the selective release of the necessary motor components from inhibition, rather than of specific motor excitation of these elements (cf. Freeman, 1948b, p. 333). We pass over these points, which we do not wish to follow into long digressions. What we wish to stress is the fact that the function of inhibition is often a process of interaction among different parts of the brain.

It is therefore altogether reasonable to suppose that such differences as we have observed between cats and dogs, which may be described as differences in the strength of the inhibitory function, are based upon structural differences in the brain. In support of this general viewpoint, we may quote the conclusion which Lashley (1947) reached, on the basis of histological studies of the brains of spider monkeys:

. . . Individuals start life with brains differing enormously in structure; unlike in number, size, and arrangement of neurons as well as in grosser features. The variations in cells and tracts must have functional significance. It is not conceivable that the inferior frontal convolutions of two brains would function in the same way or with equal effectiveness when one contains only half as many cells as the other; . . . (or) that the presence of Betz cells in the prefrontal region is without influence on behavior. Such differences are the rule in the limited material that we have studied.

Lashley's acceptance of the idea that the finer structure of the brain probably influences behavior—an idea which runs counter to his earlier views—lends authoritative support to the conjecture that differences in behavior, which can be characterized as differences in degree of impulsivity or inhibition, may result from native differences in cortical structure. This point is of fundamental importance for the understanding of human temperament.

MAJOR DIMENSIONS OF TEMPERAMENT IN DOGS

In this chapter we have seen ample evidence that fearfulness and aggressivity, the two dimensions of temperament which were most prominent in the rat, play similar roles in the life of the dog. The development of dominance relationships among dogs, as among rats, consists largely of a conflict between these opposing tendencies. We have seen new evidence that the outcome of this development, in individual cases, not only influences the behavior of an animal toward others of his species, but that it also influences the style of his behavior and the chances of his success in many nonsocial situations. However, the dog's relationship to man highlights another important temperamental characteristic, his readiness and even need to form dependent attachments. Obviously, this is not a uniquely canine characteristic, although it has undergone an extraordinary development in the dog, whose lasting attachments to human masters have become the very symbol of affectionate devotion. Basically the same need is exhibited in the relationship of every infant mammal to its mother, and in the readiness for all sorts of affiliative behavior. It is present, although less prominent, in rat nature, being as essential for the survival of a litter of rats as for one of dogs. Perhaps it is the basis for what has been called tameness, or the readiness of some rats to submit to human handling. Lacking a reciprocal attachment for rats, psychologists have been rather insensitive to this softer side of their natures, and have neglected to investigate it. In dogs, it assumes a much greater importance. We shall call it dependent-affiliative disposition, or more briefly, affiliativeness.

The dimension of excitation-inhibition, or responsiveness to external stimulation, also appears more prominently in dogs than in rats, or at least has been more extensively studied in dogs. The contrast of behavior between dogs and cats suggests that in our effort to understand this dimension, we should give more attention to the negative pole, inhibition. Depending on context, we shall sometimes call this bipolar dimension *impulsivity,* and at other times we shall call it *inhibitory control.* Unlike the other three principal dimensions, this one does not correspond to a distinctive mode of adjustive behavior. It is concerned, instead, with the more general contrast between stimulus-bound, impulsive expression of any behavioral disposition, and its controlled release or inhibition.

In summary, then, we recognize at least four major dimensions of temperament in dogs, which we designate as fearfulness, aggressivity, affiliativeness, and inhibitory control. Each of these was also present in the rat, although they were not all equally obvious there.

CHAPTER 5

The Chimpanzee

$\mathcal{W}$e turn now, as we continue our ascending march, to a study of temperament and individuality in the behavior of the chimpanzee. Among the subhuman primates, he is the psychologist's favorite. Not only his intelligence endears him to the experimenter, but his social warmth, and the sly humor which attracts crowds to his cage in many a metropolitan zoo. These qualities have often led to the surmise that a chimpanzee, raised with all the advantages of a human child, might rise above the usual limits of animal behavior. Two experiments of this type (Kellogg and Kellogg, 1933; Hayes, 1951) provide some of the most important material for this chapter. Most of the rest arises from various phases of the work of the Yerkes Laboratories of Primate Biology, in Florida. These laboratories also provided the infant chimpanzees that were "adopted" by the Kellogg's, the Hayes's, and the Finch's. Thus almost all of our scientific knowledge about the behavior of the animal species that stands closest to man, we owe indirectly to the farsightedness of one man, Robert M. Yerkes.

The experimental study of the apes is attended by many difficulties. They cannot be bred in multitudes, like rats, whose fruitful generations follow each other in quick succession, nor can they be found as captive subjects in classrooms and clinics, like children. A female chimpanzee carries her child almost as long as a human mother does, and she, or a nursery attendant, must care for it through a long infancy. Their social attachments are so strong that the effect of separating an individual from its group may be violent enough to upset any experiment. When rats are used as subjects, it is a very common practice to raise them in solitude in order to control the effects of social experience. But Köhler (1925) warns that "a chimpanzee kept in solitude is not a real chimpanzee at all." Yerkes and Yerkes (1935) state that one should not attempt to do experimental work with chimpanzees who have been removed from groups to which they have become accustomed, without gradual preparation for this painful separation. With these animals, affiliativeness can scarcely be overlooked! The intensely social nature of the young chimpanzee is the source of many of the difficulties that have been experienced by those hardy researchers who have taken infant chimpanzees into their own homes. These difficulties are usually greater than those that parents expect to meet with their own children, and in no sense comparable to the usual problems of keeping a household pet.

However, the study of the chimpanzee has much to offer us. Of all the primates he most clearly exhibits for our study the bases of our own temperament. He has, however, a very special poverty: an almost total inability to make use of language for purposes of communication. He has a few unlearned expressive sounds which reflect such basic feelings as distress, fear, or eagerness for food, and which constitute the whole of "chimpanzee language" (Nissen, 1931). Under human tutelage, he can be taught to respond appropriately to many phrases which make concrete reference to objects and actions. At the age of 2, his competence in this regard may be as great as that of the average human child of the same age, but he will continue to build his vocabulary of comprehension slowly during the third year, when that of the child advances by tremendous leaps. This is not because he is less intelligent than the child, for he can continue through this third year to hold his own on standard developmental tests, making up by his advantage on performance items all that he loses on those of a verbal nature (Hayes). Nevertheless, his speech remains limited to a very few words. Viki Hayes—as we shall call her—learned under patient tutelage to say "mama," "papa," and "cup," and to use these words appropriately when soliciting attention from her adoptive mother and father, or when asking for liquid. This practical vocabulary may in the future be extended by another few words. But it is the product of patient and ingenious training, which is like the training of a human aphasic, and not of such a drive for vocal expression as is evident in any normal child. The limiting factor is not in the vocal apparatus, but apparently in the lack of nervous mechanisms which are essential to true speech. Hayes (1950) speculates that the brain of a chimpanzee resembles that of a human who suffers from aphasia. However, the theoretical explanation of the chimpanzee's language difficulties is not the essential point for us. Even if this difficulty arises from an incapacity to master the phonetic elements of our language (Kelemen, 1949), it still imposes a severe limitation on the thought processes which are available to the chimpanzee, and which may enter into the development of individual characteristics of behavior. Hence, we see in the chimpanzee a picture of the behavioral development which might take place in a young child without the use of language in its thinking. When we observe chimpanzee behavior which is similar to that of the child, we are forced to assume that language plays no essential part in the development of such behavior in children.

Let us illustrate this point. It has often been suggested that the child's first words give him a new power of self-control, through self-stimulation. It is assumed, under this hypothesis, that the ability to repeat the word "ball," reciting it over and over, both aloud and subvocally, makes it possible for the child to carry out a search for his missing ball, which will take him through several rooms and will last a few minutes. However, Hayes tells us that Viki once responded to her request, "Give me the dog," with five minutes of searching behavior, until she had found the toy dog in the spot behind the crib where it had fallen, and brought it to her "mother" in the garden. Viki could respond appropriately to the word "dog," but she could not pronounce any approximation of it. She could not have been using sub-vocal speech to maintain the continuity of her searching behavior. Therefore we must assume that the child's ability to do the same is independent of his ability to speak. In the same way, when we observe other parallel forms of behavior in the child and the chimpanzee, we will have to assume that verbalization is not essential to the development of such behavior. This does not deny the possibility that speech *may* be utilized by the child in such situations; for although we can walk, we may prefer to ride, if we have an automobile available. But when we see the child acting in typical chimpanzee ways, we must be very skeptical of explanations in terms of language-mediated social influences.

In the remainder of this chapter, we shall give first the descriptions that are based on observation of the social life of captive chimpanzees, including both a picture of their typical behavior and of the variants that have been encountered. Next, we shall consider the behavior of young chimpanzees that have been raised in a human environment. Finally, we shall consider some of the methods that have been introduced for objective evaluation of individual characteristics, and the results obtained from them.

THE CAPTIVE CHIMPANZEE

Since it is extremely difficult to observe chimpanzees in the field, our knowledge of their behavior derives almost entirely from observation of captive animals. However, such field observations as have been made (Nissen, 1931) support the view that the behavior which is displayed in captivity, under favorable circumstances, gives a representative picture of chimpanzee development and socialization. Yerkes gives an excellent account, from which we take a summary paragraph:

The young chimpanzee is a lively extravert, active, energetic, impulsive, enthusiastic, sanguine, very sociable, ordinarily good-natured and fairly good-tempered, somewhat mercurial, timid before the unfamiliar, extremely expressive of its continuous flow of feelings and rapidly changing moods. . . . During adolescence and maturity playfulness and random, seemingly purposeless activity steadily lessen. In general, the contrast in emotionality between youth and age, or even between childhood and maturity, is similar to that we know in ourselves. There is a change from lively to sedate, impulsive to reserved, irresponsible to serious, active to relatively quiet. An individual which in the first few years of life impresses one as gay, joyous, full of life, friendly, eager for companionship, in the second or third decade may appear independent, aloof, self-centered, serious, and perhaps also short-tempered or irascible. (*Chimpanzees*, 1943.)

The reader has probably been struck by the fact that Yerkes' description of typical chimpanzee behavior draws freely upon the full vocabulary of trait description which we ordinarily use in describing the behavior of persons. This is even more striking when he describes the contrasting temperaments of some individuals: the obstinate Wendy, the timid but coöperative Bill, the trustful and energetic Chim, the distrustful and lethargic Panzee. Or, again, when he states that a youngster in the midst of a tantrum glanced "furtively" at its mother, "as if to discover whether its action was attracting attention." Such description raises two doubts in our minds, both relating to problems of scientific method.

First, we may wonder whether such descriptions are not excessively anthropomorphic—that is, whether they do not represent an addition of human thought and feeling into a situation which is not experienced in these terms by the chimpanzee, and which could be objectively reported in much simpler terms. Hebb (1946a), who has worked extensively at the Yerkes Laboratories, discusses this question at some length. He states that such anthropomorphic descriptions, even when they are made by caretakers who are without scientific training but who have had long acquaintance with the animals, have greater validity in the sense of providing better prediction of future behavior than rigorously objective descriptions by members of the scientific staff. This is because "familiarity with the animal reveals a long-term pattern of behavior *with which the observer is already familiar in man.*" The relative inadequacy of objective description is illustrated by the following example. There is general agreement among the staff, Hebb writes, that one chimpanzee is a man hater, while another is basically friendly although given to sudden outbursts of anger against men, despite the fact that the objective record shows no difference in the pattern of their attacks on humans. If such distinctions, and the many-faceted emotional portrayals given by Yerkes, have validity, it can only be because they are founded on basic points of agreement in the emotional life of men and chimpanzees. Hebb writes: "The behavior of the dog is complex enough, but lifelong familiarity with this animal does not produce the degree of 'anthropomorphism' in psychologically sophisticated persons that six months of exposure to the chimpanzee will produce."

Even granting the validity of such descriptions, a second doubt occurs. Is it not methodologically essential that we should reduce the dimensions of our description to an absolute minimum, even though this entails some loss in the richness of description, as well as in literary flavor? We shall return to this problem more than once. It seems reasonable, however, that both types of description should be carried on, even side by side. We must, indeed, make the constant effort to give rigorous descriptions of behavior in terms of a minimal number of dimensions that are unambiguously defined and objectively measured, but we must at the same time recognize how far such descriptions fall short of the fullness of behavior, whose nuances are reflected in the wealth of language. The clinician, working with human patients, faces this problem in even sharper form.

The description which Yerkes gives us, and which is borne out by all other accounts of chimpanzee behavior, reveals a typical regularity in development which encourages us in the quest for major variables. His description of the expected changes in chimpanzee temperament, as given above, should be studied alongside of his account of the typical progress of socialization.

The progress of chimpanzee socialization between birth and maturity is from a state of utter dependence to one of self-sustaining
dominance. Followed with understanding, it is a fascinating series of
events in which the paramount social need or craving undergoes
modification or replacement. Thus the necessity for something to cling
to gives place to the more obviously social expressions of need for
companionship, and this in turn is presently supplemented by the
urge to take precedence, to dominate, or just to have and to hold one's
place in the social group. Perhaps it is better to think of this as effort
to achieve and hold social status instead of as striving for dominance. . . .

The dominance drive as expressed in the endeavor to gain superior
social status is little in evidence during the early months of life,
becomes common during childhood, and is a conspicuous and highly
important chimpanzee characteristic during adolescence and maturity.
As soon as two unacquainted individuals who are well grown are
brought together they proceed to settle their social status by looking
one another over appraisingly, by trial of physical prowess and
courage, or by a combination of the two. Bluffing and physical
struggles in which teeth, hands, and feet are effectively used are
common. But often they give place to, or are supplemented by, what
looks like a contest of wills, in which self-confidence, resourcefulness,
and persistence seem to be highly important.

The process of socialization is governed by three important
principles:

. . . infantile social dependency, with its urge to cling; childish
social attachment, with its insatiable craving for companionship; and
adolescent or mature dominance, with its persistent drive for social
status—a higher place in the social hierarchy.

This synoptic statement reminds us of the account which Scott
and Marston gave of the social development of the dog. As
the puppies gain independence from the mother, they seek other
social contacts, which are at first only playful, but soon develop
into a contest for dominance. It reminds us also that Fredericson
observed his young mice engaging at first in friendly behavior,
including mutual grooming (which is a prominent feature in
the friendly interaction of chimpanzees), for a period of 10
or 12 days prior to the appearance of spontaneous fighting among

the males. Thus the process that we measure in weeks for the rodent, in months for the dog, and in years for the chimpanzee, follows the same course in all. Our own lives have a similar pattern, but we are prone to overlook its biological foundations, and to seek its explanation in the gradual surrender of the child to the competitive pattern of human society, which is judged by some of us to be evil and by others good. Particularly if we take the former view, we are reluctant to believe that what has been called "the neurotic personality of our time" (Horney, 1937) is only a variant of a pattern that is older than humanity. The chimpanzee's infantile need for mothering, and its mature need for status recognition, each of which is associated with certain characteristic behaviors, must apparently be recognized as expressions of two of the dimensions of temperament that we have already specified: affiliativeness and aggressivity. It is possible that the intervening need for companionate play, which is prominent in the prepubertal "childhood" of each mammalian species, should be recognized as an independent dimension, as Yerkes implies when he states that these "three principles" appear in the process of socialization. It seems more parsimonious, however, to regard play behavior as a complex expression of many needs, including the two that have just been mentioned, which may be characterized as dependent and aggressive social needs, as well as activity drive, curiosity, immature expression of the awakening sex need, etc.

The chimpanzee, like many other primates, exhibits a strong tendency to imitative behavior. This fact has been questioned, as a part of the general reaction of experimental psychologists against the anecdotal psychology of an earlier generation. The tests of the experimentalists took the form of trying to teach their monkey subjects how to operate problem boxes by demonstrating the necessary manipulations, or even having the demonstration performed by another monkey in a neighboring cage. The failure of such efforts only proves that imitation is difficult to evoke under these conditions, but it cannot invalidate the evidence of careful observation. Again, we quote Yerkes and Yerkes (1935):

It is well established that the animals are imitative of man and of each other. Among recorded ways may be mentioned: spitting through the teeth, hand-clapping, kissing, dancing and other social rhythmic motions, body and limb gestures, mannerisms, forms of play, manner or mode of operating mechanisms or of working in an experiment, use of objects as tools, the fashioning of objects for specific purposes. . . . Next to man, chimpanzee is the most highly imitative animal known to us.

At another point they write:

Many times . . . we have succeeded by social stimulation in eliciting positive response from an individual which previously had persistently refused to accept a certain substance or object. Sometimes another member of the species, and again a person, is used as a source of social stimulation, copysetter, or imitatee. Few primates when hungry can long withstand the mimetic influence of watching a fellow monkey, ape, or man, avidly devour some strange material which previously had been ignored, determinedly rejected, or even ejected by the individual.

The importance of imitation is not in any implication that a high order of intelligence is involved, although it is probably a fact that a fairly high level of symbolic behavior is needed for such varied imitative behavior. Its great importance is that it provides new opportunities for effective socialization. It permitted Yerkes to install push-button drinking fountains and other mechanical devices in the animals' living quarters, with full confidence that all would learn to operate them by example. In the human child it is developed to an even higher degree, and it is indispensable for the transmission of culture.

In its sexual behavior, the chimpanzee exhibits an enlightening combination of stereotyped and clearly inherited responses, along with individualized forms of social interaction. The most obvious respect in which the sexual behavior of the chimpanzee differs from that of lower mammals is in the periodicity of the receptive phase of the female. The estrous cycle of the rat is four or five days, and that of the dog or cat is half a year, but the chimpanzee approaches the monthly cycle of the human female, and is receptive to sexual approaches for a period of several days during this cycle. The copulatory act includes invitational postures by the female, and a distinctive mounting posture by the male, followed by pelvic thrusts. Individuals who have been raised in like-sexed groups of juveniles are not so quick as the lower mammals would be to perform their roles with competence, but in time they do so, without need for instruction. However, there is one very important respect in which the sexual behavior of the chimpanzee seems to foretell the shape of human events. The scope of sexual behavior becomes immeasurably broader than the episodic act of copulation. Sex is intimately bound up with every other form of social interaction. There are individual likes and aversions, acts of bullying and of bribery (the latter taking forms which have been called prostitution, in which the presenting female cozens the dominant male to secure some wanted food), seduction of young males by females old enough to have lost their preferred status, and countless other instances of the integration of sex into a status-conscious social organization! It is also worth mention that homosexual behavior has been repeatedly observed, but that it does not seem to interfere with the development of normal heterosexual behavior. (Cf. Nissen, 1951, and Maslow, 1936.)

Another aspect of chimpanzee temperament which it is instructive to consider is the maturation of the fear response. Pain, loud noises, and loss of support seem to be unlearned stimuli to fear in any young mammal, and certainly in the rat, the dog, and the chimpanzee, as well as the human. However, it is by no means certain, or even probable, that these are the only unlearned stimuli to fear in any of these animals. Let us recall that when Hall sought a standardized stimulus situation to test rats for fearfulness, he did not select pain, or noise, or loss of support, any of which could easily be inflicted, but "a strange open space." The results leave no doubt that this, too, is for them an unlearned stimulus to fear. From this perspective, it is interesting to learn that the chimpanzee (like the human child, as we shall see later) fears many "strange" things, and grows into new fears as his developing intelligence brings him to recognize an element of strangeness in stimuli that might have been accepted in matter-of-fact manner at an earlier age. Hebb (1946b) has studied this behavior in chimpanzees, and has made it one of the foundations for his general theory of behavior (1949b). Any unfamiliar object, or a familiar object seen in an unfamiliar context, may evoke the response of fear. For example, a harmless snake, or the model of a head seen detached from a body, will often evoke this response. Hebb speculates that it is not the stimulus in itself that arouses the fear, but the lack of correspondence between the nervous process which it initiates and another, already learned process, corresponding to the familiar experiences of the past. Whatever the neurological basis, it is certain that the same harmless object which will be received blandly by the infant, may evoke intense fear in an older animal.

This tendency to attach fear to unfamiliar objects, quite independently of any conditioning process, is an important basis for individual differences in temperament. Two illustrations of this fact may readily be cited. Nissen (1951) states that although most chimpanzee mothers "show an immediate, intense solicitude for the young and great skill in caring for it," there are others who "have been terrified at seeing this new wriggling, squalling object, and have run away from it." We may speculate that this difference will sometimes reflect differences in earlier experience, and particularly in opportunities to observe infants before the time of their own motherhood, but the constitutional disposition to fear strange objects must also be an important source of such panic. Hebb (1947) describes an instance of a different kind of fear, resembling a neurotic phobia, which he observed in a female chimpanzee, Alpha. Alpha had been born in captivity, and for most of her life she seemed to be a well-adjusted citizen of the Yerkes colony. When 12 years old, she suddenly showed a violent fear of any solid food. This behavior underwent fluctuation, disappeared after about two years, then reappeared as suddenly about a year later. Hebb expresses confidence that it could not have been the result of any special experience. Whatever the complete explanation may be, it seems reasonable to regard it as a special case of fear maturation. So regarded, it also fits the general principle that mental abnormalities represent extreme developments of normal processes. However, the fact that such behavior should manifest itself in one ape, and not in others who lived under very similar convictions, justifies Hebb in his conviction (which is also based on other considerations) that constitutional predisposition was a major factor.

Hebb also describes at length one other instance of mental illness in a chimpanzee, Kambi, a female who had been captured at the age of 9 months. He states that from early childhood she gave the impression of being introverted, and subject to periods of depression, which became quite severe in adolescence and maturity. The constitutional element in this abnormality is indicated by the contrast with her cagemate Bimba, who had been captured at about the same age, had the same general experiences, was rather more fearful than Kambi during the first years of her captivity, but never developed any abnormality of behavior. In this case, too, it is reasonable to assume with Hebb that an innate temperamental characteristic contributed to the determination of abnormality. In other words, Kambi would not have become a victim of pathological depression, if apes generally were not subject to depressive moods at times. In the healthy ape they are mild, and often initiated by loss of accustomed companions; in Kambi they were intense, and their basis was unclear.

THE ADOPTED CHIMPANZEE

There are a number of published accounts of chimpanzees who have shared the homes of their human masters. We shall be concerned here with the experiences of Gua "Kellogg" and Viki "Hayes," both of whom were reared by trained psychologist-observers.

Gua was brought into the home of the Kelloggs when she was

7½ months old, and she had as a companion Donald Kellogg, who was 2½ months her senior. Her visit lasted for nine months. At the start, she exhibited the clinging dependence that is characteristic of all young chimpanzees, selecting her new father as the object of her most concentrated affection. It is likely that this preference came about because the mother was more occupied with caring for Donald. Although the clinging phase passed, Gua remained extremely dependent.

Throughout the entire nine months, she was much more dependent in this sense than the child. Whether indoors or out, she almost never roamed very far from someone she knew. To shut her up in a room by herself, or to walk away faster than she could run, and so leave her behind, proved, as well as we could judge, to be the most awful punishment that could possibly be inflicted. She could not be alone apparently without suffering, whereas Donald would frequently play by himself if no one was about. When out of doors he would sometimes wander entirely away from home with a care-free abandon entirely unknown to Gua. (*The Ape and the Child*, 1933.)

Gua manifested virtually all the emotions expected of a young child. She was generally more fearful than Donald, but the authors recognize that the painful separation from her mother may have been partly responsible for this. The fear of many strange objects, and specifically of toadstools, is discussed at length. She would laugh when tickled, or when someone threatened to tickle her, when she was whirled about, or sometimes in response to Donald's laughter while they played together. Tantrum behavior was not uncommon, but it seemed to be an expression of fear rather than of rage. Fear very often also resulted in defecation or urination. There was a heartrending display of anxiety when Professor Kellogg, her preferred parent, made obvious preparations to leave the house. (Donald behaved similarly, when Mrs. Kellogg was preparing to go out without him.) When scolded, Gua continued unhappy until she was permitted a kiss of reconciliation, and then she would show her relief with an audible sigh. She was rarely angry, although often she showed impatience or irritation by such acts as slapping her hands on the tray of her high chair or throwing objects on the floor. She often exhibited jealous behavior, intruding herself into any situation in which Donald was receiving attention from others. Only in one respect, apparently, did she fail to exhibit a typical infantile reaction: when asked to perform, she did not show any bashfulness.

Throughout this period, Gua and Donald kept close pace together on the Gesell Tests for Pre-School Children. Gua excelled over Donald on the delayed reaction test, but this may have been because she was more strongly motivated, since her prize was to regain her father's company! They were about equal, at the end of the period, in their comprehension of spoken commands. Both Gua and Donald showed an early interest in the human face, and sensitivity to its expressions.

Despite the fact that ape and child were still fairly evenly matched when the experiment was brought to a close, there was evidence that Gua would be less able than Donald to accept the pattern of human living. Here are the reasons, as stated by the Kelloggs:

According to our observations, she possessed fewer inhibitory responses than the human subject. She was thus a creature of more violent appetites and emotions, which swayed her this way and that, seemingly without consideration of the consequences. Examples are her intense and almost unquenchable thirst; her frantic hunger when she had missed a meal or two, which would often lead her to gulp her food with such rapidity that much of it would spill; her inability to restrain bladder and bowel evacuations in disturbing situations, and the consequent emotional significance of these responses; and her intense affection for those who cared for her, at times amounting to an uncontrollable passion which nothing but physical contact, including embracing and kissing, would satisfy. She seemed to follow her ruling impulses with little permanent regard for restraining circumstances. In this respect she was coarser than the child and more elemental in her motives.

However, Gua was capable of altruistic concern for those she loved. She was concerned when Donald was scolded, and might make efforts to console him. She would take sides with her

preferred parent, the father, against the mother, if either one
should simulate an attack upon the other, but she would also
be ready to defend the mother against an attack by an outsider.
Of course, these situations were probably perceived by her as
part of a general pattern of social dominance, and she also made
her independent efforts to establish her dominance over other
small animals and children, by feinting attacks upon them.

Toward organisms which are afraid of her or at any rate which
retreat when she approaches, she will manifest anger and threatening behavior. Organisms which are themselves aggressive will at
once be avoided by her.

Thus we see in her play the dawning dominance behavior
which is characteristic of grown chimpanzees. Indeed, it is hard
to point out any aspect of Gua's behavior which is not typical
chimpanzee behavior. She wears the dresses of a little girl, and
has a little boy for her playmate, but she remains a chimpanzee.
As such, however, she is in many ways very like a human child.

Viki was only 3 days old when Cathy Hayes took over her
care, in the nursery of the Yerkes Laboratories. Six weeks later,
she moved from the nursery to their home, which she has shared
since. The story of her first three years has been told in a
charming manner (Cathy Hayes, *The Ape in Our House,* 1951),
and we are assured that the adoption is permanent, and the
"experiment" will go on indefinitely. Viki was raised in a family
setting which followed the usual pattern of our culture, in that
"papa" went off to work each day at the laboratories, and "mama"
was the natural focus of infant affection.

Viki never experienced the pain of separation, and perhaps for
this reason she has been "essentially a happy little thing." Her
need for affection has been just as intense, but its manifestations
seem to have been less panicky, and even though toilet training
has never been completely successful, there is no indication of
the incessant emotionally precipitated failures which Gua committed. Fears were most common when she was about 3 to
5 months old.

Like Gua, Viki held her own on the developmental tests. This is surprising, since she might have been expected to fall behind in the third year, when verbal items enter more frequently into the tests. What she lost on these, however, she more than made up by her greater ability and dexterity on motor tests, despite the handicap of poor thumb opposition. She was somewhat advanced, also, on the Vineland Social Maturity Scale (which is described in Chapter 10).

Some of Viki's apparent superiority over Gua possibly arises from the fact that we judge her at the age of 3, while we judged Gua at the age of 16½ months. For example, she seems to have a longer attention span, and we contrast the photo of Viki with her ear bent down against the picture of a watch, in a magazine advertisement, with the fact that Gua would put a watch into her mouth at an age when Donald would place it to his ear. However, it is also possible that these are manifestations of Viki's greater emotional security. She gave many indications of lively curiosity and of constructive imagination. On a trip north, she kept picking up stones, which she had never seen in Florida, "like great treasures," in very much the manner of a young child. She showed evident triumphant enjoyment when she discovered the hidden mechanism operating a problem box, even though the experimental period was long over, and therefore she could no longer collect a reward for her success. Most astounding of all is the story of the make-believe pull toy, which for a period of weeks she seemed to draw along behind her by an imaginary string, and which became caught on such obstacles as pipes and chair legs, so that sometimes mother's help had to be enlisted to untangle the string that wasn't there at all! This feat of constructive imagination in play, reported under circumstances which lift it clear of the doubts that may ordinarily be cast upon anecdotal accounts, compels us to reëvaluate the whole question of the limits of thinking without the support of verbalization.

For all this, it is clear that we are dealing with an ape, and not a child. It is not only her severe handicap in use of language which sets limits to her assimilation of human culture. Another limiting factor is her extreme hyperactivity, which makes it difficult for her to learn anything that requires restraint, rather than action. Many typical forms of chimpanzee behavior make their appearance, without any instruction or opportunity for observation. Among these are tree climbing, body grooming, and the threatening attitudes of dominance testing with children and small animals, or even with adult visitors. Compared with children, we read, "her interests are a little different, more athletic, less verbal." This understatement was undoubtedly written with tongue in cheek. However, it is true that among human children we often meet some whose "interests are a little different, more athletic, less verbal," and who set problems for their parents that are very similar to the problems that Viki sets.

Meanwhile, Viki goes on having more fun than she could ever have had in a jungle or a zoo, or even in the privileged cages of the Yerkes Laboratories. Will she ever learn that she is out of place? Her adoptive parents apparently intend to save her from the sad fate of Fin, who, being caged with other chimpanzees after having lived in a human home until the age of 2½, "did not mix with the others and sat looking longingly at people" (Nissen, 1951).

Tests of Chimpanzee Temperament

Despite the great interest and value of the material that we have considered in this chapter, it has been lacking in one aspect which is of great importance for the building of a science. We have had no quantitative measurement of behavior, although a crude measurement is implied in many of the distinctions that have been made in qualitative terms. However, some efforts are being made to fill this gap.

Over a period of several years, Kinder carried out a series of behavior sampling studies with young chimpanzees, thus applying to them a technique which was developed in the observation of children. The method of behavior sampling makes objective observation possible in an otherwise rather free situation. The observer decides in advance, usually on the basis of preliminary studies, exactly what dimensions of behavior are to be observed, and defines the steps of these dimensions. This might be in such a form as we saw used in the Klein-Hall rating scale for aggressiveness. However, instead of simply passing judgment as to whether a given type of behavior occurs or does not occur, observations are taken at systematic intervals, such as, for example, every 30 seconds. What is recorded is a symbol for the type of behavior which is taking place at that precise moment. What happens for the next 29 seconds is ignored, until the moment comes for the next observation and entry. Within the limits of the scheme that is set up, the observer is able to make reliable observations and accurate entries, and the resulting record gives a quantitative picture of the proportion of time that is spent in each kind of behavior.

Using this method, Kinder (1947) observed 15 young chimpanzees, all of whom had been reared in the Yerkes Laboratory nursery. Among the individual characteristics that she measured were the rate or tempo of activity, and the distribution of activity into such categories as social and nonsocial behavior, exploratory behavior, and stereotyped motor behavior. Relative standing on these variables remained fairly constant in repeated testing over a period of 3½ years. Thus, she states,

the marked differences in personality characteristics known to exist among adult chimpanzees are here related to similarly marked differences, appearing at an early age and persisting through childhood, in infant chimpanzees raised in a highly uniform environment.

Hebb (1949a) observed the behavior of 30 adult chimpanzees under conditions of controlled stimulation: when approached by a "timid man," when approached by a "bold man," and when presented with various pictures and inanimate objects. Hebb himself simulated the behavior of the bold and timid men, wearing masks and changing his clothes to insure that he would not be recognized by his caged friends. He used a flexible method of recording behavior, and only afterward did he attempt to classify the responses, in an effort to define the major variables of chimpanzee temperament. Responses in the social situation seemed to fall into five categories: apparent friendliness, aggression, quasi aggression, avoidance, and indifference. The distinction between aggression and quasi aggression arises from the fact that chimpanzees indulge in a good deal of feinting behavior as a technique of dominance testing, as well as in various kinds of nuisance behavior such as spitting. The responses to the inanimate objects yielded individual scores for fear or avoidance, for time spent in examining the pictures of apes and men, and for time spent in manipulating the mechanical devices. The last of these categories reminds us of the point which has recently been emphasized by Harlow (cf. Harlow et al., 1950), that monkeys as well as apes have a "manipulation drive" which can be used to motivate them in learning problem boxes and the like, without need to introduce any form of extraneous reward. It will also be remembered that Viki exhibited satisfaction at solving such a puzzle, even though the usual food reward was no longer forthcoming.

For all these categories of behavior, consistent individual trends were detected. Of particular interest is the fact that 14 of these animals had been tested eight years earlier by Yerkes and Yerkes (1936) for evidence of avoidance responses to inanimate objects, and the two avoidance scores, based on the reactions to different objects and with an interval of eight years, showed a correlation of 0.67. An agreement of this magnitude testifies not only to the validity of the dimension as defined, but also to a noteworthy persistence of early dispositions into adulthood.

These studies establish the meaningfulness of the descriptive categories used, and they also lay the basis for future experimental work on the effect of various special influences on behavior. In view of the extraordinary temperamental similarities between chimpanzees and children, one may even speculate that some day chimpanzees may be used as subjects to test hypotheses concerning the development of unfavorable temperamental characteristics in children.

SUMMARY

This review of behavioral studies of the chimpanzee leads us to a number of very important conclusions. The infant chimpanzee is a highly dependent creature, whose survival depends on his mother's devotion, or that of some surrogate. He is a panicky, fearful creature, needing reassurance to overcome his fears, but having, even in the absence of fears, a great hunger for simple companionate closeness. This leads to the establishment of strong emotional bonds to specific companions, and to the heartrending display of grief when he is separated from them. As he grows, he enters more and more, at first in play and later in deadly earnest, into the testing of dominance relationships, by which he finds his place in the hierarchy of his society. In the human home, the child chimpanzee behaves thus toward children and small animals, so that there can be no mistaking the fact that he is exercising a behavioral disposition which matures as surely as does his physique. Finally, despite the chimpanzee's very considerable intelligence, he is a "misfit" in our society because he is incapable of exercising the degree of inhibitory control which is required for civilized living. In short, he exhibits in characteristic ways the tendencies to affiliative, fearful, aggressive, and impulsive behavior. All these dispositions appear with a spontaneity which convinces us that they are expressions of chimpanzee nature, whose appearance in some form would be inevitable in any conceivable environment.

Furthermore, the material in this chapter suggests that each of these four major temperamental aspects of behavior has its own developmental history, reaching its peak development at a different stage of growth. Dependent-affiliative behavior is at its peak in early infancy. Avoidance, or fearfulness in response to external objects as opposed to the panic of desertion, seems more frequent and intense at a somewhat later period. The peak of impulsivity or hyperactivity is probably reached in still later childhood. Aggressive tendencies, although they show themselves early in dominance testing, continue to grow in strength and probably do not reach their peak before sexual maturity. These statements should be regarded as hypotheses rather than established facts, but they fit the general picture of chimpanzee social development. The details are less important than the general conclusion, which seems secure, that the temperamental development of the chimpanzee is a process in which this normal growth pattern undergoes relatively slight modifications. In all these respects, the chimpanzee shows no more than quantitative difference from the rat and the dog. As distinguished from them, however, the chimpanzee shows in addition a lively intellectual curiosity, an imitative disposition, and a capacity for humor which provide new sources of human-like motivation.

Two important general conclusions emerge from our comparative survey. First, it is clear that individuality is no more than the quantitative variation in characteristics which are shared by all the members of a species. It is the species, not the individual, which determines the important dimensions of variation. Second, there is an impressive consistency in the major outlines of the process of socialization in rats, dogs, and chimpanzees, which also offer many striking parallels to human behavior. This supports the view that human development is influenced by similar underlying biological determinants. Both conclusions coalesce in a single principle: the characteristics of the species establish a pattern which cannot be violated. The environment modifies, but it does not create, the pattern of individual life.

CHAPTER 6

The Human

Several million *sportive miracles, laid end to end in* zoölogical history, led to the appearance of an order of primates called the *Hominidae,* having (the dictionary tells us) "the brain and brain-case relatively large as compared with the face, the body erect in locomotion, and the great toe not opposable." *Homo sapiens,* sole extant representative of this order, has established his habitat in Arctic snows and tropical jungles, on high Andean plateaus and in the dry sands of the great deserts, as well as on all the plains and hillsides and seacoasts of the world. In each place, he has contrived out of that extraordinary brain case a way of life that copes with special hazards, turns beasts into his servants, and draws comfort and sustenance from all the elements—earth, air, water, and fire. So varied are these patterns of living that it is a source of never-failing wonder and frequent amusement for any man to observe the customs of his distant cousins, or even to learn about those of his not very distant ancestors. They are evidence of man's amazing flexibility, yet each of them contains a "residue" (to use Pareto's term) of universal emotional behaviors. Watching three travel films, I once in a single evening saw a 3-year-old Eskimo boy thrust his toy spear into a tiny polar bear which his father had fashioned out of snow, an African pygmy display his marksmanship with bow and arrow, and a West Indian youngster dive to retrieve coins thrown into the sea by vacationers. Each of these unrehearsed actors was then caught by the camera with the same broad grin of triumph. Goodenough (1932) has described the spontaneous appearance of delighted surprise, with its accompanying laughter, on the face of a 10-year-old girl who had been blind and deaf since birth, so that there could be no question about the complete spontaneity of this outward expression of her emotion. All around the world, men not only laugh in joy, but they also frown in anger, weep in sorrow, and open their eyes wide in fear. Each society has its own set of rules for the inhibitory control of emotional expression, but that which is to be suppressed is everywhere the same! Darwin (1872) recognized that the spontaneous emotional expressions of men represent bonds of kinship, not only among ourselves, but with our animal forebears. And indeed, in our emotional behavior we do unmistakably exhibit each of those major temperamental dimensions which we have already found in other mammals: impulsivity, affiliativeness, aggressivity, and fearfulness. We also laugh, but the chimpanzee keeps us from claiming a monopoly even here.

TEMPERAMENT AND EMOTION

A very prominent aspect of the strong upsurge of behavioristic theory during the 20's was the anti-instinct movement. Watson (1924), as its titular head, made a consistent effort to minimize the apparent importance of unlearned behavior, in order to leave as much scope as possible for environmental influences. He nevertheless defined the irreducible minimum of human neonatal behavior as including three patterns of emotional response: fear, rage, and love. For each of these he named specific unconditioned stimuli. He said that the first is released by loud noise or loss of support, the second by external restraint of movement, the third by stimulation of erogenous zones. It was not long before critics indicated that Watson had generalized too quickly from a few cases, and that human neonates do not show nearly such regularity of response to these stimuli as he supposed (Pratt et al., 1930). Nevertheless, all infants do exhibit these three patterns of response fairly early, and it is certain that their ultimate responsiveness to these stimuli is more a matter of maturation than of learning. Bridges (1932) included these three patterns in a genetic account of the development of emotion in the human infant, but said that they arose by differentiation out of the still more primitive pattern of undifferentiated excitement. Accepting this view, each of the major dimensions of temperament has its emotional counterpart in the infant's behavior: impulsivity in primitive excitement, affiliative need in love, aggressivity in rage, and fearfulness or avoidant behavior in fear.

We are thus confronted with a variant of the classic problem of the chicken and the egg: are we to regard emotion or temperament as primary? The definition of temperament usually takes emotion as its point of departure. Following this usage, Allport (1937) wrote the following careful definition:

Temperament refers to the characteristic phenomena of an individual's emotional nature, including his susceptibility to emotional stimulation, his customary strength and speed of response, the quality of his prevailing mood, and all peculiarities of fluctuation and intensity in mood; these phenomena being regarded as dependent upon constitutional make-up, and therefore largely hereditary in origin.

However, we have preferred to define it in terms of the ease of arousal of unlearned patterns of adaptive behavior, and to define its dimensions in terms of whole classes of adaptive response, rather than in terms of emotional expression. This is because the confused subject of emotion cannot itself be clarified except by reference to the organism's adaptations. Emotions, as entities, are nonexistent. Emotional behavior consists of a great many complex bodily changes, including visceral responses, postural responses, and sensory adaptations, which may have no immediate adaptive function, but which sometimes contribute to greater effectiveness and sometimes impede it. Accordingly, it is a subject of controversy whether emotion should be regarded as a disorganizing disturbance of behavior, or as purposive and integrative. The first point of view was taken by Young (1936). Most psychologists have followed his statement that "the one feature common to all emotional processes is their disorganizing effect upon behavior." The opposing view has been stated by Leeper (1948), who argues that it is misleading to judge the nature of emotion from its extreme instances, and that its usual effect is to give motivational direction to behavior. This conflict of opinion can be resolved, if we agree to interpret emotional behavior as consisting only of *the preparatory stages of innate forms of response,* by which the resources of the organism are being mobilized for one type of activity or another. According to this view, to paraphrase William James, we become inwardly afraid because we are getting ready to run, we become inwardly angry because we are getting ready to fight, and so on. These preparatory stages serve a useful purpose when the fuller execution of the response pattern of which they form a minor part is appropriate, but they are disruptive whenever this is not the case, so that the inhibition of the motor elements of the response pattern is required. The pounding heart may be quite utilitarian in either primitive courtship or primitive battle, but it reduces the efficiency of both the modern suitor and the mechanized soldier. Since the motor elements of the response often will be inhibited or dissembled, or may be imperfectly developed as in the case of the infant, temperament may be most readily detected in emotional behavior, that is, in the execution of the preparatory phases of the total response pattern. Nevertheless, it is temperament, the disposition to adaptive behavior of one sort or another, which must be regarded as primary, and emotion which must be regarded as the secondary phenomenon.

INDIVIDUALITY IN INFANTS

Because of the relative immaturity of the human neonate, we

must not expect individuality to show itself clearly in early life. Even with animals, we have seen that constitutionally determined behavioral tendencies may not be discernible until the later stages of maturation are reached. The aggressiveness of rats, or the dominance testing of chimpanzees, do not appear in their earliest behavior. This will be even more true of the human. The helplessness of the human infant far exceeds that of the newborn rat, dog, or chimpanzee, and a considerably longer period must elapse, even relative to the normal life span of the species, before the human child is able to help meet some of its own needs in anything but the simple act of nursing. Even with respect to this most essential act, although most neonate mammals are motile enough to actively seek the mother's nipple, the human infant must be helped to find it and must often be encouraged to suck it. Ribble (1944) found that 50 percent of the 600 infants she studied "had to have considerable assistance from the nurse or mother to get vigorous sucking activity established," and that "if their primary sucking was not made easy and satisfying, their sucking activities gradually diminished, and they became either stuporous or resistive." The infant chimpanzee is able, soon after birth, to help meet the problems of arboreal living by clinging effectively to its mother, but the human infant's grasping reflex is a useless vestige of such behavior. Within a few days after birth, the infant's receptor capacities are well developed, at least in the sense that all the elemental avenues of experience are open, but the development of motor abilities must still undergo a long process of maturation. It is months before the average infant can hold up its head, and more than a year before he can walk a few steps without assistance.

This long delay is not merely to permit the adequate development of bone and muscle, although the gradual change from the flexor dominance of infancy to the extensor dominance of childhood and maturity is an essential aspect of the maturation of posture and locomotion. A less obvious but profoundly important maturational process is also going on within the cerebrum. At birth, the human infant is for all practical purposes a decorticate animal, and the first few months of prenatal life are the period during which the cortex becomes functional. The process of cortical maturation is not complete for many years, but what we are now concerned with is only the relative immaturity of the human infant at birth. Compared to other mammals, human babies are all born "premies." It is a price we pay for erect posture and a bigger brain, and thus in a sense we all share in a measure the handicaps which Shirley (1939) found to be characteristic of prematurely born children.

In view of these facts, we cannot expect to find clear evidences of individuality in all important areas during infancy. Even the genetically determined aspects of individuality must often be expected to show themselves slowly in the course of growth, like baldness. Only an excess of enthusiasm, therefore, can lead to such a statement as the following:

> Infants are individuals, almost infinitely removed from a zero point of homogeneity. They differ as adults differ, and if we had an adequate biometry we should probably find that in a mathematical sense they differ as greatly and diversely as adults. (Gesell et al., 1939.)

Nevertheless, infants do differ measurably in many respects, and some of these early differences may forecast later trends in behavior. Virtually every mother who has had more than one child has been impressed by the fact that her children were different from birth. Scientists cannot add to the certainty of this well-attested fact, although for a time they did succeed, using theory rather than observation, in creating much doubt about it. Impressed by the demonstrable flexibility of the infant, and narrowing their focus to a single child at a time, the Watsonian behaviorists developed a plausible *prima facie* case for the view that all healthy babies are the same at birth, at least with respect to the factors that influence personality development—but it was a case that could not stand up long under examination of the evidence. It would surely be possible, through a questionnaire study, to set up a very long list of contemporary psychologists who earnestly believed this doctrine early in their professional careers, but abandoned it when, facing the problems of parenthood, they discovered the extraordinary persistence of a child's behavior in the face of the most sophisticated training techniques.

In the following paragraphs, we shall review a number of studies which throw light upon some of the ways in which human infants show their individuality soon after birth. We must leave aside, until Chapter 9, another phase of this problem, which is to determine how these early differences are reflected in the personalities of later life. At that time we shall have to refer again to many of the studies which will be mentioned here.

Babies differ in the amount of crying they do. Aldrich, Sung, and Knop (1945) recorded the amount of crying by 50 babies in the Johns Hopkins hospital nursery, each of whom remained in the nursery for at least eight days. The average neonate spent almost two hours in crying each day, but the range was from less than one hour to more than four hours. Since a very large proportion of this crying could not be traced to any discernible cause, it seems fair to assume that some babies are just more disposed to be crybabies. Bayley (1932) found that infants who were receiving standardized physical examinations and developmental tests each month cried, on the average, for about 15 percent of the examination time, and that records from one three-month period to the next showed individual consistency. There is strong indication that such consistency increases during the latter part of the year (see Table 6.1). Bayley states that "the children cry for different reasons at different ages," at first mainly for such reasons as fatigue and colic pain, but later from "fear of the strange situation and dislike of unusual handling." For the reasons stated earlier, it is not possible to conclude with certainty that this change is due solely to the effects of learning. Maturation may contribute to such fear and dislike, or, stating the matter conversely, the maturation of positive social tendencies

may foster a tolerance for handling by strange persons. (We shall
have another look at the interpretation of these results in
Chapter 8.)

TABLE 6.1. Correlations of time spent in crying, during monthly
examinations, between different quarters of the year (based on Bayley,
1932).

Quarters	Second	Third	Fourth
First	.38	.22	.15
Second		.26	.18
Third			.66

Babies differ in the characteristics of their sucking behavior.
We have already mentioned Ribble's finding that some infants
need much more help than others in order to establish satisfactory feeding habits. She has also stated that many of the
infants whom she studied (particularly among the 30 percent
who were prone to generalized states of muscular tension) exhibited exaggerated sucking activity. Balint (1948) made carefully quantified observations of the tempo and the intensity of
sucking by bottle-fed infants, using an ingenious technique
which directly recorded the physical suction. Most of his subjects
had been hospitalized because of illness. Retests on many of the
infants showed that the rate of sucking tends to be individually
consistent. He found that it was higher for those who were
suffering from intestinal disorders, or who were classified as
irritable, than for the normal infants and those who were suffering
from respiratory disorders. Since the characteristic rate remained
unchanged after the illness had been overcome, he concluded
that it was not a result of illness, but that it was probably related
to the predisposition to a certain type of ailment. This is quite
consistent with Ribble's thinking, that failure to establish satisfactory sucking habits interferes with healthy development.

Babies differ in the characteristics of their motor behavior.
Shirley (1931) made a two-year longitudinal study of the

development of motor behavior in 25 infants. She concluded that "the individual differences in motor development among babies can best be accounted for on the basis of a 'motor talent' or predisposition toward good coordination," and that one of the most striking differences among the babies was in "their delight in motor play." As part of this study, an examining physician rated each infant for muscle tone at each of the periodic examinations. The child who was slowest in learning to walk had consistently poor ratings, while those who learned to walk quickly had good ratings from birth. Gesell (1937) found that such traits as energy output and motor demeanor have distinctive individual character in the first months of life. However, it is his feeling that we tend to describe infant individuality in terms of motor behavior, not because individuality is strongest in this area, but because we have not developed adequate descriptive techniques to deal with other aspects of their behavior.

Fries (1944) studied the relationships between the infant's general level of activity and his adjustment. She developed two tests, a Startle Test and an Oral Test, for use with very young infants. The Startle Test consists of dropping a padded weight onto the bed, close to the infant's head, under standardized conditions which include safeguards against injury. Infants are classified as Quiet if the resulting startle response has a duration of less than 10 seconds, and as Active if it lasts for 25 seconds or more; those between are classified as Moderately Active. Both Quiet and Active children are in no sense extremes, but represent variations within the normal range. In the Oral Test, the infant's response to an interruption of feeding is observed. "The breast or bottle was presented to the infant. After he had been sucking well for one minute . . . the nipple was removed. After one minute it was restored to him." Table 6.2 summarizes her conclusions with respect to the different responses of infants who have been classified by activity types. (Shirley, too, had remarked that some infants tend to react passively to frustration, and others actively.) Basing herself in part on the continuing

TABLE 6.2. Infant response to feeding frustration (based on Fries, 1944)

Infant's activity type	Response, when the nipple was: presented	removed	restored
Quiet	May take it at once, but if drowsy or asleep, may require some help to grasp it.	Is quiet, continues the sucking act, falls asleep.	Keeps mouth closed; nipple inserted with difficulty, but then sucks.
Moderately Active	Takes it right away.	Remains awake, may move head or extremities.	Sucks at once.
Active	May continue his activity or take it right away.	May have startle response.	May continue his activity and/or cry before sucking.

observation of these same children, Fries points to the implications of her findings for child care. She tells us that the quiet child will need more stimulation, and the active child will need more comforting reassurance, for optimal development. As they grow older, the quiet child will need more help in solving problems, but the active child will need more alert watching to forestall misfortunes. (The reader may wish to consider the possibility that these types are related to the Active and Lethargic types of dogs described by James.)

This difference in the manner of response to frustration is related to a difference which Jones (1930) pointed out, in the way that children respond to mildly disturbing emotional stimulation. The sound of a buzzer, for example, may cause an infant to give a startle response, and it may also elicit a galvanic skin response (GSR). Jones observed that these two forms of response have an inverse relationship, so that the infant or child who tends to give a strong response of one kind is not likely to give a strong response of the other kind. (It was this report that led Fuller (1948) to study the relationship between heart reactivity and motor reactivity in dogs. Although he did not find the same inverse relationship which Jones had reported, his finding that there was no significant correlation between the two forms of response in dogs is not inconsistent with the view that some individuals may tend to favor one or the other mode of response.)

Washburn (1929) made a study of the development of smiling and laughing during the first year of life. She studied only 15 infants, but she felt that she could classify them with very little uncertainty into four groups: those in whom crying predominated over smiling, those in whom smiling predominated over crying, a labile or multiexpressive group in which both types of response were frequent and neither predominant, and a relatively expressionless group in which both types of response were infrequent. Spitz (1946) also studied the course of development of the smiling response. He found that from the third to the sixth month, a smile in response to a face-Gestalt—two eyes, a nose, and a forehead, with some movement—is "as unshakeably consistent as the patellar reflex," although after this time it is given discriminatively, to some adults rather than others. He attributes differences in readiness of smiling primarily to the social experience of the infant, particularly with its mother, but he also recognizes the influence of other accelerating or retarding factors. However, it does not seem possible to deny the fact that there are also constitutional differences in readiness for this behavior.

We have seen that infants differ in their crying, the tempo of sucking, the intensity and duration of their response to startle, the quality of their response to disturbance (i.e., whether primarily overt or visceral), readiness of smiling, general level of activity, and characteristic response to frustration. Undoubtedly this list could be greatly extended. However, we might only be adding examples of a few basic differences which find expression in many ways. The basic dimensions of temperament in infants are not so numerous as the kinds of activity that investigators may choose to record. What are we able to surmise about those dimensions, from the perspective we have gained through studying the behavior of several other related animal species? From this perspective, it seems reasonable that the specific reaction tendencies which we have been describing should be interpreted as only the fragments of major biological patterns of adjustment, which are very imperfectly matured at birth. Soon after birth, we seem to be able to classify infants most readily on the basis of their general excitability, or responsiveness to all kinds of stimulation. We may expect the patterns of dependency, of aggressivity, and of avoidance, which have their distinctive characteristics in each species, to show themselves more clearly as the child matures. Awareness of these dimensions permits us to go beyond the atomistic cataloguing of specific reaction tendencies, just as awareness of the future locomotor pattern permits us to understand the meaning of postural and limb reflexes, whose rudiments can already be observed in the foetus of two months (cf. Hooker, 1943). Years ago, we used to think of the patellar reflex, or knee jerk, as a defensive reflex; now we know that it is only one example of the "stretch reflex" which is present in every muscle, and that it plays an essential part in the pattern of walking. In the same way, we must see the smile as an expression of affiliative need, and the early rivalry between overt and visceral activity as perhaps a hint of the later rivalry between the adjustment patterns of aggressivity and withdrawal. Only in this way can we understand how the manifestations of individuality in infancy foreshadow the temperamental characteristics which will show themselves more clearly in the child.

CRITICAL PERIODS IN TEMPERAMENTAL DEVELOPMENT

The process of maturation is, of course, highly differentiated, and we cannot expect the different temperamental dispositions to develop at anything like an equal pace. Indeed, one of the most important tasks which we face, but one which can be only incompletely accomplished in the present state of our knowledge, is to indicate the developmental stages through which the child passes in respect to each of the major dimensions of temperament. In matters of temperament, just as much as in school subjects, when we learn and what we learn are determined as much by our readiness for such learning as by environmental circumstance. Tinbergen (1942) tells how the Eskimo dogs of a Greenland settlement seem incapable of learning the boundaries of their home territory, outside of which they are in danger of attack by other dogs, until they reach sexual maturity; then quite suddenly they show awareness of those boundaries and readiness to defend them against outsiders. We must always think of temperamental dispositions, whether they appear early or late, as providing a basis for preferential learning. It is therefore of the utmost importance to know at what period the child will be most susceptible to influence of one sort or another. It is now becoming possible for us to replace the vague generalization that the early years of childhood are a formative period, in which the major outlines of personality are established, with testable hypotheses defining relatively restricted periods within those years, each of which is of particular importance with respect to the development of a given area of behavior, corresponding to a given dimension of temperament.

With respect to *fear-avoidance behavior,* there are indications that in humans the most critical period for the reinforcement of this pattern may be in the first months or even in the first weeks of postnatal life. Because of the absence of effective cortical inhibitory processes at that time, the infant is quite readily thrown into a state of visceral upset. This normal emotional instability of the infant constitutes a predisposition to anxiety, or generalized fearfulness, which is likely to be established as a lasting disposition if it is given frequent exercise in this period. Although it is doubtful whether the infant can be readily conditioned at this time, in the sense of forming firm attachments between specific responses and specific environmental stimuli, he is certainly capable of learning in the sense that each precipitation of the emotional response of fear links the elements of this response more firmly together, and makes their recurrence more likely. Greenacre (1945) contends that the birth experience itself "seems to organize the anxiety pattern," and many other clinicians share the view that the massed painful experience of birth, and especially of a difficult birth, cannot be altogether without effect on the individual. Shirley (1939) found that prematurely born children tend to grow up to be more emotionally responsive and to show greater physical timidity, presumably because they were at birth less adequately prepared to meet the stimulations of the extrauterine world. Ribble (1943) has stressed the importance of adequately meeting the neonate's great need for oxygen, and she argues that the importance of careful nursing and gentle mothering in the first weeks lies less in the need for nutrition than in the fact that such handling helps to establish deep, healthy respiration, without which proper cortical development would be impossible. She writes, in this regard:

> If the baby's respiration fails to develop on schedule, metabolism must operate on short rations and the growing cells of the brain may suffer in consequence. The caliber of developing blood vessels may not become sufficient for the irrigation of nerve cells; the myelin sheaths which protect and nourish the nerve fibers may not complete themselves; brain metabolism itself may become established on a poor basis. Such handicaps as these can make an individual biologically unfit to meet the stress and strain of later life. In other words, his subsequent ability to "take it" may hang in the balance during this early period.

Some critics have felt that the emphasis which Ribble places on the importance of strong respiration is excessive. However, there is abundant clinical and experimental evidence of the harmful effects of even short periods of anoxia, particularly at critical stages of growth, and it is certainly not unreasonable to suppose that healthy development of the brain tissues requires better than minimal nutrition. Since cortical inhibition is an essential element of emotional control, anything which interferes with cortical development would tend also to increase emotional instability. Such a condition would constitute a disposition to anxiety, which is an aspect of fear-avoidance behavior.

The importance of early fear and anxiety occupies an extremely important place in the thinking of Sullivan (1953). Although almost unknown to the general public during his lifetime, Sullivan exercised an enormous influence on the development of psychiatric thinking in America, being perhaps more than anyone else responsible for the extension to psychotics of the same general methods of psychotherapy which had been developed in working with neurotics. He emphasizes the very diffuse and disoriented character of the sentient experience of the young infant. Within this experience he distinguishes between fear and anxiety. He regards fear as a response to the threatened catastrophic denial of the organism's needs, citing the special danger of smothering as an important example. He regards anxiety as a tension which can be aroused because of the infant's need for mothering tenderness. He asserts that *"the tension of anxiety, when present in the mothering one, induces anxiety in the infant,"* and he goes on to say that "those who have had pediatric experience or mothering experience actually have data which can be interpreted on no other equally simple hypothetical basis." Without attempting at this point to consider the implications of this distinction between fear and anxiety—which may possibly be related to the opposition of visceral and overt response to threat—it is clear that Sullivan believes: (1) that this early experience of anxiety, as an aspect of the infant-mother relationship, is of the greatest importance for the future development of personality, and (2) that it takes place before the infant experiences anything like an affectional relationship toward the mother as a person.

The critical period for the development of *dependent-affiliative behavior* starts in the third month, when some areas of the cortex have begun to function effectively, although its development is still quite incomplete. At this time the infant shows a responsiveness to social stimulation which was previously lacking. The appearance of the smiling response is the signal that this period has opened. Soon it becomes a matter of importance to the infant, not only that it be cared for tenderly, but that it be cared for by a particular person. This emotional attachment to the mother, or mother surrogate, is not firmly fixed until after the sixth month, for Spitz (1946) mentions that he has never seen mourning behavior as a result of loss of the mother—a type of reaction which he calls anaclitic depression—before that age. He also states that until then the smile will be given indiscriminately to anyone, but the persistence of indiscriminate smiling after six months is a sign of severe social retardation.

The strength of the infant's attachment to the mother continues to grow through the first year, and perhaps does not reach its climax until well into the second. One indirect way of gauging the intensity of this attachment is to study the emotional disturbance which results from weaning. On the basis of the relatively undifferentiated concept that infants are most susceptible to all sorts of disturbing influences in the earliest period, one might suppose that later weaning would be less disturbing than early weaning. Sears and Wise (1950) found, on the contrary, that infants weaned relatively late showed more emotional disturbance. Their comparison is essentially between infants weaned before the opening of the critical period which we are discussing, and those weaned during this period. Whiting and Child (1953) made a cross-cultural study which indicated that, in general, later weaning is accompanied by less emotional disturbance. Their data, based on reported observations of primitive cultures, are essentially a comparison of the effects of weaning during the latter part of this critical period and subsequent to it. Although the two sets of data show superficially opposing trends, both can be reconciled by the hypothesis that disturbance is maximal during the first half of the second year (Whiting, 1954).

The importance of mother care during the first year has been shown in important studies by Spitz and by Goldfarb. Spitz (1945) has contrasted the development of infants in a foundling home and in an institution for delinquent girls. In the foundling home, one head nurse and five assistants care for 45 babies. Food is good, and there is no lack of proper physical attention. The infants enter with a relatively high developmental status, indicating good paternity, but they show a steady decline until, at the end of the first year, they are definitely subnormal, with an average developmental quotient of 72. Infants in the institution for delinquent girls are cared for by their mothers, who compete in lavishing attention upon them, and receive instruction in child care from staff members. Starting below average, the infants show a steady rise in developmental quotient, passing the foundling children in about the fourth month, and reaching an average of 105 at the end of the first year.

Goldfarb (1943, etc.) studied the after effects of emotional deprivation as manifested in later childhood and adolescence. He showed that infants placed in institutions are severely handicapped, both intellectually and emotionally, by comparison with those who were placed directly into foster homes, where they could begin early to develop personal attachments to parent surrogates. Most important for our present problem is his comparison (1947) of a group of well-adjusted and a group of poorly adjusted children in foster homes. All the children had been placed in foster homes at about the age of 3, but most of the poorly adjusted children had been institutionalized for the first time before they were 6 months old, whereas the well-adjusted children had been institutionalized at an average age of 11 months, that is, after they had enjoyed some opportunity for the normal development of affectional relationships.

Spitz indicates that the immediate effect of early emotional deprivation is apathy, which in its extreme form becomes a serious physical depression. Goldfarb shows that in less extreme cases this passive and apathetic behavior appears in the character structure of the adolescent who has a history of early institutionalization. However, it must not be thought that loss of the opportunity for normal affection is always at the root of such difficulties. Children differ enormously in their capacity to respond to affection, and there are extreme instances of pathological unresponsiveness, constituting an innate disposition to childhood schizophrenia. Mothers of such children complain that they have never been able to "reach" their babies, although they do not themselves seem rejecting or in any way incapable of giving normal mothering (Escalona, 1948). Mahler (1952) says that in addition to such autistic infants, "for whom the beacon of emotional orientation in the outer world—the mother as primary love-object—is nonexistent," there are others who have an abnormally intense craving for a "symbiotic" relationship with the mother, joined with an incapacity to tolerate actual physical contacts. She regards both groups as constitutionally predisposed to childhood psychosis, because they possess an "inherently defective tension-regulating apparatus which probably cannot be complemented by either the most quantitatively or qualitatively efficient mother." These extreme cases are important to us because they demonstrate the fact that there is variability in capacity to develop affectional relationships. If such variability were slight, it might be utterly obscured by the admittedly important environmental influences. It is the extreme cases that help us to see that the development of affectional relationships cannot be adequately conceptualized in terms of reinforcement theory alone, but must be regarded as a phase of maturation, which is facilitated or retarded by environmental circumstances.

By the end of the first year, the healthy infant not only has a strong affectional bond to his mother, but he also shows positive social response to persons even outside his family group. Gesell and Ilg (1943) say: "Fifty-two weeks is the heydey of sociality." This becomes the basis for social reinforcement of other learning and the pattern for future interpersonal relationships. The implication of Goldfarb's findings is that if this important foundation for future personality development has not been acquired during this critical period, or within a few months thereafter, it is unlikely that later experience will make up the deficiency. If this conclusion seems too drastic, let us at once point out certain alleviating aspects. First, the nature of the evidence on which it is based does not permit us to exclude the possibility that under exceptionally favorable circumstances the child's capacity for warm and trustful social relationships may not be adequately developed during the second or even the third year of life. Clinical experience encourages us to believe that this is possible, but that it requires from the parent—or the professional parent figure—a skill and devotion far beyond what are needed in the first year. Second, although the personality in which there is a reduced capacity for affectional relationships may not meet the standards of contemporary society for optimal adjustment, it is not necessarily a "bad" personality. In fact, it may achieve an impassivity which is highly valued in some social groups.[1]

During the second year of life, the infant gives way to the child. As locomotor and manipulative responses become increasingly effective components of behavior, the child begins to act upon the environment with frequently uncontrolled and destructive energy. During the same period, the ever-continuing process of cortical maturation also brings increased powers of inhibition, but the development of inhibition lags behind the development of action, to the mother's frequent distress and exasperation. This is the age of *impulsivity,* when the child is normally a puppy-like stimulus-bound extravert, switching rapidly and unpredictably from one activity to another. Gesell and Ilg describe the child at 18 months as a "busy-body" who is "into everything." Woodcock (1941) describes the behavior of the 2-year-old as follows: "His attention span is short, his threshold of distractibility is low. His inhibitory apparatus is only slightly developed; he readily takes impulse to activity from sights and sounds around him."

Within this period, then, the child must establish a balance between impulse to action, which is usually a response to peripheral stimulation, and internal control. The outcome is not determined by physical maturation alone, for he receives a good deal of guidance in restraint. There is usually someone close at hand who is all too ready to cry "Don't do that!"—or even to

---

[1] Several weeks after writing these paragraphs, I find on my desk a news letter from an organization which does a wonderful job of rehabilitating children with severe behavior problems. With pride, they tell the story of their success with a little girl who was 10 years old when she came to them, described as "possibly subnormal, severely withdrawn, suicidal tendencies, parents committed to institution for incurable addicts." After two years, she was considered cured, and moved into a foster home where she was making a good adjustment. The possibility of this success was established by one important fact which glowed in the dismal shadows of her history. *"She was once a warm spontaneous child."* Since the early disposition to give and receive love had been nurtured at the right time, a renewal of health was possible, despite the miseries which had been experienced because of the later degradation of her parents.

provide a more physical reminder that one must not act on impulse. From these experiences the child not only learns specific rules of conduct, but, like a clever pet, he also learns that there are some things one does not do in the presence of social monitors. There is some evidence that children who are socially oriented are less impulsive in their behavior. Among the twins T and C, who were studied by Gesell and Thompson (1941), whose history we shall examine in greater detail in a later chapter, it was the less social twin who was described as more object-oriented and also more impulsive. As another example, Goldfarb observed that early-institutionalized adolescents were more impulsive than those who had better opportunity to develop adequate social relationships. It is possible that the mere fact that they have learned to give favorable attention to social stimuli has tended to weaken the impact of nonsocial experience and thus reduced the provocations to sudden acts of one sort or another. The child who does not learn to check his impulses, particularly before he enters the next period of aggressiveness, becomes a menace on the playground, and is headed for severe social conflicts. He has the same kind of difficulty in fitting into human society which was displayed by Gua and by Viki.

Aggressive tendencies come into prominence at a still later period. Impulsive behavior creates problems of discipline because of inattention to dangers and to commands, but this is not the same thing as stubborn resistance to authority and efforts to control the actions of others. By 2½, however, the child shows "imperial, domineering ways" (Gesell and Ilg, 1943). The same child who was once so sweetly obedient now says "I won't," with a determination which is quite beyond our understanding as a means of gaining any objective other than status. This is early dominance testing, similar to that which is exhibited by the chimpanzee. At a more charming moment, the youngster is ready to masquerade in his father's coat, and, with sleeves dangling from his arms and coat-tails dragging behind, to test how much authority he can arrogate to himself. The wise parent, who is sufficiently secure within himself, can afford to let his child gain some victories, knowing that the experience of this period will determine how successfully aggressive impulses can be integrated into the total behavior pattern.

Summing up, we may say that the critical periods for the appearance and control of tendencies to fearfulness, affiliative behavior, impulsiveness, and aggressiveness seem to follow one another in that order, in the development of the young human. Because of the maturational forces involved, behavior of the neonate can give only an inaccurate indication of the later strength of each of these tendencies. The manner of resolution of each of these problems in turn limits the possible solution to the later problems. Without attempting anything like a full discussion of this question at the present point, we may offer some fairly obvious illustrations. Thus an intense fearfulness developed during the first months of infancy will certainly influence the kind of affiliative relationships that are established in the following period. The love of the fearful child will have a more jealous and consuming character, and be less an immediate source of pleasurable gratification. The kind of affiliative relationships that are established will in turn influence the responsiveness of the child to social controls, during the period when impulsiveness becomes prominent. At this time, some children live in dread of the loss of parental love, and therefore never develop the spontaneity of behavior of which they would otherwise be capable. Finally, the forms of fearfulness, of affiliation, and of impulsiveness will all influence the development of aggressive behavior. The child whose development up to this point has been reasonably healthy can scarcely become one of those "children who hate" who are described by Redl and Wineman (1951) as utterly beyond the reach of education and therapy. The resolution of all four problems establishes the major temperamental characteristics of the individual in a distinctive pattern which tends to resist change in later life.

FOUNDATIONS OF PERSONALITY

The constitutional influences on behavior may usefully be divided into two categories: those which we share with other animals, and those which distinguish us from them. Up to this point we have been considering only those dispositions which we share with other animals, and which are generally called *temperament*. Those aspects of individuality which arise, on the contrary, from distinctively human capacities are called *personality*. Let us now turn to a discussion of those physiological characteristics of the human animal which constitute the basis for the development of human personality. It must be acknowledged that each of these may well be regarded as a merely quantitative difference between man and animals, for nowhere is there such a sharp break of function that we can say, "this is wholly new." Nevertheless, these quantitative differences in physiological function do give rise to new potentialities in behavior—to aspects of individuality which cannot be adequately described in terms of the dimensions of temperament.

First, there is man's slower rate of maturation. In Chapter 2, we recognized the principle that every animal must be thought of as having a characteristic pattern of temporal development, which shows itself in both physical and behavioral change. We quoted Beach's conclusion, that many response patterns which figure prominently in adult behavior are "fully organized and ready to function relatively early in life, well in advance of the time when they will normally be activated." The process of maturation is therefore largely a process of sensitization, which is brought about by hormone secretions. The typical behavior of any animal varies according to the state of physical maturation, and undergoes marked changes which are independent of experience, within wide limits. However, the longer maturational history of the human gives added force to the modifying influences of experience, including those of cultural origin, and a good deal of learning typically takes place of a character such as to inhibit the free exercise of certain behavior patterns—for example, those of aggressive or sexual nature—when they finally mature. Furthermore, the attitudes of childhood may be so strongly reinforced that they are never abandoned, so that a behavioral infantilism persists despite physical maturation. The thought is well expressed by Saul (1947): "Humans are children for so long that they never get over it." For these reasons, *level of maturity* has a meaning, when applied to human behavior, which is no longer closely tied to the physiological maturation of the individual.

Second, there is man's capacity to make himself and his actions the objects of his own attention, which has often been pointed to as the most distinctively human characteristic. It is true that the kitten discovers his tail and chases after it, in much the same way that the human infant discovers and plays with his fingers and toes. But after the kitten has learned that the tail is part of himself, it loses its stimulating value, except as the object of occasional grooming. The child, on the other hand, goes on to study himself incessantly, and to make comparisons between himself and others. Fin, the chimpanzee who "sat looking longingly at people" after his return to the caged life of the Yerkes colony, certainly never experienced unhappiness while he lived with the Finches, because of any thought of how different he was from his human companions, nor is there any indication that Gua or Viki suffered in this way. Indeed, Mrs. Hayes is openly indignant that anyone could think Viki might be less happy as her ward than in a cage or the jungle. Such blissful unawareness of difference is unthinkable in any human child above the level of idiocy. A good deal of critical self-evaluation plays an essential part in the personality development of every normal youngster. This leads to the formation of the *self-concept,* a phenomenon which we shall study at some length, along with the related process of identification. It is also the basis for true introversive trends in behavior, which are quite different from the depressed moodiness which sometimes characterizes the older chimpanzee, which probably lacks any introspective flavor.

Third, man characteristically gains a great measure of freedom from primary sources of motivation. In our introductory discussion of nonprimary drives, we stated that "the increasing complexity of the nervous system . . . provides a physiological basis for the appearance of a native 'intellectual motivation,'" which appears in the form of a need to manipulate the content of awareness. Rudimentary forms of such behavior are seen in animals below man. For example, Viki's behavior with the phantom pull toy seemed to evidence a need to exercise imagination rather than ordinary play needs, since she evidently had a variety of real pull toys available. Even in such a relatively simple behavior as hoarding, a primitive esthetic sensibility is indicated. Despite this evident biological continuity, we feel justified in stressing the fact that man, as a by-product of increased intelligence, exhibits an extraordinary amount of motivation with respect to experiences *as* experiences, independently of any direct relation to satisfaction of primary needs. Thus an important aspect of each human personality is the development of *interests,* motivating systems that instigate behavior that is not directed toward gaining gratification for primary needs.

Fourth, man has a distinctive capacity for the use of symbolism in thinking. To make our meaning clear, we must distinguish between two different kinds of symbol: the sign and the model or analogy. A symbol may be an arbitrary sign, which has no necessary relation to its referent. Thus θ stands for a central angle, "William" for a certain person, and the buzzer in a Pavlovian conditioning experiment for a situation in which food shall presently be forthcoming, each by virtue of an arbitrary designation. Man's capacity for the use of such symbols far exceeds that of any other animal, as shown by his rich endowment of language, and it is generally agreed that this is the necessary basis for any culture that is more than rudimentary, and hence also for those aspects of personality which are expressions of culture. However, it is possible to overstate the importance of this kind of sign symbolism, which is only an extension of the process of conditioning, by attributing to it some of the consequences of the other kind of symbolism, which makes use of inherent points of resemblance. Langer has emphasized the far-reaching importance of this kind of symbolism for human behavior. She writes:

> I believe there is a primary need in man, which other creatures probably do not have, and which actuates all his apparently unzoölogical aims, his wishful fancies, his consciousness of value, his utterly impractical enthusiasms, and his awareness of a "Beyond" filled with holiness. . . . *This basic need, which certainly is obvious only in man, is the need of symbolization.* The symbol-making function is one of man's primary activities, like eating, looking, or moving about. It is the fundamental process of his mind, and goes on all the time. . . . The fact that the human brain is constantly carrying on a process of symbolic transformations of the experiential data that come to it causes it to be a veritable fountain of more or less spontaneous ideas. . . . And it accounts for just those traits in man which he does not hold in common with the other animals—ritual, art, laughter, weeping, speech, superstition, and scientific genius. (*Philosophy in a New Key*, 1942.)

In this passage, we would differ with little more than Langer's nontechnical use of the word "primary," and her mention of weeping as one of the phenomena dependent on symbolization. The construction of symbols is not a mere consequence of the process of thought, but the very machinery of thinking as it is carried on at the level of human cortical function. The British neurologist Craik (1943), in a philosophic discussion which sought to define the implications of epistemology for modern neurology, pointed out that in the process of thinking the human brain must create within itself equivalent models of physical reality, as well as of possible ways of acting, and his statement in this regard has been quoted approvingly by such other distinguished neurologists as Adrian (1947) and Bonin (1950). Human individuality, and in particular human creativity, is to an important degree an expression of this incessant symbol-building activity, which Langer calls symbolic transformation. We shall call it analogical symbolism, to point up the fact that in doing this work, the brain plays the part of an analogical computing device. We shall deal with the aspects of individuality which are associated with this activity in our chapters on *cognitive individuality*.

Fifth and finally, in place of the animal's almost complete enslavement to the immediately present stimulus, man has the capacity to govern his conduct by consideration of remote consequences. Here, again, it is not difficult to find rudimentary forms of planned behavior among animals, and it might even be objected that what we are discussing is only the natural extension of the dimension of impulsivity. However, the processes of *control* assume such varied forms in human behavior, and have such great social importance, that it is useful to deal with them as constituting a major area of personality development. It may be pointed out that the exercise of increased control does not always lead to more intelligent behavior. Man may, like Buridan's ass, starve between two bales of hay, unable to choose between them. We must be very clever before we can spin lofty philosophies and allow our lives to be directed by them, in ways that gain no noticeable satisfaction for more basic needs. The capacity to respond to remote considerations brings with it the danger of responding to irrelevancies. Man's increased capacity for inhibition is directly responsible for much of his increased control over nature, but it also exposes him to the danger that he will fantasy meanings where there are none, and behave in a world of irreality. This opens new, and specifically human, vistas of personality.

These five points of difference between men and animals serve to point out as many areas of study, to which we shall turn our attention in later chapters, beginning with Chapter 10. Level of maturity, the self-concept, interests, cognitive individuality, and control might each be taken as the focal point for a full discussion of human personality, instead of the subject of one

or two chapters. However, there are no personalities which do
not have their foundations in temperament, that is, in the dispositions to love, anger, and fear, and the special techniques
which the individual develops for expressing and containing
these dispositions. The "higher" developments of personality
cannot be understood except as a superstructure raised on this
foundation.

THE IMPORTANCE OF UNLEARNED HUMAN BEHAVIOR

In the first part of this chapter we gave an account of early
human development which brought into prominence many points
of resemblance between human and animal behavior. In the
second part, we have described certain characteristics of human-
kind, which we have called the biological foundations of true
personality. Do the latter negate the first? Does their operation
make it correct to say that although unlearned responses have
an important place in the total picture of animal behavior, they
have no comparable place in that of man? Before we attempt
to answer this question, let us review what is meant by unlearned
behavior. It is a pity that we must use this cumbersome phrase
instead of the handy word "instinct," because of the stigma which
has been attached to the latter, as the price of old errors.

It should be clear at the outset that we are not talking about
a denumerable set of "instincts." The day of compiling lists of
instincts is long past, for the cat or the butterfly as well as for
man. It is impossible not to recognize, however, that the reaction tendencies of any animal, prior to experience, are not equi-
potential. There are certain predictable regularities, or—to express
the matter in a modern jargon—the elements of random behavior
under given stimulating conditions do not all have the same
statistical likelihood of occurrence. Native sensory structure
makes the animal more sensitive to certain aspects of the situation, and native response structure (broadly defined to include
the mechanisms of nervous control) assures that certain reactions
shall be linked with especially high probability to certain kinds

of stimulation. Neither is it possible to ignore the fact that these native response tendencies are very often useful to the animal, or to its offspring. This certainly does not reflect the operation of any mysterious psychic organization, implanted by Providence in the brain of the animal, to direct it into actions that are unrelated to its immediate sensory experience. Such concepts of instinct existed in the past, but they are long since defunct, and to argue against them now is to beat a dead horse. Neither is there any reason to expect an extraordinary degree of uniformity in the performance of instinctive actions. Since they are based on structure, they will vary as structure does.

If this is our concept of natively organized behavior, what may be said about its relative importance in the lives of different animal species? It is possible to single out certain living creatures, such as starfish or jellyfish, whose every action can be foretold from a knowledge of their native behavioral tendencies. These creatures are instinct-ridden, in the sense that natively organized behavior constitutes essentially the whole of their behavioral repertoire for life. We can encompass their lives in a short account, telling off their few reflexes of feeding, of defense, and the like. More complex animals, like the social insects, require longer stories, and the scientific labor of unraveling their secrets is largely still to be done. If we compare the jellyfish and the bee, for example, we must admit that natively organized responses play a proportionately larger part in the life of the jellyfish, since virtually all its behavior consists of unlearned responses, while much of the bee's work shows intelligent modification of response to certain stimuli. On the other hand, the sensory and response mechanisms of the bee are more complex than those of the jellyfish. It is sensitive to more different kinds of energy change in the environment, and it has more different ways of acting in its behavioral repertoire. These are the expressions of more complex structure, and every bit of this structure plays its part in establishing additional response tendencies. The intelligent segment of a bee's behavior is immeasurably greater than that of the jellyfish, but it is also built upon a richer foundation of unlearned behavior. Let us shift our perspective, to compare the rat and the bee. Although a decision here is much more difficult, most observers would probably incline to the view that natively organized responses play a proportionately larger part in the life of the bee. However, it does not follow at all that the bee is more richly endowed in this respect. The rat, like the bee, has numerous native responses concerned with exploration, foraging, nest building, care of the young, defense, and many other areas of adaptive behavior. We probably do not know enough about either the bee or the rat to decide which has the richer repertoire of unlearned behavior.

Let us shift our perspective once again, to compare the rat and man. We will readily agree that unlearned responses play a relatively more important part in the life of the rat. But this does not mean that man is more poorly endowed in this respect, or that in an absolute sense such responses play a smaller part in man's life. We have richer sensory organization, a more complex nervous system, and more elaborate locomotor and manipulative skills. Each bit of new structure brings with it new unlearned response tendencies. As they proliferate, possibilities of conflict among such tendencies multiply, and unlearned behavior takes on more and more the appearance of randomicity. If we were equal to the task of analyzing it into its component parts, we would find it to be made up of all sorts of prepotent responses which are successively called forth by different features of the environment. Their totality is the necessary basis for man's intelligent behavior.

However, this is not the whole story. Man also has a greater capacity for cortical inhibition. The result of this is that many natively organized responses are inhibited in their expression. The orgastic response of a woman to sexual intercourse is not basically different from that of other female mammals, but it may be totally suppressed by cortical inhibition. The nursing behavior of a human mother has the same kind of biological foundation, but she may elect to administer a formula by bottle, instead. A man's locomotion is natively organized, as truly as that of a dog, but he has an infinitely greater capacity to reorganize its elements, to create dance steps, for example, or to operate the pedals of a bicycle. In a limited way, *man* can teach animals to do similar tricks. The skilful trainer knows that the finished performance can be nothing but a mosaic of the animal's native response tendencies, which have been cued to new stimuli.

We cannot teach many tricks to a flea, because the poverty of its native equipment is such that it must remain an instinct-ridden creature. We can teach many tricks to a dog, because the greater wealth of his native endowment provides the basis for flexibility. We develop much more complicated tricks for ourselves, including such pleasant ones as ballroom dancing, and such unwanted ones as emotional frigidity. They are all modifications of natively organized response tendencies. We do not inherit the parts of a toy construction set, which can be put together to operate according to any ingenious scheme which we devise. We inherit a living machine, which has a preferred response for every situation. It is upon this broad foundation of unlearned response potential that we build our intelligent lives.

This is all very well in theory, the reader may be thinking, but could we have a more appropriate example? We are not really concerned about whether man inherits his walking pattern, or uses parts of it in ballroom dancing. How does the concept of unlearned native behavior help us to understand human culture and personality? What about, say, competitiveness in human society—doesn't this have quite different foundations from animal aggression? Let us consider this problem.

Roots of Competition

We noted at the start that by the basic pattern of their lives, animals commit themselves to an active quest for food. Each individual animal constitutes a well-balanced collection of nutrient substances ideally suited to nourish many other animals.

Hence, they are also committed to constant struggle with that old dilemma which has been succinctly stated by the humorist: *Dinner or diner?* Animals that ordinarily catch their dinners on the hoof develop considerable temperamental aggressiveness to support their way of life. However, even the vegetarians require some aggressiveness, in competitive struggle for food and for sex partners, as well as for defense. If any kind of social organization is to develop, beyond the primitive relationships of mating and early maternal care for the young, this aggressiveness must be kept in limits. The meat eater must not be a cannibal, except possibly under unusual circumstances. Lorenz (1952), in a beautiful essay on "The Wolf and the Dove," gives a vivid description of something we have all witnessed in the fighting of dogs—that the victor is unable to draw blood from the defeated animal, after the latter assumes a posture of defenseless submission. The natively organized behavior of hunters includes something which approximates an ethical injunction, "thou shalt not kill thy weaker brother." The posture of submission saves one from taking a beating. The more aggressive the species, the more essential is this control over the consequences of unrestrained aggression. Prior to experience, just as the aggressive posture of one animal arouses aggressive behavior in another, so too the posture of submission inhibits aggression.

What we have been describing is the unlearned pattern of competitive behavior. Competition between species takes on more ruthless forms. Within species, it is modified by experience, to assume the forms of dominance behavior or social hierarchies. We must stress the fact that these dominance relationships do not develop as a system of learned inhibitions to native aggression. The animal has native aggression postures, native submission postures, and a native disposition to restrain aggression in the face of submission. He needs all of this native equipment as the basis for learning which part of his repertoire to use when confronting a given individual. The adopted chimpanzees, Gua and Viki, both clearly displayed all the elements of this competitive pattern in their spontaneous playful exercise of dominance-testing behavior. It is not reasonable to suppose that the same kinds of behavior in children do not have the same unlearned basis. If they do, it is not reasonable to study even the most complex forms of competitive behavior in human society without acknowledging the influence of these dispositional factors. When we find societies in which competition among individuals is suppressed, we must study the influences which are responsible for the suppression, and avoid the wishful supposition that competition everywhere else is an artificial graft on human nature.

As a single concrete example of how the study of a problem of personality organization would be influenced by recognizing this unlearned basis for competitive behavior, we may consider the contrast of two boys, both of whom exhibit a good deal of competitive interest in sports. One of these has what we may at this point call an athletic build, although in the next chapter we shall learn to call it by a more technical name, mesomorphy. No one has ever had to urge him to take an interest in sports. He gets fun out of his games, plays hard to win, but forgets his losses soon after the game is over. The other boy has a more fragile physique, of the kind which we shall learn to call ecto-morphic. His interest in sports is less spontaneous, but he has come to appreciate the status value of winning. He spends time in practice, even by himself, to improve his chances. When he loses, his dissatisfaction endures until he has an opportunity to redeem himself with a win. Native competitiveness and learned competitiveness are merged in the behavior of both of these boys, but the proportions in the mixture are different. Whether our concern is the happiness of these youngsters, or their future contributions to society, we shall want to pay attention to this difference. How far can we safely go in cultivating competition in human society, how far in suppressing it? It is important to recognize that in either case we are cultivating or suppressing a native disposition.

CHAPTER 7

Physiological Theories
of Temperament

*W*e have defined four major dimensions of temperament. One of these, impulsivity, represents ease of arousal of
overt activity in general, and the attendant emotional behavior
is called excitement. The others are tendencies to more specific,
yet still quite broad categories of behavior: affiliation, aggression,
and avoidance. Each of these represents a mode of adjustment
to the social environment, and each includes complex innate
response patterns. The preparatory phases of these patterns
constitute the emotional behavior of love, anger, and fear. It is
not contended that these dimensions adequately describe the
whole range of temperament, but that they are four important
dimensions which are useful in its description. Our general
review of the principles of animal behavior, in Chapter 2, indicated many more sources for constitutionally determined differences in behavior. We have chosen these as most indispensable
for our purpose. And, since we are concerned about achieving
a rapprochement of clinical and experimental viewpoints in our
own thinking, we are pleased by the fact that these dimensions
of temperament also correspond to areas which frequently give
rise to problems of adjustment in children as well as in adults:
the management of impulsiveness, of love, of hostility, and of
anxiety.

It should be clear that no set of abstractions can ever encompass the infinite variability of real events. However, it is equally true that we cannot deal effectively with nature except by introducing an artificial simplicity, to serve as a frame of reference. Whether such a set of dimensions as we have outlined has practical value depends on how well it orients us in dealing with the individual case.

In this chapter and the next, the reader will have an opportunity to compare this treatment of the problem of selecting the principal dimensions of temperament with the results of other methods. In the present chapter, we shall consider those treatments which resemble our own in that they emphasize a small number of dimensions selected on some conceptual basis, leading to relatively simple theoretical structure. Most of these theories, though not all, relate the dimensions of temperament to definite physiological foundations. In the next chapter, we shall consider those treatments which are basically empirical in their derivation, and which therefore tend to develop longer lists of traits, which exhibit confused interrelationships. Both chapters will serve to introduce the reader to the general problem of the representation of behavior by mathematical models. We shall begin with very simple models, which are invented by their authors as aids to clarity and vividness in exposition. Later we shall see how the mathematical method of factor analysis is used to construct models which help us to understand the relationships among the phenomena we are investigating.

Two-Dimensional Models

Many different authors have used two-dimensional models to represent the major aspects of human temperament. Although these different models have been conceived independently, we shall see that they have certain important features in common, and thus attest to some small degree of harmony on the theoretical front.

Elizabeth Duffy (1949) contends that every act of behavior

can be classified with respect to two hypothetical dimensions: a dimension of intensity, whose poles are Very Active and Inactive, and a dimension of directional reference, whose poles are Approach and Withdrawal. She believes that every useful descriptive trait name should relate unambiguously to one or the other of these dimensions, and that those which relate to both simultaneously should be dropped from scientific usage. To us, this simple model seems inadequate because it does not provide for an unambiguous representation of hostile behavior. Such behavior cannot be classified as Approach, since this side of the behavior space is reserved for responses that indicate a positive or acceptant relationship toward external reality. Neither does it seem appropriate to classify it as Withdrawal, since there is an essential difference between the passive rejection of retreat and the active rejection of attack, over and above the mere difference in intensity of physical activity. For this reason, it does not seem likely that any two-dimensional schema can be psychologically adequate to represent the major aspects of behavior.

Stagner uses essentially the same schema for a more limited purpose, namely, to represent the affective aspects of behavior. He assumes that there are four innate patterns of affective response—excitement, depression, pleasantness, and unpleasantness—and he discusses in physiological terms the relationship between these responses and the Activity and Approach-Withdrawal dimensions. (See Figure 7.1.) Excitement and depression fall at opposite ends of the activity continuum. High excitement is accompanied by generally high muscular tonus, increased reactivity to stimulation, and inability to restrain oneself from even irrelevant acts which seem to provide needed outlets for excessive energy. Depression, on the other hand, is characterized by a general reduction of muscular tonus, a lack of ordinary alertness, and difficulty in carrying out the most essential tasks. In the same way, pleasantness and unpleasantness correspond to the poles of the approach-withdrawal dimension. Pleasantness

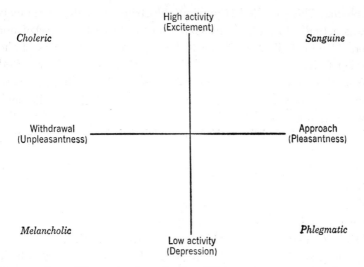

FIGURE 7.1. Illustrating how the four Hippocratic temperaments may be regarded as resultants of the interaction of two basic dimensions of behavior. The "four innate feelings," given in parentheses, have been placed as suggested by Stagner (1040), but the position of the temperaments, given In italics, has been rotated 45 degrees counter-clockwise.

is the subjective correlate of the satisfaction of bodily needs for assimilation of nutrients and affiliative social behavior, the basic forms of approach behavior. Unpleasantness, on the other hand, is the correlate of the sympathetic-adrenal pattern of emergency response, which prepares the organism to fight or to run, the basic forms of withdrawal or rejection. Although some of these relationships are certainly valid, the failure to distinguish between the basic patterns of hostile attack and fearful withdrawal still appears to us to be a basic defect.

GALEN'S FOUR TEMPERAMENTS

Stagner goes on to state that "the traditional four temperaments of Hippocrates—the sanguine, choleric, phlegmatic, and melancholic—correspond fairly well to the major points" of this schema. This so-called Hippocratic doctrine of the temperaments was actually formulated by Galen, in the second century of our era (Irwin, 1947). He based it, however, on the theories of the great father of medicine, who believed that various ills resulted from the excess or deficiency of the different bodily fluids, whose proper balance was essential to health. These fluids, or humors, were identified as the blood, the yellow bile secreted by the liver, the "black bile" supposedly secreted by the spleen, and the phlegm or mucous secretion. Galen stated that individuals differ in their temperaments according to which of these humors is relatively more abundant. Accordingly, persons may be classified as sanguine; as bilious or choleric, the Greek root *chol* meaning bile; as splenetic or melancholic, the root *mela* meaning black; or as phlegmatic. This ancient theory of psychosomatic relations survives in our language, in the common usage which most of these words still enjoy.

A first hasty glance may seem to support Stagner's assertion that these four temperaments correspond to the four poles of the 2-dimensional schema which we have been discussing. However, it takes only a short second glance to discover that the two systems do not really jibe. Each system has four polar points, but they cannot be made to coincide. When sanguine temperament is paired with pleasantness, the first must tone down its implied enthusiasm, and the second must forego some of its relaxation. Excitement and choleric temperament also fit uncomfortably together, since the former does not necessarily imply the hostile aggression essential to the latter. Although melancholy and depression fit fairly well, unpleasantness and phlegmatic temperament do not fit at all. It is interesting, however, to see what happens when Galen's four temperaments are superimposed on the Activity-Approach two-dimensional schema with a rotation of 45 degrees. (See the italicized words in Figure 7.1.) Now the sanguine temperament lies in the upper right quadrant, where it partakes of both excitement and pleasantness. Choleric lies in the upper left, partaking of excitement and unpleasantness.

Melancholy lies in the lower left, where unpleasantness and depression, or reduced activity, are both represented. Phlegmatic temperament lies in the lower right, partaking of pleasantness and depression. Except for this final quadrant, the fit of the two systems is quite satisfactory. If we were to think of depression as unresponsiveness, so that typically depressed behavior would be consigned to the melancholic quadrant, the four temperaments of Galen would all be satisfactorily accommodated by the two dimensions of the Duffy-Stagner schema. In the next chapter, we shall refer back to this as an illustration of the factorial approach: the two dimensions of Activity and Approach, or Excitement and Pleasantness, may be regarded as factors, through the use of which it is possible to define four different temperaments. Note also that in order to reconcile the two systems, we had to make use of a "rotation of axes," a device which plays an important part in factor analysis.

AUTONOMIC BALANCE AND THE APPROACH-WITHDRAWAL DIMENSION

It will be convenient at this point to give a fuller statement of arguments favoring the view that the most fundamental aspects of temperament have physiological foundations which are closely bound up with the dimensions of the schema which we have been studying. We shall consider first the relation of autonomic function to the Approach-Withdrawal dimension.

The autonomic nervous system plays an important part in the regulation of many physiological processes that are directly involved in emotional behavior. Each of the viscera is supplied by nerves from both major divisions of the autonomic system, the sympathetic (or thoracic-lumbar) and the parasympathetic (consisting of both the cranial and the sacral divisions). The effects of innervation from these two sources are everywhere antagonistic. Sympathetic innervation speeds the heart rate, but depresses the tone and activity of gastric muscle. The vagus nerve, which is part of the parasympathetic division, will on the contrary depress the heart rate and increase the tonus of gastric muscle. In general, predominantly parasympathetic innervation favors the functioning of normal digestive and life-sustaining processes, while predominantly sympathetic innervation subordinates those processes to others which are concerned with mobilization for aggression and defense. There is an anatomical distinction between the two divisions, which influences the nature of emotional phenomena. The parasympathetic division has ganglia which lie close to the innervated organs themselves, permitting a fair degree of specificity in the innervation of this organ or that. The ganglia of the sympathetic division are close to the vertebral column, and they are interconnected by preganglionic fibers, with the result that any sympathetic discharge tends to be diffuse, involving several of the viscera or all of them. One of the effects of sympathetic discharge is the release of the adrenal cortical hormones, adrenin and nor-adrenin. (For the distinction between these, see page 135.) Since the direct effect of sympathetic innervation of any organ is similar to the effect of these hormones on that organ, their spread through the body constitutes a diffuse and lingering reinforcement of the sympathetic pattern of response.

These physiological factors all contribute to the efficiency of what Cannon (1927) defined as the emergency response, which includes such diverse but coördinated aspects as relative immunity to fatigue, facilitation of blood clotting, increased respiration and faster blood circulation, withdrawal of blood from the viscera in order to supply the brain and the skeletal muscles more generously, etc. However, the activation of this pattern interferes with the proper functioning of the digestive and reproductive systems, or (as we recall from the open field test) the exercise of normal control over eliminative processes. It also interferes with the performance of fine manipulative processes or involved thinking. In short, it is part of a primitive defense pattern, but it is rarely useful in facing the dangers of modern life. It sustains the physical stamina of runners or football players, but in other competitive situations, such as school examinations and employment interviews, it is decidedly an impediment. As we recall from the last chapter, such facts led Young to define emotion as disorganizing behavior.

These and other related considerations have led to the concept of autonomic balance: that individuals may be characterized as having a chronic tendency to dominance of the sympathetic or parasympathetic innervation, the first group being predisposed to anxiety and the second being resistant to it (Eppinger and Hess, 1915). Wenger (1941) stated this hypothesis in a form which avoids the implication that people are to be classified in two sharply contrasting groups. He assumes that autonomic balance is a characteristic which is normally distributed, with relatively few individuals showing marked dominance of either the sympathetic or parasympathetic division. From a variety of possible physiologic indicators of autonomic function he selected seven as constituting a useful battery of tests, whose composite score may be taken as an autonomic index. These seven measures are: heart rate, pulse pressure, respiration rate, salivary output, dermographic persistence (persistence of a red mark when a line has been drawn with standard pressure on the upper arm— an indicator of capillary response), and two determinations of galvanic skin resistance, one taken while the subject stands and the other while he rests. Wenger and Wellington (1943) showed that the scores of children on this autonomic index have a significant correlation (about 0.70) from one year to the next. Jost and Sontag (1944) found evidence of hereditary influence in the fact that the scores of twins correlated better than those of ordinary siblings.

Wenger (1947) compared 14 children showing sympathetic dominance with an equal number showing parasympathetic dominance, and found many indications of psychological differences between these groups. He summarized his findings as follows: "Children with autonomic scores indicative of functional parasympathetic predominance were found . . . to manifest more emotional inhibition, less emotional excitability, and a lower frequency of activity with less fatigue; and proved to be more patient and neat than those children with autonomic scores indicative of functional predominance of the sympathetic system." The two groups also showed differences on a number of other traits which, though not significant, corresponded in direction to the predictions set up in advance of the experiment.

These results seem to be in conflict with those obtained by Jones (1943). He classified adolescent boys and girls into groups of low reactors and high reactors on the GSR, which should presumably correspond to parasympathetic and sympathetic dominance. He found that the low reactors were rated as significantly less calm, more impulsive, more irresponsible, and less constant as to mood. In other words, those who have more successful inhibitory control over their overt behavior tend to show greater autonomic responsiveness than those who more readily "act out" their feelings. The two sets of results may not be irreconcilable, since Wenger's measurements of galvanic skin resistance and the other elements of the autonomic index are taken under conditions of rest, while the measurement of the galvanic skin *response* (which depends on a sudden drop of skin resistance that presumably results from otherwise imperceptible activation of the sweat glands) is taken under conditions of mildly disturbing stimulation. However, Wenger's thesis would seem to require that these two kinds of measurements should show some correspondence.

There are two main considerations which point against accepting autonomic balance as the major factor in determination of temperament. These are (1) lack of consistency in the sympathetic pattern of response, and (2) the dependence of autonomic response on cortical control.

1. Difficulty in finding consistent patterns of visceral response during emotional behavior has led most investigators, unlike Wenger, to regard these visceral phenomena as secondary rather than primary components of the emotional response. The very

fact that Wenger found it necessary to use seven indicators of autonomic response shows that we are dealing with a complex group of phenomena rather than a unitary response. After many efforts to define emotions in terms of their physiological components (such as changes in blood pressure, heart rate, respiration, etc.), Landis (1934) reached the general conclusion that "the disturbance in emotion lacks pattern in the sense that essentially the same pattern should be shown by all individuals. What is found, then, is an individual rather than a common pattern." Lacey (1950) has provided evidence supporting this view. His subjects were examined in various contrived situations, which might have been expected to produce a variety of emotional responses, but the results revealed that each individual showed a characteristic consistency in the pattern of response to different forms of psychological stress. This finding, of course, favors a genetic theory of emotional development, in which the individuation of emotional behavior would be achieved as a result of experience. The concept of the feeling habit, which we shall introduce in Chapter 9, fits the requirements of such a theory. However, this sort of consistency, which represents a sort of personal signature on any emotional experience by a given individual, must necessarily remain a relatively subordinate part of the total response, and the fact that it exists does not at all exclude the likelihood that, with increasing knowledge, we will discover satisfactory criteria for distinguishing the visceral components of different emotions. Along these lines, it has recently been shown that what we have thought of as one hormone, adrenin, actually consists of two, one of which is now called nor-adrenin. It has been demonstrated that a preponderance of nor-adrenin is characteristic of angry, aggressive response, while a preponderance of adrenin is characteristic of fearful response (Funkenstein, 1955). It has also been found that aggressive animals secrete more nor-adrenin, while those that rely on flight secrete more adrenin (von Euler, cited by Funkenstein). This new knowledge may mark the beginning of a successful analysis of the sympathetic complex into discrete patterns, which will certainly necessitate revision of the concept of autonomic balance. Already, however, it suggests that closer knowledge of the physiological substrate of behavior supports the behavioral distinction between fear and rage as different temperamental characteristics, despite past difficulties in distinguishing the visceral components of these behaviors.

2. Turning now to the second point, we must recall the nature of the reciprocal influence between the autonomic system, which is controlled by hypothalamic centers, and the cerebral cortex. In keeping with the principle of anterior dominance, the cortex may be excited, but not inhibited, by stimulation of autonomic origin, whereas the autonomic functions can be and normally are inhibited by the cortex (Grinker, 1939). What superficially appears as "ease of arousal" or "sympathetic dominance" may therefore actually be a relative instability of the cortical inhibitory process which normally holds in check the primitive emotional response. In that event, the so-called balance between parasympathetic and sympathetic innervation would be only a reflection of the rivalry between autonomic excitation and cortical inhibition. Hence, to think of emotional instability as an expression of a balance within the autonomic system is quite misleading. We shall consider this point at greater length in the chapter on Control.

VOLUNTARY MUSCLE RESPONSE AND THE ACTIVITY DIMENSION

If one axis of the two-dimensional schema of behavior seems to have as its physiological correlate the opposition of sympathetic and parasympathetic divisions of the autonomic system, the other axis seems to be related to the characteristics of voluntary muscle response. We have already seen that Shirley, Gesell, and Fries were all impressed by the fact that infants differ strikingly in their motor behavior, and we shall see in Chapter 9 that these differences are predictive of later behavior trends. We may also recall that the background for Jones' study of the relationship between GSR and overt activity in adolescents was his much earlier observation of an apparently reciprocal relationship between these two modes of response to disturbance, on the part of infants. Wenger (1938) has sought to define a second major physiological component of temperament, in his hypothesis that "characteristic levels of muscular tension are related to various forms of personal behavior." He offered evidence, based on an intensive study of a small group of very disturbed children, that muscular tension is a dimension which is related to performance on a variety of psychological as well as physiological tests. He has subsequently performed a number of other researches tending to support this thesis. Ever since Luria's (1932) basic work in this field, in which he demonstrated how the presence of conflict can be detected by the measurement of minimal changes in muscular tension, there has been no doubt about the fact that this is a rich field for psychological experimentation. Nevertheless, all the work still seems to have a certain preliminary character, in which the promise is repeated but never realized.

It should be clear to the reader that Wenger's views also fit into a two-dimensional schema which greatly resembles those of Duffy and Stagner. However, the Activity dimension is labeled by him as Muscular Tension, and the Approach-Withdrawal dimension is called Autonomic Balance or Emotional Lability.

Another investigator who has worked along somewhat similar lines is Freeman (1948). Starting from the proposition that all behavior should be studied in the general framework of homeostatic regulation, he examined the responses of individuals to stress situations. His names for the two basic dimensions are Autonomic Arousal and Discharge Control. The latter dimension relates to the degree of inhibitory control over voluntary muscle response, which is an indirect consequence of the autonomic arousal. It is therefore homologous with the dimensions of Activity and of Muscular Tension, and does not constitute a recognition of the role of inhibitory control over the autonomic functions. Freeman takes express note of the fact that extremely effective discharge control may mean that the excitation must be discharged through visceral channels, increasing the likelihood of various psychosomatic disturbances. At this point, he is in agreement with the position taken by Jones.

It is evident that the supposed dimension of Activity is far from being psychologically or physiologically simple. Activity may be vigor, but it may also be impulsiveness, and it may thus reflect either or both of what we have come to regard, in earlier chapters, as two separate dimensions of temperament.

In summary to this point, we may say that the two-dimensional representation of human temperament appears inadequate, except as a descriptive device of limited applicability. The categories which it provides are too superficial for the proper analysis of behavior. We turn, therefore, to the study of a three-dimensional scheme.

PHYSIQUE AND TEMPERAMENT

There have been many attempts in the history of medicine to define a relation between temperament and physique, or gross bodily build. Some such relationships are widely believed by the general public. Shakespeare did not have to wait for Kretschmer's *Physique and Character* (1925) to know that his Falstaff must be quite fat, and his ruthless Cassius have a lean and hungry look, at least to achieve the most convincing theatrical effects. Kretschmer's contribution was to break away from the centuries-long custom of describing temperament in terms that stayed close to the Hippocratic system, and to use instead a classification based on the modern system of psychiatric diagnosis which had been introduced by Kraepelin. He stated that the pyknic or rounded type of body build is characteristic of persons predisposed to manic-depressive psychosis, while the leptosomatic or thin, fragile build is characteristic of those predisposed to schizophrenia. This psychological dichotomy was not essentially altered by his addition of a third body type, the athletic build, which was psychologically allied to the schizoid group. A good deal of controversy has raged about Kretschmer's theories, and there has probably been a slight preponderance of evidence in its favor, as a valid generalization whose practical import had been greatly overstated. However, Sheldon's more elaborate typology, which is free from the statistical naïveté of its predecessor, shifted the debate to other grounds. We propose to examine Sheldon's work in some detail, because it is all quite relevant to the definition of major temperamental dimensions. If the reader feels his resistances bristling beyond control, he is quite at liberty to turn directly to the beginning of the next chapter.

Let us first review Sheldon's system for the classification of physique (1940). He distinguishes three components of body build, which he calls endomorphy, mesomorphy, and ectomorphy. These three names have an obvious reference to the three tissue layers that are distinguished in the early developmental stages of vertebrate embryos. From the inner layer of cells, or endoderm, there develop the vital organs of digestion, respiration, and reproduction. The middle layer, or mesoderm, gives rise to the skeletal structure and the striped musculature that are involved in posture and movement, as well as the heart and blood vessels. The outer layer of cells, or ectoderm, gives rise not only to the skin, but also to the central nervous system and to all the sensory organs which maintain contact with the outer world. Hence there is some justification for thinking of these three systems of organs as having a relative independence of each other, and being capable of differentiations that might arise from hereditary or early developmental influences that might affect one system more than the others.

To determine an individual's somatotype, he must be separately rated for each component, on a seven-point scale. Sheldon's system of rating is based on measurements of 17 anthropometric characteristics, in addition to the ponderal index, or ratio of height to the cube root of weight, which is the best single indicator of somatotype. These 18 measurements give rise to three separate indices, one for each of the morphological components. At least, Sheldon cannot be accused of setting up "simple" types. In fact, he describes 76 different somatotypes, each representing a different combination of the three morphological components, and these may be further complicated by "dysplasias," or instances of inharmonious development of different major regions of the body. Although three independent seven-point scales can give rise to 343 different combinations, most of these combinations never exist in life. For example, an individual who scores 7 on one scale rarely scores as high as 3 on either of the others. The sum of the three index numbers which identify a somatotype (always given in the order: endomorphy, mesomorphy, ectomorphy) is never less than 9 nor more than 12. If the three components are regarded as dimensions defining a cube, then the 76 observed somatotypes all lie within an area which may be thought of as resembling a portion of a melon, so cut that it has three equilateral sides. The corners of this occupied area lie in three nonadjacent corners of the cube, as shown in Figure 7.2. The area is fairly thin along its edges, and becomes progressively thicker, as well as more densely populated, toward its center. Only about one individual in five belongs to a somatotype which has any index number lower than 3 or higher than 5.

Although careful measurements are needed to determine somatotypes with accuracy, we are told that it is possible to recognize a high mesomorphic component by "uprightness and sturdiness of structure," a high endomorphic component by "softness and sphericity," and a high ectomorphic component by "stooped posture and hesitant restraint of movement." (Sheldon, 1944.)

Sheldon (1942) also describes three temperamental components, which are associated with these morphological components and have a similar distribution. He declares that their discovery and definition proceeded independently. From a large number of descriptive behavioral traits he selected a few, which fell

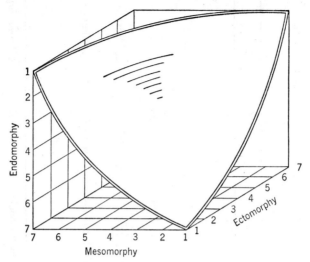

FIGURE 7.2. The distribution of observed somatotypes in a three-dimensional space. The area occupied is a solid, whose outer surface approximates a spherical triangle. Moving in from the edges toward the center, both thickness and density increase. The apexes are occupied by the rare extreme types (7-1-1, 1-7-1, and 1-1-7), and the types falling elsewhere along the edges are also relatively rare. The middle is occupied by the more common "balanced" types, with the perfectly balanced 4-4-4 at the center.

into well-defined clusters. Those within each cluster had high positive correlation among themselves, and negative correlation with each item in any other cluster. He states that he was surprised to find only three such clusters, because he had expected to find four, including one for masculinity. He hunted assiduously for traits which would satisfy his statistical criteria, until he had 20 in each group. These traits constitute scales for the measurement of the three temperamental components, which are designated as *viscerotonia, somatotonia,* and *cerebrotonia.* Table 7.1 gives a few items from each of these scales, and hence serves to describe these variables. For the complete determination of a somatotype, an individual is to be rated on a seven-point

TABLE 7.1. Definition of Sheldon's temperamental components, in terms of a few characteristics selected from the scales for their appraisal.[a]

	Viscerotonia	Somatotonia	Cerebrotonia
Posture and movement are	relaxed	assertive	restrained
Primary orientation is toward	childhood and family relations	goals and activities of youth	the later periods of life
Has a strong love for	food and comfort	exercise and adventure	solitude
Behaves toward others with	indiscriminate amiability	competitive aggressiveness	inhibited social address
In emotional life, shows	greed for affection and approval	psychological callousness	secretiveness of feeling
When troubled, needs	people	action	solitude

[a] Adapted from Sheldon, William H., "Constitutional Factors in Personality," in J. McV. Hunt (ed.), *Personality and The Behavior Disorders*, Ronald, 1944.

scale for each of the 60 traits, by a rater who has had the opportunity for long observation, including many intimate interviews. Working by this method, Sheldon has found very high correlations between morphological and temperamental components. His results have been received with a good deal of skepticism, because it is obviously impossible for anyone familiar with the general theory to carry out this long process of appraisal without being influenced by his knowledge of the body build of the subject. It must therefore be assumed that a strong halo effect is present in all of Sheldon's ratings, but it is not possible wholly to dismiss his conclusions on these grounds. Adcock (1948) found strong indications of this halo effect in the mathematical difficulties which he encountered in an effort to factor analyze some of the correlations which Sheldon reports among various temperamental traits, but he nevertheless concluded "that there is a sound basis to it all and that with all allowance made for halo there is still something substantial left." However, if Sheldon's theories are to be credited with any validity, they must be confirmed under stricter scientific controls. Fortunately, there are some recent studies in which his views have been subjected to thorough and unprejudiced test.

Child (1950) used items of Sheldon's temperament scales to construct a 66-item personality questionnaire. Each item called for a stepwise rating, rather than for a yes-or-no answer. The questionnaire was answered by more than 400 Yale sophomores, all of whom had been somatotyped by Sheldon during their freshman year, and who had no suspicion that it was related in any way to this earlier experience. In advance of the experiment, Child prepared a list of 96 predictions of positive relationships between answers to individual items and standing on morphological components, all in strict accordance with Sheldon's theories. (Some items permitted more than one prediction, since a high rating on the trait would be hypothetically related to one component, and a low rating to another.) Ten of these predictions were confirmed at the 1 percent level, 10 more at the 5 percent level, while 54 more were confirmed in direction although they did not individually satisfy conventional criteria of statistical significance. One prediction was disconfirmed at the 5 percent level, and none at the 1 percent level. The overall result constitutes an overwhelming confirmation of the general validity of Sheldon's theories. Few propositions in the field of personality can claim to have stronger experimental support.

Dividing his subjects into random halves, Child examined the records of one group in order to determine which items were most closely related to the morphological components. He set up three scales of seven items each. He then scored the remaining subjects, on the basis of their completed questionnaires, on these brief scales, and thus obtained a rating for each subject on each dimension, which could be correlated with the morphological indexes of the same subjects. The resulting correlations appear in Table 7.2(a), while Table 7.2(b) gives the corresponding correlations that were reported by Sheldon. Child's data leave

TABLE 7.2(a). Correlations between self-ratings for temperament and morphological components (Child, 1950).

| | Dimension of Physique | | |
	Endomorphy	Mesomorphy	Ectomorphy
Viscerotonia	.13	.13	−.15
Somatotonia	.03	.38	−.37
Cerebrotonia	−.03	−.38	.27

TABLE 7.2(b). Similar correlations reported by Sheldon (1944), based on his intensive study of 200 cases.

	Endomorphy	Mesomorphy	Ectomorphy
Viscerotonia	.79	−.23	−.41
Somatotonia	−.29	.82	−.53
Cerebrotonia	−.32	−.58	.83

no doubt about the reality of the relationship between soma-totonia and mesomorphy, on the one hand, and cerebrotonia and ectomorphy, on the other. Furthermore, there is a clear negative relationship between each of these temperamental components and the physique that is associated with the other. These relationships are not nearly so strong as indicated by Sheldon, but their direction is consistent with his theory. The relationship between viscerotonia and endomorphy is weaker. This circumstance is probably related to the fact that ratings for endomorphy are less consistent, during adolescence and young manhood, than ratings for the other components of the somatotype (Zuk, 1956).

Paradoxically, the more moderate relationships reported by Child may persuade us to more serious consideration of the temperamental variables that Sheldon has defined. Sheldon's claims were too sweeping for acceptance. The results reported by Child (like those reported by Glueck and Glueck, which we shall consider shortly) transport the theory to the plane of reality.

The really important aspect of Sheldon's work, in the long run, is not the demonstration of a correspondence between physique and temperament, but the definition of temperamental syndromes. We may recall, at this point, the observations by Stockard and by James, that in the second generation offspring of crosses between German shepherds and bassett hounds, it would sometimes occur that the temperament of one breed would appear in a dog that had many of the physical characteristics of the other. Such observations imply that a very close cor-respondence between physique and temperament, in a population that has not been selectively bred, is not to be expected. The constitutional determinants of temperament are undoubtedly more deep-seated than the external characteristics that have been used as their indicators. However, the definition of tempera-mental syndromes in adults has an importance which is quite independent of the question of correspondence between physique and temperament. Wells (1947) has stated, on the basis of his experience in the Grant Study, a very intensive psychological study of a selected group of Harvard undergraduates, that the usefulness of Sheldon's categories of temperament is such that they represent a major contribution to psychological theory, even if it should turn out that they are not at all related to somatotypes.

Sheldon's (1949) report that mesomorphic dominance is extraordinarily frequent in a population of delinquent youths, and particularly so among those of persistent criminal inclination, demands attention. We must point out that he does not contend that the somatotype in itself determines delinquency. He says:

It should be clear that the somatotype alone has virtually no predictive value. To try and predict such a thing as criminality from the somatotype would be like trying to predict where a bullet will strike by describing only the gun and the bullet and powder charge. You still have to deal with such variables as how the gun is aimed.

Mesomorphic dominance, he states, "means energetic vitality and freedom from inhibition, two cardinal factors in success at most of the things men undertake," including, he says, fiction writing as well as crime.

Again, we must turn to better controlled studies than Sheldon's to judge the validity of his conclusions. Glueck and Glueck (1950) directed a many-sided inquiry into the determinants of delinquency, in which approximately 500 pairs of boys, delinquent and nondelinquent, were studied from psychological, sociological, and anthropometric points of view. The anthropometric part of the work was done by Seltzer, a co-worker of Sheldon's, but under stricter controls than are found in Sheldon's work. Working from randomly intermingled photographs, he rated each boy for dominant physique characteristics, leading to the results shown in Table 7.3. Almost twice as high a proportion of the delinquent boys were classified as dominantly mesomorphic. On the other hand, more than twice as many nondelinquents as delinquents were classified as dominantly ectomorphic. An

TABLE 7.3. Distribution of dominant morphological components among delinquent and nondelinquent boys (based on Seltzer, in Glueck and Glueck, 1950).

Dominant component	Delinquents		Nondelinquents	
	Number	%	Number	%
Endomorphy	59	11.8	72	15.2
Mesomorphy	298	60.1	148	30.7
Ectomorphy	72	14.4	191	39.6
None dominant	67	13.5	71	14.7

examination of the more detailed tables in the original, which give a finer classification of physique types, strengthens the conclusion that mesomorphic constitution does represent a predisposing factor to delinquency, in the environmental circumstances under which these boys have grown up. The magnitude of this relationship is great enough so that we cannot afford to ignore it, but it is not so great as to detract in any way from the importance of other determinants, such as family, neighborhood, and economic influences.[1] Indeed, it may help us to understand better how these other influences operate. It tells us that temptation to delinquency is strongest for boys who are temperamentally disposed to active physical self-assertion, if not, indeed, directly to challenge authority in a test of dominance. Such boys are made to feel most rebellious by restraints imposed upon them, for example, in the classroom. They are not "born" delinquents, but it is quite possible that they have a stronger need for physical adventure, and it would be wise for us to take extra pains to provide it for them in acceptable ways. Such a conclusion rep-

---

[1] By a series of deductions which it would be pointless to repeat here, the data in Table 7.3 may be used to support the interpretation that in a population such as that represented by these subjects, approximately 20 percent of variance in delinquency may be traced to the influence of physiological factors reflected in the somatotype. Hence, 80 percent remains to be accounted for in other ways. If we understand this multiple determination of a complex phenomenon, we may feel less threatened by the proof that physique is one of the factors which influence it.

resents no more than a logical extension of the admonition expressed by Fries, to the effect that the Active child will require more alert watching as he grows up, if he is to be kept from disaster.

SHELDON'S TEMPERAMENTAL COMPONENTS AND BIOLOGICAL MODES OF ADJUSTMENT

Sheldon's three-dimensional system obviously cannot be accommodated by the two-dimensional schema that was discussed earlier in this chapter. However, it seems quite likely that it permits a more adequate conceptualization of temperament than any two dimensional scheme can achieve. In addition, there is a remarkable correspondence between the dimensions or components which Sheldon has defined, and those that we found prominent in the behavior of animals. Let us consider this relationship.

An important condition for the survival of any mammal is the presence of strong affiliative response tendencies in both the mother and the infant, directed toward one another. In the infant, such responses are associated with nursing, but not limited to it. Survival depends on more than a sucking reflex in response to stimulation of the lips. The maintenance of conditions for successful nursing, as well as proper body temperature, and, as Ribble points out for human babies, proper respiratory rhythm, requires a constant seeking for bodily contact. In the chimpanzee, our closest living relative, this shows itself also as a tenacious clinging behavior, which is essential for survival in arboreal life. In short, all infant mammals show the antecedent forms of the "need for love" which we have come lately to recognize in our own babies. The satisfactions of eating and sleeping and social interstimulation are blended together in this one complex of dependent-nutritive behavior. It corresponds, of course, to the viscerotonic temperament as defined by Sheldon, in which love of comfort, and especially of food, is joined with delight in sociability and distress in its lack.

The maturational history of every mammal is marked by a decline of the initial dependent attitudes, and the appearance of dominance behavior. Aggressive elements appear, at first in play, later in earnest, and with greater vigor in the male than in the female. Fredericson (1950) observed the spontaneous appearance of fighting, at the beginning of puberty, among pairs of male mice who had until that time been exhibiting friendly behavior toward each other. Scott and Marston (1950) describe the appearance of aggressive play and later dominance behavior as definite stages in the development of dogs. Yerkes (1943) and others vividly describe this aspect of chimpanzee behavior, and Hayes' (1951) account of its appearance in her ward Viki, who was reared without contact with other chimpanzees, leaves no room for doubt about its innate character. There is no possible scientific justification for clinging to the view that when such behavior occurs in children it is solely as a response to the competitive spirit of contemporary society. The evidence from social anthropology proves that such behavior can be effectively suppressed—though not without cost to the individual—but this does not alter the fact that the dominance-aggression complex represents a second great temperamental variable. It corresponds, of course, to Sheldon's somatotonia, which is characterized by aggressive adventurism and by a vigorous erect bearing which is directly reminiscent of the dominance posture in animals.

A third important category of temperament which we have recognized in each of the animals that we have studied is that of fear and avoidance. We have discussed its relation to the emergency response described by Cannon, and have concluded that it must not be thought of as solely or even primarily an autonomic pattern of response. In the intact animal, these visceral reactions are always triggered by impulses of cortical origin, and the total behavior pattern includes the posture of shrinking retreat, cautious restraint of action, or flight. This aspect of temperament corresponds to Sheldon's third component, cerebrotonia, which is characterized by "hesitant restraint of movement" and timidity in social relationships.

Thus, the results of a comparative approach to the problem of temperament, along the lines of the first few chapters of this book, and of Sheldon's very differently oriented work with human adults, coincide in important respects. We should take note of the fact that impulsiveness, which we have considered an independent dimension, is regarded by Sheldon as one aspect of somatotonia. (The fourth component which Sheldon says he had anticipated, but for which he found inadequate evidence, was masculinity-femininity. This will be discussed in Chapter 13.) Unfortunately, Sheldon's views have had so poor an audience among psychologists that some moral courage is required to confess to this degree of agreement with them. In honesty, however, they cannot be ignored.

CHAPTER 8

The Factorial Approach

*B*efore we go any farther in our consideration of rival theories of temperament, it will be necessary to digress for a while, to discuss the method of factor analysis. Some acquaintance with this method is essential to an understanding of the work of Guilford, Thurstone, Cattell, Eysenck, and others. Besides, this general method is being adapted in many ingenious ways for use in other areas of personality study, as will appear in later chapters. A good deal of current research on personality must remain quite unintelligible without an understanding of the objectives and the limitations of factor analysis.

Actually, we have already seen several examples of the factorial approach, which is the modern counterpart of "type" theory. The Hippocratic temperaments were first thought of as four types, each dependent on a special physiological mechanism, but we have seen that it is possible to regard them as the outcome of the interaction of two factors, of which one is the direction of affect and the other is the rate of activity. Wenger and Freeman make explicit use of the method of factor analysis in interpreting their findings, and we have to some extent done them an injustice by failing to acknowledge this in presenting their views. One can make use of the factorial approach in the analysis of a problem, without making explicit use of the mathematical method of factor analysis. Although Sheldon's conclusions on the relations between physique and temperament have often been disdainfully dismissed as type theory, it would be more correct to say that he uses a factorial approach, since each of his numerous types is defined in terms of only three postulated fundamental factors. There is, however, another classic application of the factorial method of thinking with which all students of psychology are familiar, and which provides a very clear illustration of both the power and the limitations of this method. This is the theory of color vision.

The color spectrum contains hundreds of distinguishable hues, which are chosen fastidiously for ties, curtains, and automobiles. It is common knowledge that each of these hues may be reproduced on the color wheel by mixing the light reflected from only three standard papers. Furthermore, there is more than one such set of standards which may be used. Young first advanced the idea that all color vision could be explained as the fusion of three processes. Helmholtz elaborated the theory, and postulated the existence of three different types of nerve elements, each sensitive to virtually the whole of the visible spectrum, but each having its peak sensitivity in a different part of the spectrum, corresponding to the three colors which he selected as primaries. In a modern variant of this theory, Hecht showed that the facts could be as well explained by assuming three sets of sensitive elements which differed only very slightly from one another with regard to the location of their peak sensitivities in the spectrum. Thus the factorial approach to the study of color vision started from a recognition of the fact that the multiplicity of colors could be regarded as the results of fusion of only three color processes. This led to the development of several different theories, which are alike in their reliance on three separate color processes, but nevertheless define these processes quite differently. Furthermore, the fact that three primary colors suffice to explain color vision does not eliminate the possibility that four or five primaries may be involved, as postulated by some other theories. (Cf. Geldard, 1953.)

The mathematical techniques of factor analysis are employed in order to construct and to test hypotheses about how a smaller number of determining factors may explain the relationships that are observed among a larger number of empirical phenomena. The starting point of such an analysis is a set of correlation coefficients, each of which represents an empirical (and hence fallible) determination of the strength of association between two of these phenomena. We may assume that behind each significant correlation there lies at least one causal influence which affects both of the variables that are involved. However, the same causal influence may express itself in several of these correlations. For example, hot weather may increase the incidence of ice-cream sales and swimming-pool attendance, as well as the sale of camping equipment and week-end automobile accidents. On the other hand, a single correlation may be the result of more than one common influence. The correlation between grades received in different school subjects results partly from the influence of general intelligence, and partly from the influence of study habits. In the effort to arrive at a parsimonious explanation of the observed relationships, we may ask ourselves the question, "What is the minimum number of separate causal influences which must be assumed to underlie the matrix of correlation coefficients between all the variables which we have observed?" Assuming that the correlations themselves are accurate, it is possible to give an unambiguous mathematical answer to this question. Usually, the number of factors which are so indicated will be smaller than the number of variables with which we started, and this fact represents a simplification of the problem we face in trying to understand the relationships among all the variables. As soon as we have answered the first question, we are confronted by another: "To what extent does each of the factors influence each of the variables?" Just as it is possible to construct a variety of color vision theories each of which is based on the assumption of three color processes, so it is possible in every case to set up a large number of mathematically correct hypotheses as to how the influence of the different factors might be distributed. Fortunately, many of these hypotheses can be dismissed immediately as psychologically implausible, but sound judgment is needed to select the most likely hypothesis among those which remain, and in complex situations agreement is not easily reached. Like other statistical methods, factor analysis will offer its best yield when an investigation has been designed to give proper scope to its powers.

Let us now illustrate the application of factor analyses to a very simple example in the field of temperament. In Chapter 6, we reported certain findings by Bayley on the consistency of crying by human infants. Table 8.1 reproduces the correlations

TABLE 8.1.   Correlations of crying scores for successive quarters of the first year of life. (Based on Bayley, 1932.)

	II	III	IV
I	.38	.22	.15
II		.26	.18
III			.66

which she reported between crying scores for different quarters of the first year of life. Examining this table, we may reason as follows: The sizable correlation between scores for the first and second quarters of the year gives some evidence of temperamental consistency even at that early stage. The much higher correlation between scores for the third and fourth quarters demonstrates the presence of an even stronger factor which is making for consistency in later infancy. However, the negligible correlation between scores for the first and fourth quarters shows that whatever is responsible for consistency in early infancy is not the same as what is responsible for consistency in later infancy. Hence, at least two different factors are responsible for the observed correlations.

When we deal with a large number of variables, it is rarely possible to perceive the relationships among them without making resort to the mathematical technique of factor analysis. The data of this illustrative example are inadequate for a serious study of this sort, first because of the small number of variables, and second because the correlations are based on too few cases, and are therefore not sufficiently stable. Nevertheless, they do yield results which have all the clarity that might be desired in a demonstration problem. In the next few paragraphs we shall explain the purpose of the different steps of the analysis in a general way, but the serious reader, if he is not already familiar with the technique of factor analysis, will be asked to turn to the Appendix of this chapter to read a more detailed explanation.

The first part of a factor analysis consists of two alternating phases, which may be called the "extraction" and "testing" phases. In the extraction phase, one factor is extracted at a time; in the succeeding testing phase, a check is made to see whether this factor, together with all other factors that have been previously extracted, suffices to explain all the common variance which is represented in the correlations. When that appears to be the case, the determination of the minimum number of common factors that must be assumed, is completed. In the present case, the computational routine leads, as expected, to the unambiguous indication that at least two factors are present, and that no more than two need be postulated to explain the observed relationships.

As each factor is extracted, a set of coefficients or "loadings" is obtained, one for each variable. These are, in effect, coefficients of correlations between the empirical variables and the hypothetical factor. The loadings for all the factors in the problem (in this case, two) constitute a full restatement of the information in the correlations. Just as the factors, with their loadings, have been derived from the correlations, so the correlations can be calculated from the factor loadings. However, these loadings

(which are called the loadings of unrotated factors, in Table 8.2)

TABLE 8.2. Summary of results of a factor analysis of the
correlations in Table 8.1.

Test	Loadings of unrotated factors		Loadings of rotated factors		Proportion of variance explained		
	A	B	A′	B′	by A′	by B′	h^2
I	.470	.399	.61	.10	.37	.01	.38
II	.499	.363	.60	.15	.36	.02	.38
III	.748	−.322	.23	.78	.05	.61	.66
IV	.687	−.438	.11	.81	.01	.66	.67

represent only one way in which two factors could give rise
to the correlations with which we started. As a matter of fact,
the distribution of loadings has a pattern which depends more
on the computational method than on the underlying psychological realities. In particular, the negative loadings on the second
factor are an inevitable consequence of the method of analysis
which was used, and they do not imply the presence of a bipolar
psychological dimension. In other words, the first part of the
analysis results in a mathematically sound but psychologically
misleading hypothesis.

(It is at this point that we would urge the reader to study
the Appendix to this chapter, where the computations for this
example are given in detail, and explained for those who are
willing to pause just a little as they read.)

Since there are only two common factors, the relationships
among the four tests may be represented in a two-dimensional
mathematical model. In Figure 8.1, the vertical and horizontal
axes represent the two factors which emerged from the preliminary solution. Each test is located according to its projections on these axes, which are its loadings on the factors. The
interpretation of the factors proceeds by manipulation of this
mathematical model, and is quite literally a "rotation of axes."

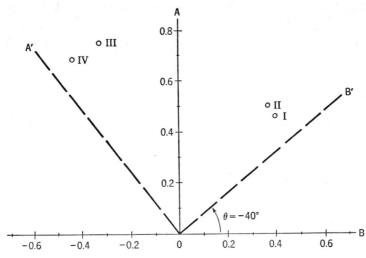

FIGURE 8.1. Graphic rotation of factors.

When we put the axes into new positions, we get a "new slant" on the relationships among the tests, without changing their absolute positions relative to each other. Therefore no rotation can be called wrong, but some rotations may be better than others, because they define factor dimensions which are more meaningful to us.

The dimensions which we have selected are defined by a counterclockwise rotation of both axes through an angle of 40 degrees. The projections of the tests upon these new axes appear, in the table, as their loadings on the rotated axes, A′ and B′. The rotated factors explain neither more nor less than the unrotated factors, but they offer an explanation which is superior in the sense that it seems more consistent with the general body of our knowledge about crying infants. It seems especially consistent with Bayley's statement that "the children tended to cry for different reasons at different ages," at first mainly for such reasons as fatigue and colic pain, but later "from fear of the strange situation and dislike of unusual handling." Following this clue, we designate the factor which is prominent in early infancy (Tests I and II) as *physical health,* and the one which is prominent in later infancy (Tests III and IV) as *social adjustment.*

The next two columns of Table 8.2 give the squared values of the loadings of the rotated factors. These represent the proportion of variance in each variable—that is, in each quarter of the year—which is associated with each of the factors. The sum of these values for each test is the communality, and it is gratifying that these sums agree closely with the original estimates (see Appendix). The extent by which these figures fall short of unity indicates the proportion of the variance in each test which cannot be attributed to either of the common factors. This is a reminder of the incompleteness of our knowledge. We must never slip into the error of supposing that a phenomenon has been explained because we have found 2 or 20 factors which, taken together, still account only for the lesser part of the total variance.

This simple case illustrated the two separate phases of any factor analysis: determining the number of factors that must be assumed, and then attempting a psychological definition of the factors. The larger the number of factors, the more difficult will this second task become, so that differences of interpretation will frequently arise.

THE ANALYSIS OF INTROVERSION

The first application of factor analysis to problems in the field of temperament and personality dealt with definition of the concept of introversion. The terms introversion and extraversion were introduced into modern psychology by Jung (1923). He defined them as two opposing trends in mental activity, one or the other of which often predominates to the point that it may properly be called the person's typical mode of response. The mental activity of the extravert is outward-directed—"the object works like a magnet upon the tendencies of the subject." In extreme cases, the person loses himself altogether in the things of the outside world, so that his own character seems to be determined altogether by them. The mental activity of the introvert is inward-directed—"as though energy were flowing away from the object, as if the subject were a magnet which would draw the object to itself." In these brief summary statements, we have spoken of mental activity rather than of thinking, because Jung himself distinguishes four basic kinds of mental activity—thinking, feeling, sensation, and intuition—and four corresponding kinds of introversion or extraversion. But whether an individual tends to deal with reality basically in terms of logic or of value, as sensory experience or on the basis of unconscious intuitive dispositions, he may still do so in either an introvert or an extravert manner, turning attention chiefly toward inner or outer reality.

The distinction which Jung made between what he called the four function types has received little attention except from his immediate followers, but the concept of the opposition of intro version and extraversion, which he called general attitude types, became not only a focal point of research but also a commonplace addition to the conversation of every educated layman. Tests of introversion soon became the most popular form of personality test, although it was evident from their very low intercorrelations that there was very little agreement as to the meaning of this term. These tests were almost all of the self-inventory type, with items which would give a score for introversion if answered in one way, for extraversion if answered in the other. Thus the unidimensionality of introversion-extraversion was assumed in their construction. This is consistent with Jung's own statements, which always emphasize the diametric opposition of introvert and extravert tendencies, and certainly seem to imply that any person can be located, at least as regards his conscious attitudes, on a continuum stretching from one extreme to the other. It is unjust to charge him with the error of assuming that the distribution of men on this continuum is bimodal, for he freely recognizes that most people occupy intermediate positions. However, he does think of introversion and extraversion as having a necessarily reciprocal relationship, so that if we know the extent to which an individual is introverted in his attitudes, we also know the extent to which he is extraverted. It was therefore reasonable to devise tests which were intended to measure the single dimension of introversion-extraversion.

In the hands of American psychologists, the concept of introversion soon became almost identical with that of neurotic tendency. Downey (1926) found that psychologists who characterized themselves as introvert also tended to characterize themselves as emotionally less stable than those who characterized themselves as extravert. Heidbreder (1930) showed that introverts quite generally agreed that extravert traits were more desirable. The Thurstones (1930) found that "the less serious forms of neurotic maladjustments have the characteristics ordinarily known as introversion." On Bernreuter's Personality Inventory (1933b), which included scales for Introversion, Neurotic Tendency, Dominance, and Self-sufficiency, the agreement between the first two scales was so high that they must be regarded as practically identical. These findings were not really in conflict with Jung's definition, for he himself described the introvert as not merely shy, but ineffectual and fearful in his relationships with other persons and with inanimate things. This is the more remarkable since he frequently shows a strong preference for introversion over extraversion as a way of living. In *Modern Man in Search of a Soul* (1933), he implies that the introvert's disadvantage is a fault of our culture because of the premium it places on extraversion.

This was the situation which invited some of the first applications of factor analysis to a problem in the sphere of personality. The questions which such analysis might answer, in whole or in part, were: Is there a unitary dimension of introversion-extraversion? If not, what are the principal factors that influence behavior which is ordinarily classified as introversive? To what degree do neurotic behavior and introversion have the same determinants?

Actually, the very construction of the Bernreuter Inventory implicitly recognized something of the factorial approach. Its four dimensions were defined by criterion groups of subjects who were high and low scorers on as many different tests: the Thurstone Personality Schedule, which is a measure of neurotic tendency (Thurstone and Thurstone, 1930); the Allport A-S Study, a measure of the ascendant-submissive dimension (Allport, 1928); Laird's C2, a test of introversion (Laird, 1925); and the Bernreuter Self-sufficiency Test (Bernreuter, 1933a). The 125 items of the inventory were assigned different weights for each of the four scales, depending on how well each item distinguished between the "highs" and the "lows" on each of the criterion tests. This implies some recognition that each of the items has multiple determination. There would of course be no assurance that the set of dimensions adopted a priori was the best for the purpose of showing this multiple determination.

By factor analysis, Flanagan (1935) showed that virtually all the information gained from the Bernreuter Inventory, which owed much of its popularity to its omnibus character, could be adequately stated in terms of two scores instead of four. He developed two relatively independent scales, called Self-confidence and Sociability. Introversion, as measured on the Bernreuter Inventory, represents a low position on both of these scales, and it is thus shown to consist of at least two distinct elements. The active interest in subjective experience which is the central point in Jung's definition does not even appear as a factor in the Bernreuter Inventory. It is an amusing fact, as well as an indication of how the factorial approach is generally misunderstood, that as an outgrowth of Flanagan's research, guidance workers now often interpret the Bernreuter Inventory to their clients as if it yielded *six* independent scores!

The Guilfords (1934) constructed a questionnaire of typical items taken from various tests of introversion-extraversion, and ministered it to college men and women. The factor analysis of correlations between the items gave evidence of a large number of factors. Three factors which were clearly indicated are: a tendency to emotional depression or moodiness, which approximates Flanagan's dimension of Self-confidence, the negative pole of which is heavily loaded with emotional instability; social introversion, or tendency to avoid wide social experience, which corresponds to Flanagan's dimension of Sociability; and thinking introversion, or tendency to reflective behavior. The last-named factor is the nearest to introversion in Jung's original sense, although we must remember that it is his contention that emphasis on intellectualization may have either an introvert or an extravert expression.

It is evident from such analyses that what was instrumentally defined as introversion, through the medium of tests, is almost identical with the syndrome of cerebrotonia which Sheldon was later to describe as displaying inhibitedness, desire for concealment, and high intellectual interest. However, Jung's theoretical justification for this syndrome is very different from Sheldon's, and more difficult to sustain. For Sheldon, defensiveness is the central feature, and this can be seen to be operative in each of the factors defined by Flanagan or by Guilford. For Jung, the central feature is the subjective orientation of interest, which leads to defensiveness as a secondary consequence. (Compare his use of the concept of compensation, p. 292.)

These pioneer applications of factor analysis to problems of temperament were the forerunners of many others.

THE FACTORS OF TEMPERAMENT

In this section, we shall chiefly consider the contributions of three men who have pursued the problem of the definition of the major factors of temperament, through the technique of factor analysis, with exceptional vigor. A thorough evaluation of their results would involve us in a difficult technical discussion, and would in any case be premature. We shall try, however, to indicate the extent of their agreements, and to understand the reasons for their disagreements. What comes out of a factor analysis depends, of course, on what is put into it at the start, and the important differences between the findings of Guilford, Cattell, and Eysenck do not depend so much on differences in the factoring technique as on the different ways in which they choose the basic data for their studies.

The work of Guilford and his collaborators has been concerned with practical problems of test construction, and it consists essentially in a refined cluster analysis of the types of items that are commonly included in questionnaire tests of personality. It has led to the definition of 13 temperamental variables, and to the construction of a battery of tests for their measurement (Guilford, 1948). The Guilford Inventory STDCR yields scores for social introversion, thinking introversion, and emotional depression, as well as cycloid disposition, or tendency to fluctuation of mood, and rhathymia, or carefree and excitement-loving temperament. The Guilford-Martin Inventory GAMIN similarly measures general activity drive, ascendance-submission, masculinity-femininity, inferiority feeling or self-confidence, and nervousness as opposed to calm. The remaining dimensions are agreeableness or friendly disposition, coöperative disposition, and objectivity as opposed to subjectivism in general outlook.

A process of this sort can be continued indefinitely and, as the dimensions multiply, one must either make a more or less arbitrary decision as to their relative importance or attempt, by some analytic procedure, to reduce their number without sacrificing any significant amount of their predictive value, in much the same way that Flanagan reduced Bernreuter's four dimensions to two. Lovell (1945) undertook such a reductionist study. She obtained the intercorrelations of the 13 scores as found in a population of 200 college students, and discovered that underlying these 13 factors there were 6 superfactors, or second-order factors, as they are now more commonly called. Two of these proved, after rotation, to be of relatively little importance. The names which Lovell proposes for the others are Drive-restraint, Realism, Emotionality, and Social adaptability. We may regard them as the approximate equivalents, respectively, of aggressiveness, inhibitory control, fearfulness, and affiliative tendency.

Lovell's basic data were also utilized by Thurstone (1951), in a somewhat differently oriented investigation of the question whether Guilford's 13 variables could be regarded as reasonably independent. He reached the conclusion that at most nine dimensions were justified, and that two of these accounted for so little of the variance that for practical purposes they could be ignored. He designated the remaining dimensions as Active, Vigorous, Impulsive, Dominant, Stable, Sociable, and Reflective, and he used these as the dimensions of the Thurstone Temperament Schedule.

Cattell's work has been marked by an effort at exhaustive exploration of the whole field of individuality. He has not been content to analyze only those aspects of behavior which have already drawn the attention of psychologists. Instead, he took as his starting point the list of almost 18,000 trait names and related terms in the English language which had been compiled by Allport and Odbert (1936). By eliminating repetitious terms and clustering those that are closely related, Cattell (1946) reduced the Allport and Odbert list to 160 traits. However, he also noticed some gaps in this extensive vocabulary of personal description, which had been built up by many generations to serve the varied needs of social intercourse, literary communication, and medical diagnosis. He found it necessary to make 11 additions in order to take account of certain aspects of individuality which figure prominently in contemporary psychological research, but have not yet found their way into the standard dictionaries. He regards these 171 traits as comprising "a kind of Basic English for the complete description of personality" and he designates them as "the personality sphere." This is a puzzling term for anyone who is unaccustomed to think of a sphere otherwise than as a three-dimensional object. Cattell's personality sphere is actually a hypersphere in a space of 171 dimensions, and all his further research may be regarded as an effort to reduce the dimensionality of this hypersphere, by isolating a smaller number of dimensions which may be adequate for the description of at least the major aspects of individuality.

More than 100 of these traits are expressed in terms of opposite poles, such as patient-impatient, cynical-idealistic, enthusiastic-apathetic, courageous-cowardly. Each is accompanied by a cluster of related terms, and these are rarely so synonymous that one feels quite satisfied to have them all absorbed into a single dimension. It is doubtful, therefore, whether a basic vocabulary for the description of personality can be reduced to fewer than several hundred words. (As an aside, we may mention that Gough (1950), basing himself largely on Cattell's prior work, has prepared an Adjective Check List of 300 words. This is designed to facilitate obtaining personality descriptions from relatively untrained persons, and it has proved to be a valuable research instrument.) However, a useful list need not necessarily be exhaustive, and Cattell pressed steadily forward toward his objective of defining the primary dimensions of personality.

He next organized the 171 traits of the personality sphere into 35 clusters, trying to retain all the major "surface traits" of personality, whose relationships might reveal the underlying source traits. These 35 traits became the basis of ratings which were assigned to 208 adult male subjects, of varied social backgrounds. Each subject was rated by 2 judges, and each judge rated only 1 group of 16 men whom he knew well from long acquaintance. The analysis of the resulting correlations indicated a need for 12 factors. However, a number of these proved in the process of rotation to be "coöperative factors," which overlap to a considerable degree, so that the final list includes several factors in which the cyclothyme-schizothyme (that is, sociable vs. seclusive or hostile) contrast is prominent, and several in which the major contrast is between mature control of emotion and an immature absence of control. It is difficult, with all good will, to form a clear conception of the distinctions which Cattell makes among these presumable "source" traits. Of course, Cattell does not pretend that they are clear, but only that something very like them appears to be necessary, and that further research should help to clarify them. An attempt is made in Figure 8.2

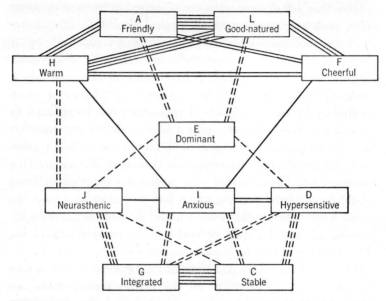

FIGURE 8.2. How Cattell's primary source traits, or factors, share relatively high loadings of the surface traits from which they were developed. See text for explanation.

to show their interrelations, by indicating the extent to which they share the same surface traits. This chart is based upon Cattell's listing of five to eight surface traits for each source trait, as an aid to its definition. Each line on the chart represents the sharing of one surface trait by two source traits, in that listing. A broken line indicates that the loadings are opposite in direction. Factor B, Intelligence, and Factor K, which is defined as Cultured mind vs. Boorishness, have not been included in the chart, because they are obviously not factors of temperament, and including them would make the chart needlessly more complicated without changing its basic pattern. The short names that are given to the source traits, or factors, are meant to be only suggestive, and not to replace Cattell's longer bipolar designations.

If we examine this chart with the expectation that the major temperamental dimensions which were indicated by the comparative and developmental approach of the earlier chapters should be represented here, we are not disappointed. At the top of the chart there is a strong constellation of factors reflecting affiliative tendency. The negative poles of these factors all express in varying degrees the coldness, aloofness, and hostility of the schizoid temperament. At the bottom of the chart, there is a pair of related factors which represent inhibitory control. Incidentally, the factor of intelligence, which we have omitted, is also strongly bound to each of these, as might be expected. Between, there is dominance, which stands relatively apart, and a weaker constellation which might be termed emotionality, which centers on anxiety or fearfulness. It might be objected that if the emotionality factors were designated by their favorable poles, their bonds to the control factors would be positive rather than negative. However, the choice of polarity was not arbitrary, but follows Cattell's own usage by selecting the first pole named by him in each factor designation, and this may be presumed to be the one that is more prominent in the factor. In any case, there is abundant evidence from other sources that control and emotionality are two distinct, though interacting, aspects of temperament. Thus while Cattell's work indicates the need for more detailed analysis of temperamental dispositions, it does not invalidate the simpler overall picture which we have already formed.

It is interesting to compare Cattell's results with those reported by Fiske (1949), who analyzed three sets of ratings which were based on 22 rating scales that were taken, with only a few slight ifications, from Cattell. The scales were chosen so that each of Cattell's 12 factors should be represented by at least 2 variables, and thus have a chance to evidence itself. The subjects were 128 clinical psychologist trainees engaged in an intensive week-long assessment program. Hence, they were individuals who had some psychological sophistication, and who had already been screened in such a manner that one would not expect to find obvious unfavorable personality characteristics in any of them. The three sets of ratings included self-ratings by these trainees, ratings of each by several "team-mates" in the group who had close contact during the program, and ratings by highly qualified psychologist observers. Each set of ratings yielded five factors, and two of these proved, after independent rotations, to be strikingly similar in all three sets. These are identified by Fiske as Social Adaptability and Emotional Control, the parallels to Cattell's A and C factors. Two factors in each set showed a less striking correspondence, and these were designated as Conformity and Inquiring Intellect. Perhaps the appearance of these factors is due to the special population used and the very special situation in which the study was carried out. The fifth factor in each set of ratings contains some elements of assertiveness, initiative, confident self-expression, or the like. We may therefore look upon it as an expression of Dominance, but it took rather different forms in the self-ratings, ratings by team mates, and the ratings by psychologists.

In Cattell's recent work, ratings have given way to objective tests, or behavior samples derived from experimental test situations. He still makes the same effort to cover the whole domain of personality in a broad, random fashion, and still arrives, therefore, at rather lengthy lists of factors which are not too clearly defined. His interpretation of these tends still to be influenced by his confidence in the 12 factors which he defined on the basis of what may be called his pilot rating study.

The work of Eysenck (1947, 1952, 1953) is not exploratory, but is a planned effort to demonstrate the pervasive influence of certain selected dimensions. He has given most attention to the dimension of control, which he prefers to define in its negative sense, as neuroticism. His basic project (1947) in an extensive program of research was the analysis of psychiatrists' ratings of 700 hospitalized neurotics, on 39 selected variables. Data on many other variables were equally available, and it is difficult to understand why he elected to include such dimensions as "age above 30" and "exposure to bombing," which turned out in any case to contribute very little to the definition of factors, in preference to such others as "rebellious or aggressive" and "psychopathic personality." Whatever his principle of selection was, it must have influenced the outcome, which was already determined in part by the circumstance that the population being studied consisted wholly of seriously neurotic persons. The factorial analysis of this data led to the extraction of one general factor, and three bipolar factors of progressively diminishing importance. This factor pattern is the direct result of the method used, and might be altered considerably by rotation of the axes. However, at the time when he first reported this study Eysenck was openly skeptical of the rotational methods which had been introduced by Thurstone and which were in general use by American factorists. His methodological approach led him to dismiss two of the four factors as inconsequential, and to concentrate his attention upon the general factor, which he called neuroticism. He called the first of the bipolar factors hysteria-dysthymia, and regarded it as an expression of the introvert-extravert dimension, which is here defined in terms of the symptomatology which may be expected of extraverts and introverts, respectively, when they become neurotic. Subsequently (1953), Eysenck recognized the correctness of Thurstone's position, but he saw no need to revise his early interpretation. However, Cattell (1945) rotated Eysenck's factors, and concluded that they were probably the equivalents of his own Factors B, C, F, and I. (For these, see above.) He expresses an understandable surprise that Factor A, the schizothyme-cyclothyme or sociability dimension, is absent, since in research with normal subjects it is usually the most prominent dimension. Its absence not only in this study but in all of Eysenck's work must be taken to indicate the limited range of the domain which he is investigating. Cattell is also quite positive in his judgment that none of the four factors in Eysenck's study may properly be identified as introversion-extraversion. However, Eysenck is supported on the main point, namely, that he had isolated a dimension of control, which he called neuroticism.

In his later work, which still revolves largely around the neuroticism factor, Eysenck introduced a method which he calls criterion analysis, as a means of guiding the interpretation of factors. Having determined, for example, that neurotics in general tend to score high on a test of body-sway suggestibility, and low on a test of darkness vision, he then fixes the position of the supposed neuroticism dimension in a factorial study with normal subjects, by rotating it so that suggestibility has a high positive loading on the rotated axis, and the test of darkness vision a high negative loading. More precisely, he employs a rotation which results in the maximal positive intercorrelation between loadings of the tests on the rotated axis, and their relative efficiency in discriminating between the criterion groups, that is, between neurotics and nonneurotics. Unfortunately, in its present development this method is applicable only to the interpretation of one factor in any study, and Eysenck's demonstration of the neurotic and psychotic factors, in two separate studies, using a different selection of tests in each, does not meet the need for a meaningful organization of the total domain. Criterion analysis, which he describes as an hypothetico-deductive method, is quite in contrast to the empirical tendency of most American factorists, who are striving to develop more effective formal criteria for blind rotation which can lead to consistent results in the hands of different workers. Its results deserve serious attention, but they leave us to a degree uncertain whether the investigator has penetrated the mystery of nature, or forced it to his will.

In any discussion of this kind, it should be borne in mind that any set of axes, rotated or unrotated, is just as correct as any other, although one may be more useful than another. Indeed, with the same data, one set of reference axes may be more useful for one purpose, and another set for a different purpose. In the long run, those interpretations are most useful which give rise to similar reference axes for different sets of comparable data—that is, to points of view that have wide application. It is too early for dogmatism; we are still trying to find our way about in the shadowy multidimensionality of a hypersphere where, before everything has been resolved into clear hyperplanes, we shall probably find some hypercorners that we have yet to turn!

Under these circumstances, the amount of agreement that we find among these different factorial analyses of adult human temperament is not inconsiderable. They contain repeated assurances of the importance of dispositions to affiliative, aggressive, fearful, and controlled (or impulsive) behavior. One may be called friendliness, sociality, or cyclothymia; another may be ascendance, dominance, or assertiveness; the third may be timidity, depression, or, in Cattell's phrasing, "agitated melancholic desurgency"; the fourth may be impulsiveness or maturity or neuroticism; yet in some way the same dimensions which appear as basic in the behavior of animals and of human infants show themselves repeatedly in these analyses of adult human behavior.

DIMENSIONS OF MALADAPTIVE BEHAVIOR

Through the years, psychiatrists have wrestled with the task of classifying the varieties of mental disorder. In the modern period, the viewpoint has gained ground that the differences between the mentally ill and the mentally well are not differences of kind, but of degree. According to this view, the forms of neurosis and psychosis must be regarded as extreme developments of the same processes of adjustment which healthy persons use. The categories of psychiatric diagnosis should therefore constitute a useful system of dimensions for the description of normal personality.

One consideration which may be urged against such a recommendation is the fact that the categories of psychiatric diagnosis are unsatisfactory even for their primary purpose. Experience shows that they are unreliable in application, and one evident reason for this is the fact that the characteristic symptoms of different abnormalities, and not infrequently of those which are thought to be incompatible, are seen together in the same person. Although this circumstance demonstrates that these categories cannot usefully be taken as representing *types* of people, it offers no impediment to accepting them as definitions of *factors* of individuality. Perhaps it remains true that each of us may see the multiple personification of *all* his behavioral tendencies in the full population of a mental hospital.

Whether or not this is a sound point of view (and we prefer to withhold judgment upon it at this point), it is certain that some acquaintance with the dimensions of maladaptive behavior, as they have been defined by psychiatrists, is a necessary part of the background of any psychologist who works with problems of normal personality. It would be inappropriate for us to attempt anything approaching a full exposition of even the most common varieties of abnormal behavior. Nevertheless, we shall try briefly to characterize the nature and scope of one important and influential effort to measure the dimensions of maladaptive behavior in normal persons.

The Minnesota Multiphasic Personality Inventory (MMPI) is one of the most ambitious, carefully prepared, and widely used of all psychological inventories. It is an omnibus-type test, and its authors (Hathaway and McKinley, 1943) were so confident of its future success that they boldly retained in the published form many items for which they had no immediate use, predicting that they would be found useful in the development of future scales. Events have shown that their expectations were justified, and in later chapters we shall take note of some examples of such special scales which have been developed for the MMPI, in the course of many research applications. Here we are inter- ested only in eight basic scales which purport to measure the dimensions of abnormal behavior. We shall not consider either the masculinity-femininity scale, which is sometimes useful in the detection of homosexuality, or the several validation scales, which constitute one of the test's most important contributions from a technical point of view.

Each of the scales with which we are concerned represents a selection of those items, from more than 500 which are included in the inventory, which significantly differentiate hospitalized patients who carry a given diagnostic label from a control group which is a sample of the nonhospitalized population. The cri- terion groups were taken from the population of a large state mental hospital. The principal dimensions of the test were there- fore never in doubt. They are the administrative categories established by the hospital. An important reason for this plan is that the test was intended primarily as a diagnostic instrument in studying hospital admissions. But the subsequent acceptance of the MMPI in general use for the study of normal persons is based, as we have already indicated, on the assumption that the factors of normal behavior are the same as those of abnormal behavior.

Capsule descriptions of the eight scales with which we are concerned are given in Table 8.3. One cannot read this table

TABLE 8.3. Descriptions of Certain MMPI Scales
(Based on Tyler, 1951)

Depressed:	Depression, dejection, discouragement, de- spondency.
Hypochondriasis:	Concern over bodily functions, concern about health, tendency toward physical complaint.

TABLE 8.3.   Descriptions of Certain MMPI Scales—(*Continued*)

Hysteria:	Immature, unrealistic, amenable to group ideas, kindly, courteous, naive, needs social acceptance.
Psychopathic deviate:	Irresponsible, undependable, impulsive, egocentric, defiant, asocial, individualistic.
Paranoid:	Aggressive, critical, irritable, moody, sensitive, sensitive to criticism.
Psychasthenic:	Apprehensive, tense, hesitant, insecure, self-conscious, feelings of inadequacy.
Schizoid:	Bashful, withdrawn, oversensitive, secretive, cautious.
Hypomanic:	Confident, hypersensitive, not persistent, aggressive, charming, expansive.

carefully without becoming aware that there is much overlap among these categories. This is particularly evident with respect to depression and hypochondriasis, and also with respect to schizoid tendency and psychasthenia. These are actually eight symptom complexes with many common elements. If we select almost any arbitrary pair, it is possible to find items of the inventory which contribute similarly to both scales. This is due in part to an essential ambiguity in many items, which permits them to be interpreted differently by differently-minded persons. A very striking example of this is provided by the one item which, when judged "true," scores for both depression and hypomania. When the manic individual says, "I work under a great deal of tension," he is testifying to the inner excitement which drives him, but when the depressed individual says the same thing, he is testifying to the great effort he must expend to do anything at all, against the weight of his physiological inertia. With all possible allowance for confusions of this sort, it remains true that these are not basic behavioral tendencies but symptom syndromes. The general factorial approach prompts us to inquire whether they may be the expressions of a smaller number of basic determinants.

Before considering the available evidence on the factors which underlie the dimensions of maladaptive behavior, we should like to point out certain relationships which exist among these syndromes. Some, though by no means all, of the contrasts and similarities among them are schematized in the following listing. Here each category is to be thought of as in some important sense opposite to the category with which it is paired horizontally, and in some important sense similar to the one with which it is paired vertically.

Depressed	Hypomanic
Psychasthenic	Psychopathic
Hysteric	Paranoid
Hypochondriac	Schizoid

We shall consider them first line by line. Depressive and manic trends are known to occur in the same person at different times, and the reader is probably already familiar with the fact that this circumstance has given rise to the terms manic-depressive psychosis and cycloid personality. However, these two types of behavior fall at opposite ends of the Activity dimension which we studied in the last chapter, and they cannot occur simultaneously. The opposition of psychasthenic and psychopathic personality rests upon the fact that the first (which is more commonly called compulsive personality) is characterized by an overstrong conscience and obsessive worries, and the second by a lack of social conscience and a nonchalant brashness of behavior. The hysteric is a basically friendly and quite suggestible individual, in sharp contrast to the paranoid, who is hostile, suspicious, and negativistic. Finally, the hypochrondiac utilizes his worrisome self-concern in order to extract sympathy from others and tie them emotionally to him, while the schizoid individual withdraws from social contacts and exhibits at least superficially a lack of social responsiveness, finding his gratifications in fantasy rather than in social relationships. Turning now to a consideration of the vertical pairings, we note that depression and psychasthenia are both marked by tendencies to self-blame. Hysteria and hypochondria are partners in self-pity. The manic and the psychopath may both be classified as self-promoting or self-aggrandizing individuals. The paranoid and the schizoid (so often joined in paranoid schizophrenia) show a common tendency to the elaboration of intellectualized fantasies. When we compare the left-hand and right-hand columns, we see that all the entries on one side are characterized by strong social dependency, while those on the other side show a variety of aggressive or hostile behaviors.

Such schematic characterizations can scarcely do justice to the complex symptomatology of these diseases. A few items taken from the test will not go a long way toward clarifying them, but they will help the reader to appreciate the general character of the test. (The items which appear below are quoted by permission of The Psychological Corporation, which publishes the MMPI, the copyright for which is held by the University of Minnesota.) Two items have been taken from each scale. Of these, one would be symptomatic when answered "true," the other when answered "false." They were selected by arbitrarily taking the shortest items which would meet these criteria, excluding those items which figure on more than one scale. It should be remembered that the assignment of items to one scale or another is based on empirical findings with the criterion groups, and not on logical or systematic grounds. The items are arranged here in alphabetical order, and the reader may test his intuition by seeing if he can decide to which scales they belong. To make the task less difficult, it has been indicated for each item whether it is symptomatic when answered "true" or "false." The correct answers will be found at the end of the chapter.

1. Everything tastes the same. (T)
2. I almost never dream. (F)
3. I am an important person. (T)
4. I am easily embarrassed. (T)

5. I brood a great deal. (T)
6. I enjoy children. (F)
7. I feel uneasy indoors. (T)
8. I hardly ever feel pain in the back of my neck. (F)
9. I have a great deal of stomach trouble. (T)
10. I have no enemies who really wish to harm me. (F)
11. I have used alcohol excessively. (T)
12. I liked school. (F)
13. I like to flirt. (F)
14. It is safer to trust nobody. (F)
15. Much of the time my head seems to hurt all over. (T)
16. Sometimes when I am not feeling well I am cross. (F)

The simplest manner of use of the MMPI is to take note of those dimensions of the test on which the individual's score rises above the expected normal limits, and approaches that of the relevant hospitalized groups. However, it is not uncommon to have several such scores in a single record, and it is therefore better practice to base a judgment on the total profile, rather than simply to accept the highest score as indicating the dominant trend in the person's behavior. The MMPI is very far from being a "self-interpreting" test. It should be interpreted only by trained clinicians who are familiar with much of the extensive literature which has accumulated about its use.

Let us return now to the problem of determining the basic variables which underlie these syndromes. In pointing to certain contrasts and similarities among them, we in effect hypothesized as many group factors. It has been shown by Thurstone (1947) that to determine a given number of factors, one always needs a much larger number of variables. The application of his formula shows, for example, that a minimum of 13 variables would be needed to determine 8 factors and define them in a satisfactory manner. A much larger number of variables would be desirable, and they should be chosen in a way that gives promise of throwing light on the relationships being studied. Unless the number of factors present in the MMPI is very small (and this would imply that the construction of the test is extremely wasteful), it would not be possible to define them clearly except by a large-scale research which would include a number of other variables along with the MMPI scales. In a well-conceived program of this sort, some of the variables would be specifically designed to serve as reference variables to assist in the later interpretation, in accordance with some preliminary hypotheses being subjected to test. There have been no such thorough factor analyses of the MMPI and related data, and its full factor structure therefore remains unknown.

However, there have been two attempts to study its structure which do deserve attention. Wheeler, Little and Lehner (1951) used the scores of 12 MMPI scales, including the Masculinity-femininity scale and several internal validation scales which we have not described. They used two separate populations, one consisting of male neuropsychiatric patients, the other of male college students. Tyler (1951) based his analysis on 15 scales, omitting the validation scales, but including half a dozen scales developed by other research workers, called Social introversion, Status, Prejudice, Academic achievement, Responsibility, and Dominance. His population consisted of female college students. As would be expected, more factors were indicated in Tyler's study than in the other. The results of both studies are not sufficiently clear to justify detailed presentation here, but they do seem to coincide in one important point: the two major factors indicated seem to be identifiable as a "neurotic" factor and a "psychotic" factor. These factors might also be designated as "discomfort" and "irrealism." This is not to suggest that all of the many forms of personality disturbance may be assigned to one or another of these two major categories, but rather that they may all be profitably looked upon as containing different admixtures of these two basic forms of maladjustment.

Key to MMPI items. The first item listed for each scale is symptomatic when answered "true," and the second when answered "false." Depression, 5 and 13; Hypomania, 3 and 16; Psychasthenia, 4 and 2; Psychopathic deviate, 11 and 12; Hysteria, 15 and 14; Paranoia, 7 and 10; Hypochondria, 9 and 8; Schizophrenia, 1 and 6. (See pages 176-177.)

APPENDIX TO CHAPTER 8:   A CLOSER LOOK AT FACTOR ANALYSIS

The operations of factor analysis are ordinarily explained in terms of matrix algebra. However, they can be given a much simpler rationale, if one is willing to overlook some fine points of controversy in order to make the essentials more readily understandable. In the illustration that we offer, the usual computational routine has been changed somewhat in order to facilitate this simpler explanation, but the result obtained is identical with that of a centroid analysis carried out by Thurstone's method. Indeed, the change consists of little more than reversing the order of two steps in the process! In this account, we shall refer to the separate parts of Table 8.4 as (a), (b), etc.

The correlations which appear in (a) are those that were reported by Bayley (1932), between amounts of crying by infants during developmental examinations in successive trimesters of the first year of life. Hereafter, we shall speak of the set of scores for each trimester as constituting a "test." Each correlation appears twice, so that on any row, or in any column, one may read the correlations of one test with each other test. It will be noted that the cells of the principal diagonal are empty. The pattern of the table suggests that some sort of self-correlation should be entered into each of these empty cells. However, before we proceed any farther, let us stop to consider the meaning of any one of the correlations that has been empirically determined.

TABLE 8.4.   Computations for illustrative factor analysis. The Appendix gives a step-by-step explanation.

		I	II	III	IV	Sums
(a) Original	I		.38	.22	.15	
correlations	II	.38		.26	.18	
	III	.22	.26		.66	
	IV	.15	.18	.66		
(b) Completed	I	.38	.38	.22	.15	1.13
matrix	II	.38	.38	.26	.18	1.20
	III	.22	.26	.66	.66	1.80
	IV	.15	.18	.66	.66	1.65
						5.78

TABLE 8.4. Computations for illustrative factor analysis.—(*Continued*)

(c) Expected values,	I	.221	.235	.352	.322	1.13
first hypothesis	II	.235	.249	.374	.342	1.20
	III	.352	.374	.560	.514	1.80
	IV	.322	.342	.514	.472	1.65
						5.78
(d) First-factor	I	.159	.145	−.132	−.172	.00
residuals	II	.145	.131	−.114	−.162	.00
	III	−.132	−.114	.100	.146	.00
	IV	−.172	−.162	.146	.188	.00
(e) Residuals	I	.159	.145	.132	.172	.608
after	II	.145	.131	.114	.162	.552
reflection	III	.132	.114	.100	.146	.492
	IV	.172	.162	.146	.188	.668
						2.320
(f) Expected values,	I	.159	.145	.129	.175	.608
second	II	.145	.132	.117	.159	.553
hypothesis	−III	.129	.117	.104	.142	.492
	−IV	.175	.159	.142	.192	.668
						2.321
(g) Second-factor	I	.000	.000	.003	−.003	.000
residuals	II	.000	−.001	−.003	.003	−.001
	III	.003	−.003	−.004	.004	.000
	IV	−.003	.003	.004	−.004	.000
(h) Loadings of	A	.470	.499	.748	.687	
unrotated	B	.399	.363	−.322	−.438	
factors [a]						

[a] For loadings of rotated factors, and communalities, see Table 8.2, page 156.

A correlation coefficient is a measure of concomitant variation, or covariance. If a single causal factor is responsible for all the covariance between two tests, then the resulting correlation is the product of two numbers, each of which states the degree to which this factor is present among the determinants of one of the tests. For example, the correlation of .38, between the first and second trimesters, *may* arise because some one factor is responsible for 76 percent of the determination of one of these variables, and 50 percent of the determination of the other. Any other two proportions whose product is .38 would serve equally well. Furthermore, a correlation often represents the sum of concomitant variations which arise from different sources. For example, the correlation of .38 *may* also arise because Factor X has a loading of .56 on one test and .25 on the other, while Factor Y has loadings of .48 and .50 on these two tests. This possibility is shown by the following computation:

$$(.56) \ (.25) \ + \ (.48) \ (.50) \ = \ .38$$

There is no limit to the number of such hypotheses which can be created to explain a single correlation. However, when we are dealing with a number of related correlations, many of these hypotheses are mutually inconsistent. By factor analysis, we construct a consistent set of hypotheses for all the observed correlations.

Let us now return to a consideration of the empty cells in the principal diagonal. To be consistent with the pattern of the table, each of these cells should contain the sum of the squared (that is, self-multiplied) loadings of one test for all the common factors. This value is called the communality of the test, and it is symbolized h^2. It is not influenced by any of those unique determinants which the given test does not share with any of the other tests being studied. At the start of our work it is an unknown value, but fortunately we are able to estimate it with fair accuracy. Much experience supports the convenient rule that a usually satisfactory estimate of the communality of any test is the highest correlation of that test with any other. Writing in these values, we obtain the completed matrix shown in (b). It should be emphasized that this method of estimate has not been guided by any hypothesis regarding the outcome of our analysis. We have simply made some guesses, which are justified because similar guesses have proved helpful in the past. If these guesses are grossly inaccurate, that fact will appear, as we shall see, at the end of the analysis, and we would then face the prospect of starting over again with new estimates. In this case, the first estimates prove to be very satisfactory.

Having thus completed the matrix, we sum each row, and enter also the grand sum for the entire table. Since the table is symmetric, column sums would be identical with row sums. Although we shall refer to column sums, we shall omit writing them.

We now adopt the working hypothesis that there is only one factor which is common to all the tests. We do not know the loadings of this factor, but we do know that if the hypothesis is correct, each entry in (b) is the product of two such loadings, plus a discrepancy which is due to experimental error. Furthermore, the hypothesis implies that the true correlations, undisturbed by error variance, will show the same row-to-row and column-to-column proportionality which appears in the marginal sums. If the reader is familiar with the method of computing expected values for contingency tables, he already knows the method by which these values may be obtained. The necessary formula is

$$\text{expected cell value} = \frac{(\text{column sum})(\text{row sum})}{(\text{grand sum})}$$

For example: (1.13) (1.20) ÷ 5.78 = .235. The results appear in (c), and we call them the expected values for the first hypothesis. These expected values represent the correlations which would arise among the four tests under the following conditions: (1) that all of their common variance is the result of a single factor; (2) that the loading of the factor in the several tests is proportional to the row sums in the original matrix, including the estimated communalities; (3) that the overall influence of the common factor is correctly reflected by the grand sum of correlations in the table; and (4) that all error variance is excluded.

The factor loadings which are implied by the hypothesis are the square roots of the expected communalities, that is, of the entries in the principal diagonal of (c). These loadings have been entered in the first row of (h). They may be regarded as coefficients of correlation which would exist between the separate tests and the hypothetical factor. The reader should satisfy himself that cross-multiplication of these loadings does give rise to the entries shown in (c). (It may be mentioned here that the usual procedure is to compute the factor loadings first, by a formula whose logic is more difficult to explain, and then compute the correlations to which they give rise. When this is done, (c) is called a Product Matrix rather than a table of expected values.)

It was stated above that under our one-factor hypothesis each entry in (b) is the product of two loadings, plus a discrepancy which is due to experimental error. We wish now to consider the magnitude of these discrepancies. To do this conveniently, we subtract each entry in (c) from the corresponding entry in (b), and we write the resulting differences as a table of First-factor Residuals, in (d). Note that the sum of the discrepancies in each row is zero, as it must be, save for errors due to rounding numbers, if our computations are correct. The magnitude and the distribution of these discrepancies are such that we must reject the hypothesis that they are simply the results of error variance. We therefore conclude that one factor does not suffice to explain the original correlations. However, although Factor A does not quite live up to the expectations formulated in the single-factor hypothesis, it evidently suffices to explain a large part of the common variance. Therefore we need not discard the results of the work that we have done. Instead, we set up an auxiliary hypothesis, namely, that a second factor will suffice to explain all the residual common variance.

The residual common variance, that which Factor A could not explain, is represented in (d). However, the rows of this table all add to zero, as already noted, and it is therefore impossible for us to repeat the earlier procedure on this table in its present form. There is an easy way out of this difficulty. For the next stage in our analysis, we "reflect" tests III and IV, that is, we pretend that the high-scoring and low-scoring ends of these dimensions have been interchanged. As a result, all their negative correlations with other variables become positive, while correlations between these two variables remain unchanged in sign. Giving effect to these sign changes, we obtain (e). (It is sometimes not possible to remove all the negative signs, but one can always attain a positive sum for every row.)

The expected values for the second hypothesis, shown in (f), were computed by the same formula used above: expected value = (column sum)(row sum) ÷ (grand sum). The square roots of the entries in the principal diagonal of (f) are the loadings of the second factor, and they have been written into the second row of (h), as the loadings of Factor B. It will be noted that the loadings for tests III and IV have been entered as negative, in recognition of the fact that our recent operations were actually being performed with tests III and IV taken in a reverse sense.

Once again, we construct a table of residuals, by subtracting the entries in (f) from those in (e). This time, the discrepancies, which appear in (g), are negligible, and they must therefore be regarded as the results of chance. The hypothesis of two common factors is therefore not rejected.

We are ready now to turn to the second major part of our analysis, the problem of interpretation. For this, the reader should turn back to page 156.

CHAPTER 9

Individuation of Temperament

*T*he temperamental characteristics of a human adult are the end products of a developmental process in which original endowment, maturation, and learning have all entered in important degree. Although research and theory may concentrate for a while on one or another of these determinants, whose influence is then brought more forcefully to our attention, this in no way diminishes the real importance of the others. Whatever increase of knowledge we attain with respect to temperamental endowment and maturation should help us better to understand how experience sometimes reinforces and sometimes alters original dispositions. In the present chapter, we shall look first at the evidence for the view that individuation of temperament takes place very early in life, so that within the first year of life it is possible to identify behavioral characteristics which the individual is likely to retain into adolescence. However, this evidence is not to be interpreted as simply demonstrating the importance of hereditary or even congenital influences—the latter term embracing the effects associated with the conditions of pregnancy and childbirth. In part, they reflect the importance of very early experience in modifying original dispositions. It is difficult to separate these factors, but it is certain that both play their parts. The kind of learning which we are here interested

in is not a matter of habit training, but of exerting influences
which help to select one disposition in preference to others. How
could we teach love to one who had no disposition for it? Or
fighting, to one who had no disposition whatever to fight? However, since each human child is endowed with both of these
dispositions, timely experiences may serve to emphasize one or
the other. In an attempt to understand this process, we shall,
in the second section of this chapter, review some of the known
facts about this kind of learning. In the third section, we shall
consider several different ways in which the lasting influence of
quasi-permanent dispositions formed in childhood may be conceptualized. Finally, we shall look at some recent efforts to
demonstrate the importance of early infant experience by
comparing the typical personality structures which appear in
different social classes and different nations or cultures as the
result of different child-rearing practices.

THE EVIDENCE OF EARLY INDIVIDUATION

In this section we shall briefly report four studies which deal
directly with the problem of persistence, into childhood or
adolescence, of characteristics noted in infancy.

Margaret Fries (1944) continued the observation of some of
the children who had been classified by her according to activity
type in very early infancy. She writes:

> After following the same children for 5 years, it was found that
> the Activity Pattern of the so-called normal child could be modified,
> but only within certain limits, and that the most important factor for
> modifying it (excluding organic pathology) is the parents' emotional
> adjustment, their relation to each other and to the child.

The children of adjusted parents were observed to retain their
original position or to swing toward the median, while the children of maladjusted parents tended to deviate farther from the
median, without crossing it. In other words, children who had
not been subjected to special emotional stress would tend to grow
more like the general norm, which may be taken to represent

better adjustment, while those who had experienced the special emotional stress induced by their parents' disturbance would tend, if quiet, to become more so, and if active, to become hyperactive. However, very startling changes were seen in those few children who themselves developed neurosis at this early age, so that, for example, a basically active child might present a false appearance of being quiet, as a result of repressions, or a basically quiet child might display an unhealthy forced activity. However, Fries emphasizes that these cases must not be allowed to obscure the general rule, that most children conform to the activity pattern which they manifested early in infancy.

Gesell (1937), in a study in which he was assisted by Louise Ames, compared the ranking of 5 children on 15 different aspects of behavior, as infants and as 5-year-olds. Some of these 15 variables seem to be fairly direct expressions of major dimensions of temperament. Thus, reaction to restriction appears to be a measure of aggressiveness, emotional maladjustment of fearfulness, family attachment of affiliativeness, and energy output of impulsiveness. Some of the remaining 11 variables are almost equally direct expressions of single temperamental dimensions, a fact which gives rise to high correlation among some of the variables. Others, such as emotional expressiveness and communicativeness, are probably influenced by several aspects of temperament. A very interesting variable, which yielded highly consistent ratings, is humor sense. The rater was someone who had not known these children as infants. She made the first set of ratings from a study of motion pictures which had been taken during the first year. She then observed the children, at the age of 5 years, in their own homes, and together with their mothers at a garden party. Precautions were taken that the two sets of ratings should be independent. When the ratings were compared, it was found that on a number of the variables, the five children had retained their original relative positions without change. These variables were motor demeanor, self-dependence, humor sense, emotional maladjustment, reaction to restriction, and family attachment. For two other variables, energy output and emotional expressiveness, the only disagreement was an interchange between two children who held adjacent positions, neither being at an extreme. For only one of the 15 variables, communicativeness, did it happen that there was a displacement of three ranks, for a single child. If we consider the results in terms of children, rather than in terms of behavioral characteristics, we find that two children, who initially received 25 of the 30 extreme ratings, together underwent a total of only five one-position displacements in the later ratings. The other three children, who received predominantly intermediate ratings, underwent 22 shifts, including five of two positions and one of three positions. Although consistency is evident in the record of any of these children, it is far stronger in those who exhibited pronounced characteristics at an early age.

Shirley's report (1933) of her developmental study of the first two years of childhood includes personality sketches of the 19 children who were still under her observation at the end of that period. Fifteen years later, Patricia Neilon (1948) was able to locate 16 of these children, who were now young men and women, 17 years of age. She gave each of them a battery of personality tests, and had a single interview with each of their mothers. Then, without knowing the pseudonyms that Shirley had used, and without reference to the original sketches, she prepared new sketches. Excluding one boy from her study (as somehow "not comparable"), she was left with 10 boys of the original 13, and five girls of the original six. Judges who were asked to match the old and new sketches had far greater than chance success. The judges who worked with the girls' sketches, matching five against six, were highly successful with four of the five. However, not one made the correct match for the fifth girl. Thus while Neilon's study gives strong support to the view that valid forecasts of future personality characteristics can be made in very early childhood, it also gives evidence that some individuals do undergo considerable change.

The judges who worked with the boys' sketches were less successful, although they also had much better than chance results. Neilon attributes the difference in success to the fact that matching a set of 10 sketches against 13 was a far more difficult task than matching five sketches against six. However, one cannot dismiss the possibility that within our culture the temperamental characteristics of boys are in general less firmly set at the age of 2, than is the case with girls. Methodologically, it would have been better to have divided the boys into two groups, each comparable to the girls' group. This would have made intersex comparison possible.

Gesell and Thompson (1929) studied two twin girls, designated T and C (Training and Control), primarily with a view to determining the effects of early training on motor performance. At the same time, they made note of consistent differences in such traits as placidity, length of crying, vigor of protest, tolerance of physical discomfort, and social responsiveness. They continued their study of these twins, and years later (1941) they were able to report that these identical twins showed slight but consistent differences in personality which conformed to the differences that had been observed in infancy. At 6 weeks of age, the impression had been recorded that C was more placid and less tense, and that T was more reactive to objects. At 8 weeks, it was noted that T was again more alert in fixating objects, and more active in the prone position. At 28 weeks, when the decision had just been made to use these twins in the training experiment, fuller notes were taken. At that time, T was described as more active posturally, and quicker to respond to motor test situations, while C was more responsive to social situations. C vocalized more, and spent more time looking at the examiner and at her co-twin, while T directed her attention more to the stimulus objects. At the age of 14 years this difference still persisted, with C still exhibiting a livelier interest in people, and T still showing a stronger interest in things. C is still the more tranquil, T the more restless. "The typical emotional coloring of C's mental processes appears to be softer and warmer than that of T—more often suffused with personal and social reference." For example, the two girls were asked to write a composition a few days after their graduation from school. Although no topic was assigned, both of them chose to write about that event. But whereas T wrote a very detailed factual account of the graduation program, C wrote that she "never had so much fun" in all her life, and continued in this bubbling vein, with references to fun in almost every sentence. A subtler expression of the same basic difference appears in the fact that T tends to use straight lines in drawing, where C tends to use curves by preference.

EMOTIONAL LEARNING

We wish now to consider the probable nature of the learning experiences which are at least in part responsible for the early individuation of temperament. In the efforts to understand this early learning, too much emphasis is commonly placed upon the reinforcement which results from the satisfaction of the infant's needs by those who care for him. We wish to remind the reader that reinforcement of this kind is not essential for learning, and may even play a very negligible role in the kind of learning that we are now considering, the selective emphasis on dispositions rather than instrumental actions.

Let us take note, first, that the recognition of the function of critical periods helps us to understand this process. It is evident that learning proceeds most readily when it is parallel to and reinforced by maturation, and when the responses that are reinforced by experience are those that have a great likelihood of appearing spontaneously in the behavioral repertoire. At an earlier point, for example, we looked at certain evidence for the view that affectionate attitudes may be readily fostered during the latter part of the first year, but that they are not very available for training during the first three or four months. It is not necessary to repeat here what has already been said in

Chapter 6 about critical periods in human infancy, but it should be understood that an appreciation of their importance is essential for understanding the process of temperamental learning in general.

Another important factor is the circular interaction of the infant and his environment, which tends to restimulate whatever kinds of behavior have already been exhibited. Stewart (1953) says that infants who cry excessively provoke insecurity in their mothers, which is then retransmitted to the infants by a sort of contagion—to which Sullivan also made reference—and represents a new stimulation to crying. In the same vein, but with more concrete description of the interpersonal stimulation of mother and child, Escalona (1953) shows how the spontaneous smiling of infants, long before it has any authentic social character, elicits an empathic response in the mother, which leads to desirable playful stimulation, which in turn facilitates the favorable social development which the mother *thought* she saw in the early smile! Thus dispositions tend to be strengthened in experience (obeying the maxim that "the rich get richer") because they create the opportunities for their own reinforcement. It is doubtless as a result of such influence, rather than as a direct consequence of behavioral inertia, that the initially stronger dispositions do tend in most cases to retain their advantage, leading to results like those that we have just surveyed.

It would be generally agreed that the relative strength of temperamental dispositions can be changed by early environment, at least in unfavorable directions. To understand how this takes place, let us consider the nature of emotional learning. The phrase *emotional learning* may be interpreted in two senses. First, it refers to the conditions under which emotional responses can appear as learned rather than as spontaneous behavior. Second, it refers to the effect which the presence of strong emotion has on the progress of learning in general. We shall want to pay attention to both of these aspects.

With regard to the first aspect, it seems to be fairly well

established that emotional responses are subject to conditioning in the pure sense, that is, they tend to be called forth by stimuli which have been associated with them in past experience, regardless of whether or not such association was followed by any form of tension-reduction. The importance of this point may not be immediately obvious to readers who have been accustomed to assume that the conditioned response formulation of learning has almost universal validity. Actually, there is a good deal of question whether this formulation does not omit essential aspects of the learning situation. Rather than attempt to survey the voluminous evidence here, let us quote Hilgard's conclusion on this point:

> The theory of simple conditioning is an inviting one. It says in effect that partial cues reinstate stimulus-response situations just as fully as they reinstate perceptual ones—that what was *done* in the presence of the stimuli as well as what was *perceived* tends to recur in their presence. Despite all the attention commonly given to simple conditioning in learning theory, the evidence for it is very fragmentary. There is no doubt that learning takes place under the arrangements of the conditioned response experiment, but the results may usually be given alternative explanations. The fact is that *there is little evidence that the simultaneous occurrence of an incidental stimulus and an unconditioned response is the sufficient condition for establishing a sensorimotor association between them.* The conditioning of muscle twitches in spinal preparations comes nearest to the pure case, but it is scarcely typical. (*Theories of Learning,* 1948.)

Many learning theorists have been content to draw the less sweeping conclusion that conditioning is not a factor in the learning of skills, but that it does occur in the learning of emotional responses. Schlossberg (1937) stated his conclusion, which was based on a painstaking series of experimental studies, in the following terms:

> It is thus possible to make a rough, and perhaps superficial distinction between diffuse preparatory responses, to which the laws of conditioning apply in a direct fashion, and precise adaptive responses, in which the law of effect seems relevant.

Skinner (1938) made a more carefully reasoned distinction

into *operant* and *respondent* forms of behavior. The former may be likened to expressive dispositions, whereas the latter has an instrumental or purposive character. Operant behavior is "emitted" by the organism in response to internal drive, whereas respondent behavior is "elicited" by external stimuli. Operant behavior is said to be subject to pure conditioning, whereas changes in respondent behavior are brought about by the consequences which follow them.

Mowrer's statement of the two-factor theory of learning has been the most influential, but his earlier effort to retain a one-factor theory of learning is also relevant to our topic. How can one explain instances of habit formation in which the fixated act seems to bring punishment, rather than reward, as its consequent? It does not suffice to say that it formerly brought reward, because this leaves unexplained the fact that it resists extinction, and may grow stronger with repetition, though each repetition leads to disappointment and failure. Mowrer's (1939) ingenious attempt at solution of this problem assumed that the act, although unsuccessful in the broader sense, does bring about an immediate reduction of the anxiety which the subject feels in the situation, and that it is this reduction of anxiety which fulfills the requirement of Hull's general theory of reinforcement by need reduction. This theory plays an essential part in the efforts of Dollard and Miller (1950) to apply Hullian behavior theory to problems of personality and psychotherapy. Mowrer (1946) defended it in a symposium in which Allport (1946) also participated. There he heard Allport say in rebuttal that if a man used some cleaning fluid in his kitchen, and the house suddenly blew up, he would learn quite quickly not to repeat the operation, but no tension reduction would be involved in the act of learning. This vivid illustration convinced Mowrer of the need to rethink his position. The result was an essay on the dual nature of learning (1947), in which he stated that tension reduction is essential only for learning of a problem-solving character, while learning of an emotional character is subject to pure conditioning.

If we accept emotional conditioning as a fact, it follows that the frequent evocation of an emotional response tends to make its recurrence more likely, by linking it each time with new stimuli, and thus introduces an important modification of temperamental disposition. Because such behavior is readily conditioned, it is also readily generalized to all sorts of attendant stimulating circumstances, and every new occurrence gives rise to new reasons for recurrence. The consistently fear-evoking or consistently love-evoking environment must therefore tend to produce a fearful or a loving child. Within very wide limits, the efficiency with which an infant's needs for food and warmth are satisfied will be less important than the kind of social stimulation which accompanies these ministrations.

Let us now turn our attention very briefly to the second aspect of emotional learning, namely, the way in which strong emotion influences learning in general. The reader will recall Maier's (1949) demonstration in rats of a type of learning which he called abnormal fixation. I wish to emphasize again that we are not concerned with instances of convulsive or erratic behavior, which some of his rats exhibited, but with the frequent occurrence of stereotyped responses of such fixity that they might be repeated for hundreds of trials, in the face of repeated frustration, even though the animal gave clear evidence of knowing that a different response would be correct in the situation. The writer (Diamond, 1934) has also demonstrated that when a choice is made under conditions of fear, the course of action selected may thereafter be repeated with extraordinary perseverance. Maier has discussed at length the implications of such behavior for the handling of children who have acquired undesirable habits. As long as the frustrating aspect of the situation continues, a purposeful modification of behavior is impossible. Punishment produces a rigidity which we often interpret as wilful stubbornness, though it is actually helplessness in the emotionally charged situation. We are therefore led to conclude that chronic frustration or repeated punishment may cause a marked reduction in problem-solving ability, and a tendency to remain fixated at infantile levels of adjustment.

It is possible that the rigidity which is induced by frustration is related to another important learning phenomenon, which also seems paradoxical when it is viewed from the standpoint of a monistic reward or tension-reduction theory, and is no better explained by a conventional two-factor theory. This is the fact, which has been demonstrated many times experimentally in recent years (e.g., Grosslight and Child, 1947), that habits which have been acquired under conditions of occasional reward interspersed with occasional frustrations are far more resistant to extinction than those which have been acquired under conditions of consistent reward. The determination to "keep on trying" for some hoped-for satisfaction must be acquired on a basis of frequent disappointment. Needless to say, real life situations approximate the conditions of intermittent reward far more often than the regularity of the usual well-ordered experiment. It is possible that, given the optimal emotional accompaniment, a very few strategically placed satisfactions may suffice to establish lasting dispositions in the face of almost total frustration. Certainly, this is what appears to happen in the lives of many persons who keep striving for satisfactions rarely experienced.

Patterns of Temperament in Adult Behavior

We have seen evidence that quasi-permanent patterns of temperament are ordinarily established in early childhood, and we have considered some of the characteristics of the learning process by which this takes place. We may now ask ourselves what the variety of such patterns is, and what is the scope of their influence on adult behavior.

The simplest way to characterize an individual pattern of temperament would be to say that tendencies to responses of an affiliative or aggressive or defensive nature predominate over others. It is obvious that his could be only a coarse approximation to the description of an individual temperament. One reason for this is that it is only the rare individual in whom one of these tendencies predominates to the almost total exclusion of the others. If the major dimensions of temperament are regarded as so many factors, each of which can be independently appraised, then it is evident that in combination they do not give rise to four types, but to dozens of distinctive patterns. To be highly aggressive and moderately affiliative is not the same thing as to be highly aggressive and strongly affiliative, or highly aggressive and weakly affiliative. Any one of these may be further modified by the rating for avoidance, or for impulsiveness. If each individual is rated as high, average, or low on each of four temperamental components, 81 combinations are mathematically possible. Most of these, and perhaps all, are psychologically possible as well. This multiplicity of "types" defeats the purpose of type theory, which is to attain simplicity in description. It is evident that the modern approach through factor theory, that is, to select a minimum number of dimensions as a basis for description, but to allow these to vary independently in the individual case, is more promising than the attempt to classify individuals into types on the basis of their most prominent characteristics.[1]

There are two further reasons why it is unsatisfactory to classify an individual according to his one strongest temperamental disposition. First, the various temperamental dispositions are in constant rivalry, and they do not stand in the same relative

---

[1] It is interesting to consider how a theoretical population would be distributed in 81 such patterns, on the assumptions that the four factors are independent—i.e., a knowledge of an individual's score on one does not help us to guess his score on another—and that each is normally distributed. We reserve the designations "high" and "low" for scores that are at least 1 standard deviation above or below the mean. A large population would then be expected to distribute itself as follows: 1 percent would fall into 16 patterns in which there are no average scores; 9 percent would fall into 32 patterns having 1 average score in each; 28 percent would fall into 24 patterns each having 2 average scores; 40 percent would fall into 8 patterns having 3 average scores each; 22 percent would fall into the single pattern having 4 average scores. Thus, about 6 persons in 10 are consigned to the mediocrity of having average standing, as here defined, in at least 3 of the 4 dimensions.

strength from moment to moment. Every wise wife is supposed to know that she should withhold an account of her shopping expenditures until after dinner, and perhaps also until her husband has taken the first puffs at his cigar. The man who might be described as ordinarily angry and excitable, may then be fairly complacent. Second, individual experience may have made the individual highly responsive to some kinds of social stimulation, and much less responsive to others. For each person, we need to know the kinds of situations which have become, through conditioning or other learning, releasers for certain kinds of temperamental or emotional response. For example, a competitive challenge may evoke aggressive behavior from one individual and avoidance from another. On the other hand, a display of dependent weakness may cause the first individual to cease being aggressive, and become affiliative, in a protective manner, while it may cause the second individual to cease being avoidant and to become aggressively dominant. Such differences among chimpanzees were observed by Hebb, when he posed as sometimes "bold" and sometimes "timid," and they are obvious in human relationships. This illustration is based on learned dominance behavior, but other such differences might arise from special interests or from differences in the self-concept, aspects of the personality which we have yet to explore.

It would be false, however, to conclude from this that an adequate statement of the temperamental characteristics of a person would have to include a sort of catalogue of typical circumstances, with a notation of his characteristic mode of response under each. Clinical experience indicates, rather, the need to recognize that for each person there is likely to be some one type of situation which has a special and disproportionate importance. Furthermore, by a process of perceptual distortion or overgeneralization, many other situations may be reacted to *as if* they conformed to this especially significant situational pattern. In a healthy individual such distortions are slight, and appropriate responses are given to most situations.

In cases of mental disorder, distortions are greater, and inappropriate behavior is therefore more frequent. Such a person may feel himself threatened by a friendly smile, or perceive the intent of courtship in a scolding from the boss. Sullivan (1953), borrowing a technical term from the grammarians, speaks of such distortions as *paratactic,* that is, as invested with a meaning which the perceiver is disposed to provide, rather than the one which is conveyed by the situation itself. In severe cases of psychosis, every imaginable situation may be perceived in the same stereotyped pattern.

The most useful way to characterize the temperamental pattern of an individual is to discover this dynamic pattern which tends to repeat itself in his experience under many diverse circumstances, calling forth the person's characteristic mode of response. Adler (1929) coined the very useful phrase, the "style of life," to designate this consistent resort in the face of every difficulty to a device that was learned in childhood. One child learns to put his reliance on a show of strength, another on a display of helpless weakness, a third puts his faith in cunning, and a fourth in the disarming power of a friendly smile. Horney (1945) has said that such life styles fall into three major categories, which represent basic tendencies to move "toward people," "against people," and "away from people." (These three tendencies clearly correspond to the three modes of adjustment that we have discussed in earlier chapters, i.e., affiliation, aggression, and defensive withdrawal.) In neurotic behavior, we show such strong preference for one or another of these modes of response that we lose normal flexibility of adjustment.

Another important approach to the definition of such pervasive dispositions may be found in the "dynamic formulas" which we often read in psychoanalytic literature, and which are meant to tell us in one or two sentences the essence of the patient's innermost attitude toward life. Thus, for example, Alexander (1934) characterized the different attitudes of patients suffering from various psychosomatic digestive disorders in the following dynamic formulas, which have since served as focal points of many research studies:

> In the case of duodenal ulcer: "I do not wish to take or receive. I am active and efficient and have no such wishes."
>
> In the case of colitis: "I have the right to take and demand, for I always give sufficiently. I do not need to feel inferior or guilty for my desire to take, because I am giving something in exchange for it."
>
> In the case of constipation: "I do not take or receive and therefore I do not need to give."

One may question whether such dynamic formulas may validly be applied in this manner to whole classes of patients differentiated by their somatic disorders. There can be no doubt, however, that they may be validly stated for certain persons. There is no more important step toward understanding the individuality of a person, that which Allport (1937) called the individual's *uniqueness* and which, as he said, escapes description in terms of scores on any number of standardized traits, than to discern the nature of such a characteristic, persistent attitude. Rather than use the term dynamic formula, which emphasizes the intellectual task of analysis by which such an attitude may be uncovered, we should like to speak of *feeling habits,* to emphasize their basis in emotional learning. The statement of such habits should not be couched in intellectual terms, but neither should they be thought of as altogether devoid of intellectual content. In the feeling habit, a vague yet unmistakably intellectual appraisal of the environment is linked by a process of conditioning with a strong emotional response, that is, with the intimations of a tendency to action in accordance with some innate disposition. Since the feeling habit therefore represents a firm integration of both an intellectual attitude and an emotional response, either part is able to evoke the other. Thus some slight emotion-arousing situation often calls forth this characteristic attitude, while the attitude in turn reinforces the emotion and helps to determine its characteristic quality. The feeling habit is like a well-worn rut in the road we travel. We can stay out of it as long as the road is smooth, but as soon as we meet a few bumps we are likely to slip into this readiest form of response. Such a habit may continue to shape our behavior in all the major events of our lives.

At this point we shall give a single example of such a habit of feeling, withholding other examples until our discussion, in the next chapter, of regressive behavior. A woman in her 50's had always been extremely dependent on her parents. The only way in which she had ever displayed any independence of them was in clinging to an improvident husband, despite her mother's encouragement to leave him. She had expended her energies in clinging alternately to mother and husband, never using her own considerable abilities to improve her situation. Her behavior becomes understandable when we recognize that all through life her strongest motivation had been the fear of abandonment. Her most vivid childhood memory is of an occasion when she was temporarily "abandoned" by her parents in a field, when tho family had gone for a Sunday ride in the country. This abandonment was a pretended and disciplinary measure, but it filled her with great fright at the time. The feeling of that moment, when she was about 3 years old, is akin to the feeling that has governed her actions in crucial moments throughout her life. We cannot often be successful in discovering the specific events that have shaped the temperament of the individual, whom we meet for the first time as an adult. It is often possible, however, as in this case, to establish the continuity of temperament from childhood. In our efforts to do this, we are helped by an awareness of the major dimensions of temperament, since these help us to understand the basis for the development and the nature of the continuity. In this specific case, a domineering mother evidently succeeded in suppressing the child's tentative efforts at aggressive independence. The child "learned," in an emotional sense, that efforts at independence bring on the danger of abandonment by one's protectors, and directed her life by this feeling habit.

It may not be amiss to add the hint that in our efforts to

understand ourselves, we would do well to catch ourselves in spontaneous response to sudden minor frustrations, and try to define their pattern. After having done this a few times, we may try to think back to our responses to major frustrations that we have suffered, to see if they were not also more the outcome of feeling habit than appropriate ways of meeting the actual situations. One of the important services of a psychotherapist is ordinarily to observe and clarify consistency of this sort.

CULTURAL SELECTION OF TEMPERAMENT

The environmental factors that favor the individuation of temperament in one direction or another may be so generally operative in a given cultural milieu as to produce a pattern of behavior which is characteristic of virtually all the members of a given social class or national group, and yet strikingly different from the typical behavior produced by another culture. The observation of such differences provides the most irrefutable evidence for the strength of environment in modifying temperament, for it is now generally accepted that the constitutional differences between different peoples cannot be responsible for more than a very minor part of such differences. However, this observation must be considerably refined before it can tell us how much of this influence takes place within the span of infancy, and very early childhood.

In recent years, largely under the influence of psychoanalytic theory, many attempts have been made to point to relationships between specific practices of child rearing and what have been called the "basic personality structures" or the "modal personalities" which they produce. Although we cannot doubt the reality of such effects, a great question still remains as to their extent. As Whiting and Child (1953) point out, the usual difficulty of establishing the direction of causal relationship that underlies an observed correlation exists here. Are the child-rearing practices the cause of the adult behaviors, or are they merely one expression of the adult personality that is more effectively shaped by later experiences in the culture? Unless the effects of child rearing are demonstrated in early childhood, before other socializing influences have been felt, the answer to this question can be no more than a guess. Orlansky (1949) concluded from a review of the general subject of the relationship between infant care and personality that there was very little evidence to support the idea that infancy in itself was a period of crucial importance for personality formation; on the other hand, he does not question the importance of postinfant experience in early childhood. The answer to this problem is vital, and we believe that it will be given in terms of critical periods. According to the hypothetical formulation of these periods which we gave in Chapter 6, fearfulness and affiliative disposition are most subject to influence during infancy, while impulsivity and aggression are the central problems of early childhood.

Because of the tenuous nature of the results that have so far been attained, we shall give only brief mention of some outstanding examples of research in this area. However, we must acknowledge the importance of this approach, and the likelihood that with further refinement of method it will yield information of decisive value.

Kardiner (1939, 1945) has tried to demonstrate how societies cultivate specific types of "basic personality structure" in their members, through the ways in which they are handled as children. He has worked in collaboration with a number of anthropologists, including especially Linton and DuBois. He contends, for example, that Alorese children grow up to be slipshod and suspicious as adults, because the care that they experience as infants is neglectful and sporadic.

Erikson (1950) has contrasted the early training and later personalities of the Sioux Indians, who live on the Dakota plains and are traditionally hunters, with the Yurok, who live along the Klamath River and depend upon salmon fishing for their livelihood. Sioux mothers are very indulgent toward their infants, and indeed nurse them well into childhood, until the child himself rejects the breast. The adults grow up to be generous, and the men to be energetic hunters. The Yurok are weaned at 6 months, earlier than any other American Indians, and they are taught to be quite formal and restrained in their eating habits. They grow up to be stingy, suspicious, and hostile in their attitudes. The Yurok assumes that the success of his fishing depends more on whether he has a proper prayerful attitude than whether he is energetic and skilful.

Studies such as these may be compared with others which have been concerned with class and national differences within the limits of Western civilization. Davis and Havighurst (1946) compared the manner in which middle-class and lower-class Chicago mothers, both Negro and White, treated their infants. They found that middle-class parents were stricter than lower-class parents with respect to both feeding and toilet training, as well as in other areas. Within the same social class, Negroes tend to be more permissive than Whites in respect to feeding and weaning, but more rigorous in respect to toilet training. Gorer and Rickman (1949) believe that the manner in which the people of Great Russia swaddle their infants helps to produce the impassivity and covert hostility which appear as prominent traits in their adult personalities.

Finally, Whiting and Child (1953) made an extensive cross-cultural study, in which they used the reported data on 52 primitive societies to test several hypotheses concerning the relationship between child training and personality. This study is of particular interest to us, because the authors made a series of roughly parallel tests of two general hypotheses concerning the mechanism by which early training influences later behavior—hypotheses which they designate as positive fixation and negative fixation. The first hypothesis assumes that those kinds of activity which have been especially rewarding as sources of satisfaction in infancy and early childhood will continue to have great importance to the person in adult life. They found relatively little evidence to support this view, and what they did find stemmed from early childhood rather than from infancy. The hypothesis of negative fixation, on the other hand, assumes that those kinds of activity that have been the sources of frequent frustration will have a particular importance in later life. They found clear evidence for this, much of it stemming out of the experiences of infancy. The most conclusive of all their findings was a strong relationship between "oral socialization anxiety" as a characteristic of early training and "oral explanations of illness" as an index of persisting oral anxiety in adulthood. They sum up with the statement that "the most important and definite conclusion in comparing the two types of fixation is that the two are not the same process and do not have the same result." This is in general agreement with what we have already said about the nature of emotional learning, and will have an important bearing on a central problem of our next chapter.

CHAPTER 10

Levels of Maturity

*I*n behavior, as in physical maturation, there is a normal and well-recognized pattern of development from infancy through childhood, puberty, adolescence, and adulthood, into senility. The major outline of this developmental history is determined by factors of physiology and physique which all mammals have in common. The infant's total dependence on his social environment, and specifically on his mother or a mother surrogate, is reduced as the growing child acquires capacities for action and for judgment. With the coming of sexual maturity, the possibility is created for new forms of social relationship, and the young adult normally becomes a principal in a new family organization, in which he fulfills the protective role of parent toward his own offspring. These developmental stages are obviously closely related to the stages of sexual development, and we must therefore anticipate that they will not have identical manifestations in both sexes. This differentiation is especially evident in the exercise of the parental function, since care for the young is a focal activity of the adult female, whereas the male—consistent with his greater aggressiveness—may show only a not too dependable tolerance for the young, free from any special solicitude. Although such differences between the sexes will be given some attention in this chapter, they will be

204

dealt with more extensively in a later discussion of masculinity-femininity as a complex variable of both temperament and interest. They do not alter the general fact that for both sexes there is an expected progress from early attitudes of total dependency through stages of increasing independence and aggressiveness, until in adulthood the individual assumes responsibility for others. Such behavioral change implies corresponding change in temperament, that is, in relative readiness for different kinds of action at different periods of growth.

However, the correspondence between maturity of physique and maturity of behavior is by no means absolute, and some of the most important differentiations which we make between persons are based on our observations of discrepancies in these respects. The big, strong man who sometimes surprises us by acting "like a baby" in the face of some emergency is the accepted stereotype for a kind of childishness which we all exhibit at different times, in different degrees. For example, a young woman who sought the help of a counselor when she learned that her husband was having an affair with another woman, was surprised to discover that her strongest feeling in this situation—and one which prevented her from dealing effectively with it—was her dread of her mother's attitude toward this threatened failure of her marriage. Most of us, if we are able to recognize our feelings truly, will discover that we are very frequently being similarly motivated, behaving like children when we think ourselves adult.

Immaturity of behavior is sometimes the direct consequence of developmental retardation, and, on the other hand, precocious physical development is always attended by a parallel precocity of interests and behavior. Although the extreme clinical instances of 5-year-old stubble-chinned, cigar-smoking youngsters do not directly concern us, they are instructive as showing how impotent our normal social training procedures are in the face of abnormally strong biological drives. Even more important though less dramatic are the frequent instances of physical infantilism which have their basis in more common forms of glandular pathology. These persons quite commonly exhibit an absence of strong motivation of any sort, and hence, though they may be docile in the sense of being obedient, they also are nonresponsive to the more important aspects of social training, which are directed toward preparing them for responsible maturity. The principal value, for us, in taking note of these extreme instances is that they make us aware of the possible importance of individual differences of the same kind, within the normal range. One illustration of this is the fact observed by Kinsey (1948) that it is possible to make more accurate prediction of the educational careers of young men from a knowledge of their high-school sex habits than from a knowledge of their intelligence. However, the effect of inequalities of physical development is complicated by the person's awareness of these differences—an aspect of the problem which we shall not consider until the next chapter. In this chapter, we shall be concerned only with those kinds of disturbance to the usual pattern which represent instances of failure to develop an expected psychological maturity, or lapses in mature behavior, which take place in spite of normal physiological maturation.

The background of our problem is the simple fact that the continuance of any culture presupposes the existence of more than the minimal biological dependence of children upon their parents, in order to foster the transmission of culture from one generation to the next. Different human societies display a great variety of economic and emotional relationships between parents and their children. The research of anthropologists reveals that human intelligence can devise, and the human constitution accept, many diverse patterns of such relationships, but it also demonstrates that no society can survive without institutions which in some way reinforce the basic biological fact, that the mature mammal must raise its young. Everywhere, this leads to some degree of prolongation of the child's dependence on the parent generation beyond what is physiologically necessary, and to a strengthening of the emotional bonds between the generations. Everyday observation of our domestic animals shows us how the mother loses interest in the offspring almost as soon as they are capable of independent survival, while the young as quickly abandon their dependent relationship to the mother. The relative constancy of child-parent attachments among humans is not simply a consequence of greater intelligence, nor can it be regarded wholly as a product of culture. Its beginnings are apparent in the long-term friendships of the chimpanzee, and it undoubtedly has its basis in a modification of the physiological foundations of affiliative behavior, which shows itself also in the relative constancy of sexual interest among the primates and in human life, in contrast to its episodic character among other animals. It has undoubted practical advantages, which we do not need to consider here. It also yields deep satisfactions which provide real enrichment to our lives. But it also may and often does interfere with normal emotional maturation, leaving the grown person temperamentally unfitted for adult responsibility. Such phrases as "momism" and "the silver cord" attest to the fact that this is not a rare phenomenon, but one frequent enough to constitute a social problem, providing the army sergeants and the judge in the court of domestic relations with some of their most difficult problems. It is this cultural modification of the process of psychological maturation which we wish to understand, as it manifests itself in the individual.

Three quite different approaches have been taken to the problem of describing the nature of psychological maturity. The *normative* approach concentrates its attention primarily on the measurement of individual differences, which can best be accomplished in terms of rather specific, clearly defined behavior components. This approach often allies itself with a behavioristic understanding of the process of development itself, as being composed of the separate acquisition of a great many specific acts in a series of learning experiences, the bit-by-bit accretion of attitudes and skills in a continuing history of social interactions. It may equally well be allied with an emphasis on the importance of maturation, in which case the norms of social behavior are regarded as a developmental scale of social growth. The *psychoanalytic* theory of personality gives rise to a different type of genetic emphasis. It views social development as a maturational process, but one in which the maturation of motivation is far more important than the maturation of capacities. It is also concerned especially with the interruptions and distortions of development which take place under what may be termed unnatural conditions. The *phenomenal* approach emphasizes the descriptive study of each developmental stage for and by itself, without regard to its relationship to preceding or following stages. The causal relationships it seeks are only those that explain the present act by the present psychological structure, not those that link past experiences to future action. This approach is allied with "field theory," as developed by Lewin and his followers. In future chapters, we shall meet again and again with these three quite different ways of studying the more complex problems of human personality.

Undoubtedly the best-known example of the normative approach to the study of maturity is the work of Gesell and his collaborators. (Cf. Gesell and Ilg, 1943, 1946.) Their pictures of 2-year-oldness, 3-year-oldness, 4-year-oldness, etc., are known to many thousands of American mothers. However, we should like to illustrate this approach by another very important contribution, which is less widely known.

The Vineland Social Maturity Scale (Doll, **1935**, 1953) consists of 117 items of graded difficulty, which are assigned to age levels at which their performance may be expected. Its construction is roughly similar to that of a standard intelligence test such as the Stanford-Binet, and the scoring procedure is designed to yield a "social age" and "social quotient" which are analogous to the MA and IQ derived from the intelligence test. It deals with social maturity as "social intelligence," in the same sense in which we also speak of "verbal intelligence" and "spatial intelligence." A random selection of items from ascending age levels will indicate what is here operationally defined as social maturity: walks about a room unattended—eats with a fork—helps with little household tasks—is trusted with money—disavows a literal Santa Claus—makes minor purchases alone—engages in adolescent group activities—follows current events—provides for the future—shares community responsibility. Just as with the Stanford-Binet, it is only the superior person who can be expected to attain the higher reaches of this scale, whose last items are stated to represent a social age of "25 and above."

The Vineland Scale grew out of a practical need for an intrument which would supplement the intelligence test as an indication of an individual's capacity to get along in society, without special protection. Experience had shown that factors of personality development, as well as mental development, had to be taken into account in making a decision whether mentally handicapped persons could take jobs in the community, or would have to be kept in institutions. It is to the credit of its author that the scale was not limited in its scope by this practical consideration, but that it was extended to give fuller expression to the concept of social maturity by including evidences of superior social responsibility. Nevertheless, the scale does have a very important defect, in that it includes no items relating to courtship, marriage, and parental behavior. It thus omits what seems, from the genetic viewpoint, to be the very core of the maturational process.

We may also question whether it is possible to measure a phenomenon in which so much ambivalence is present, while paying attention only to the evidences of increasing self-sufficiency and the acceptance of community responsibilities, but neglecting to take stock of the instances of immature behavior which may continue to occur, and, perhaps even more important, the hidden emotional dependency which may only reveal itself in behavior at just the crucial moment. There is, in the scale as it exists, an implicit assumption that as examples of mature behavior make their appearance, the tendencies to immature behavior are being progressively displaced. This reciprocal relationship is not necessary. To measure psychological maturity successfully, we must find clues that will detect the survivals of childish attitudes even when they are not obvious in everyday behavior. Even within the framework of its own structure, the Vineland Scale might have approached this task by including at higher age levels such items as "makes important purchases with reluctance or great hesitation" or "reads the comics before the news."

Although quite useful for certain purposes, the Vineland Scale of Social Maturity represents a quite limited approach to the whole problem. Its limitations seem to arise from the fact that it views social maturity as the result of the successful acquisition of habits of independent, responsible behavior, while giving no attention to the dynamic factors which underlie such behavior and which frequently upset it.

PSYCHOSEXUAL DEVELOPMENT

In view of the obvious importance of sexual development for psychological maturity, it is not surprising that the whole process has been described as primarily one of psychosexual development, that is, of psychological or behavioral changes which take place as the accompaniments of somatic sexual change. It is obvious that for such a viewpoint to be meaningful, the concept of sex itself must be greatly broadened, to include elements which appear in childhood, and even in infancy. Freud in his *Three Contributions to the Theory of Sex* (1905, 1938c), introduced this broader concept, and at the same time drew the initial outlines for the psychoanalytic theory of psychosexual development. This extraordinary essay is packed with original conceptions which have formed the foundation for the psychoanalytic theories of personality. In it, Freud defined three major sources of sensual experience for the child, and he asserted that each of these represents a source of energy (libido) which continues to play its part in later sexual behavior. He emphasized the distinctive roles played by the three anatomical zones which are the focal points for the child's sexual experience in successive periods of his development: the oral, the anal, and the genital. To the child, these are areas which, each at a given age, offer maximal opportunities for pleasurable exploitation, but the realization of these pleasures is gained only in struggle against the repressive discipline of adults, who force the child through the experiences of weaning and toilet training, and threaten him with punishment for masturbation. It is in deference to this repressive and civilizing discipline that the child finally enters into a "latency period," during which these energies are deflected toward other aims by the process of sublimation. Despite such deflection, the strivings that were present in these early periods continue to exert their influence in later life. "Every step on this long path of development may become a point of fixation" to which some of the libidinous energy becomes permanently attached, with the possibility that such fixations may impede or completely obstruct the normal course of development.

Soon after, Freud himself showed how these concepts could be used in the further development of personality theory. His paper on "Character and Anal Erotism" (1908, 1924a) described what has become known as the anal personality, a behavior syndrome which includes the traits of compulsive orderliness, parsimony, and stubbornness. Such persons, he said, are those who would have been classified as anal erotics in childhood, because of a prolonged and intense interest in anal pleasures. The adult traits represent reaction formations, through which they finally achieve a superficial control over anal-bound impulses. Their overt interest in orderliness and cleanliness, which is the least constant element in the syndrome, is a denial of interest in unclean things; while money is a socially acceptable symbolic equivalent for the fecal matter which they once, as children, stubbornly saved up within their bowels to achieve heightened satisfaction in the ultimate act of excretion. In contrast to such persons, there are others in whom the anal traits persist in relatively undisguised form, and still others who have achieved more acceptable sublimations. (It is scarcely possible to overemphasize the importance of the concept of reaction formation for the study of personality. It will be discussed at length in Chapter 12.)

The progress through the later stages of psychosexual development is bound up with the Oedipal situation, that is, with the child's experience of conflicting feelings of love, jealousy, fear, and hatred toward his parents, and his confusion regarding his relationships with them. (See Chapter 11.) The failure to resolve these conflicts is often held responsible for the person's inability to attain a *genital* level of development. There is an intermediate level of pregenital development, called the phallic stage, which is marked by intense sexual interest which appears superficially to be genitally oriented, because of the heightened narcissistic concern with the pleasurable potentialities of genital stimulation. However, at this stage the capacity for mature sexual behavior, including the capacity for a love experience which shifts the focus of attention from one's own gratifications to the person loved, is absent. (The Freudian term *object-cathexis* seems peculiarly cold to convey this meaning of unselfish love.) The person for whom sexual experience is the main focus of interest has not yet passed beyond the phallic stage of development. In mature behavior, genitally generated libido is released for creative effort in other spheres. (Whatever the reader may think about the value of this distinction, it is important to remember that the words phallic and genital do have quite different meanings in psychoanalytic parlance. Here, as in many other instances, great confusion may arise from attaching to technical words the meanings which they might be expected to have on the basis of everyday usage.)

The principal personality types, or character types, that have been described as characteristic of the various developmental stages and of persons who have remained psychosexually arrested at these stages include the following: oral-dependent, oral-aggressive, anal-compulsive, anal-sadistic, phallic, and genital. In the isolation and description of most of these types, the most important contributions other than Freud's have been made by Abraham (1927).

The oral-receptive character is one which remains dominated by the basically dependent attitudes of early infancy. The oral-aggressive character is similarly dependent and parasitic, but exhibits in addition hostilities and resentments, like those of the teething infant, who wishes to bite the breast as well as to suck nourishment from it. Where the first may give a picture of amiable and trusting helplessness, the second is more treacherous and threatening in its demands. The anal-compulsive character often includes, besides the elements of orderliness, stinginess, and stubbornness which Freud mentioned, an additional quality of suspicious aloofness which seems quite in place as a survival of overstrict toilet training. The anal-sadistic character, in whom these repressive reaction-formations have not taken place, continues to exhibit the undisciplined, impulsive behavior of the child who uses his excretory powers as a weapon against his mother, and takes his principal satisfactions from asserting his power in ways that cause pain to others. The phallic type was described by Reich (1933, 1949) as vain, insolent, and domineering in behavior, though fundamentally dependent. Each of these types of character structure represents a kind of immaturity due to the predominance of a behavioral trait which either in unaltered form or in the disguise of a reaction formation has retained its primacy into adult life. Each of them includes a strong element of narcissism, or self-love. The mature individual attains genital character, which means not only a capacity for full enjoyment of heterosexual intercourse, but also the capacity to develop true love relationships, free from narcissism, the ability to direct both love and hate appropriately, efficient utilization of sublimated energies outside the sexual sphere, and ability to withstand frustrations.

An interesting statement of the stages of psychosexual growth is given by Erikson (1950). The oral-dependent stage is more fully labeled by him as the oral-respiratory-sensory stage, and it is also called the first incorporative mode, in which there is an emphasis on *receiving* from the environment whatever it is prepared to give. In the oral-aggressive stage, or second incorporative mode, the emphasis shifts from passive reception to more actively *getting.* The third or anal-compulsive stage is characterized as retentive, in which the principal effort is to *hold on.* In the anal-sadistic stage, which Erikson characterizes as eliminative, the child learns to *let go.* After passing through these early stages, the active child enters the *intrusive* stage of infantile genitality, in which the release of creative impulses constitutes an important parallel to later mature genitality.

The contemplation of this elaborate theoretical structure raises many questions. Is there sufficient justification for the importance that is attributed to the various bodily zones? What is the nature of the process of fixation, or arrested development? What is the relationship between this process and the modification of temperament, which we have already observed taking place in animals and children?

Let us first consider whether Freud places undue emphasis on the part that the different bodily zones play in the development of personality, so that the resulting picture is, as sometimes charged, an uncouth grotesquerie, a caricature rather than a portrait. We must grant, on the contrary, that he was the first to recognize the importance of seeing the child's experience from the child's own point of view, giving to each kind of experience an importance commensurate with its place in the child's life, not in ours.

With respect first to the importance of oral experience, we must not forget how largely the waking moments of the infant's day are taken up with nursing, and how he "drinks in" the social features of his environment as incidental to his sucking. As Dollard and Miller (1950) take pains to calculate, oral gratifications and the mother's face are linked in at least 2000 reinforcements during the first year of life. This intimate joining in experience of oral needs and gratifications and dependent feelings is a concrete fact of growth, which amply justifies the use of the phrase, "oral dependency." However, we do not appreciate the full importance of this phrase unless we recognize that the primacy of oral experience is determined by the child himself, and not by external circumstances. The powers of modern science are scarcely equal to the task of training an infant to keep his thumb out of his mouth. When the child gains in motor dexterity, it will be not only the thumb, but every object that comes to hand, that must first of all be mouthed. As the dog sniffs his environment, so the infant tastes it, never satisfied that he has explored an object properly until he has put his lips to it. Still, the phrasing of this last sentence is wrong, for the lips play no part in active exploration of the environment. They are an avenue of reassuring contact, and as long as they occupy a position of primacy in experience, the infant continues to be utterly dependent. When the older child puts his thumb into his mouth, we know that he is retreating from the responsibilities which growth have imposed upon him, and we do well to let him cuddle up to us, to satisfy his need, rather than to slap his hand or ridicule him.

Nor does the emphasis on the anal zone lack equally concrete foundation in the reality of child life. From late in the first year until early in the third, the child copes incessantly with the problem of bowel control. During this same period he also develops a sense of physical self-mastery, and begins to use his developing motor skills in outwardly directed aggressions. The intimate physiological relationship between the growth of motor skills and of control over the processes of elimination is described by Gesell and Ilg (1943), who show how the stages of the one give rise to vicissitudes in the other. Motor mastery and sphincter mastery both call for new powers of inhibition and disinhibition, and in one field as in the other, through the exercise of these powers, the child comes to feel that he has a will, and seeks in both for opportunities to test this will against external coercion. It is not difficult for us to recognize this in the child's physical play, and in his stubborn resistance to parental commands. However, the designation of this period as the "anal phase" makes us sense also the child's thrill of power when he produces, in response to his own effort, a fecal mass. It also reminds us of how frequently the retention of feces or the soiling of clothes are expressions of the rejection of outside authority. The concrete physical experiences of bowel evacuation, maturation of bowel control, and submission to bowel training provide much of the basis for the development of the child's aggressive impulses. Anyone who finds it implausible that children should really have a positive interest in fecal matter, may perhaps ask himself what factors would make them indifferent, despite their otherwise active curiosity, to the odorous stuff whose coming coincides with sudden relief from cramping discomfort. Only a delicate sensibility to the proprieties of the situation, which they have not yet acquired! Generally speaking, if we return to the frame of reference of our earlier chapters on animal behavior, the fact that an animal possesses strong sensitivity to any stimulus assures his responsiveness to it, and no one can deny that humans are quite sensitive to the odor of feces.

We conclude, therefore, that the "anal phase," like the "oral phase," is no empty theoretical construction. These apt phrases help us to become sensitive to the predominant temperamental dispositions of the periods to which they refer. They represent an important first effort, correct in its major outlines, at the description of the sequence of critical stages in the life of the young child.

We turn to our second question: What is the nature of the process of fixation, or arrested development? This phenomenon has been explained, within the general context of psychoanalytic theory, by two quite different hypotheses, which we may call the "spoiled child" theory and the "starved child" theory. The first stems most directly from Freud's own writings, and it is also based on the conventional concept of learning by positive reinforcement,—Freud's "pleasure principle." Freud warned that "excessive parental tenderness 'spoils' the child and makes him unfit to renounce love temporarily or to be satisfied with a smaller amount of love in later life." According to this theory, it is assumed that the child is more strongly attached to periods that have been especially pleasurable. Following this tradition, Alexander (1952) defines *fixation* as "the tendency to retain previously successful behavior patterns," and *regression* as "the tendency to return to them whenever new adjustments are required" which are beyond the individual's capacities at the time. Wolf (1943) invoked the same principle in the effort to explain the results of his experiment on the effects of sensory deprivation in infancy (which was described at length in Chapter 3). He said that when the rats were confronted with the necessity to struggle for gratification in a rivalry situation, there was "a tendency to return to the use of older infantile patterns that were once associated with gratification and mastery. These were the conditioned reflexes of the nursing period when security involved an exploitation of the mother." However, we need feel no compulsion to accept this explanation of his findings, for what was actually observed in the behavior of the rats was only the inhibition of response to the crucial signal. A more direct test of Freud's formulation of the phenomenon of fixation is to be found in Levy's study of *Maternal Overprotection* (1943). Levy distinguishes between mothers who are domineering and those who are overindulgent, and we are concerned only with children of the latter type of mother. Typically, "their behavior toward the mother was marked by disobedience, impudence, temper tantrums, excessive demands, and the exercise of varying degrees of tyranny." However, Levy also finds that the prognosis for such children is rather good, that although they are severe behavior problems in the home they are likely to get along well at school, that although they have difficulty in forming friendships as children they often become socially successful as adults, and that the group as a whole "shows a normal growth of heterosexual interest and activity." These results certainly do not indicate that the spoiled child is hopelessly retarded in his psychosexual development.

The alternate hypothesis states that fixation occurs because adequate satiation of natural needs is *not* received. This, too, may be illustrated by an important study by Levy (1934). Using six puppies of a single litter, he allowed the mother to nurse two, and fed the others by bottle. Two puppies were fed from nipples which had openings so large that the milk flowed freely, and they had very little sucking activity in their feedings. The other two were fed from nipples which had small openings, so that they had to suck long and vigorously to get their milk. It was observed that the two pups which had little opportunity for sucking in their feedings did a good deal of sucking of other objects, while those which were required to do a good deal of sucking on their bottles, did little sucking otherwise. The experiment was designed to test the hypothesis that thumb sucking would be encouraged by a lack of adequate nursing experience. Because other experiments dealing with the same problem, some with animal and some with human subjects, have led to conflicting results, this specific problem must be regarded as unsettled. However, Levy's experiment, without being conclusive, serves well to illustrate the theoretical proposition that fixation at an oral level may result from *lack* of oral gratification at the proper time. This supposition is based on the genetic viewpoint, which postulates that entrance into each successively higher stage of development is in some sense conditioned upon a satisfactory completion of the prior stage, like the process of promotion through school. Fixation, or arrested development, therefore takes place where needs have been unsatisfied, not where they have been too well or too easily satisfied. It is, accordingly, the child who is "starved for love" whose life is dominated by a continuing need for affection. Hence we may call this the "starved child" theory, in contrast to the "spoiled child" theory.

Fenichel (1945) acknowledges that the concept of fixation as a result of frustration falls within the scope of orthodox psychoanalysis. He explains the effect as follows:

> One gets the impression that at developmental levels that do not afford enough satisfaction, the organism refuses to go further, demanding the withheld satisfactions. If the frustration has led to repression, the drives in question are thus cut off from the rest of the personality; they do not participate in further maturation and send up their disturbing derivatives from the unconscious into the conscious. The result is that these drives remain in the unconscious unchanged, constantly demanding the same sort of satisfaction.

A more parsimonious explanation of how deprivation leads to fixation can be based upon a recognition of the fact that learning can take place with respect to feelings and emotional responses as well as with respect to action and perception. We turn, therefore, to a consideration of the third question stated above, namely, the relationship between the process of fixation and the modification of temperament. We have already reminded the reader more than once that learning which takes place with respect to emotional responses seems to be extraordinarily resistant to extinction. What is repeatedly experienced, and hence in a very real sense practiced and learned during a period of deprivation, is the feeling of need for the unexperienced satiation. The temperamental disposition toward a continually unconsummated response persists as a felt need. Since emotional responses may be conditioned without reinforcement, simply on the basis of temporal contiguity, such feelings become associated with multiple cues. The child whose dependency needs are satisfied feels them acutely only for short periods, and has them quickly supplanted by perhaps more intense feelings of gratification. The child whose dependency needs are unsatisfied continues to feel them over long periods, and under conditions of emotional disturbance which, we recall, are conducive to abnormal fixation.

It is thus that what might be a passing phase of temperamental development becomes instead a fixed feature of adult temperament. Strong support for this viewpoint is given by the findings of Whiting and Child (1953), which were cited at the close of the last chapter, to the effect that it is much easier to detect the operation of negative than positive frustration in the consequences of early child training.

We can readily admit that the hypothetical statements of the last paragraph may be wrong in detail, yet insist that there is abundant proof for the correctness of the general thesis, that the important early training which influences later personality is not the learning of motor responses, but the learning of feeling habits, which are too often entirely disregarded. This hypothesis, which we believe has reached the status of a fact, has enormous implications for educational practice. It means that we must always be more concerned about the emotional experience or feeling that we are fostering, by any disciplinary or tutorial procedure, than about the actions that we are suppressing or inducing. How does the child inwardly *feel* as we force him to obedience? Is the induced feeling, which is being fixated as the pattern for later character structure, best stated as "I must give in now, but not always," *or* "I must always be giving in," *or* "It never pays to be disobedient," *or* "I hate you." We must learn carefully to observe such feelings, and judge the effects of discipline not by the conduct induced, but by the feelings aroused, which will be far more permanent. How often we violate this simple precept of effective teaching! An illustration may be taken from the experience of a young woman who came for marital counseling, and whose difficulties were connected with her fears of pregnancy. She recalled an incident when, returning from school, she found her mother talking to a neighbor outside the house. The neighbor was obviously pregnant, and the self-conscious girl avoided acknowledging her presence. Later she was sharply reprimanded, and told that women in "that condition" were especially sensitive. It was an effective lesson in social decorum—and served besides to instil more deeply the young girl's feeling that pregnancy should be feared.

From this standpoint, we may readily acknowledge the validity of the concept of oral and anal levels of personality development, that is, of levels characterized by a preponderance of feelings that are normally associated with those developmental stages. Such emotional immaturity would be the expected consequence of conditions which favor the fixation of these feelings, at the time when they first occur. Overprotection may provide such conditions in a degree, by fostering the retention of dependent attitudes; however, this implies learning by positive reinforcement, and since such learning is readily susceptible to extinction, its effects do not persist into later life. It is frustration, or deprivation, which favors abnormal fixation (in Maier's sense), with its extraordinary resistance to extinction. For this reason, we believe that the "starved child" theory is more generally applicable than the "spoiled child" theory. However, both appear to be consistent with the general principles of the psychoanalytic theories of psychosexual development.

MATURITY AS MENTAL STRUCTURE

We have seen psychological maturity defined, first, from the normative standpoint, in terms of the growth of behavioral capacities by maturation and by learning, and second, from the psychoanalytic genetic viewpoint, as a process primarily of motivational development. It may be described also, from the phenomenological standpoint, as a difference in mental structure, as a different way of perceiving the world, which gives rise to consequent differences in behavior. This type of approach developed first within the European academic tradition, in which the subject matter of psychology is thinking, rather than behavior. Transplanted to American soil, it has had a vigorous growth, and has shown itself capable of bearing rich fruits in the understanding of children's behavior. It is in this tradition, that one must place the influential work of Piaget (1929, 1932, etc.), who stresses the fact that the child's perception of the world about him must not be dismissed as merely rudimentary or mistaken, by contrast with the more accurate perceptions of the adult, but must be understood as different in certain important qualitative respects. When we study the development of the child's thinking, we must not suppose that it consists of no more than a gradual assimilation of what adults can teach him. Before he learns our tricks of reasoning he has his own ways of perceiving reality, and without our tutelage he would pass through his own stages of growth to more complete understanding. As seen in Piaget's voluminous work, this growth starts from the child's early total egotism and his animistic interpretation of all things as essentially like himself. Step by step, the child takes himself out of the external world and the world out of himself, and thus he becomes more and more capable of objective judgments.

We shall be concerned here only with the Lewinian concept of mental structure. It has its antecedents in the speculations of Lévy-Bruhl and others regarding supposed differences in the thinking of primitive and civilized man; in Werner's (1926, 1940) emphasis on the concept of structure as essential for the definition of developmental levels of thinking; in Koffka's (1924) formulation of the intellectual development of the child in terms of growth to increasing levels of complexity, rather than by accretion of knowledge. Although Lewin himself takes his point of departure from the Gestalt school, one does not find in his work their usual insistence on the inviolability of wholes. On the contrary, Lewin is at all times eager to undertake the analysis of the relationships which exist between the parts of the whole, conceived as a dynamic field. In his personality theory, therefore, he represents the individual as being a composite of many separately organized systems, and he particularly emphasizes the fact that intercommunication between these systems may sometimes be rather poor. In his topological models, each disposition or aversion toward any kind of activity is represented as a bounded *region*, and the ease of communication, or likelihood of interaction between such relatively self-contained parts of the personality, is represented by *boundaries* having different degrees of permeability. If a system, or region, is scarcely subject to outside influence, its boundary is shown by a heavy unbroken line, whereas if it is quite susceptible to such influence, its boundary will be thin, or even broken. The topological scheme of representation of course permits a single region to have a variable boundary, one which is more permeable to influences from one quarter than another. Within this framework, the process of development is conceived as a process of *differentiation*, or the progressive establishment of more and more sub-systems within the individual, and in general also of increasing *rigidity*, or relative independence of the systems (or regions) from one another. This relative segregation of the different systems is recognized as essential for orderly behavior. However, it can be excessive, and the feeble-minded child is said to differ from the normal child in being both less differentiated and more rigid. If the regions are thought of as representing so many different potentialities for behavior, then the less differentiated individual is capable of less varied response. The systems, or regions, are also thought of as occupying different strata, including those of reality and irreality, and of past, present, and future. For the child, the level of irreality is far more accessible than for the adult, so that an increased rigidity in this respect is definitely an accompaniment of maturation.

Lewin regards regressive behavior as being simply an instance of dedifferentiation, that is, a reversal of the process of differentiation. Such dedifferentiation would be a natural result of the collapse of boundaries which had been established in the process of differentiation. This is presumably one of the consequences of emotional stress. The consequence, of course, would be a more diffuse perception, with a relative blurring of the distinctions between present and future, between irreality and reality, and between different regions generally.

An experimental demonstration of this kind of regression was given by Barker, Dembo, and Lewin (1941). They had 30 child subjects, ranging in age from 2 to 5 years. Each child was first observed in a controlled individual play situation, in which a number of moderately attractive but not unusual toys were available. The observer took careful notes, and the child was scored for the "constructiveness" of his play. Some steps of the rating scale which was used for this purpose were:

Constructiveness 2: the toys are examined superficially.
Constructiveness 4: somewhat more complicated manipulation of the truck.
Constructiveness 6: the truck is used as a means to haul other things.
Constructiveness 8: play showing more than usual originality.

At the end of this period of preliminary observation, the observer pushed aside a partition, thus opening up another section of the room in which there were a number of highly exciting toys. A little later, the observer explained to the child that he could not permit him to go on playing with these toys, and led him back into the first part of the room. A folding gate was drawn across the room, permitting the child to see but not to reach the toys which were now denied to him. Once again, the child was rated for constructiveness of his play with the more ordinary toys. (Before each child left, he was given another period of play with the attractive toys, in a postfrustration situation which was not part of the experiment, but was designed to prevent any undesirable aftereffects of the frustration experience.)

Comparing the behavior of the children with the first group of toys, before and after the interpolated experience with the more attractive playthings, a highly significant difference in "constructiveness" appears. The mean score declined from 4.99 to 3.94, which, the authors state, is equivalent to a regression of more than 17 months in mental age. That is, the child who was experiencing frustration played on a less mature level than that of which he had previously shown himself capable. The authors consider this regression to be the consequences of dedifferentiation, a sort of blurring of the life space. They speculate that all of the phenomena of "fixation" and "regression" can be explained in the same way, in terms of the present situation and present mental structure, without appeal to explanatory concepts that are based on the special experience of the individual subject at a relatively remote time.

Lewinian theory, like Freudian theory, claims the distinction of being "dynamic," but whereas, in the latter case, the word refers to emphasis on motivational or dynamizing factors, in field theory it refers to the fact that explanations are "ahistoric," each event being explained as the resultant of forces immediately present and acting, and hence in a cause-and-effect context which is comparable to that of the physical sciences. From the standpoint of genetically oriented psychoanalytic theory, such explanation neglects one of the most essential aspects of the problem, namely, that the greater susceptibility of one child or another, to the effects of frustration, is to be attributed in large part to influences which cannot be effectively studied otherwise than genetically. The contrast between these two different kinds of explanation can be illustrated by applying them to a real life situation which often leads to regressive behavior—the arrival of a baby brother or sister, who very nearly monopolizes the mother's attention. Does the older child, whom we may suppose for purposes of illustration to be a 4-year-old, more or less wilfully put on babyish ways, in a planned campaign to hold his mother's love? By this it is not meant that he consciously adopts a program of action, but only that in his diffuse perception of the situation these elements enter: "I am not getting enough love; the baby is getting more love; it is good to be a baby; I can be a baby again." This would constitute a return to earlier patterns of response partly because they had been successful in experience and partly because their value was being demonstrated by the sibling. Or does the older child, because of the emotional disturbance accompanying his frustration, simply lose some of what he has gained in maturity, so that his behavior becomes less adequate, more infantile, less differentiated, without constituting a turning back to earlier ways? Perhaps this is a good point at which to appeal to the psychoanalytic principle that all psychological events are "overdetermined," and hence explicable as outcomes of many converging processes. It is therefore not unreasonable to suppose that the basic realities of regression in behavior include both those genetic elements that have been emphasized in the theory of psychosexual development, and the perceptual factors that are emphasized by Lewin and his co-workers.

However, if the Lewinian and psychoanalytic concepts of regression are to be reconciled, this can more readily be achieved with respect to the "starved child" theory than the "spoiled child" theory. Indeed, certain early experiments of the Lewinian school can be invoked as supporting the "starved child" theory of regression. Zeigarnik (1927) and Ovsiankina (1928) studied the aftereffects of the interruption of activities that had been assigned to their subjects. Zeigarnik permitted her subjects to complete some of the tasks which she had assigned, but she interrupted them before the conclusion of others. Later, she asked them to recall all the tasks on which they had been working, and she found that the unfinished tasks were more likely to be recalled than the completed tasks, despite the fact that more time had been spent in working on the latter. The "tension of the uncompleted task"—which is called the Zeigarnik effect—was therefore a more important determination of recall than the number of repetitions. Under similar conditions, Ovsiankina found that when her subjects had the opportunity to do so, they tended to resume the activities at which they had been interrupted earlier, apparently to fulfill an inner need. Both experiments point to the existence of a "tension system" corresponding to the uncompleted task, a felt need to return to such tasks and to complete them. (Later research has shown that there are large individual differences in susceptibility to this phenomenon, but this fact does not lessen its importance. See page 284.) Barker, Dembo, and Lewin utilize these findings to construct an auxiliary hypothesis for the explanation of their findings, to wit, that if "a certain part of the person (is in a) state of more or less permanent tension," regression will be more likely to occur. This conclusion is quite in harmony with Levy's position, that when there is inadequate opportunity for the exercise of a native disposition—in that case, specifically sucking—the need for such activity will persist. The tension of the uncompleted activity and the motivational force of the unsatiated need have much in common.

Feeling Habit as a Basis of Psychological Immaturity

We should like to take this opportunity to expand somewhat further on the relationship between the feeling habit and retardation in emotional development, or regression to childhood patterns of behavior. In clinical experience, it often appears that the attitudes which influence the conduct of a grown person seem to be survivals from childhood. Understanding the pattern of psychosexual development helps us to penetrate the secret of such survivals in many cases, but the understanding of an individual case is not reached by fitting it into such a schema, but rather by formulating it in such concrete detail, drawn from the person's own experience, that the schema with its pigeonholes becomes superfluous. We gave one example of such a regressive feeling habit in the last chapter. Let us add two others here.

A young married woman has had repeated difficulties in her social relationships, especially with women, both on the job and in her personal friendships. In childhood, she had practiced certain deceits upon her mother, felt ashamed of them, and perpetually feared the consequences of discovery. Now, whenever a minor incident brings a small criticism from a friend or superior, she falls into a panic—a sort of belated realization of her old fear that her deceit has been discovered, she is found out, she is no longer loved.

The second example is that of a young man who had recently been divorced. He readily acknowledged that he had precipitated the divorce without real reason. He was also afraid to enter into another marriage, because of an unreasonable expectation that his wife would surely be unfaithful to him. It developed during the counseling interviews that this fear was based on the knowledge which he had had as a child, that his mother was unfaithful to his father, to whom he felt closely attached. The feelings associated with this suppressed knowledge had become so fixed in his mind that he transferred them to the present situation, without being immediately aware of their origin.

We may recall, also, the example, early in this chapter, of the young wife who feared that the failure of her marriage would displease her mother!

Each of us, if we explore the motivations of our own actions, can find within ourselves some such habitual readiness to slip into patterns of feeling that were important in our childhood. If such survivals dominate much of our behavior, we are relatively immature. If they are rare, so that our conduct is determined by the requirements of the present situation rather than by our expectations in the old one, we are mature persons.

Maturity, then, might be defined as *freedom from restraints arising from the emotional experiences of childhood.* This is a quantifiable dimension, which permits us to rank individuals as more or less mature. Beyond this, however, we still wish to understand the individual case in its concrete particularity, which will tell us what kind of situation can be expected to precipitate immature behavior in that person. In a clinical situation, the understanding of such a unique dynamic pattern is more important than all the information that can be gained from standardized tests yielding trait scores.

SUMMARY

We have considered several different theoretical approaches to the problem of describing behavior in terms of "level of maturity." The normative approach, as exemplified by the Vineland Scale of Social Maturity, has a limited usefulness. The Freudian concepts of psychosexual development are illuminating, but the orthodox "spoiled child" theory of fixation and regression seems less useful than the alternative which we have called the "starved child" theory. The Lewinian representation of maturation as a process of differentiation, and of regression as dedifferentiation, was found to be compatible with the latter theory. From our own point of view, in dealing with individual cases, we find the formulation in terms of "feeling habit" to be most useful. However much we may rely upon one theoretical formulation or another, it remains true that an important part of the characterization of any individual must be in terms of the level of maturity exhibited in his behavior, and particularly of the level to be expected in the face of frustration.

CHAPTER 11

Formation of the Self-Concept

*T*he human capacity to observe onself and to judge oneself gives rise to a variety of complex phenomena, which are perhaps more distinctively human than any other aspect of our behavior. For more than one psychologist, these phenomena have seemed to constitute the core of human personality. Wolff (1947) describes the child's early years as revolving about "the child's search for his self." Lecky (1945) said that the major determining force in personality is the need to maintain self-consistency. It is with the first part of this dual process, the search for the self, that this chapter will be concerned. The next chapter will deal with the defense of the self, which is always a partly illusory concept, against reality.

Our discussion of the formation of the self-concept will begin with a consideration of the body image, or the self-concept in the most concrete sense, together with those aspects of the self-concept that are most intimately related to it. There will follow a discussion of identification, or modeling of the self-concept after ideal figures, which is one of the most decisive factors in personality development. Later sections will deal with role taking, the views of the neo-Freudian school, and the self-concept in field theory. Finally, there will be a short discussion of introversion, or self-observation *per se* as a personality variable.

THE BODY IMAGE

The very first use we make of our capacity for self-observation is to gain some acquaintance with our external body parts, and to form a connected body image. All through life we go on revising this image, which can never be altogether free of distortion. We never have quite enough mirrors, or mirrors clear enough, to see ourselves as others see us, even in the simple physical sense. The infant's discovery of fingers and later of toes, and such later events as the young girl's concern with her developing breasts or the often surprising first acquaintance with one's own profile, are incidents in a never-ending process. Many factors complicate the problem of forming an accurate body image. Probably the most important of these is the circumstance that our bodies undergo a constant process of change, which is especially rapid during the years of childhood and adolescence. The child is not only aware of his body, but also of its growth, and inevitably he develops concern as to whether this growth will leave him finally with an acceptable body, one which conforms to the demands of his cultural environment as well as to his own needs. An element of immaturity of attitude, which the reader can readily fit into the framework of the last chapter, is the tendency to continue thinking of oneself as relatively immature, as having the body and appearance of a child rather than of a man or woman. Perhaps it would be better to say "feeling" oneself immature, because what is important is not the intellectual assessment of one's age, stature, and general appearance, but one's spontaneous feelings of bigness or smallness, strength or weakness, skill or awkwardness, and the tendencies to dominance and submission which are linked with them. The young child compares himself to those about him, and measures his feeble potentialities against the things that are possible for them. From his position, the perspectives of size and time are such that he must exaggerate the differences between himself and slightly older children, and underestimate the difference between these other children and adults. He is small in a world of giants, and hence he suffers from an inevitable sense of inadequacy, which may easily become the foundation for damaging feelings of inferiority (Adler, 1933). As he grows older, this objective inferiority is lessened, but the old habits of thinking tend to linger on. From year to year, as birthday follows birthday, he is called upon to see himself always differently, and to accustom himself to the fact that others see him differently. He never quite gets used to it. At 30 he is amused that his young son thinks him old; at 50 he is annoyed that his fellow-workers no longer recognize that he is young. In most individuals, the feeling of one's own age tends to lag behind actuality, at least during the younger years. Where this lag is extreme, it shows itself in a tendency to be submissive toward one's own age peers, as a child might be toward adults.

Another complication is the fact that we are under pressure to make the body image conform to what may be termed a mythology or popular stereotype of physical appearance and body functions, in which some parts of the body are accorded great prominence and special significance, while others are screened out of our attention. In this stereotype, the body's clothing also plays a part, and if our mental image of a lovely woman or a handsome man includes such details as flowing skirts or casual tweed jackets, it is obvious that we must expect the counterparts of these embellishments to play a part in the body image.

As the child forms his body image, he wrestles in concrete, instrumental terms with the profound philosophic problem of distinction between the "self" and the "not-self," and with the equally profound problem of the temporal continuity of the self. Although we may gain an intellectual understanding in early childhood that our toys, for example, are not a part of our true self, we probably never reach a satisfactory solution to the problem of delimiting the self. William James (1890), who sought his empirical self most earnestly, could find it only in the muscular tension of his forehead. Horowitz (1935) asked some young children the repeated question, "*Is this you?*" as he pointed to different parts of their bodies. One little girl, aged 2½, located herself in the mouth region; another who reported her age as 3 was insistent that only her lower right jaw was truly herself; a third, at 3 years and 8 months, regarded the abdomen and lower thorax as herself; a fourth, aged 4 years 2 months, seemed to locate herself in the head. All these children seemed to regard other parts of their bodies as simply belonging to themselves, as possessions belong, and not as domiciles of the self. It is interesting to note that these few cases give some support to the idea that the early self may be given an oral localization, and that in an intermediate stage the self may sometimes be given an anal (abdominal) localization, before the child comes to accept the culturally approved theory that the head is the seat of the self. Horowitz pursued this problem further, by more formal experimentation with college men. They were instructed to give three answers to the question, "If you *had* to locate yourself at some point that 'is you,' where would that point (or area) be?" The head was named most frequently, the brains, the eyes, and the heart almost as often. Other fairly common answers were the face, the hands, and the genitals. Perhaps William James' preference for his knitted brow was as much a matter of individual difference, or the occupational stereotype of a philosopher, as the result of more sophisticated introspection.

With respect to the temporal continuity of the self, we probably all remember puzzling in childhood over the problem of whether one is really the "same person" from one year to the next. How can the same self include so many diverse experiences, even with the continuity of memory? But then how can it extend beyond even the limits of memory, into a forgotten infancy? As we lengthen our time perspective, we become concerned over the possible existence of the self after the disintegration of the body. The strength of the body image never shows itself more clearly than in the fact that the imagined immortal self cannot shuffle off the appearance of its mortal coil. It may, of course, be extended by a pair of wings, to fulfill a common childhood fantasy.

It is not too difficult for us to understand the confusions which a child experiences with respect to the problems of age and bigness. After all, there is a continuum of age and size, and a growing child might not be sure of his true place along the scale. It is more difficult for us to understand the confusions that take place with respect to sex. At a relatively early age, the child becomes aware of sex distinctions, of his own physical sex, of social expectations that are connected with it, and of his inadequacy to meet those expectations. He does not have the time perspective which can enable him to understand confidently that some day he will overcome these inadequacies. The sex role is something mysterious, envied, and—at least in our middle-class culture—forbidden in some of its aspects at the same time that it is enforced in others. Sex is not seen by the child as a category to which one belongs, but as an achievement which one may easily fall short of. Many factors, of which the body image is one, influence the child in his feeling that he will fail or succeed in reaching the goal of desired sex status. There are many degrees of certainty with which the conviction of one's maleness or femaleness may be held, just as there are many degrees of doubt about the desirability of the sex role which has fallen to one's lot. We shall return to this question later, when we deal with the subject of identification.

A very important adjunct to the body image is the estimate which each of us forms as to how attractive he is to the opposite sex. This estimate is subject to much revision as a result of experience, and to much distortion as experience is inaccurately perceived. It is not an uncommon event in clinical experience to meet a pretty girl who thinks of herself as unattractive and even repulsive in appearance. Such exceptional cases should not, however, obscure the general rule that by and large the individual who possesses the physique and the features that conform rather well to the social ideal experiences less conflict in the development of a satisfactory body image. Loomis and Green (1947) concluded from a survey of their counseling experience on a typical state university campus, that "there is a tendency for most of the boys' conflicts, of whatever origin, to channel into despair of not being handsome and virile; the girls', into mortification at not being beautiful and charming." The case studies supporting this conclusion certainly indicate that the boy or girl who is unfortunate enough to be physically exceptional, in a negative sense, has a severe handicap in the development of a healthy adult personality. Jones (1949) has described the problems of the adolescent boy whose maturation proceeds either faster or slower than that of his classmates, and who thus finds himself for a while with a body that is not standard. The more severe problem, of course, is that which is occasioned by delayed maturation.

Schilder has discussed the development of the body image from the standpoint of orthodox psychoanalytic theory. According to this theory, the prominence which different parts of the body acquire in the body image is a consequence of the role which they play in psychosexual development.

In the whole structure of the schema of the body, the erogenic zones will play the leading part, and we have to suppose that the image of the body, in the oral stage of development, will be centered around the mouth; in the anal stage, around the anus. . . . Individuals in whom a partial desire is increased will feel the particular point of the body, the particular erogenic zone belonging to the desire, in the centre of their body image. It is as if energy were amassed on these particular points. (*The Image and Appearance of the Human Body*, 1935.)

It will help us to understand the force of this phenomenon if we think of how quickly we start to itch at a point of the body to which worrisome attention has been directed.

One should be wary of the easy generalization that the primary erogenic zones hold the most prominent places in the body image. The secondary sex characteristics, such as breast and hair for the girls, and hairy development for the boys, also become focal points of interest, especially in early adolescence. Besides this, it is possible for any part of the body to achieve paramount importance in the body image of a given person. Any facial feature or aspect of physique may become the focus for an individual's concern, and become as such a preoccupying element in the development of the self-concept. A large or small ear, fingers that are thought to be clumsy, hair that is too straight or too curly, a nose that is thought to be misshapen, legs that are not straight enough, being too tall or being too short—any bodily characteristic may become the psychological center of the body image. We must always be alert to the possibility that the concentration of energy on such a point, especially when the deformation is more imagined than real, is in reality a displacement of feeling, and that the important underlying concern is the conscious or unconscious fear of sexual inadequacy. Again, however, we must not permit such an easy generalization to stop us from exploring the distinctive experiences which have led to the emphasis on a particular feature. For example, a woman who showed an obvious self-consciousness about her nose, when asked about it, said that it had always bothered her because it was a strong point of resemblance to her brutal father. For her, it had become the symbol of everything evil in herself. An illustration in a lighter vein is provided by some of the lines of a song in the musical comedy *Guys and Dolls,* in which one of the "dolls" complains to her dilatory suitor that "a person," however well bundled in gowns and in furs, can feel naked "just from looking at her left hand." The ring finger may also become a prominent part of the body image!

Almost any personality disturbance which is not inconsequential will express itself in part by giving rise to some distortion of the body image. This, in turn, will often lead to symptomatic postural mannerisms, or to peculiarities of dress. Such distortions are perhaps also responsible for the special difficulty which depressive, schizoid, and anxious subjects have in dealing with that phase of the Wechsler-Bellevue Intelligence Scale in which the subject is required to reconstruct, as in a jigsaw puzzle, a mannikin, a face, and a hand. (Cf. Rapaport, 1945.) These simple tasks are quite confusing to subjects whose body images are fuzzy and attended by much self-consciousness.

The clinical tool which is most useful in exploring disturbances of the body image is the drawing of the human figure. This very penetrating instrument is a development of the Draw-a-Man test which Goodenough (1926) devised as a nonverbal test of intelligence. She standardized it to yield a mental age score, based on the number and nature of the details that were included in the drawing. Her discussion at that time was limited to a consideration of the intellectual factors that might influence a child's performance on the test, and she gave no intimation of an awareness that the drawings might also be emotionally revealing. However, psychologists who used the test with disturbed mental patients became aware of its diagnostic possibilities. To augment these, Karen Machover (1949) introduced an important change in the form of the test, by instructing the subject only to "draw a person," leaving sex and age indeterminate. After the first figure is drawn, the subject is asked what it represents, and if, for example, it is a man, he is then asked to draw a woman; or if a girl, he is then asked to draw a boy. Although the subject rarely makes a conscious attempt at self-portraiture in these figures, the self-concept exerts a strong influence on the outcome. This is illustrated in Figure 11.1, which presents four drawings made by sixth-grade girls, and three that were made by college women. Both sets of drawings from which these examples were chosen were produced in response to the "draw a person" instruction given to a class group. As to the college women, I have no hesitancy in asserting that any judge would find it easy to match these unconscious self-portraits with their authors, if the three women were first pointed out as a group. I do not have the same personal

FIGURE 11.1. Drawings of a person. Above, sixth-grade girls; below, college women.

acquaintance with the sixth-grade girls, but certainly the riding costume, the party dress, the housewifely apron, and the big bow and short skirt of the last childish figure, all suggest that the self-concepts of these girls are finding rather clear expression.

The drawing of a person is only one part of the H-T-P technique which was devised by Buck (1948), and which constitutes a more elaborate procedure for the exploration of the self-concept. In this test, the subject is required to draw a house, a tree, and a person on separate sheets of paper. In interpreting the results, Buck regards the drawings of the house and the tree, as well as that of the person, as fundamentally self-portraits. Machover and Buck both recommend rather extensive inquiries to help in the interpretation of the drawings, but in both techniques the major interest is in the symbolic content of the drawings themselves. The use of the inquiry represents an acknowledgement that such symbolism often has a highly individual character, so that it is not easy to set up general rules for interpretation. However, one need have little doubt about the meaning of a drawing in which the genital area is left as a gaping hole, with legs oddly disjointed. Such drawings, which are not rare, provide a forceful illustration of Schilder's statement that "we experience our body as united, as a whole, only when the genital level is harmoniously reached."

IDENTIFICATION

The process of formation of the body image passes over, without sharp division, into that of identification. Just as in childhood we examine our bodies, and avidly observe the bodies of other persons for comparison, so we also observe actions and the evidences of feeling. We learn about ourselves not only by experiencing our own actions, but also by experiencing the actions of others, who serve us both as mirrors and as models for imitation. The effectiveness of this vicarious experience seems to depend on the strength of the felt emotional bond with the person observed, and therefore the most important early models are the members of our own family group, who are "close" in both the emotional and physical sense.

For the initial conceptualization of this process, we are again indebted to the genius of Sigmund Freud. It was his insight that instructed us that the most effective disciplining of the child does not take place by instruction, but by the child's unconscious incorporation of the parent image—an image founded partly on reality and partly on fantasy—which then becomes, as "superego," the template of his own conduct. Freud believed that this process was primarily an outcome of the Oedipus situation, and that it was chiefly motivated by the child's fear of hostile retaliation by his powerful parent rival. This theory of Oedipal conflict has been the object of a great deal of skepticism, not only in academic but also in psychoanalytic circles. It was one of the aspects of Freudian theory which both Jung and Adler rejected. It is rejected today by the neo-Freudians, who emphasize the fluidity of family relations in different cultures. However, not even so orthodox a Freudian as Schilder is limited to a narrow interpretation of identification as exclusively a parent-child relationship. He writes:

In identification the individual identifies himself with persons in his actual or imagined surroundings, and expresses his identification in symptoms, whether actions or phantasies. He plays a role, enriches himself by the experiences of others without knowledge of the procedure. The identification takes place with persons whom we admire and with whom we are in love. In the development of infantile sexuality the little boy admires the father and wants to take his place. We may be dealing with a conscious wish. But often this wish will never come to a clear conception. He will only betray it by taking over gestures, habits, and trends of the father, which then become symptoms of identification. Since he does not know about the tendency to take the place of his father, he may not feel changed at all in his conscious personality. The imitation remains again in the unconscious, but it is not so much imitation as taking the place of another person. But the fact that identification is in the unconscious makes it possible to identify with several persons at the same time. We know that in the little boy there are not only tendencies toward identification with the father, though they may predominate, but also tendencies toward identification with the mother. This tendency toward identification with the mother may come into the foreground in cases of homosexuality. But the boy may also identify himself with his nurse, with his uncle, with the footman, and with anyone else in whom he is interested. By identification one may play the part of an enormous number of persons, at the same time. We know that this is not only a possibility, but a psychological fact which is typical in every psychic development.

From this account, we see that the concept of identification is not at all limited by the Oedipal situation. This is not to imply that it is not influenced by it, as we shall see farther on in our discussion.

Although at the opening of this chapter identification was defined as a modeling of the self after ideal figures, this should not be taken to mean that only admired figures are used as objects of identification. We shall soon see that hated or despised figures may also become the objects of unconscious imitation. The young child may also identify himself with an animal. It is not uncommon for parents to be driven to distraction by a daughter's insistence that she is a pony, or a son's insistence that he is a dog. (The child's choice of a model is certainly not accidental. For example, girls seem to be much more likely than boys to imagine that they are ponies, or that they have pony playmates.) In such cases, one may feel sure that there is at least some temporary disturbance in the basic process of identification with the parent, which leads the child into this hostile denial of his membership in the human race. The intensity with which these fantasies are defended attests to the force of the motivation which has created them.

There can be no doubt that the most important aspect of the process of identification is the acceptance of the parent of like sex, by boy or girl, as a model for imitation. Clinical experience supports the conclusion that when a young boy accepts his father, or a young girl accepts her mother, as a suitable model for his or her own development, a favorable condition for healthy personality development is established. When the child, for whatever reason, rejects the like-sexed parent as a model, considerable emotional disturbance is certain to ensue. These generalizations are meant to apply only to children in our own culture, or in other cultures which resemble our own by providing at least equal opportunity for parent-child relationships to develop. It would certainly be foolhardy to attempt to apply them to cultures in which sons had no contact with their fathers, or those in which mothers play a very minimal part in caring for their own children after the immediate nursing period is ended. However, most such cultures do provide a surrogate parent figure, and it seems safe to assume that the identification process is only deflected onto another model, but not otherwise essentially altered. In our own culture, however, the child who is forced to take a substitute model feels himself greatly deprived as a result. This appears most clearly in the cases of orphans and of adopted children. The boy who has not known his father, or the girl who has not known her mother, is likely to feel as if some part of himself or herself remains undefined, even unformed. One instance of the strength of this need appeared in a recent newspaper account of the success of a young man's 20-year search through every state of the union for the father he had never known. The early fantasies about such unknown parents exercise a powerful formative influence of which the person is usually quite unaware. For example, one young man's friendliness for "black sheep" was traced in the counseling process to his unwillingness to accept the idea that his father, who had apparently deserted his mother early in their marriage, was not a worth-while person. Another interesting example of the strength of identification by fantasy is offered by the following case. A college student asked for help in meeting his responsibilities toward his wife, who was supporting him. Discussion revealed that his parents had been divorced when he was about 2½, and that until very recently he had known virtually nothing about his father except what he had heard in the conversations of his mother and grandmother. From them he learned to think of his father as a shiftless and selfish person. Resisting domination by the mother, his self-concept was formed by identification with the fantasy of an irresponsible father. Perhaps the very circumstances which made it possible for him to contemplate a change in himself, and to ask for help in effecting this, was the fact that he had recently discovered to his surprise that his father was a successful and respected businessman in another city.

Schilder alluded, in the lengthy quotation above, to another danger which threatened this boy, and which is not infrequently realized. When a boy is raised in a household of women, and has very little contact with his father or with any effective father surrogate, he may grow up with interests that are predominantly feminine. In extreme cases, this leads to a bewildered feeling that his sex is confused, that he cannot really be male despite the evident maleness of his body. This type of cross-identification is only one of the many avenues to homosexuality. It should not be necessary to point out that such feminization is not an all-or-nothing phenomenon, but exists in many degrees of severity. It is almost inevitable that the boy's early identification shall be directed toward his mother rather than toward his father. Since some degree of feminization is an essential part of education for living in modern society, this is not in itself bad. It is only when circumstances prevent the transition to normal identification with the male parent that the problem of homosexuality arises. The sexual make-up of every individual includes a latent tendency to homosexuality, which may easily become the preferred outlet if the normal development of heterosexual interest is blocked.

Another circumstance which may block the normal development of heterosexual behavior is the child's conscious rejection of the parent of like sex as an object of identification. It is a short step from this to the conscious or unconscious generalization that all men are brutal, or that all women are nagging, and hence to a very determined refusal to accept one's own membership in the hated group. It is one of the most ironic paradoxes in the whole spectrum of human personality that this rejection of one's own sex leads not infrequently to failure to develop the heterosexual attitudes of that sex, and hence in the end to emotional dependence on one's own sex for sexual gratification! The girl's contempt for her mother makes her renounce womanhood, and so she ends by becoming the mistress of another woman! Even in the statistically more likely case that she does enter upon normal heterosexual living, latent homosexual tendencies will have been made relatively more prominent due to the renunciation of her sex. Another, not dissimilar disturbance of identification is the case of the boy who consciously rejects his father as a weakling, and who nevertheless develops a self-concept in which this same weakness is a central and disabling feature. Many of us are able with very little effort to find in our own lives similar evidence of the strength of the process of identification, and of its independence from our conscious control. Though we may not have rejected our parents *in toto,* it is likely that we found some one characteristic much less desirable than others. Through trying to avoid this characteristic in our own behavior, we fix our attention upon it, and develop it even more inevitably than those things which we consciously imitate.

The strength of positive identification with the like-sexed parent, plus the emotional stress of a home filled with dissension, opens a more obvious path to homosexuality, through hatred of the opposite-sexed parent. Even in this case, a full acceptance of the parental model would probably lead to a happier outcome, for the renunciation of love for the other sex is based upon pity for the preferred parent, and a consequent determination not to accept the same role.

Stoke (1950) has listed many factors which influence the course of identification. The purpose of his discussion is to show that this process can be understood without reference to the hypothetical Oedipus situation, in terms of a learning situation which is influenced by the clarity of the precepts involved, the strength and consistency of reinforcement for different kinds of behavior, social prestige factors, and the like. One factor which is of particular interest to us is the degree of similarity in temperament between the child and the model for identification, which makes conformity to the model easy or difficult. However, while acknowledging the effectiveness of all these factors in the total process, we should   not allow them to detract from the importance of the Oedipus situation.

For the child normally experiences all these influences, and the inward repercussions of his own emotional attachments and hostilities, within the setting of a family situation which also provides many restraints upon his actions and upon the expression of his feelings. We do not need to think of the family as fixed in some immutable biological pattern to find within it all the elements of love, jealousy, and hatred which Freud described. In the first period of complete dependency, the mother is inevitably the focus of the infant's emotional responses. In the next period, she becomes also the convenient target for his maturing aggressive impulses, whose exercise implies no diminution of the continuing positive feelings. But then, with the beginning awareness of its own sex role, the boy child recognizes a new appropriateness in his love for the mother, and the girl child recognizes that this kind of appropriateness belongs to her expressions of love for her father. (It is true that most children will continue to profess equal love for both parents, whether the question is put to them by a visiting aunt or as part of a psychological questionnaire. Nevertheless, the clinical evidence seems overwhelming. We may offer the following bit of objective support for this view. When college students are asked to guess who made the remarks that "My mother was a wonderful woman," "My father was a tyrant in the family," and "My father was the kindest man I ever knew," there is a strong concensus that the first two remarks were spoken by men, and the last by a woman.—Diamond, 1955.) At the same time, the child also senses an inappropriateness, an overpretentiousness, in its exercise of this role. There is ambivalence of feeling, a desire and a timidity, with one or the other predominating in the individual case. How sensitive the child must now be to the least sign of disapproval (and what parent so perfect as to show no sign?), how ready to direct all of its hostility against the "rival," how eager to copy the charmed devices that are the secret of the rival's success! Every child wishes to be "a member of the wedding," and senses with resentment the determined exclusion which his parents direct against him. These are the elements of the Oedipal conflict. It does not seem to be stretching the case too much to say that most of this is an inevitable part of each child's experience.

This does not mean that it is a universal pattern which is subject only to rare and minor variations. It is as general as our typical family structure, and this is general enough to set a pattern of expectation for all of us. The child for whom any of the elements of this typical family structure are missing— the adopted child, the institution child, the child in a broken home—is keenly aware of the lack, and provides the missing elements in fantasy. The Oedipus situation of the individual child may only exceptionally correspond in full detail to the pattern which Freud outlined, but it will aways constitute a recognizable variation of this major theme.

The process of identification does not end in early childhood. It plays a continuing part in personality development, as long as the individual remains sufficiently flexible for change. In its later phases, just as in the earliest years, it is guided by the person's own needs, just as much as by external circumstance. The school-age child finds a favorite teacher to supplement his parent ideal where he finds it lacking. The adolescent, in his struggle for individuation, may find the inner sense of identification with his parent even more irksome than the obvious restraints of parental authority. He then readily discovers what he had difficulty in perceiving before, that the gods of his childhood have feet of clay. This rejection of his old images is so essential to further growth, and may be accompanied by such pangs of guilt if it cannot be adequately rationalized, that Blos (1941) is led to exclaim, "Pity the adolescent with understanding parents!" However, the independent young man is by no means ready to be simply himself. He must choose a friend, or a friend's father, or some admired public figure, to serve as his new model.

Although we commonly use the term identification almost exclusively in connection with the child's imitation of certain prominent figures in his social environment, the same process plays a part in virtually every instance of social learning. Mowrer (1950) has hypothesized that it is even present in some instances of learning by animals. The first important step in teaching a parrot to talk, he says, is to make it fond of you; thereafter it will imitate you in your absence, practicing the elements of speech to give itself a fraction of the pleasure it might have from your company. Whether or not this is a valid statement as applied to the parrot, it is an insightful description of an early phase in the learning of speech by human infants. In the child's babbling we hear the intonations of his elders, and in these wordless incoherencies we recognize his determination to become like them. From this time forward, the element of personality growth is present in every learning situation. In the classroom, the child who learns becomes more like teacher, and also more like older children in higher grades. On the playground, he has a chance to become more like some popular athletic hero. At home, he is under pressure to become more like father—or not to become like father. The student of a foreign language has to overcome not only the physical difficulties of learning to make a new set of sounds, but also his resistance to being the foreign-like person who makes such sounds. (A student once offered the following excellent illustration of this point. In his shop, there were many old machinists of German extraction, all rather scornful of the abilities of Americans at their trade, and all talking in heavy accents despite many years in America. But a youngster who had come from Germany six months before, imbued with the idea that Americans could do anything, had dropped almost every trace of accent in that time.) On the other hand, the language arts major who regards his ineptitude in mathematics as an expression of his innate mental structure, must change his self-concept before he can assimilate any mathematical skill. In these and other instances of learning, there is always present at some level of consciousness the desire to be or not to be "that kind of person." The process of identification is therefore the constant accompaniment of learning. We may state with confidence that willing identification is a satisfying form of act reinforcement. It is easier to acquire any act which is describable in terms that we would accept as self-description. Thus the young girl learns to dance more readily than the boy, because she accepts being "graceful" as part of her self-concept, while he does not. With only a shade less confidence, we may state the companion hypothesis that the obsessive thought of being something distasteful to ourselves is likewise reinforcing.

There is a phase of the later history of identification which deserves special mention. This is the phase called transference, when it appears as an aspect of a client-therapist relationship. The name derives from the fact that the attitudes and prestige which were originally attached to the parent figure are displaced or transferred to the therapist. To describe it merely in these terms is an inadequate formulation, for it suggests that the transference blocks a rational, adult approach to the client's problem, and must be removed before any progress can be made. In some forms of therapy at least, quite the opposite is the case! The transference phenomenon creates an emotional climate which is favorable to learning. Whatever learning takes place in therapy must be guided by the patient's sense of identification with the therapist, which is necessarily an echo of the childhood identification with a parent. In therapy, the patient relives the process of identification with a new model, striving this time for a different outcome. The skilful therapist watches this process with awareness, and is sufficiently flexible in his behavior to offer his patient a model suited to his needs.

To explain the phenomena of identification in terms of learning theory is a challenging problem. Miller and Dollard have attempted to do this from the standpoint of Hullian reinforcement theory, in the course of their treatment of *Social Learning and Imitation* (1941). They lay the basis for their argument by demonstrating that rats can be taught to "follow" or "not follow" other rats in order to obtain gratification for their hunger, and that children also can readily be taught to imitate under a variety of conditions. They contend that this is an important aspect of socialization, and they analyze such complex phenomena as crowd behavior and social diffusion as being based on a learned tendency to imitate prestigeful leaders. They make a distinction between two kinds of imitation. When the subject is conscious of the sameness or difference of his response relative to that of his model, the imitative behavior is called copying. They introduce the phrase "matched-dependent behavior" to denote imitative behavior of a more primitive type, in which the follower has a much narrower perspective of the total situation, and is merely conditioned to respond to cues which the leader provides. It is surprising that after having made this distinction they ignore the invariable psychoanalytic insistence that the process of identification is unconscious, and they suggest that copying, rather than matched-dependent behavior, is the key to identification. Then comes the following footnote, which emphasizes their conviction that the entire process can be explained in terms of reinforcement theory:

In this connection, it is interesting to note that psychoanalytic observations seem to indicate that identification is most likely to occur with parents or other loved, prestigeful people. These loved people with prestige are the very ones who control the rewards and punishments which are most important to the child. They are thus in the best position to give acquired reward value to conformity with their behavior, and acquired anxiety value to non-conformity with their behavior. . . .

Such an explanation fails to account for the strength of identification in those cases where the parent is absent, or where the model is otherwise provided by fantasy, or where the child steadfastly resists the influence of the immediate authority figures despite their punitive measures to enforce it. We do not wish to suggest that the problem of identification lies outside the scope of learning theory, but only that it serves to demonstrate the limitations of a learning theory which seeks to explain all fixations as the consequences of tension-reducing reinforcements. These difficulties vanish if we are willing to admit the existence of other kinds of reinforcing states. It is not enough to admit the possibility of self-administered reductions in anxiety level. The facts call here, as in the experimental work on abnormal fixation, for a recognition that there are conditions of high emotional stress which are fixating or reinforcing in their effects. This seems to us to be one of the major keys to a rapprochement of theories derived from experimental and clinical sources.

In this discussion of identification as the central aspect of the development of the self-concept, we have not found it necessary to refer to the part that identification plays in the development of conscience, or a sense of guilt. This is an important by-product of identification, which we will discuss in later chapters. However, it seems to us an error to make this "punishing superego" the basis on which all identification develops. Whiting and Child (1953) suppose that the origin of identification is in the child's need for parental approval, which the parents often withhold. Therefore, the child learns

. . . to substitute self-love for love from others when and if the latter is withheld at a time when the child strongly needs to be loved. The reward of self-love is obtained by imitating the evaluative behavior of the parents, and is provided by the child to itself in conditions in which the parents have provided special indications of love. Under these conditions self-love is thus tied to conformity with cultural rules, for it is conformity rather than non-conformity which has previously led to parental love.

We should like to suggest that the motivation to identification has a different source than the need to avoid punishment or to solicit love. From time to time, as we deal with the problems of personality development—as distinguished from the development of temperament—we shall meet with the concept of self-actualization as a motivating force. Something like this surely arises out of the human child's capacity to wonder about himself. To understand oneself is a hard riddle, even for a child, who might be content with a less-than-book-length answer! He looks to the people around him, who seem so sure of themselves, for hints at the solution. Their voice and posture often echo one's own feelings, or offer taunting reminders of one's own inadequacies. It is good to be loved, but it is also good to be big and powerful and skilled, quite without regard to secondary gains of food and affection. If the infant needs to be loved, then the child also needs, as his aggressive impulses awaken, to be feared, as adults are feared. Add to all this motivation the child's dawning ability to make comparisons, and to think in terms of abstract categories. Slowly, the objects of the world are catalogued into the living and the nonliving, the two-legged and the four-legged, the big and the little, the male and the female. We must leave the closer study of this process to a later chapter, but it is already at work in the child's brain, for all that. There is plenty of reason for obsessive thinking about parents, without being incessantly concerned about retaining their love.

Role Taking

When the formation of the self-concept is explained primarily in terms of identification, there is an implication that a very few personal relationships serve as the instruments by which society shapes a given individual to become one of its own members, different in many ways from the citizens of any other sociocultural group. Social psychologists, as distinguished from clinical psychologists, tend to place greater emphasis on an alternative explanation of this process, which does not ascribe such overwhelming influence to a few conspicuous persons in the child's environment. According to this view, we are molded by the constant, day-by-day experience of the expectations of the people with whom we are in contact. Taken together, such expectations form the definition of a social role. Aunts and uncles expect something different of a boy than of a girl, and so the brother and sister soon learn their separate roles. A boy's mother and his playmates do not expect the same things of him, and soon he learns to act in different ways at home and on the playground. People generally do not expect the same things of the banker's son and the gardener's boy, and before long these different expectations are being justified in actions. All these partial roles fit together, by the logic of the social structure, into a major role or social function which assigns to each individual the part that he must perform in the division of labor that is characteristic of any organized society. Furthermore, the picture we form of ourselves is filled in, line by line, as we perceive what people expect of us, and how well they seem to think we fulfill their expectations. It is in large part, as Cooley (1902) called it, a "looking-glass self," found in the eyes of other persons, which serve us as mirrors. Newcomb (1950) defines the self as "the individual as seen by that individual in a socially determined frame of reference." The expectations that we meet at every moment, whichever way we turn, are like the trees of the social forest, in which we are striving to find ourselves.

Sherif (1936) succeeded in using this social frame of reference—the expectations of the group—as an experimental variable. His subjects thought they were being used in a study of some recondite aspects of the problem of visual perception of movement. Actually, unknown to themselves, the movement they perceived was completely illusory: it was the apparent movement of a stationary pinpoint of light in an otherwise darkened room, which is known as the autokinetic effect. When one observes this light fixedly, it seems to move, but since there are no reference points by which to judge the extent of the movement, estimates will usually be accompanied by a fair degree of subjective uncertainty. With the help of some "stooges" who were instructed to give either higher or lower estimates than those which the subject originally offered, Sherif was able to show that individuals quickly modify their judgments to conform to the expectations of even a casual group. He drew the conclusion that our acceptance of the social norms which regulate our lives derives from the cumulative effect of such experiences.

What Sherif observed in the laboratory, Newcomb (1943) observed in a real life situation. He describes how students who entered the fairly closed community life of a New England college came to accept its dominant values as their own. The study was carried out during depression years, when the atmosphere at this particular college was strongly liberal. The degree to which one "belonged" to this community depended to a great extent on one's active interest in the progressive side of current events. The student daughters of patrician Boston families sometimes spent their week ends on factory picket lines. To earn a diploma, one marched leftward across the campus. In 1936, 62 percent of freshmen and only 15 percent of upper-division students favored the Republican presidential candidate; 9 percent of freshmen and 30 percent of upper-division students favored either the Socialist or the Communist candidate. In this social atmosphere, much of the influence of family training was submerged, and new roles were learned.

In all such situations, individual differences will be conspicuous. Newcomb describes the overall process, but he does not neglect to point out also that many individuals resisted the group pressure, some with and some without awareness. Asch (1951) has recently employed a modification of Sherif's experimental design to test for the quality of independence of judgment. He discarded the illusion, and confronted his subjects with a real test of spatial perception, but each subject found himself a solitary voice for reason, surrounded by a dozen complacent companions who all seemed to agree that black was white—or, in this case, that long was short. Under these conditions, most men can be induced to deny what is evident to their eyes. How-

ever, there are those independent souls who, though they may
fidget with discomfort, still speak the truth as they see it. This
kind of independence, which enables the individual to resist the
pressure of the group with whom he sits, must have its basis
in the strength of the self-concept which he brings into the
room, the result of all his past identification and/or role
acceptances.

The concept of role taking or role acceptance, as we have
defined it and seen it exemplified in the experimental work of
Sherif and of Newcomb, should be clearly distinguished from
the concept of role playing. When a child plays at being a grown
up, he is acting a role, but he is certainly not accepting the
role which is currently defined for him by social expectations.
It is true that such role playing prepares him for his future
role in society, but there may be more of rebellion than of
conformity in its motivation. He is deliberately pretending to
be something other than a mere child—perhaps a policeman,
or a nurse, or a truck driver. His play is not directed by what
others expect of him, but by what he wishes to make of himself,
by discarding the child role for one of greater status. These
aspirations are still unclear, and they exist—to use a very descriptive Lewinian phrase—on a plane of irreality, but they are
nevertheless more vividly present to the child's mind than any
thought of what others expect him to become in future years.

Role playing is actually a form of identification, and it is
a much more active and spontaneous process than role acceptance. It probably plays some part in every form of therapy, as
the patient gains in expressiveness and venturesomeness in
response to the permissive atmosphere of the therapeutic situation. All therapy represents an effort to escape the limitations
of a role that has been found too unrewarding, but the patient
is usually afraid to risk the dangers and embarrassment of
presenting a different face to the world. In the privacy of the
counseling room or the psychiatrist's office, or in the small circle
of a coöperative group, he may venture to exchange the familiar
but distasteful mask for another. This therapeutic use of role

playing has received its fullest elaboration at the hands of Moreno (1946). In the method of psychodrama, which he developed, the patient learns to correct his misperceptions of social relationships, and discovers his own resources of spontaneity, by acting out parts whose general outlines only are prescribed by the psychiatrist-director.

The role concept has stimulated many recent research studies. We shall give space to two examples. Unlike Sherif's ingenious use of a controlled laboratory situation, these represent experimental modifications of the master clinical instrument, the interview.

Rabban (1950) studied the sex role identification of young children. His carefully planned study had 300 subjects, half of whom were drawn from what sociologists call the "upper lower" class, and is more commonly called the working class, while the others came from upper-middle-class families. The preschool children of the first group were attending state-operated day nurseries for the children of working mothers, while those of the other group were enrolled in private nursery schools in a suburban community. Five different age levels were investigated, the lowest averaging 3 years, the highest representing the eighth year. Each child was asked to make six successive choices out of an array of 16 sex-typed toys. They were also asked the question, "When you grow up, would you like to be a mamma or a daddy?" The author states the following conclusions:

1. Boys are more clearly aware of sex-appropriate behavior than are girls in both middle-class and working-class groups.
2. Boys and girls of the working-class group are earlier and more clearly aware of the sex-role pattern than are both boys and girls of the middle-class group. This class difference is especially great between the girls.
3. (a) Three-year-old boys and girls of both groups show incomplete recognition of sex differences and as a group are unaware of any appropriateness of sex-typed toy objects. (b) The fourth and fifth years are periods of growth in clarification of sex role for working-class boys, while the sixth year is particularly significant for middle-class boys. (c) Working-class girls accept the sex-appropriate pattern by 6 years of age, but middle-class girls do not fully acquiesce to the

definition of appropriate sex patterning even by the eighth year, when all other groups have accepted the social expectations.

These conclusions may be questioned in so far as they seem to imply that acceptance of the sex role and awareness of it go hand in hand. The choices made under the permissive conditions of the experiment must at every age be interpreted as expressions of preference rather than knowledge. It is interesting, indeed, that the little daughters of working mothers, whose perception of the sex role must surely be influenced by the fatigue and harassment of their parents, have nevertheless outwardly given up the initial protest against their role long before those whose mothers are leading a more leisurely existence in what Rabban calls "Suburbia." It is possible that this difference reflects a greater tolerance for deviant attitudes and behavior in this sample of upper-middle-class homes, where there was a very high level of general education among the parents. Certainly, further investigation would be necessary before one could feel reasonably sure that this sample gives a true picture of sex-role acceptance in the middle class generally.

Bugental and Zelen (1950) asked their adult subjects to write three short answers to the question, "Who are you?" They designate this procedure as the W-A-Y technique. Answers are classified in a system of empirically derived categories. Name, sex, and occupation are given very frequently, while metaphysical references, descriptions of appearance, and affectively toned comments may serve as examples of some of the less frequently used categories. There is as yet no adequate fund of data to judge the significance of responses to this technique, but it seems safe to speculate that the individual whose answers all fall in popular categories is one who accepts his social role without question, while the answers in less frequent categories point to more individualized features of the self-concept. Here are a few examples of responses received from students in a college class, in which the writer used this technique for demonstration purposes: "I am a member of the Fellowship of

Reconciliation"—"I am a person with a destiny to fulfill, who is unsure of his strength for the task"—"I am the girl William loves."

THE NEO-FREUDIANS

We shall include at this point a brief statement and evaluation of the theories of the neo-Freudian school, concerning the manner in which personality development is influenced by the larger social context. Although they do not conceive of this influence taking place through the mechanism of role taking, there is considerable affinity in the two viewpoints. Both diminish the importance of identification as the dominant force in personality development, and both see the individual as tending to assume a socially defined role, in response to social pressures. In different ways, each of the neo-Freudians strives to define the way in which the particular cultural milieu of a given time, place, and social class exerts its formative influence. The extent to which these theories differ from the role-taking concept will become apparent as we proceed.

Horney's definition of *The Neurotic Personality of Our Time* (1937) is based solely upon a consideration of contemporary culture, and the effects of its pressures, as she observes them in the emotional difficulties of her patients. She is led to believe that the competitiveness of modern society fosters interpersonal hostilities and emotional isolation of the individual even within his own family. She believes that Freud placed too much emphasis on biological determinants of behavior, because he lacked an adequate understanding of these sociological factors. From our own point of view, we must add a reminder that Horney is at least equally guilty of neglect of the deep biological roots of competitiveness, which we studied in the earlier chapters. She also seems insufficiently aware of the fact that competitiveness is hardly a distinguishing characteristic of contemporary Western civilization, since it exists in all societies, although it takes different forms of expression. Where it is least obvious on the surface, as among the Zuni and Hopi Indians of the south-west, this is only because the culture has developed efficient controls for its suppression. The picture which these cultures present is not an absence of competitiveness, but universality of self-control, which eliminates competition from public view. This is not at all the same thing as a simple absence of com-petition because the culture has not fostered it, which is what Horney apparently believes would be the case. It is certainly necessary to study in concrete detail the interaction of social pressures and biological dispositions, but one should not leave either of these sets of determinants out of account.

Fromm (1941, 1947) has a broader perspective, and though he finds essentially the same faults in contemporary civilization, he recognizes that the problem is rooted in man's nature and in economic necessities, and is not an artifact of modern times. The very names of the character types which he describes— the Exploitative, the Hoarding, the Marketing, the Productive— show how his attention, like Horney's, is focused more upon the adult world than that of the child. He regards these character types as forms of adaptation to the competitive socioeconomic organization. In the Oedipal situation, the child struggles against parental authority as a representative of irrational authority generally, the element of sexual rivalry being altogether sec-ondary. Under these conditions, all psychiatry is merely palliative, and true health can be attained only by the establishment of a society in which man's potential for moral and coöperative conduct can be realized. In modern life, the very norm is a mass neurosis.

Ansbacher (1953) has pointed out that these theories bear an essential resemblance to those of Alfred Adler (1917, 1933), who also rejected Freudian views as inadequate from a socio-logical standpoint. Adler's thinking was undoubtedly influenced to a great extent by social-democratic political theory. He felt that the fostering of competition accentuates the effects of neurotic inadequacy, and that the cultivation of social interest and truly coöperative attitudes is an important aspect of therapy. He saw the origins of the neurotic power drive in the inevitable inferiority of the young child, which gives rise to compensatory efforts to gain a position of strength and superiority. Since this experience is inescapable, there is need for a wise educational program to overcome its effects. Mental health must be gained by education, and not simply by economic reform. The function of the therapist is to provide such education.

The teachings of Fromm and Horney, as well as those of Adler, lead directly to an emphasis in therapy on the immediate social relationships in which a patient is involved and in which he experiences difficulties. This is quite different from the Freudian expectation that any improvement in adjustment which is more than superficial must be based upon the uncovering of the emotional entanglements of the early family constellation.

Like Horney and Fromm, Kardiner also feels that Freud's orientation was too exclusively biological. He differs from them, however, and remains close to Freud, in that he still places great emphasis on the importance of infant experience in shaping what he calls the basic personality structure—a constellation of traits which are shared by all the members of a culture by virtue of the similarity of their very early experience. (See page 201.)

We may summarize the viewpoint of the neo-Freudians as follows. They believe that typical character or personality traits are developed in the members of a given social group, not as a result of any imitative process, but as a common form of response to environmental conditions. Sons grow up to be like fathers, not because of identification with them, and not as a result of training in role behaviors, but because they have been subjected to like influences of the same cultural milieu. It is a doctrine which has an optimistic aspect, since it suggests the possibility that through improvement of social conditions we may effect real improvement in our children, even though we cannot succeed in remaking ourselves.

Alexander (1952), who has sometimes been classified as a neo-Freudian because he shares the belief that Freud gave inadequate attention to sociological factors, nevertheless criticizes all the members of this group because they "underestimate the specific influence of the parental personalities." We concur in this judgment. The neo-Freudians have drawn our attention to important factors which had been neglected, but they have been too extreme in their rejection of the part played by the parent figures, that is, the process of identification.

The Self in Field Theory

Lewin gave a good deal of attention to the question of how the person's self-concept is influenced by his own perception of his membership status in different social groups. His discussions of the psychological problems of members of minority groups, and of those interstitial or displaced members of society who are uncertain to which groups they truly belong, are couched in the terms of his topological system, with which we made some acquaintance in the last chapter. In this system, the many groups to which a person belongs are represented as overlapping regions of his life space—overlapping to the extent that they include like groups of people. Adjacent to these are other groups in which he has potential membership. Farther removed are groups of whose existence he is aware, but which are or appear to be firmly closed to him. These regions are more or less sharply differentiated from each other, and they offer more or less opportunity for entrance or escape across their boundaries. Different degrees of valence also attach to them, for membership in some groups may be highly desired, while membership in other groups may seem a reason for shame and discomfort. These articles (1948) provided an important impetus to the study of the psychological problems of minority groups, which is now a brilliant facet in the work of American social psychologists.

In this construction, the perceived social structure is directly taken over as a part of the internal structure of the person. A diagram of the person, and a diagram of the world in which he moves, as it is perceived by him, are essentially the same. As the person matures, his self-concept becomes more complex, for maturation—as we remember from the last chapter—is also represented as a process of differentiation. Bit by bit, the child recognizes his membership in family, sex, nation, social class, and the like. Before reaching adulthood, he learns to think of himself as belonging to many other groups. Ultimately he may be a veteran, a Rotarian, a lover of Shakespeare, a gourmet, a Democrat, and a thousand other things. There may be no other man who has just this combination of belongingnesses, but this may be his only claim to uniqueness. There is not a bit of him which does not represent a sharing of social roles. A characteristically Lewinian aspect of this field-theoretical analysis of the self in terms of vectors and topology is that it can be made entirely in terms of the person's present affiliations and aspirations. These have a history, but it need not be taken into account in explaining present behavioral tendencies. This is of course in sharp contrast to the childhood-oriented concept of identification.

INTROVERSION

The self-concept, in all of the aspects which we have discussed, is important in every personality. However, its formation is largely a result of unconscious processes, and individuals differ greatly with respect to the degree to which their own acts, feelings, and attitudes become the objects of their conscious attention. Jung's term, introversion, seems like an appropriate designation for this important variable in human behavior, and it is reasonable that we should try to measure people on a scale of introversion, that is, that we should try to determine whether behavior of this type is strongly or weakly developed in the individual case. In his effort to define this dimension, Jung made the assumption that it must be bipolar, with extraversion as the opposite of introversion. (Cf. page 159.)

The reciprocal relationship of introversion and extraversion was disputed by Rorschach (1921, 1942). He used the terms *introversive* and *extratensive,* in order to emphasize that these do not represent states or conditions, but tendencies to certain ways of acting or perceiving. The terms introversion and extraversion, he said, should be reserved to designate conditions of pathological dominance of one of these tendencies over the other. He maintained that introversive and extratensive tendencies should not be thought of as opposites, but as two quite different forms of mental activity, "as different as thinking and feeling." It is quite possible, according to this conception, to be at the same time highly introversive and highly extratensive, or, on the other hand, to have a poverty in both kinds of experience. He described the very restricted (coarctated) individual as suffering from incapacities in both directions, while persons of great talent, who are simultaneously both creative and skilful, rate high in both.

With such a concept of introversive tendency, there is less likelihood to confuse it, in the way that has been so general, with neurotic tendency. Nevertheless, one must be prepared to face the problem of explaining the frequent association in a single syndrome of introversive self-preoccupation, emotional instability, and timidity in dealing both with things and with people. There is good reason to believe that the force which converts the initial capacity for self-study, which is the foundation for so much that is distinctively human, into the frequent correlate of neurotic tendency, is the fear of one's own unworthiness, a subject which is reserved for the next chapter. Although introversive and extratensive behavior do often show a roughly reciprocal relationship, this is no proof that they are polar opposites. Let us say, rather, that the individual is introversive to the extent that he consciously utilizes the distinctively human capacity for self-conceptualization, and extratensive to the degree that he develops interests in things outside himself. However, the mention of "interests" is an allusion to a whole new aspect of personality, which we are not yet ready to discuss. We must give our attention first to the ways in which the self-concept is defended. When this defense becomes too preoccupying, then indeed the extratensive side of the personality will be limited in its development.

CHAPTER 12

Defense of the Self-Concept

*T*he self-concept is a blend of fiction and reality. Wishes, misconceptions, and distortions enter into it easily, and are removed with utmost difficulty. A young man may come to his college counseling center and say with evident sincerity, "I would like to take a series of tests to find out what kind of work I am best suited for,"—but the counselor knows that taking the tests and learning the scores will be a very small part of any significant reappraisal that may take place. This is not to say that the self-concept does not undergo change. It is changing all the time, partly from obsolescence as we grow older, partly by the reluctant acknowledgement of our limitations, often happily by recognition of virtues we had not previously suspected in ourselves. It changes in response to many different influences, but logic plays a minor part in the process. It changes mostly on the periphery, as if its parts were inventoried and storaged on a "last in, first out" basis, which makes it hard to get down to the original elements at the bottom of the stockpile. There, under many layers, lies an old and probably quite irrational concept of the self which is highly resistant to change. Ask a young man if he would rather be changed into a stallion or a woman, and you aim a question very close to the heart of the system.

We are not all equally comfortable in our self-concepts, but none of us would find it easy to shed this garment, and to stand up quite naked in the public gaze to receive a fresh appraisal. If the young man who came asking for tests could be quite honest, he might say: "I would like to take some tests, to see if I cannot patch up my self-concept where it has been wearing thin." Or perhaps (since we often find it necessary to cling to our faults as well as our virtues, if we are to go on being comfortable with our Selves) he might say instead: "I would like to take some tests, so I can show my folks that I really don't have the brains to do everything that they expect out of me." In either case, it is evident that he is under some strong environmental pressure to revise his self-concept. That being the case, it is possible that with wise guidance—and a minimum of testing—he may be helped to change it in such a way that it will conform more closely to reality, and hence become even a more comfortable garment than the old one.

The young man may be quite sincere in his conscious intention to learn the truth about himself, and to face up to it squarely, and yet have a great deal of difficulty in assimilating the implications of such relatively simple matters as aptitude and achievement scores, let alone such complex matters as why he can't seem to carry on a civil conversation with his father. There are "resistances" within him, which make him very obtuse to any implication that his self-concept is mistaken.

In the present chapter, we wish to study first certain aspects of the self-concept itself, in which this incessant struggle of the self to maintain itself unchanged in the face of the critique of reality is especially clear. These are, first, the self-esteem, and second, the level of aspiration. In the latter part of the chapter, we shall consider the many different devices or "mechanisms"— a Freudian term—to which we may resort in the defense of the self-concept. Since so much of this defense is carried on below the level of consciousness, we shall have to include also a brief discussion of what we mean when we speak of thinking as "conscious" or "unconscious."

SELF-ESTEEM

From its very beginnings, the self-concept is not merely descriptive, but also evaluative. The parent-ideal is not only a model but also a standard, and for the young child the discrepancy between this standard and his own feeble potential appears to be insurmountable. At this time, feelings of inadequacy and inferiority are indeed, as Adler (1933) pointed out, normal and inevitable. Whether they persist into later childhood, and extend their paralyzing effect even into adulthood, depends primarily on whether there is a sufficient experience of successful achievement and of acceptant approval by others, at an age before the feeling of inferiority has been deeply entrenched. Or, stated in the terms that we have used earlier, it depends on whether the early experience of these feelings is accompanied by anxiety-provoking, frustrating events that would "fix" them as feeling habits. If this does not take place, if the child meets acceptance rather than rejection, the phase will be a transient one. For, although the child's initial helplessness predisposes him to feelings of inferiority, an antidote is soon offered in the form of his awakening aggressiveness. The child's initial sense of weakness and inadequacy is the proper complement to the complete dependency of his earliest years, but by the middle of the third year he is ready to hold a chip upon his shoulder— if the world does not shake its finger too threateningly at him. This new aggressiveness leads him into dominance-testing behavior which is quite like that of the chimpanzee. He tries to stand his ground against small animals, just as Gua and Viki did, and he is very appreciative of a pet in relation to which he can feel big and powerful.

Thus the roots of a positive self-esteem, a healthy sense of his own worth and strength, are provided in the child's natural pattern of growth. It is necessary only that this development should not be crushed while it is still a tender growth. It seems a reasonable assumption that the continuance of a warm, permissive, acceptant social environment is favorable to the development of a healthy positive self-esteem, while a critical, judgmental, rejecting environment—which meets every playful sign of challenging aggression with a cold rebuff and a reminder of weakness—fosters the development of negative, self-derogatory feelings of inferiority, unworthiness, and guilt. We think of this first as a matter of parental acceptance, but this is not the whole story. We must be alert to the kinds of social interaction among children which tend to parallel those conditions which give rise in litters of rats and of dogs to dominance hierarchies that have timid and victimized scapegoats on their bottom rungs.

The early history of self-esteem therefore offers an interesting example of the interaction of maturing temperamental dispositions and social influences. The latter, needless to say, are themselves not constant. As the child outgrows his original babylike proportions and locomotor awkwardness, he becomes less and less a "releaser" for nurturant attitudes in adults, and faces an increasing exposure to whatever forms of discipline the culture prescribes or sanctions. Stoke (1950) recognizes the part that native aggressiveness plays in this interaction, in the following passage:

> Given parents who reject a child, the response of the child will be determined in considerable part by its own temperament. Vigorous children . . . react aggressively toward those who reject them. Less vigorous, outgoing children may attempt to hide their hurts and simply withdraw from the reality of the situation as far as is compatible with other conditions.

Maslow (1939) even more explicitly recognizes the essential relationship between dominance and self-esteem. He distinguishes between dominance behavior and dominance feeling, making the former more or less synonymous with learned social adjustments in face-to-face situations, while the latter represents the temperamental component of dominance behavior. He says that dominance feeling is virtually identical with self-esteem. This analysis is based upon an experimental study of the relations between measures of social dominance and self-esteem in college women.

The defense of the self-concept may be observed to operate in the building of psychological theories as well as in other fields of human endeavor. One of its most interesting repercussions is the reluctance of psychologists to recognize the reality of innate aggressivity, because this does not fit our own concept that we are really, through-and-through, utterly nurturant and coöperative persons. The consequence is that we are unable to recognize the positive contributions of this disposition, of which positive self-esteem is one. On the one hand, we are led to believe that the primary source of self-esteem is in the opinions of others, as if we were by nature so modest that we cannot think well of ourselves except by acceding to the generous appraisals of our friends. On the other hand—and this is the more serious distortion—we are led to suspect that all our self-aggrandizing feelings arise as compensations for our initial feeling of small-ness—that there can be no "feeling of superiority" except as the expression of a deeper-lying feeling of inferiority. Although there are certainly a great many cases in which this Adlerian theory is applicable, we should not deny the possibility that feelings of self-satisfaction may grow directly out of our positive achievements. To illustrate how prevalent this tendency is, let us juxtapose two passages from Erikson (1950). Early in his book (on page 83), he describes the period in which we are now interested, the end of the third year, in the following terms:

> The *intrusive mode* dominating much of the behavior of this stage characterizes a variety of configurationally "similar" activities and fantasies. These include the intrusion into other bodies by physical attack; the intrusion into other people's ears and minds by aggressive talking; the intrusion into space by vigorous locomotion; the intrusion into the unknown by consuming curiosity.

He goes on to suggest that a key word to characterize the tendency of this, period would be "'making' in the sense of 'being on the make.'" For, he says, "the word suggests head-on attack, enjoyment of competition, insistence on goal, pleasure of conquest."

Much later, on page 360, we read:

Every adult, whether he is a follower or a leader, a member of a mass or of an elite, was once a child. He was once small. A sense of smallness forms a substratum in his mind, ineradicably. His triumphs will be measured against this smallness, his defeats will substantiate it. The questions as to who is bigger and who can do or not do this or that, and to whom—these questions fill the adult's inner life far beyond the necessities and the desirabilities which he understands and for which he plans.

There is nothing wrong in this passage, except for the implication that the original basis for enjoyment of triumphs—the satisfaction in head-on attacks, competition, and pleasure of conquest—has been forgotten. The "smallness" phenomenon is true of all of us in some degree, and of some of us in great degree, but so too is the pleasure of conquest, and the rise in our self-esteem which stems directly from it. Many children enjoy these satisfactions in competitive sports. Without forgetting the caution that we expressed a few paragraphs earlier, about the need to protect children who are in danger of becoming underdogs, we must also preserve these opportunities for self-inflation. Those of us who wish to diminish them should ask themselves whether, besides their concern for the losers, they are not also engaging in the defense of *their* self-concept.

The continuing dependence of self-esteem on temperamental factors is underlined by the instances of sharply deviant behavior which have a clearly physiological basis. In manic psychosis, the patient is elated and self-satisfied; in depressive psychosis, he is overwhelmed by the sense of his utter worthlessness. Many persons of cycloid temperament undergo less extreme swings, exhibiting tendencies sometimes toward one and sometimes toward the other direction, while staying within the bounds of normality. We may all experience something of the same kind in the effect of a bad cold on one day, or a buoyant sense of good health on another. These things remind us that we do not see ourselves exclusively through the eyes of others.

It is an important empirical fact that low self-esteem is frequently associated with feelings of sexual inadequacy and with guilt over masturbation or sexual desires. It could hardly be otherwise, when we remember how important the problems of sex role and parental status are as aspects of identification, how much needless worry is attached to the process of masturbation, and to what extent sex is used in our culture as virtually a synonym for sin. Often it appears as if low self-esteem is no more than a minor symptom of the deeper anxiety associated with the whole sexual area, but even in these cases one must acknowledge that the sexual disturbance is at least aggravated by the presence of feelings of inadequacy that have other origins. Impotence (defined solely as inability to carry out the sexual act because of anxiety in the situation, and without any reference to fertility) is a psychic mutilation which, like any physical mutilation, will usually act as a handicapping deterrent to any activity whatever, but will occasionally lead to an extraordinary mobilization of compensating effort. In either case, whatever course of action is taken will be in the service of the paramount need to defend the self-concept. Whether the individual shrinks into the shadows or fights his way into the limelight, his actions will be intended to keep the world from suspecting this vital defect.

For many persons in our society, an important source of self-derogation is the impact of hostile and discriminatory attitudes which are directed against ethnic groups to which they belong. These attitudes, which are unfortunately so widespread, lead to the formation of popular stereotypes which attribute undesirable characteristics to the members of many minority groups (cf. Allport, 1954). Within our own country, the American Negro is the most conspicuous victim of such misjudgment. There is a naïve popular belief that the major source of intergroup frictions, including such prejudices, is a general tendency which all of us have to believe in the superiority of the particular group to which we belong. This belief is based on giving too much credence to surface protestations. There is abundant experimental and clinical evidence to show that the members of minority groups that are the objects of hostile discrimination unconsciously tend to accept this majority opinion as valid, and incorporate it into their self-concepts. Clark and Clark (1940) showed that even very young Negro children place a high value on light skin color, when they are given a choice of dolls to play with, and the darker children are especially likely to make such escapist responses. Kardiner and Ovesey (1951) have shown the deleterious effects of this process on personality development in clinical case studies of Negro patients. Sherif (1948) states the conclusion that "a great many members of groups to whom are attributed certain 'traits' to justify their low position come to accept, in time, stereotyped characterizations of themselves." The mechanism by which this self derogation is brought about brings us back again to the phenomenon of identification. The social degradation of the parent figures undermines their value to the child as objects of identification, and thus interferes with optimal personality development.

SELF-ESTEEM AND CLIENT-CENTERED THERAPY

The importance of self-esteem as a factor in personal adjustment has received a great deal of attention from the client-centered (or nondirective) school of counseling. As is well known, this school originated with the work of Carl Rogers (1942), who maintained that in so far as practicable the course of therapy should be controlled in its minor details as well as in its broader aspects by the patient rather than the therapist. Rogers introduced certain important technical innovations (most notably: the "reflection of feeling") which made it possible for the counselor to assume this nondirective role, by systematically stimulating the patient to more active participation in the therapeutic interview. The influence of his views has served to draw the attention of clinicians generally away from themselves, and toward their clients. Of course, they were always concerned with the client's *problem,* but not with the client's efforts to resolve it. Before the influence of Rogers had been felt, the report of a series of therapeutic interviews would usually contain little more than the history of the problem, as it had been unearthed in the therapeutic process. The focus of attention was the interpretive ingenuity of the therapist. Now this focus was shifted to the client's utterances, and especially to the feelings expressed in them, more than to their content. Fittingly, Rogers and his co-workers also introduced the practice of electronic recording of interviews, which made the content of the interview much more amenable to scientific analysis, since it was no longer influenced by the selective note taking of the therapist himself.

This is the background for a series of important researches in which the self-attitudes of the clients have been the objects of study. True to the general principles of the client-centered school, little attention has been given to the source of these attitudes. The approach is almost purely phenomenal, dealing with the here and now. Raimy (1948) analyzed the verbatim records of a number of series of counseling interviews which were judged to have been successful in their outcomes, and he compared them with others that were judged not to have been successful. He concluded that the progress of personality "growth," as it takes place in successful therapy, can be described as a movement from negative, rejectant attitudes toward the self to more positive, acceptant attitudes toward the self. This result was a highly satisfying one, since it could be taken as an endorsement of the client-centered counselor's effort always to be permissive, nonjudgmental and acceptant—goals which he believes his technique permits him to attain more fully than is possible by any other therapeutic technique. Sheerer (1949), analyzing a new group of records, confirmed Raimy's finding, and she went on to indicate that as the self-concept changes in a positive direction, toward increasing self-acceptance, parallel changes take place in the attitude toward others. Thus the client not only feels better about himself, but he also modifies his attitude toward others in ways that will make it easier for him to enter into satisfying social relationships. (This parallelism between self-derogation and the derogation of others has also been suggested by clinically oriented studies of prejudice, and may be based on the mechanisms of "projection" and "displacement" which we shall consider later in this chapter.) Pursuing this idea, Phillips (1951) constructed a questionnaire which included some items concerned with attitude toward the self and other items concerned with attitude toward others. His test included such items as these:

I find it hard to accept some minority group members as equals.

One soon learns to expect very little of other people.

I feel inferior as a person to some of my friends.

I think I would be happier if I didn't have certain limitations.

He gave this questionnaire to several groups of high school and college students, and in each group he found a moderately high positive correlation between the score for self-esteem and the score for attitudes of respect toward others.

These results and others of the same character have led Rogers (1951a) to restate his theory of client-centered therapy. He now bases it on a general theory of personality and behavior in which the growth of the self-concept occupies a central position. He presents this theory in a series of 19 propositions. It will suffice for our purposes to quote four of these (actually, numbers 9, 16, 17, and 18):

As a result of interaction with the environment, and particularly as a result of evaluational interaction with others, the structure of the self is formed—an organized, fluid, but consistent perceptual pattern of perceptions of characteristics and relationships of the "I" or the "me," together with values attached to these concepts. . . .

Any experience which is inconsistent with the organization of structure of self may be perceived as a threat, and the more of these perceptions there are, the more rigidly the self-structure is organized to maintain itself. . . .

*Under certain conditions, involving primarily complete absence of
any threat to the self-structure, experiences which are inconsistent
with it may be perceived, and examined, and the structure of the self
revised to assimilate and include such experiences. . . .*

*When the individual perceives and accepts into one consistent and
integrated system all his sensory and visceral experiences, then he is
necessarily more understanding of others and is more accepting of
others as separate individuals.*

The first of the propositions which we have quoted states the
simple fact that a self-concept is formed; the second, that it is
defended; the third, that this defense may be relaxed in the
nonjudgmental atmosphere of the client-centered counseling
session; and the fourth, that one phenomenon which will result
from such relaxation is the greater tolerance of others which has
been noted in several of the investigations which we have just
reviewed.

Rogers (1951b) also shows how it is possible to measure shifts
in the self-concept, as a means of evaluating the progress of
therapy. It will be worth while for us to look in some detail at
the method which he uses for this purpose, because the same
basic procedure is being applied in an increasing number of
researches in the field of personality. The client, a young woman,
was asked to describe herself in terms of 150 prepared statements,
such as the following:

I have all the assurance and self-confidence I need.

I sort of only half believe in myself.

Most of my problems revolve around dealing with people.

To me life is interesting, rich, and colorful.

The method by which such a set of statements can be used
to obtain a useful description of the person was introduced by
Stephenson (1935, 1953), and is called the Q-sort. Each statement is written on a card, and the subject is instructed to sort
the cards into a series of piles, ranging from those which seem
most true about himself to those which seem most untrue about
himself. He is also told how many piles to make, and exactly
how many cards to place in each pile. Perhaps just two cards

are to be placed in each of the extreme piles, just five in each of the next adjacent piles, etc. The middle pile will be the largest, and will contain those statements about which the subject feels most uncertain, or which seem least relevant. Thus the cards will have been distributed into an approximately normal distribution—a very different result from what we obtain if we simply ask for judgments of "true" and "false." If we use nine piles, each trait may now be given a score of 0 to 8, and if we have two such Q-sorts, we may compute a correlation between them. Indeed, if we have many such correlations we may use them as the basis of a factor analysis. Since the correlations are between persons, and not between tests, this is often called an inverse factor analysis. However, we are not now concerned with this aspect of Q-technique. We are interested only in the fact that it is possible to measure the degree of similarity between two different sortings of the same cards, and express this as a coefficient of correlation. The different sortings may be for different persons, or they may represent different opinions about the same person.

Now to return to Rogers' illustration. Before therapy had begun, the client was asked to sort these statements in two different ways: first, to form a description of herself as she was, and again, to form a description of the kind of person she would like to be. At these initial sortings, the correlation between the "self" and the "self-ideal" was .18, indicating only slight resemblance. At the conclusion of therapy, after 31 interviews, the client repeated this process, and this time the correlation was .81, indicating a very strong resemblance. The self-ideal had changed, but not radically. The principal change was in the self-concept, for the initial self and the terminal self correlated .15, while the initial self and the terminal self-ideal had zero correlation. Evidently, the client thinks of herself as changed, and as being much more the kind of person she wants to be. (Other applications of this general method are to be found in Rogers and Dymond, 1954.)

INSIGHT

This evaluation of the effects of therapy in terms of alteration of the self-concept brings us face to face with the problem of insight: the correctness of the self-concept. How do we know whether the client has really changed in the ways that she indicates? From one point of view this does not matter. Her feelings of change and her reduced unhappiness with herself are worth while in themselves, and they may be expected to lead to positive changes in behavior even if the reported changes are still largely illusory. However, the accuracy of the self-percept is often a matter of importance. The Q-technique has been used in another recent study which throws some light upon it.

Friedman (1955) has compared the "self," the "self-ideal," and the "projected self" of normal, psychoneurotic, and psychotic subjects. The self and the self-ideal were obtained in the manner that we have just described, using a collection of statements about persons which had been taken out of typical stories which are told in the Thematic Apperception Test—a test in which the subject is shown a series of pictures, and is required to use each one as the basis of a short story (Murray et al., 1943). In addition, the investigator himself sorted these same statements to represent a projected self for each subject, on the basis of a reading of the stories which that subject told in the Thematic Apperception Test. For the normal self, all three sortings—the phenomenal self, the ideal self, and the projected self—showed substantial resemblance. For the neurotic subjects, only the phenomenal and projected selves showed resemblance. This indicates a reasonable accuracy in self-perception on their part, although low self-esteem is shown by the lack of resemblance to the ideal self. Most of the psychotic subjects, who were suffering from paranoid schizophrenia, were like the normals in that they described themselves as resembling their own self-ideals. However, there was no resemblance between these and the projected self, leading to the important conclusion that their positive self-esteem is based upon an unrealistic perception of themselves.

Most studies of insight have been concerned not so much with assessing it in the individual as with demonstrating the part that it plays in personal adjustment by means of group comparisons. In the following paragraphs we shall look at a few examples of such research.

Wright (1944) investigated the degree of insight shown by high school students who were asked to rate themselves on a large number of traits. Lack of realism appeared in the fact that on the average only about 11 percent placed themselves in the least desirable fifth of the class distribution for the various traits. This tendency to overrating of the self was by no means uniform for all the traits considered. Only about 1 percent put themselves in the bottom fifth of the class with respect to honesty. This is no accident, for it is only with the help of this fiction that they can take any subjective profit from all their other misrepresentations. On the other hand, 32 percent gave themselves this low rating with respect to the ability to speak up in class. If the same trend to overestimation of the self operates here as elsewhere, we must assume that even a larger proportion of students feel themselves at a marked disadvantage in this area. This comes as no surprise to the counselor, who over and over again has the experience of listening to students who put up a good front to their families and their classmates, but in confidence express the fear that no one is quite so hopelessly inadequate and miserable as themselves.

Taylor and Combs (1952) tested the hypothesis that children with relatively good emotional adjustment should be able to face up to their shortcomings more honestly than those who were emotionally disturbed. They found confirming evidence in the fact that when school children were classified as well adjusted or poorly adjusted on the basis of answers to a personality inventory, it was the well-adjusted group which was more ready to admit to various kinds of misconduct.

Norman (1953) carried out an unusually extensive study of the relationship between the ratings which a person gives to himself on personality variables and the ratings which he receives from others. He took his basic data from the Veterans Administration research project for the assessment of clinical psychologist trainees (Kelly and Fiske, 1951). In this project, groups of trainees (about 20 at a time) lived together closely for a week, during which time they took an extensive battery of psychological tests. They were rated on a variety of traits by highly trained observers, who had access to the test results. They all rated themselves and one another on the same traits. In addition, each trainee received an "acceptance" score, which indicated his relative status and popularity in the group on the basis of a series of sociometric judgments. From a study of the correlations among these different kinds of ratings, Norman arrived at the following conclusions, which give further support to the view that self-acceptant attitudes are an important aspect of personal adjustment:

> There is a positive significant correlation between the degree of acceptance by other individuals and insight into oneself. . . . There is a positive significant relationship between insight into oneself and realistic perception of others. . . . Those with highest acceptance significantly overestimate others in comparison to their peers' ratings of others. We have postulated that a high degree of acceptance is related to a generous appraisal of others because there is also a generous appraisal of self.

It should hardly be necessary to state, particularly with Friedman's results on psychotic lack of insight so freshly in mind, that these results should not be interpreted as negating the obvious truth that overestimation of the self may also be a symptom of maladjustment. Frenkel-Brunswik (1951) describes two girls included in the California Adolescent Growth Study who illustrate the opposite types of error in self-appraisal. Their histories also serve to show how self-derogation and excessive self-approbation both tend to correct themselves as better adjustment is achieved. In this study, the children involved were studied over a period of years, and there were repeated assessments of behavior. One of the girls is described as talkative and attention-seeking. Early in the study she rated herself high in popularity, but her schoolmates gave her low ratings on this scale. Toward the end of the study, with increasing insight and clearer social perception, she began to rate herself lower, and at the same time she modified her behavior so that she rose in the ratings of others. The other girl, on the contrary, was judged by others to be good looking and received highest ratings on popularity, yet she thought herself to be plain and unpopular. As time went on, she did in fact lose some of her early popularity, but she continued to be rated more favorably by others than by herself. It was true of both cases that greater insight led to improved personal adjustment.

LEVEL OF ASPIRATION

An essential aspect of the self-concept is the appraisal of our capacity for achievement. Through the trick of identification, the child may escape the full burden of his inadequacy and assume in his imagination some of the power of the parent figure. Reality, however, brings a steady succession of challenging situations which enforce continuous revaluation. His own aggressiveness and the pressure of social incentives—a pressure which varies in form and strength in different cultures, and according to many special circumstances—urge him to strive for achievement and recognition. To enjoy the exhilaration of success, he must set himself goals that are within his capacity to achieve. To escape the consequences of failure, he must limit the scope and height of his ambition. The subjective aspect of this goal-setting behavior is called the level of aspiration.

Lewin and his co-workers have distinguished themselves in both the theoretical formulation and the experimental investigation of this aspect of the self-concept, but many other workers have added to a very extensive literature on the subject.

Hoppe (1930), a student of Lewin's, demonstrated that the experience of success or failure cannot be defined solely by the objective difficulty of a task and an objective evaluation of the outcome. The subject's expectations are an essential element. The thrill of success cannot come from completion of a task that seems too easy, nor the disappointment of failure from lack of completion of one that seemed unreasonably difficult. Success and failure, as subjective experiences, are relative to the individual's own expectations of achievement. This pioneer investigation only served to give a preliminary definition to the problem: how do people set their goals, or aspirations?

The subjective importance of personal goal setting had been recognized years before by William James (1890), when he said that for a man who had set his heart on being the world's champion prize fighter, to be second best was bitter defeat. "That he is able to defeat the whole population of the globe minus one is nothing; he has 'pitted' himself to beat that one; and as long as he doesn't do that nothing else counts." James goes on to define self-esteem as the ratio of success to pretensions, and he wisely recommends diminishing the denominator in this proportion as an easier means of raising its value than increasing the numerator!

The general method that has been used in level of aspiration experiments has been to assign some unfamiliar task, which is or appears to be a learnable skill, and to ask the subject between successive trials what score he expects to make on the next. Often the situation is given a competitive character, and the subject is told that he will not get credit for any achievement in excess of his stated goal, but that if he fails to attain the goal he will get no credit at all. One favorite task has been dart throwing; another is a kind of modified shuffleboard called the Rotter board, after the experimenter who introduced it (Rotter, 1942). Group experiments have used ordinary tests in school subjects, as well as a variety of paper-and-pencil tasks such as cancelation of letters, tracing maze patterns, and the like. In the analysis of the results, attention is usually not given to the absolute goal, but to the discrepancy score, that is, the difference between the individual's stated goal for each trial and his just preceding achievement. However, many other measures have been suggested, in the effort to quantify what is obviously a very complex phenomenon.

Frank (1935) pointed to three principal factors which influence the setting of goals: the need to keep the goal high enough to maintain self-respect, the need to conform to reality, and the need to avoid the experience of failure. In other words, our aspirations simultaneously express the striving for an ego ideal, the acceptance of reality, and the capacity for tolerance of frustration. The general pattern which has appeared in work with normal subjects, and which has been accepted as typical of well-adjusted individuals in our own culture, is the tendency to fix a goal slightly above the level of achievement. For example, Pauline Sears (1940) studied the level of aspiration of school children, using tasks that were like classroom exercises. She found that children who were generally successful in their school work conformed to the expected pattern, but those who were generally unsuccessful set goals that were either too high or too low.

Irrational goal setting is a frequent characteristic of persons who have a poor adjustment to reality. Cohen (1950) has defined 12 different patterns which may appear in the setting of aspiration levels. Along one dimension, he distinguishes between tendencies to goal setting considerably above the achievement level, within the range of achievement, and well below achievement. On another dimension, he defines four different forms of responsiveness to the immediate experiences of success and failure. Those who pay no attention to these experiences are called rigid; those who tend to raise their goals after failure and lower them after success are called arbitrary; those who are moderately responsive to these experiences, but in the expected direction, are called flexible; and those who are very strongly influenced by these momentary experiences are called conforming. He found 11 of these 12 patterns represented among his subjects, who included a high proportion of neurotics, some psychotics, and a good many patients who were suffering from hypertension, asthma, and other illnesses which are generally acknowledged as being largely psychological in their causation. However, his 50 patients provided no instance of the pattern of high positive goal setting of the conforming type— a pattern which would seem to require a simultaneity of submissive and aggressive attitudes.

The notion of a general level of aspiration is a useful clinical concept, but no one has yet devised a test situation which will yield a meaningful score for all subjects. Gould (1939) pointed out that it is not possible to establish a generalized level of aspiration which is characteristic of a person in all situations. She demonstrated that the same individual may have quite different levels of aspiration for different tasks, presumably because of different degrees of ego involvement. Indeed, there is a logical contradiction between the very concept of the subjective basis of success and failure, and the attempt to find a single test that would provide a score, for any subject, which would enable us to predict that subjects characteristic method of goal setting in other fields. Some occupational interest inventories do attempt to measure the subject's level of aspiration as it is expressed in his indicated interests. An index of occupational level is one of the useful scores derived from the Strong Vocational Interest Tests. It would be interesting to study the degree to which aspiration level varies between the field of chosen interest and other occupational fields that are not unreasonable for the subject.

Gould also pointed out that some subjects apparently take satisfaction from the fact that they have high goals, even though they never achieve them. This is an attitude which certainly finds frequent expression in unrealistic vocational planning, in the stubborn striving for an unattainable objective. Such individuals prefer to fail at a level of distinction, rather than to succeed at one of mediocrity. (I recall an advisee who could not do better than average work in freshman mathematics, or in any other area, but was quite determined to become nothing other than an atomic physicist.) In every aspiration, the element of wish is blended with the realistic appraisal of likelihood. Marks (1951) showed for children, and Irwin (1953) for college students, that their guess at an outcome of known probability, in an event over which they had no control, was influenced by whether the outcome was regarded by them as desirable or not desirable. This defiance of reality is much less extreme among college students than among children, but the annual take of the lotteries, the race tracks and the gaming tables proves that it is still a potent factor in the adult mind. In Lewinian terms, the positive valence of a slim chance to win is greater than the negative valence of the more probable loss. This buoyant optimism protects humanity against the impervious logic of the pessimistic philosophies. However, when this wishful thinking gets out of reasonable bounds we must suspect that it is no longer an expression of a healthy euphoria, but of some deeper motivation of the compulsive kind that is usually fostered by experiences of frustration. Perhaps the long-shot gambler is one who cannot restrain himself from testing again and again his unconscious childish belief in a protecting parent figure that will show its love for him in a special act of showering generosity. The satisfaction of an occasional confirmation of this belief is worth the hardships of many rebuffs by reality. Similarly, the phantom goal of an aspiration that lies beyond possible reach may exercise an irresistible fascination. Most of us succeed in confining these utterly unrealistic aspirations to our daydreams, where they can be a harmless source of gratification.

It is the controlled daydream—that is, the fantasies which subjects create when, in the Thematic Apperception Test, they are instructed to tell stories which suggest themselves in response to picture materials—which has been used by McClelland and his associates in an effort to penetrate the characteristics of *The Achievement Motive* (McClelland et al., 1953). On the basis of their studies, they conclude that the lack of high achievement motivation must often be interpreted, not simply as representing a relatively low need for the satisfactions ordinarily associated with success, but as indicating a relatively high need to avoid the experiences of failure. Atkinson (1953) found evidence to support this view in an experiment in which the Zeigarnik effect (the better recall of incompleted than of completed tasks; cf. page 226) was measured both under relaxed conditions and under conditions which were structured to suggest that failure to complete the task was truly a "failure." Those subjects who had been judged to be high in achievement motivation, on the basis of the TAT fantasies, showed the effect more strongly under the latter condition, whereas those who had been judged to be low in achievement motivation actually showed a reverse effect—that is, better recall of completed than of uncompleted tasks—under the stronger motivation. That is, the relatively low achievement motivation of these subjects seems to be part of a generally defensive orientation, which shows itself also in a greater readiness to forget failure experiences.

MECHANISMS OF DEFENSE

In so far as the self-concept is realistic, it needs no defense. The defense of the self-concept is the defense of an illusion, which must be waged on an internal front, against our own doubts, even more determinedly than against any external criticism. It must be waged, therefore, outside the glare of consciousness—it would be false to say beneath the level of consciousness, because that would imply a less complex type of mental process—by devices that escape our understanding when we employ them. For the description of these devices, we are more indebted to Freud than to anyone else.

Freud attached paramount importance to the phenomenon of repression, by which we keep our primitive, socially inadmissible, desires from entering awareness. The self-concept is therefore vitally important, since it is only to spare ourselves the knowledge of our own depravities—or what we have been led to regard as such—that we deny ourselves the direct satisfaction of our basic desires. It was formulated by Freud as the ego ideal, in an important essay on the subject of narcissism (1914, 1925a), from which we quote at length:

We have learnt that libidinal impulses are fated to undergo pathogenic repression if they come into conflict with the subject's cultural and ethical ideas. By this we do not ever mean: if the individual in question has a merely intellectual knowledge of the existence of these ideas; we always mean: if he recognizes them as constituting a standard for himself and acknowledges the claims they make on him. Repression, as we have said, proceeds from the ego; we might say with greater precision, from the self-respect of the ego. The very impressions, experiences, impulses, and desires that one man indulges or at least consciously elaborates in his mind will be rejected with the utmost indignation by another, or stifled at once even before they enter consciousness. The difference between the two, however—and here we have the conditioning factor in repression—can easily be expressed in terms of the libido theory. We may say that the one man has set up an *ideal* in himself by which he measures his actual ego, while the other is without this formation of an ideal. From the point of view of the ego this formation of an ideal would be the condition of repression.

This ego ideal, which came to be called the superego in Freud's later writings, is also the instrument of conscience, the embodiment of parental and other social criticism. The person is therefore usually painfully aware of discrepancy between this ideal and reality, just as in childhood he was aware of his inadequacy by comparison with the parent ideal. Repressive devices are employed to reduce the evidence of this disparity to tolerable dimensions. Freud regards this process as being motivated entirely by the economics of pleasure, as stated in the following paragraph, which follows directly after the one already quoted:

To this ideal ego is now directed the self-love which the real ego enjoyed in childhood. The narcissism seems to be now displaced on to this new ideal ego, which, like the infantile ego, deems itself the possessor of all perfections. As always where the libido is concerned, here again man has shown himself incapable of giving up a gratification he has once enjoyed. He is not willing to forego his narcissitic perfection in his childhood; and if, as he develops, he is disturbed by the admonitions of others and his own critical judgment is awakened, he seeks to recover the early perfection, thus wrested from him, in the form of an ego ideal. That which he projects ahead of him as his ideal is merely his substitute for the lost narcissism of his childhood— the time when he was his own ideal.

At this period, Freud believed that one of the principal effects of repression was the conversion of the energy of the repressed drives into anxiety. Repression does not dissolve their energies, which still strive for expression. Thus, to gain the narcissitic pleasure of preserving our self-ideal, we must undergo not only the austerities of abnegation but often also the martyrdom of anxiety. Later, in *The Problem of Anxiety* (1927, 1936), he changed his views, and stated that the principal purpose of repression was to reduce anxiety. This is a problem which we shall discuss at length in a later chapter. Whatever the relative merits of these explanations, there can be no question about the value of Freud's descriptions of the different forms which repression can take. Most of them are indispensable to any psychologist, and many of the words he used to designate them, or their translations, thereby acquired new meanings in the vocabulary of all educated persons. They are found scattered through his writings, but the reader who wishes to study them together in an extended treatment may turn either to Anna Freud's important contribution, *The Ego and the Mechanisms of Defense* (1936), or to Symonds' book on *The Dynamics of Human Adjustment* (1946), which is very largely devoted to their exposition.

The basis of every repression is the danger that some forbidden intent or desire, something that is quite incompatible wth the ego ideal, shall make its appearance undisguised in consciousness. Simple repression usually does not suffice to exclude the unwanted thought. It has its own motive energy, and continues pushing itself forward—a circumstance which leads many a worried student to complain that he cannot concentrate on his books, because within a few minutes after he opens them his mind begins to wander, that is, chaotic thoughts begin pushing their way into consciousness. One way to verbalize the thought, without compromising the self-concept, is by the method of *denial.* "I don't wish to disagree with you," we say, as we begin what we hope will be a thorough annihilation of our opponent. The client says, "I have never had any tendency toward homosexuality," and we know at once that the fear of homosexuality is the central problem with which we shall have to deal, although it may be many hours before it will be broached again. This is a kind of rhetorical magic, by which we declare the unwelcome thought to be nonexistent. Since the unconscious is a poor grammarian, it can sometimes be satisfied in this easy way. The sophisticated listener ignores the statement of negation, and looks to the affectively toned words of the communication for evidence of the real motive.

The mechanism of denial, as well as some of the others that we shall discuss, can often be used in defense against other dangers than those to the self-concept. "It can't be true" is our first response to an unwelcome piece of news, as we prepare to brace ourselves for inescapable reality. The grieving mother may refuse for years to believe the report of her son's death, and there can be no doubt that the belief in immortality receives support from our very strong inclination to deny both the death of those we grieve and our own inevitable end.

Another device, which may have far-reaching effects upon social conduct, is that of *displacement.* Often it is not the intent which is unacceptable, but its object or direction. Many revolutionary movements have owed much of the enthusiasm of their leaders to the fact that we may permit ourselves to hate tyrants, but not our fathers. The richest ecstasies of religious experience have been reserved for those who, rejecting carnal love as sin, have let themselves be overwhelmed by love for a Divine Being. On a humbler plane, we bang out our aggressions with a constructive hammer, or, less usefully, we fume at the driver of the car in front of us, after being meekly acquiescent to the boss.

Displacement should not be confused with *projection,* which is another device that most of us exhibit at least occasionally on the highway. The other fellow's maneuvers are always so much less considerate and permissible than our own! It is not simply a matter of relative emphasis, that "I am resolute, but he is stubborn; I plan, but he connives." It is rather that, in interpreting the actions of other persons, we read into them the motives that clamor most for expression in ourselves. When, as small children, before we clearly understood the difference between living and nonliving things, we attributed feelings and intentions to inanimate objects, it was of course our own feelings and intentions that we projected onto them. As adults, when we interpret the behavior of other people, we can only attribute to them more or less of what we have found in ourselves. The deaf or blind from birth cannot understand the nature of the experience of sound or light, and if we were quite without love or anger, we could not recognize these feelings in others. Therefore the trick of projection is not a novel device, but one which we are all well prepared to practice. Becoming aware of a feeling that we do not wish to acknowledge as our own, we simply put it outside ourselves, and attach it to some other person. This device is of particular importance to the paranoid individual, who sees himself as threatened by others, when the hostility he senses is in reality his own. In war, the enemy is always the aggressor, and his soldiers most brutal and disorderly. In business, our competitors are usually scamps. (Again, we must warn the student against a possible verbal confusion. Projection signifies either the false perception of one's own feelings as belonging to some one else, or the display of thoughts and feelings by means of actions whose revealing nature is obscure to the behaver. The use of one word for such distinct meanings is perhaps unfortunate, but there is no reason why it need lead to any fuzziness in thinking, if we are alert to the fact.)

Reaction formation is another important mechanism of defense, which has already been mentioned in connection with

Freud's description of the anal character. It is scarcely possible to exaggerate the importance of this concept as an aid to our understanding of people. Whenever we face the problem of interpreting a bit of behavior, whether it be a formal test response or some casual action or remark, we must always seriously consider the possibility that this particular bit of behavior, instead of being a direct expression of a seemingly obvious motive, is a reaction formation, that is, an effort at the denial of a motive toward the opposite kind of conduct. Just as compulsive cleanliness may grow out of anal interest, so ostensible love may signify hate, and ostensible hate may signify love. The little boy who finds himself embarrassingly interested in the girl next door does not content himself with a display of indifference, but may try to prove his point by the violence with which he rejects her friendly overtures. The mother who inwardly rejects her child may outwardly appear to be the most solicitous of its welfare (cf. Levy, *Maternal Overprotection*). The young woman who prides herself on her independence and self-sufficiency, who has left home and is working her way through college although her parents are willing to pay the cost, learns with the help of a psychologist that she has been fighting a stubborn battle against acknowledging her great emotional need to be cared for by others. On every hand, we see people who recoil from some course of action which they cannot accept as suitable for themselves, and then resort to a conspicuous display of the opposite kind of behavior.

Sometimes it is not necessary for us to revise our behavior, because we can find an acceptable motive by which to justify it to ourselves and others. We buy an expensive car "just to please the wife," punish our children because it is "good for them" although it "hurts us more," and keep the extra change because the railroad makes too much profit, anyway. We justify our prejudices by accusing our victims of villainy. This invention of plausible and socially defensible reasons for our behavior is called *rationalization*. The reasons adduced are often quite impressive, but they are false in the sense that they do not include the true motive behind the act. More often they are shallow and contradictory, like the excuses of the man who answered his neighbor's complaint by saying that he had not used his neighbor's lawnmower last week, that in any case he returned it in good condition, and besides that it was damaged already when he borrowed it. Rationalization is frequently used to explain away our failures. The teacher had a grudge; I wasn't really trying; the competition was unusually severe; I had no time to prepare; the opposition was unscrupulous; I had a blister on my toe—there is always a good reason for failure of any sort, which makes it unnecessary to confess a personal inadequacy.

This listing of defense mechanisms might be extended considerably, but the half dozen that we have described probably include all those that are encountered most frequently and that have a predominantly defensive character. *Sublimation* is sometimes included among the defense mechanisms, but it stands apart from them because of its constructive character. It will be discussed in the next chapter, as an aspect of the development of interests.

Compensation is a mechanism whose importance was stressed by Adler, and which plays a key role in all his thinking. It was not as psychiatrist, but as internist, that Adler (1907) first turned his attention to the problem of how the body meets the stress created by any type of organ inferiority. The relative weakness of any organ constitutes a possible basis for future illness, but it often leads to compensatory processes which not only serve to protect the vulnerable organ but may sometimes achieve the result of rendering it especially strong. Adler transferred this physiological concept, which bears an obvious relation to the general homeostatic theory of a self-regulating organism, to the psychological sphere. He recognized the part which the central nervous system played in these adjustments, and before long he was led to the concepts of inferiority feeling, and of neurotic compensatory goals (1917). This conception is a rather narrow base on which to support a whole theory of personality and a system of therapy, but it does draw attention to a kind of motivation which had been overlooked by Freud, whose orientation at that time was still exclusively hedonistic. Adler observed that quite frequently it is some apparent weakness of the individual which serves to mobilize his efforts, and which thus in the end becomes a source of strength. Sometimes the compensation sought is quite direct, with the individual selecting just that goal which seems least reasonable or appropriate in light of the handicap—but it is the attainment of such a goal which is most prized, because it proves to the world that the supposed handicap is not real, that the self is sound and whole. By patient training, Demosthenes became an orator despite his stuttering. The world of sports provides many instances of such direct compensation for physical handicaps. Annette Kellerman, having been told as a child that she might never walk normally again, not only struggled to regain the use of her limbs but went on to win world renown as a swimmer and diver. In very recent years, Ed Furgol, playing with a deformed arm, won a national golf championship. Usually the compensation is less direct and it may often be symbolic. Napoleon, the little Corsican, became the ruler of a continent, and Walter Scott, stricken by paralysis in childhood, commanded the armies of the crusaders in his fantasies.

The same dynamic is at work in each of us. Half of the world's population is motivated in varying degree by the need to compensate for the seeming inferiority of being female, while most of the other half worries about its virility. This "masculine protest" (another phrase due to Adler) is not so different from the Freudian hypothesis of penis envy and castration fear. However, Adler rejected these hidden sexual origins, and regarded the child's littleness and enforced dependency, things that are obvious and readily admitted to awareness, as sufficient basis for all the far-reaching effects of compensation.

Jung uses the concept of compensation to explain the tendency of unconscious mental processes to produce results that seem antithetical to conscious attitudes. He writes:

> The contents that are excluded and inhibited by the chosen direction [that is, the overtly introvert or extravert orientation] sink into the unconscious, where by virtue of their effective existence they form a definite counterweight against the conscious orientation. The strengthening of this counterposition keeps pace with the intensification of the conscious onesidedness until finally a noticeable tension is produced. . . . The more one-sided the conscious attitude, the more antithetic are the contents arising from the unconscious; in which case, compensation appears in the form of a contrasting function. Such a case is extreme. Compensation by the unconscious is, as a rule, not so much a contrast as a leveling up or supplementing of the conscious orientation. (*Psychological Types,* 1923.)

This compensatory process compels the extreme extravert to adopt a subjective attitude, which shows itself as "pronounced egocentricity and personal bias," and it compels the extreme introvert to view objective facts in "terrifying dimensions" despite his conscious depreciation of them. In one respect, we may observe, such behaviors are consistent rather than contradictory. Even the compensations of the extravert lead to greater effectiveness at least in the immediate satisfactions of daily needs, while the compensations of the introvert lead to reduced effectiveness!

CHAPTER 13

Interests

*T*he biblical phrase, "Man doth not live by bread alone," expresses an important psychological truth. The person whose day-to-day activities are largely motivated by primary drives is immature, for such behavior is normally typical only of very young children, and clinical experience indicates that when it is observed in older children and adults it is the result of long-standing drive frustration. The process of maturation, and the formation of the self-concept, are attended by the development of interests and values, which largely displace the drives as sources of motivation. From one point of view, interests may be regarded as specialized ways of satisfying the non-primary drives. When his primary needs are satisfied, the human child, like the chimpanzee, exhibits in spontaneous play a delight in rhythmical movement, and a curiosity about all kinds of sights and sounds and feels of objects. Doubtless there are individual differences in the pleasurable potentialities of the different nonprimary drives, which may contribute to the fact that ultimately we find one man tinkering in his garage on a Sunday afternoon, while another is listening relaxedly to the broadcast of a symphony concert, and a third is playing golf or tennis. Potentially, all these forms of interest activity are capable of development in each of us, and the man who doesn't like machinery, or music, or sports, has "missed something," though he may have found a more or less adequate compensation in literature, mathematics, or pinochle. Strong and suitable interests are an essential part of the healthy personality, and hence any descriptive account of personality is incomplete if it does not include them.

We may define an interest as *the disposition to engage in some culturally elaborated activity without regard for any consequent gratification other than through the mere exercise of this disposition.* In this definition, the phrase "culturally elaborated" has been introduced in order to distinguish between the complex phenomena of personality and the more primitive manifestations of stimulus hunger which are the direct expression of the nonprimary drives. It is not a distinction of principle, but one of convenience, and it will not at all eliminate the possibilities of confusion between late-maturing drives and concurrently developing interests. The most obvious instance of such confusion is between the burgeoning sex drive of adolescence, which has a hormonal basis, and the simultaneous display of sex-linked interests which are in part prescribed by social custom. Another is between innate curiosity and cultivated intellectual interests. In all such cases, social education takes advantage of opportunities offered by maturation, as the drive or temperamental disposition provides the basis for development of related interests.

How Interests Are Acquired

As interests develop, and take over more and more of the motivational direction of everyday behavior, they seem to supersede the person's primary drives. The process may therefore be conceptualized as one of need substitution, rather than simply as the acquisition of additional behavior dispositions. However, this substitutive process is explained in diverse ways by psychologists of different theoretical orientations. Again, we will find it convenient to give separate consideration to the contributions of reinforcement theory, field theory, and psychoanalysis.

Thorndike (1935) felt that the acquisition of interests could be embraced in the general framework of learning theory without the need for any special principles. He maintained that

a person can be taught new attitudes and tastes as surely though not as easily as he can be taught tacts and skills. The basic principles of learning by repetition and reward seem to operate with wants, interests, and attitudes as they do with ideas and movements.

In a typical experiment to support this viewpoint, he demonstrated that subjects could be influenced to shift their esthetic preferences among poetic excerpts to conform to the standard which was fostered by the experimenter, who commented "right" or "wrong" after each of the subject's judgments. However, the Thorndikean experiments seem coldly distant from real life situations, and few critics are willing to accept his premise that the comments "right" and "wrong," under these conditions, can be equated to the experiences of reward and punishment. The persuasive value of prestige is a well-established fact of social psychology, but even if we could reduce prestige effects to reward effects—and we should probably have to ignore many of the facts that we have learned about identification in order to do this—we should still have to face the fact that many interests are developed without this sort of reinforcement.

Wolfe (1936) showed that if chimpanzees are first trained to use tokens to obtain food rewards from a kind of vending machine, they will soon be motivated to perform work to obtain the tokens. This is true even when the conditions of the experiment are such that the tokens cannot immediately be used to obtain the reward. In fact, they seem to take some satisfaction in the mere possession of the token during the delay period. Miller (1951) gives a tabular summary of many experiments of this general plan. Cats and dogs also have learned to respect the value of token rewards, and the conclusion seems unassailable that man's interest in money is not the characteristic which places him above the rest of the animal kingdom. It is, however, far from demonstrated that man's interest in money always has such a rational basis as that which Wolfe provided in his research design. We know that some interests arise as secondary motives which are learned through the process of reinforcement by tension reduction. We do not have a convincing demonstration that all interests are acquired in this manner.

The difficulties which must be faced by anyone who hopes to prove that all secondary motivation is based on learning through the effects of reward, or tension reduction, are of two kinds: first, most interests seem unrelated in their origins to primary drives; second, interests seem to be extraordinarily resistant to extinction effects—a clue which, on the basis of much material that we have seen in earlier chapters, warns us that a different type of learning is probably involved.

The first of these difficulties has been clearly recognized by Seward (1953), himself a behavioristically oriented learning theorist. He writes:

Experiments strongly imply that the chief sources of motivation are a few bodily needs, a variety of ways of satisfying them, and a large number of fears. Common experience, on the other hand, suggests that the bulk of our activity is directed toward things we want rather than away from the things we don't want, and that many of the things we want have little to do with bodily needs.

It seems clear to us that the answer to this paradox lies in a recognition of the importance of nonprimary drives, as we have defined them. It is these, and not the "bodily needs" to which Seward refers, that provide the foundation for a major part of the development of interests. The chimpanzee can indeed be taught to "work" for tokens, but we should also remember that if the task is one which intrinsically intrigues him he will work at it even if no reward is dangled before him. Most of the activities which we label as interests have this same independence of bodily needs, not only in their later histories, but in their origins. Furthermore, we do not regard them as means of achieving tension reduction, but as ways of feeling ourselves more responsively alive. If reward plays a part in the acquisition of such interests, the reward is excitement, and not tension reduction.

A more serious shortcoming of this approach is its inability to explain the extraordinary persistence of interests in the face of prolonged frustration. Dollard and Miller (1950), who treat the problem of "learned drives" from the standpoint of a consistent reinforcement theory, state as one implication of this position that "learned drives should be weakened by nonreinforcement." They do not discuss the subject further, but Miller (1951) has elsewhere acknowledged the importance of this difficulty. He seeks to minimize it by offering a demonstration that when rats have been taught a bar-pressing habit on the basis of fear, the extinction of this habit, although slow, does finally take place. This does not meet the essential problem. Actually, persistent motivated behavior in the face of prolonged nonreinforcement is such a commonplace of living that we feel driven to conclude that their theory fails to pass this test which they propose.

Indeed, other writers have been impressed above all by the fact that learned motives apparently become independent of reinforcement, or, better stated, are self-reinforcing. This fact is in a way implied in our definition of interest as involving no gratification other than through the mere exercise of the disposition. Allport (1937) introduced the phrase "functional autonomy of habit" to express the thought that likes and habits which have been acquired in the service of one need, when no longer useful for that purpose, survive as independent or autonomously motivated behavior, that is, they have no need for further continued reinforcement to prevent their extinction. For example, the retired worker with a good pension still prefers to carry on the activities of his job, as in themselves satisfying. Murphy (1947) appeals instead to the principle of canalization, by which one comes through experience to have a preference for more and more specific ways of satisfying originally diffuse drives. This is illustrated with particular ease in the gastronomic area, where a person who has become accustomed to certain foods may be unable to tolerate other "outlandish" foods even under conditions of extreme hunger. One might also appeal to canalization, rather than fixation, to explain the development of sexual habits. Freud (1905, 1938c) calls the infant "polymorphously perverse," because it has the potentiality of experiencing gratification in many different ways, most of which are socially condemned as perversions. However, after some of these ways are experienced, they become charged with additional motivational force, and the likelihood that others will occur is reduced. The principles of functional autonomy and canalization both seem to imply that the mere performance of an activity gives it interest value, but both Allport and Murphy warn against such a conclusion, and point out that it is not hard to find examples of acts which become boring and distasteful as a result of repetition. Possibly Lewin (1935) has given the most cogent statement of the conditions under which interests develop. He emphasizes that the cultivation of a new interest takes place most effectively when the activity is embedded in a behavioral whole which already has positive valence, rather than as a result of repetitions or the administration of rewards. This is undoubtedly true, and there is no more significant and highly charged "behavioral whole" than the self-concept. If the sailor cannot leave the sea, if the professional soldier (quite unlike the conscript) finds it hard to lay aside his uniform, and the merchant is unhappy away from his shop, it is not because sailing or fighting or selling has become functionally autonomous, but because these activities have become embedded in self-concepts whose integrity is threatened if the activities should lapse.

The development of interests has been envisaged by Freud (e.g., 1908, 1924a) in an entirely different manner. According to his conception, the decisive event which determines the appearance of substitutive interests is the occurrence of conditions which prevent the continued gratification of the original drive by the accustomed means. Under such conditions, the performance of the accustomed activity is blocked, but the unstemmed energy of the drive is only deflected into new avenues of expression. The social restraints that are imposed by society on the direct gratification of sex desires, whether in their infant or adult form, lead to the "sublimation" of their energy (libido) into other activities which, in the fortunate case, are socially more acceptable. These substitutive activities usually have some symbolic resemblance to the forbidden act. Thus oral tendencies may be sublimated by chewing gum or operating a restaurant, and anal tendencies by thrift and punctuality or by spreading paints on canvas. In art, science, and industry the motive forces of achievement are presumably, according to this view, the transformed energies of the sex drive. Psychoanalysts conceive of this process as being so extensive that Symonds writes (1946): "Sublimation is practically the equivalent of education in its customary usage." Not all the sublimated activities are homologous with their repressed antecedents, for some are reaction formations—as classically illustrated by the excessive orderliness and cleanliness which are associated with the anal character structure. The Freudian theory of need substitution emphasizes the permanence of motivation, almost to the point of indestructability, and the ephemeral nature of specific need gratifications. Thus Roheim (1933) was led to declare: "Life consists of finding a series of substitutes for the things we really want to do." It is a theory which regards the surface motivations of adult life as illusory, and views the acts which serve them as subtle clues to the hidden dynamics.

Lewin's extraordinary genius for devising experimental tests of crucial problems has shown itself again in this area. Lissner, Mahler, Sliosberg, and others have worked under his general direction on the problem of what determines whether a substitutive activity can satisfy the tension of the original need. A good summary of these experiments is available in English (Escalona, 1943). In Chapter 10, we mentioned the work of Ovsiankina and Zeigarnik, who showed that when an activity is interrupted, there is often a felt need to bring it to completion, which shows itself in a tendency to resume the activity when opportunity offers. The experiments on substitutive activities begin by setting up such tensions, but immediately upon interruption the subject is assigned another task, which he is permitted to complete. The crucial question is to what extent this substituted activity will satisfy the existing tension, as evidenced by a reduced tendency to resume the previously interrupted task. In various experiments with this general pattern it was found that the substitutive value of an act increases not only with its similarity to the prior interrupted activity, but also as a function of its difficulty, and of its reality; it decreases as the intensity of the original need is greater. Lewin (1935) sums up these results by saying that the substitutive value of nonspontaneous substitutions "is the greater the more the substitute action corresponds, not to a new goal, but to another way of reaching the inner goal." It is possible to view this conclusion as a confirmation of the psychoanalytic doctrine of symbolic substitutions.

Maslow (1943) has proposed a maturational theory of human motivation, according to which what are commonly regarded as derived motives are seen instead as the expression of "higher" needs, which do not show themselves until the "lower" needs have been satisfied. Most basic in this hierarchy of needs are the physiological tissue needs, including hunger. When these have been satisfied, the need for safety or security becomes paramount as the motivating force. When this has been met satisfactorily, love needs appear. Following in order are the need for esteem, the need for self-actualization, and finally —as might be expected of a research scientist—the intellectual need for cognition or understanding. It is characteristic of our culture that basic needs are satisfied for all, and security needs for most. Most of us are at least partially frustrated in our needs for love and esteem, and therefore these appear to be the dominant motives in our society. Only those who escape these frustrations can live the richer life of self-actualization. In a primitive society where security needs are less adequately met, or in a Utopia where all advance to the level of self-actualization, love would seem far less important as a motive. This theory probably contains a good measure of truth, although it has been elaborated beyond the point at which it is easily tenable. It is interesting to note that Maslow's successive needs not only correspond to the major dimensions of temperament, but that their hierarchic ranking corresponds to the order of their critical periods. The needs for security, love, and esteem express the dispositions to avoidance, affiliation, and dominance behavior, and the later needs for self-actualization and cognition may be regarded as corresponding to the nonprimary drives. One point at which Maslow's theory runs into difficulty is in its implication that the satisfaction of love needs is a prior condition for self-actualization. This is a doctrine which appears to be diametrically opposed to the Freudian concept of sublimation. Neither theory seems to meet the facts of artistic and scientific creativeness satisfactorily. It is proper to mention here that Goldstein (1935) contends that all of the motivating forces of men and animals, including the most basic drives, must be regarded as manifestations of one universal organismic tendency to self-actualization in the larger sense, that is, to maximal realization of the organism's potentialities.

In this section, we have sketchily presented a number of different theories about the sources of human interests. Most of these theories, and certainly those in widest acceptance, imply that the manners of men are stretched and chopped to fit a Procrustean bed of social expectations, and that men delude themselves when they regard as their "own" the purposes which they pursue in daily living. However, Maslow reminds us that the course of development is influenced by an

underlying maturational trend, and Lewin suggests that substitutive behaviors will only be retained if they do somehow
contribute to the attainment of the person's "inner goal." The
behaviorist's view that the infant becomes amenable to social
influence because of the frequent experience of need reduction
at his mother's breast, and the Freudian view that the child
reluctantly submits to social discipline because of his fear of
parental retaliation against any expression of his primitive wishes,
both contain truth, but neither gives adequate recognition to
the strength of influence of the individual's own dispositions in
determining which of many possible substitute behaviors he
shall adopt. These dispositions are partly temperamental, partly
based upon nonprimary drives, and partly formulated in the
self-concept.

OCCUPATIONAL INTERESTS

A good deal of research in the field of interests has had a
very pragmatic orientation, being concerned with the development of tests for the measurement of occupational interests, to
serve the related purposes of personnel selection and vocational
guidance. We shall consider several of the most widely used
tests, what they indicate about the place of occupational interests
in personality, and their apparent shortcomings.

Perhaps the outstanding leader in this field is Strong (1943),
whose persistence in the pursuit of a single problem, through
three decades, represents a rare example of thoroughness in
psychological research. His Vocational Interest Blank is based
on a purely empirical approach. The hundreds of items were
not chosen according to any prior definition of the dimensions
of interest, nor deliberately as representing elements involved
in any particular occupations, but simply as offering choices of
preference on which people might be expected to vary. The form
for men may now be scored on more than 40 different occupational scales, each of which is the outcome of a separate research study. There are 19 occupational keys available for use

with the form for women. Each of these keys is based on the distribution of responses by the members of a standardization group which consists of people actively engaged in that occupation. Thus, for example, to say that you would like to be an actor scores +2 on the Artist scale, but −1 on the Carpenter scale; a dislike expressed on the same item scores +1 on the Carpenter scale, 0 on the Chemist scale, −3 on the Musician scale. These weights are not logically determined, but simply reflect the finding that very few professional musicians express disinclination to be actors, that chemists do not show any preference either way on this item, etc. An interest score must be computed separately for each of the many scales. A score of "A" on a given scale means that most of the subject's answers are similar to those given by most members of that occupational group, and therefore suggests that he would find that occupation agreeable.

Of special interest to psychology students is the fact that a psychologist scale prepared in 1948 differs in important respects from the one prepared 10 years earlier, reflecting the shift from an academic to an applied emphasis in the profession. The 1948 group is described as "more interested in, more tolerant of, and more willing to help people, and less interested in mechanical and methodical work and in solitary activity" (Kriedt, 1949). It was also found worth while to establish subkeys for clinical, experimental, guidance, and industrial psychologists, in recognition of the partly divergent interests of these different groups. One can judge from this that a good many keys are needed to canvas adequately the occupational possibilities for a given subject, although a single key may suffice where the interest is in personnel selection for a particular kind of job. It is in fact recommended that when the test is used in vocational guidance, a profile be prepared of scores on all the available keys, rather than for the few occupations that may be under active consideration.

However, many of the scales fall into a few obvious clusters, a fact which suggests the need for an analysis in terms of interest factors. Thurstone (1931) performed a factor analysis based on Strong's data on the 18 original scales, which indicated that four major interest factors were present. He identified them as interest in Science, Language, People, and Business. Subsequent factor analyses, including the data from additional scales, have led to essentially the same results. None of these factors can be said to be altogether unambiguously defined. The first factor is named from its heavy loading in many scientific occupations, but it is also present in strong degree among artists. Since artistically inclined persons do not often have a strong manifest interest in science occupations, this is something of a puzzle, whose solution should contribute to a better understanding of the foundations for success in both areas. The language factor may perhaps better be defined as bipolar, that is, as an interest in work which involves language vs. work which involves handling things. Strong prefers a slightly different rotation of the axes, which leads to a definition of this factor as work with people vs. work with things. The third factor is described by Strong as "working with people for their own presumed good." The fourth, interest in Business, proves especially elusive during rotations, and it seems to be a composite of inclinations to "contact" and "system," which find their highest loadings, respectively, in the personnel man and the certified public accountant.

Three special nonoccupational scales have also been developed for use with the Strong Vocational Interest Test for Men. These are masculinity-femininity (which is also available for the women's form), interest-maturity, and occupational level. The problem of masculinity-femininity will be considered at length later in this chapter. The interest-maturity scale is a measure of the degree to which responses resemble those of 25-year-old men rather than those of 15-year-olds. Sollenberger (1940) found that in teen-age boys, interest-maturity correlated more highly with hormone activity than with chronological age, which is certainly a very forceful demonstration of the ineffectuality of social motivation which is not supported by temperamental disposition. The occupational level scale is a measure of the degree to which responses resemble those of business and professional men generally rather than those of unskilled workers. When the test is being used in vocational guidance, the score for this scale may be regarded as an indication of the general level of aspiration.

The Allport-Vernon Scale of Values employs a very different approach to the problem of measurement in this field (Allport and Vernon, 1931). Its starting point is a classification of major interest areas which is borrowed from Spranger (1928), and includes the following "values": Theoretical, Economic, Esthetic, Social, Political, and Religious. Spranger's intent was to classify all men according to innately determined interest types, and although his system seems to be based more on the traditional list of faculties in a German university than on the observation of mankind generally, it has proved useful in work with college students. However, Political interest as measured by the Scale of Values does not represent interest in world affairs so much as social dominance, and Religious interest does not reflect institutional observance or a theological attitude so much as a cosmic world outlook. Some of the items of the Scale call for paired comparisons, while in others the subject must give preferential rankings to three activities which represent as many different interest areas. The final scores only indicate the relative importance of these six areas for the individual, and they provide no measure of absolute intensity of interest. This is a failing from which nearly all interest inventories suffer, despite the obvious need for an instrument which will take into account the intensity of interests, as well as their relative strength in the individual.

Many validation studies have demonstrated the meaning-fulness of the dimensions of the Scale of Values. For example, Sarbin and Berdie (1940), found positive correlation between

Scientific interest, as measured by the Strong Blank, and the Theoretical score of the Scale of Values, and also between interest in "working with people for their own good" and the Religious score. Seashore (1947) reports distinctive profiles for two groups of students at Springfield YMCA College: students who are majoring in "applied social science" stand exceptionally high in Religious value, and the Physical Education majors in Political value, which we have already described as a measure of social dominance—an expected attribute of the mesomorphic physique. Stagner (1948) has presented a composite profile for the department of psychology at Dartmouth, which has interest for us even though it is based on only six cases. This group was found to be very high in Theoretical, high in Social, low in Political and Economic values. The writer has found this profile to be representative of advanced psychology students, although women students tend to have Social interest higher than Theoretical, and to score higher than the men in Religious interest. In contrast, business majors will be highest in the Economic and Political areas. Summarizing many such studies, Super (1949) writes: "Values are related in expected ways to choice of training in fields such as art, business, drama, education, law, literature, medicine, natural science, psychology, the priesthood, social studies, and social work."

The Kuder Preference Record (1946) is probably the most widely used of all interest inventories. An amazingly high proportion of recent high school graduates will remember it as the test they took by punching their answers through the booklet with a pin. This is one aspect of an ingenious format which not only permits students to score their own tests rapidly in class groups, but also makes it possible for each student to prepare quickly a profile which shows him his standing on each dimension of the test, relative to an appropriate norm group—for example, high school senior boys or girls. Each item of the test requires a preferential ranking of three activities which are transparent representatives of different occupational fields, so that the final scores never produce any surprise, unless they are interpreted by the subject—as they too often are—as recommendations rather than as the direct reflection of their own expressed preferences. The dimensions lend themselves readily to use in vocational counseling, except for an unfortunate overrepresentation of the art areas. They are: Mechanical, Computational, Scientific, Persuasive, Artistic, Literary, Musical, Social Service, Clerical. The typical profile for a given occupation will have several high or low points. Psychologists, for example, stand relatively high in both Literary and Scientific interest, and relatively low in Persuasive, Mechanical, and Clerical interests (Baas, 1950). Unfortunately, the results are often used in vocational guidance with inadequate reference to the information about such profiles, and it is to be regretted especially that the test manual, although it provides such information, also encourages students to consider seriously any occupational field in which they rank above the 75th percentile rank in interest. Such scores in Artistic, Literary, Musical, and Scientific areas, particularly on relatively flat profiles, usually reflect an intensity of interest which is quite inadequate to support the intensive efforts needed for success in those areas, whereas experience shows that low average interest in the less competitive Mechanical and Clerical fields is altogether compatible with success in them (Diamond, 1948). Here again, we see the practical need for a measure of the intensity of an interest, rather than its relative strength. To construct a more obvious illustration, a high school girl who shows above average interest in civil engineering, and below average interest on a scale for "motherhood," both relative to other girls of her age, might still have a much stronger interest in home and babies than in bridges and waterworks. The 75th percentile rule makes no allowance for the fact that mechanical and clerical fields, like motherhood, offer opportunities for a large proportion of the population, whereas some of the other fields are extremely restricted.

More immediately interesting to us, however, are the relationships between the test variables and other aspects of personality. Clinically oriented counselors have frequently suspected that basic personality factors find expression in the responses to interest inventories, and some published data are available to support this opinion. Triggs (1947) found that in a small group of college men there were significant positive correlations between clerical interest, as shown by the Kuder Preference Record, and trends to depressive, schizoid, and compulsive behavior, as indicated by the relevant scales of the MMPI. He also found that expressed Musical interest correlated with the indications of schizoid and compulsive trends. On the other hand, Mechanical, Scientific, and Computational interests, and Social Service Interest, all yielded negative correlations with various indicators of personality disturbance on the MMPI. Forer (1953) studied the Kuder Preference Record profiles of 400 veterans with psychiatric disabilities, and concluded that in this group, high scores on Persuasive, Artistic, Literary, Musical and Social Service scales (the last alone being in disagreement with Triggs' results on a very different and also much smaller population) were "indicative of maladjustment rather than vocational fitness," and were motivated by a wish to avoid "routine activities or activities calling for specific duties and compliance to standards set by others." Guidance counselors in schools should be alert to the fact that the interest scores are contaminated in this way. From the theoretical standpoint, such findings inevitably suggest that a system of interest dimensions which is based on a purely occupational classification may be psychologically unsound.

In summary of this section, we may say that there are two important problems whose solution is needed before interest tests can fulfill the expectations of vocational counselors. One of these is to define dimensions of interest which correspond to true dimensions of personality. The method of factor analysis, applied to the right kind of data, should be adequate to this problem, but there is no reason to suppose that inventory tests of preferences actually yield all the necessary data. In a serious approach to this problem, interest indicators and other measures of personality should be combined in the same study. The other major problem is to measure the intensity of interests, rather than their relative strength. Thorndike (1940) attempted this by having his subjects equate their interest in various kinds of activities to sums of money. It does not seem likely that this technique could be successfully applied in tests for mass use, but some device of this sort is needed. It is well-nigh meaningless to say, for example, that a student's strongest interest is scientific, if the general level of his motivation is such that this strongest interest is very little above the level of bland indifference.

MASCULINITY-FEMININITY

Another topic in the general field of interests which has been the object of extensive research is the differentiation of typically masculine and feminine attitudes. Nowhere are the elements of temperament and social training more inextricably interwoven than in the complex of behavior which is designated as the M-F dimension. We also venture to say that no other topic which could be included in a book of this sort arouses more decided opinions in readers generally, as if each had a personal stake in the question under discussion. In a sense, each of us does, for this is a question on which we cannot accept any modification of the views we already hold, without at the same time experiencing a change in a very sensitive part of the self-concept, in the jealously guarded inner core of the self.

It is obvious that men and women, as groups, differ in certain attitudes and behavioral tendencies which are related only indirectly, if at all, to their roles in the reproductive process. Within each sex it is possible to distinguish some individuals who bear greater resemblance to the norms of the other sex than do their sex mates generally, and a very few who seem to fit the norms of the other sex, in some particulars, better than those of their own. We have, therefore, a dimension on which the two sexes overlap, although they have central tendencies which are clearly distinguishable. Where an individual lies on this M-F dimension is in part a result of innate physiological factors, which are largely endocrine in nature, and in part a result of social pressures. As always when the question of interacting hereditary and environmental factors arises, it is more profitable to be alert to the manner of their interaction than to pit them against each other like gladiators, with the partisan hope that one of these forces may annihilate the other. The simple truth is that they are both invincible. In fact, they have been living peacefully together for a long time, except in our minds.

It is not a difficult matter to devise a test which distinguishes between men and women, as groups, on the basis of interest. Terman and Miles (1936) constructed an Attitude-Interest Analysis Test of 456 items, every one of which differentiates between the sexes. The items are organized into seven groups, and although the agreement between scores that are based on these different parts is not very high—a fact which points to the complexity of the phenomenon with which we are dealing —it is worth noting that the part which differentiates the sexes most effectively is that which is specifically labeled "Interests." Many other interest inventories and personality tests include M-F scales. Although the items of the Strong Vocational Interest Blanks were not selected with the M-F variable in mind, most of them proved to be useful in establishing such a scale. Likewise, when it was deemed desirable to add such a scale to the Kuder Preference Record, it was necessary only to give weights to the existing scales, for experience had shown that Mechanical, Persuasive, and Computational interests tend to be higher among men, while Clerical, Artistic, and Social Service interests tend to be higher among women (Kohn, 1948). The MMPI

eyes, because they have given up fighting and taken to pageantry as their major interest, but they are still striving for personal distinction in activities which they regard as giving prestige. Furthermore, how nature deals with such a development may be judged from the fact that "they had fled their ancestral territory, in fear of the warlike Iatmuls, and gone . . . to live with the bush people." If not for the protective intervention of the British Empire, this society of effeminate men might by now be quite extinct. Nature may have had many such experiments, but they have not survived.

With respect to the implications of this difference between men and women, Margaret Mead writes: "If women are to be made restless and questing, even in the face of childbearing, they must be made so by education. If men are ever to be at peace, . . . they must have, in addition to paternity, culturally elaborated forms of expression that are lasting and sure." It is possible to agree with this point of view, even without accepting the hypothesis regarding the origin of this difference. In effect, Mead agrees with William James that men need "a moral equivalent of war," while women can find complete satisfaction in activities close at home. This is the difference which finds its symbolic expression in the Franck and Rosen test, in which women tend to elaborate the interior of each stimulus design, while men tend to build the designs outward, each sex giving evidence of its basic orientation. Even the Tchambuli men should indicate their basic masculinity by such a test.

The Arapesh and the Tchambuli represent striking examples of the modification of interest which takes place in both men and women, in every society, because of the pressure which is placed on individuals to assume their "proper" roles. We have seen some evidence that in our society this pressure is felt more strongly by women than by men. Possibly the difference is only that the feminine role is defined in greater detail, leaving women fewer areas for individual expression without social conflict. However, we should not overlook the fact that both men and women are also subject to pressures which tend to minimize the differences between them. The fact that masculine qualities are commonly held in greater esteem constitutes a part of that very education which does make some women "restless and questing." On the other hand, the extremes of aggressiveness are also devalued, and many feminine qualities are admired in men, when they occur in moderation. Furthermore, every boy's first identification is with his mother, and the conditions of our family life are not such as to obliterate this influence. Thus our society brings about a partial blurring of the temperamental differences between men and women, probably with some benefit to both in most cases.

That social pressure to accept a prescribed sex role is very far from being the whole answer to the question of how men and women generally acquire distinctive interests is demonstrated most clearly by those unhappy persons who find it impossible to respond to those pressures. For example, the sturdy son of a career officer in the Navy would have liked nothing better than to follow in his father's footsteps, but he confessed with shame that his mind turned more readily and with greater delight to curtains and bric-a-brac. He had evidently been influenced more by an early unconscious identification with his mother than by all the social teachings as to what a man should be, despite his strong conscious desire to accept those teachings. Such cases of feminine identification are not uncommon among boys who have been reared in a predominantly feminine environment. This fostering of feminine interests does not always lead to overt homosexuality, although that is not an uncommon outcome. However, the point we wish to make is that effective teaching of the sex role is by example, and not by the pressure of social expectations. The boy with three or four older sisters and no brothers is in danger of learning too well how to be a girl, although it is clear to him at every moment that he is expected to be different, in a way that may be very difficult for him to master.

The preponderant role of experience, or learning, in the development of homosexuality is indicated by the lack of any strong relationship between M-F and physiological sex characteristics. The reader is undoubtedly familiar with the fact that only a small proportion of homosexuals show any marked divergence from physical norms for their sex. The appearance of secondary sex characteristics of the opposite sex is so rare that it need scarcely be considered as an important determining factor. Terman and Miles state that there was no relation between M-F scores and physique, within either sex alone, in the populations they studied. On the other hand, Seltzer (1945) found that among Harvard undergraduates, those who were described as weak in the physical characteristics which were defined as the "masculine component"—and who constituted about 10 percent of the men included in the intensive Grant study—were more likely to show "sensitive affect," cultural interest, and other aspects of femininity in attitude. They were more likely to select majors in the arts and in philosophy, and less likely to select the natural sciences. Lurie (1953) gives several examples of the use of endocrine therapy to overcome effeminate characteristics in teen-age boys. What is significant in his examples is that a shift of interests is observed to take place coincidentally with the physical changes in secondary sex characteristics, in much the same way that interests normally shift during early adolescence.

A thorough study of all the evidence on this involved problem would probably serve only to emphasize principles with which we are already familiar from our study of temperament and of the self-concept. Every individual has dispositions to varied types of behavior. Certain dispositions, including aggressivity, are natively more prominent in males, and within each sex such dispositions vary in strength in direct relation to the degree of physical masculinity, that is, to the quantity of masculine hormones. Others, including, for example, the tendency to nurturant behavior, are more prominent in females, and again they show variation in strength within each sex, associated with definable physiological characteristics. However, these dispositions are modifiable by experience, so that we do not expect to find a strong direct relationship between their development in later life and this single set of determinants, the physiological. Among the most important modifying influences are those which we have considered under the headings of self-concept and identification. Effeminacy in the male, or masculinity in the female, reveals itself fairly readily in gesture and mannerism, but these are by no means regularly linked to abnormalities of physique. Such linkage as does occur, in men, between lack of masculine component in physique and effeminacy in either mannerism or interests is certainly in large part the result of the person's thinking of himself as insufficiently masculine. Worry about a supposed lack of masculinity is far more common among boys and young men than is generally realized, and of course those who lack the physical development which might give them needed reassurance suffer more in this regard. (The unconscious fear that this sort of inadequacy may be apparent to others is a not uncommon cause of inability to talk in front of a class.)

The ideal man and ideal woman certainly do not stand at the extremes of the M-F dimensions. Even in the sexual act itself, two such extreme individuals would probably find each other unsatisfactory partners. Freud said that there are four persons present in every act of intercourse, thus dramatically drawing attention to the feminine side of the male partner, and to the masculine side of the female partner. In a successful relationship, all four must be satisfied, or, to state the matter otherwise, a normally bisexual individual would be ill-matched with a "perfect" monosexual one! This mixture within each of us is not simply the result of multiple identifications and other educational influences, but has its biochemical basis in the fact that normal adults secrete substantial quantities of the hormones responsible for the special characteristics of the opposite sex. Indeed, "normal women secrete almost as much androgen as men," although "the androgen: estrogen ratio in the male is two to five times that in the female." (Cantarow and Trumper, 1949.) In both sexes, this mixed biochemistry is the evidence of latent dispositions which render each normal individual susceptible to the effects of social training in diverse directions.

Let us make some summary remarks concerning M-F as a behavior variable. It is not a unitary dimension. Some of its aspects are fairly direct expressions of temperamental variables on which sex differences appear in all mammals. Since all such dispositions are present in every individual, and their varying initial strength is only one of the determinants of their later development, we cannot be surprised to find frequent instances of noncorrespondence between secondary sex characteristics and the behaviors that we might naïvely expect to find associated with them. Other aspects of the M-F dimension, such as cultural and occupational interests, have no direct relation to temperamental variables, although dispositional factors may facilitate the acquisition of one or another type of behavior. We have conjectured that our contemporary culture often tends to blur rather than to sharpen some of the psychological differences between the sexes, by discouraging the extreme manifestations of masculinity in men and by encouraging each sex to acquire, in moderate degree, certain characteristics of the other. It is impossible to state any general rule with respect to the relative strength of innate and environmental forces as determinants of sex-linked behavior. The imbalance of physiological factors is marked for some individuals and slight for others; the exposure to environmental influences is also unequal. The two sets of factors interact in complex ways. The most important determinant seems to be identification, but the choice of models for identification is often influenced by temperamental factors. A simple measure of M-F will contribute something, but relatively little, to the understanding of a given person. However, if we can make separate appraisal of the temperamental and interest aspects which are included in this behavior, if we take note whether these are in harmony or in disharmony, and above all whether they are integrated with a self-concept that is acceptable to the person, then the study of this aspect of the personality can be of considerable value.

CHAPTER 14

Cognitive Individuality, I

Mental Abilities and Perception

*I*n earlier chapters, the motivational determinants of behavior have always been most prominent in our discussion. That is the expected emphasis in any treatment of personality, and one that only a few years ago might have been used without question in a definition of the field. However, recently there has been an increasing recognition that it is as one-sided to describe a man without intellect as one without desire. In the next few chapters we shall try to give an account of individuality as it appears in the intellectual sphere. We shall see, however, that motivational factors will constantly intrude themselves into this discussion, partly because of the influence of all kinds of motivation on the progress of thought, but also partly because the very machinery of thinking gives rise to new forms of motivation.

INTELLECTUAL ABILITIES AND THEIR ORGANIZATION

The normative approach to the study of individuality in this area is through the analysis of intellectual capacity into its components, devising tests for their separate measurement, and studying their organization and the relative importance of their contributions in the thinking of different persons. Logically, this is a division of the study of personality, and Cattell (1946) quite properly includes general intelligence and special mental abilities as dimensions of the personality sphere. We should therefore summarize in a general way what is known about these dimensions, and consider the implications of this knowledge, although its application lies chiefly in the fields of education and industrial psychology.

The results in this field parallel those that we have studied in so much more detail in the field of temperament. This parallel may be stated in a series of 3 propositions. First, it is possible to define a few major dimensions of mental ability which should be kept in mind whenever we try to assess the intelligence of a person. Second, it is also possible to isolate a very large number of highly specific abilities, which are concerned with the handling of special kinds of materials or with special ways of handling materials of any kind. Third, the organization of cognitive functions in the individual undergoes a process of differentiation, so that a reasonably full account of its structure in the adult must include reference to some factors which do not appear, at least with any prominence, in the child. The reader should keep all 3 of these propositions in mind while reading the following pages, since it will not be practical to present the evidence with respect to each of them separately.

The problem of unity vs. diversity in the definition of intelligence has troubled workers in this field from the very beginning. In the early development of his tests, Binet thought that judgment was the one "fundamental faculty" upon which it was necessary to focus. Although he included some tests in which judgment played no obvious part, such as memory tasks, he said that "so far as we are able, we shall give these tests such a turn as to invite the subject to make absurd replies, and thus under cover of a test of memory, we shall have an appreciation of their judgment" (Binet and Simon, 1905). Later, however, he came to think of intelligence as a manifestation of a number of relatively independent aptitudes. Terman therefore wrote:

Binet fully appreciated the fact that intelligence is not homogeneous, that it has many aspects, and that no one kind of test will display it adequately. He therefore assembled for his intelligence scale tests of many different types, some of them designed to display differences of memory, others differences in power of reason, ability to compare, power of comprehension, time orientation, facility in the use of number concepts, power to combine ideas into a meaningful whole, the maturity of apperception, wealth of ideas, knowledge of common objects, etc. (*The Measurement of Intelligence,* 1916.)

This was a pragmatic solution to the tester's problem rather than a theoretical resolution of the question. The technical advance of intelligence testing might still have taken either of two paths: it might have developed in the direction of a clearer definition of the "one fundamental faculty" and toward the discovery of one kind of problem best suited to assess it, or, on the contrary, toward defining the separate components of intelligence and devising methods for measuring them independently. As it turned out, the man who argued most decisively for the former course laid the technical foundation for the great progress which has been made in the other direction!

Spearman (1904, 1927) was the proponent of what is called, rather misleadingly, the two-factor theory of intelligence. According to this theory, there is a single factor of general intelligence, g, whose operation can be detected in every test of mental ability, and may be thought to correspond to Binet's fundamental faculty. However, this general factor never accounts for all the variance in any test. Besides g, there is always a specific factor present, which depends on the exact nature of the test. Since there are as many specific factors as there are distinctive types of test, this might more understandably be called a multifactor theory, or even, as Thurstone (1947) prefers, a one-factor theory. Spearman and his followers did a vast amount of research in support of his views. Their results never lifted the cloud of controversy which still surrounds the question of *g,* but they did lead to some other very important developments. Spearman himself devised an ingenious mathematical method for testing the relationships among a number of tests, in order to discover whether a single factor could account for all their common variance. His "tetrad difference" criterion rests upon a study of four correlations at a time, so chosen that each of four tests is represented in one pair of the correlations, and the same tests in different combination are represented in the other pair.[1] Thurstone's extension of this method gave rise to factor analysis. Meanwhile, the mass of experimental data produced led Spearman and his followers to the discovery that there were also general factors of a nonintellective nature. The most important of these are a volitional factor, *w,* which is described as "purposive consistency," and a kind of mental inertia called *p,* or perseveration. These factors are measures of temperamental rather than intellectual characteristics, but they influence the results of most ability tests. British psychologists in general accord them considerable importance, while American psychologists tend to disregard them.

Thurstone's coördinated experimental work and contributions to factor theory provided the strongest support for the opposing view, that intelligence consists of many overlapping factors, which may better be described as group factors, rather than as

---

[1] Consider 4 tests, A, B, C, and D. Let g be the only nonspecific factor which is present in these tests, and let g_a, g_b, etc., represent the loadings of this factor on the respective tests. Then $r_{ab} = g_a g_b$, $r_{bc} = g_b g_c$, etc. Now consider the equation

$$r_{ab}r_{cd} - r_{ac}r_{bd} = x$$

This can be expanded into the form

$$g_a g_b g_c g_d - g_a g_c g_b g_d = x$$

and it is seen that the 2 terms of the left-hand member are identical, and their difference must be zero. However, this is the case only under the condition which we have assumed, namely, that there is no other nonspecific factor which results in an increment to any of these correlations. For example, if there is some factor f which contributes to the variance of both A and B, but not to the variance of C or D, and if there is no other nonspecific factor in the 4 tests, then the expansion takes the following form:

$$(g_a g_b + f_a f_b)(g_c g_d) - g_a g_c g_b g_d = x,$$

and the "tetrad difference" will no longer be zero.

either general or specific factors. He isolated a moderately large number of these, and called them primary mental abilities (1938). They include verbal facility (V), numerical facility (N), spatial visualization (S), rote memory (M), perceptual speed (P), word fluency (W), and reasoning (R). His analysis also justifies a distinction between inductive reasoning (I) and deductive reasoning (D). The conflict between these findings and Spearman's theory of a general intellective factor is largely resolved by Thurstone's later acceptance of what is called a second-order factor, which underlies the primary abilities, and which bears at least a very close resemblance to g.

Such factors are not to be regarded in any sense as entities, but rather—as in the case of temperamental variables—as types of consistency which become apparent to us in our analysis of intellectual activity. The conclusive demonstration of a single general factor would simply mean that there is such underlying consistency in all mental work that the observation of any instance of it helps us to predict the outcome of any other instance. Types of test which have high saturation in g would therefore be the best general predictors, and conversely, prediction would be most difficult for types of activity which have low saturation in g. The problem from a practical standpoint is whether, in studying a person, we would do best to concentrate our efforts on measuring general intelligence, or plan to distribute our effort so as to obtain separate estimates of special abilities. In the construction of tests for different purposes this question has been answered in different ways. Thurstone's PMA, which yields a separate score for each of the primary mental abilities mentioned above, is widely used for testing in the upper elementary grades and in high school. However, the ACE (Psychological Examination of the American Council on Education), which is planned as a test of academic aptitude at the college level, consists of only two parts, one Linguistic and the other Quantitative. As might be expected, the scores on these two parts have differing significance in prediction for different types of college curricula. The Miller Analogies Test (MAT), which is often used to select students at the graduate level, stresses a type of content which has been found most predictive of reasoning ability. The Wechsler-Bellevue Intelligence Scales (Wechsler, 1941), which were planned for use in a clinical rather than an educational setting, are based on the assumption that there is a general factor which can best be approximated by using many varied types of test material, but it also makes an *a priori* distinction between a general verbal and a general performance factor. Besides this, the separate scores of the 11 subtests of the Wechsler Scales are used to support many types of inference about the person's mental organization, few of which have received any satisfactory experimental verification.

Garrett (1946) presented a differentiation hypothesis, according to which the general factor is very strong in early intelligence, or at least in the early school years, but declines in importance with age. He therefore believes that it is inadvisable to "fractionate the IQ" into special abilities at the elementary school level. He says:

> At the high school and college levels, abstract intelligence breaks down . . . into a number of relatively independent factors. It would seem to be theoretically more defensible, therefore, and practically more useful, to measure verbal, numerical, perceptual or spatial ability, and perhaps other factors at these ages, than to give the subject a single over-all score. . . . In the case of adults, tests designed to measure aptitudes for special kinds of work are to be preferred to blanket measures of general ability.

The most important evidence which Garrett adduces for this theory is the fact that many investigators, using different types of intelligence tests, have reported generally higher correlations among subtests at younger ages than at older ages. He might have pointed also to the fact that the Thurstones found fewer primary abilities among younger children. Their test for 5- and 6-year-olds (Thurstone and Thurstone, 1946) measures only the factors V, P, S, and Q—quantitative, the precursor of numerical aptitude—besides M, motor ability, which could certainly have been isolated at the older ages if there had been any interest in doing so. However, the evidence which Garrett considers is almost wholly limited to the school years, and where college students are included, we must reckon with the possibility of distortion resulting from restriction of the intelligence range within this selected population. The exception is some data from the Army draft, but Garrett himself recognizes that the reported correlations among different parts of the AGCT (Army General Classification Test) are too high to fit his theory. He says: "This probably resulted from the fact that many soldiers were undoubtedly closer to the elementary school child than to the superior adult in the facility with which they handled abstract test material." The implication is that the differentiation of mental abilities takes place as a result of the educational process rather than as an aspect of maturation.

A consideration of certain results reported by Balinsky (1941) suggests that the process of differentiation probably reaches its peak, at least for the average person, in early adulthood, and that from this point forward the general factor may tend to regain its early prominence. Balinsky made separate factor analyses of Wechsler-Bellevue subtest scores for five different age populations. The average intercorrelation of the subtests at the different age levels was as follows:

Age	9	12	15	25-29	35-44	50-59
Mean *r*	.37	.34	.23	.18	.31	.43

He found evidence for a strong general factor at age 9 and again in his oldest group, but not in the intermediate groups. There seemed to be only two nonspecific factors at age 9, three at ages 12 and 15, four at age 25-29, and then again only three in the older groups. This suggests that differentiation not only does not progress after early adulthood in the average person, but that some of the gains of earlier differentiation seem to be lost in middle age and later life. This is not to gainsay the likelihood that it does continue, as Garrett implies, in the superior and mentally more active adult population. This apparent difference in mental organization, not only between children and adults but also between the educated and the relatively less educated, conforms to the expectation of Lewinian theory.

It appears likely that the "fractionation of the IQ" can be carried to any desired point of complexity, by applying the technique of factor analysis to more and more extensive batteries of tests, each consisting of a distinctive kind of problem. With the increasing application of high-speed electronic computing devices to psychological research, we may expect before long to see factor analyses based on tens of thousands of correlations. A foretaste of the results to be anticipated is given by Guilford and Zimmerman (1947), who list more than 20 aptitude factors which appeared in the analysis of tests used by the Army Air Force for the assignment of cadets to specialized tasks. They define three kinds of reasoning, four kinds of memory, and several different aspects of ability to deal with spatial problems —the abilities to visualize shapes, to estimate lengths, and to recognize relative positions. It is interesting to note that this differentiation of aptitudes for dealing with spatial problems runs parallel to the clinical recognition of visual *dis*abilities or agnosias. Nielsen (1946) distinguishes visual form agnosia, visual distance agnosia, and visual direction agnosia—that is, conditions in which one or another of the spatial abilities is much more seriously impaired than the others.

Guilford (1950) has pointed out that one of the intriguing possibilities opened up by factor analysis is to discover whether the extraordinarily creative thinker, or genius, thinks in different ways than other men. The definition of genius solely in terms of high IQ has never seemed satisfactory, and Guilford proposes to search for special factors which may explain their exceptional productivity, or at least be useful in the early identification of persons with great creative potentiality. He suggests that it should be possible to construct tests for such characteristics as sensitivity to problems, ideational fluency, novelty of ideas, flexibility of mental operations, capacity for reorganization of organized wholes, and the capacity to deal with complex conceptual structures. Then, with the help of factor analysis, one can determine whether some of these play an essential role in the thinking of genius. In a report on the progress of this research program, Wilson, Guilford, and Christensen (1953) describe a number of tests which they have devised, such as writing clever titles for a short story whose plot has been sketchily presented, or imagining remote consequences of some very unlikely event. Since the effort is to discover originality, it is essential that the problems give free scope to the subjects, rather than calling for set answers which might have been anticipated by the test constructors. They find that the correlations among scores on these tests do indicate the presence of a common factor of originality. Ultimately, they hope to be able not only to measure this ability, but also to describe the characteristic mental organization of persons with exceptional capacity for creative thinking.

GESTALT PRINCIPLES OF PERCEPTION

We turn now from the study of abilities to the study of proclivities or dispositions in thinking, as they are expressed in the phenomena of perceptual selection and perceptual attitudes. It is not possible to discuss these topics without some familiarity with the general principles of perception. Therefore we shall first review some salient points of cognitive theory which have special relevance to the problems of personality.

One of the foundations of modern cognitive theory is the doctrine of perception that has been developed by the Gestalt school. Everyone who works in the field of thinking and perception is forced to acknowledge the importance of the principles which have been so brilliantly demonstrated by the

Gestalt experimentalists. There are differences of opinion as to how broadly these principles should be applied. Gestalt theory stresses the autocthonous determinants of perception, that is, the factors whose operation is independent of experience. Many psychologists therefore believe that they do not give enough attention to experiential influences. This conflict of opinion is not merely analogous to the conflict over the importance of unlearned behavior, but is actually an aspect of that conflict, since the basis for many unlearned adjustive responses by higher animals and by man is the immediacy of perception for certain configurational patterns of stimulation.

The basic concepts which are of importance to us can be seen in operation in four important investigations of visual perception and memory: Wertheimer's study of illusory movement (1912); Rubin's study of reversible figures (1915); Wulf's study of memory for designs (1922); and Köhler's study of responses to size and brightness relationships (1918). It is essential for us to have a clear understanding of the major implications of each of these, although it is not necessary to accept all the theory that has been developed from them.

Illusory movement, or the stroboscopic phenomenon, had been the object of a good deal of study during the 19th century. For the introspective psychology of that period, nothing seemed more important than to discover the fundamental elements of mental structure, which presumably combined as chemical elements do to form all the complex experiences of our mental life. With respect to movement experience, the question was whether it could be reduced to other elements of visual and kinesthetic sensation, or whether it must be regarded as a distinctive quality of experience. In his attack on this problem, Wertheimer turned away from the more complex forms of stroboscopy, and reduced the illusion to its essential minimum: two lines, or two spots of light, seen in succession at different points. The brightness of the stimuli, their angular separation, and above all the time intervening between their exposures, influence the forcefulness of the illusion. Two young men who served as the principal observers in this experiment—Kurt Koffka and Wolfgang Köhler—were destined to form with Wertheimer the future triumvirate of the Gestalt school. Their protocols showed that it was possible to have a pure experience of seen movement, not associated with any moving object. There had been other demonstrations of Gestalt character in experience before (the concept had been emphasized above all by Ehrenfels) but this became the starting point of what was to be the Gestalt school. The major point which the experiment illustrates for us is the fact that it is not possible to define an experience as the sum of the separate experiences which would be aroused by all the parts of the stimulus situation, considered one by one. The experience, or the response, is unitary, and the effects of the stimuli cannot be studied except in their dynamic interaction, which has an organismic character. Lest the point be overlooked, let the reader be reminded that it is of the very essence of this doctrine that this unity of experience is not achieved through learning, but is a fundamental characteristic of perceptual response, due to the inherent organization of the physiological mechanisms involved. Everyone will agree that this is true "to a point," but there will be a great deal of disagreement as to where that point should be placed, on the continuum from the "buzzing, blooming confusion" of the infant's early experience, as James described it, to the painstaking syntheses of scientific theory. The Gestaltists emphasize the essential unity of perceptual structure at every stage of development.

At almost the same time, Rubin was engaged in another investigation of how the elements of a visual field organize themselves into unitary perceptions. His experiments gave rise to the very useful concepts of *figure* and *ground*. Many readers will recall Rubin's famous figure of a white goblet on a black ground, which can almost as readily be seen as two black facial profiles separated by a white space. The same basic point can also be illustrated by this simple drawing:

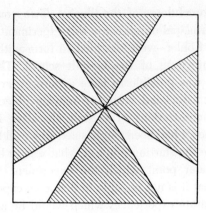

Inside the square, one sees a cross whose arms are shaded equilateral triangles. As one continues to look at the figure, the field suddenly becomes restructured, so that one sees a cross of four pointed and diagonally placed arms, which appear to stand out in relief above the shaded ground. Having had both experiences, one may alternate them more or less at will, but it is no longer possible to stare fixedly at the figure for any length of time without the shift from one structure to another occurring involuntarily.

Such reversible figures provide a forceful illustration for certain characteristics which inhere in every stimulus situation. (1) Every stimulus field is spontaneously structured by the perceiver into figure and ground. (2) The field is often ambiguous, in the sense that it can give rise to many figures, and unstable, because these figures tend to displace one another. (3) Some figures are extremely unstable, while others can be altered only with difficulty. Rubin's goblet figure, the well-known staircase illusion, and the simple drawing which we have just been looking at are all examples of unstable figures, for they undergo repeated spontaneous reversals while we look at them. An example of a very stable field is the puzzle picture which presents the appearance of an ordinary landscape, within which we are supposed to find, let us say, the face of George Washington, whose features are lost in the lines that seem to depict only clouds, shrubbery, and a grazing horse. (4) The restructuring which discloses such a figure is always sudden and complete, rather than gradual and piecemeal. All at once, the man's features leap out at us, and in that very instant every line of the drawing undergoes a change of meaning. Even some cloud puff in the corner, though it may still be a cloud puff, is no longer quite the same, because it has changed from being a natural part of a rural scene to being a bit of stylized background for a hero's portrait. This principle of the dynamic restructuring of ambiguous stimulus fields applies far outside the sphere of visual perception, to every instance of reinterpretation of facts, which is a constant aspect of our intellectual activity.

One consequence of the figural structuring of a field is that the figure exhibits greater constancy than the ground. For example, Rubin showed that a shadow thrown upon the figure seems to have less darkening effect than a like shadow thrown upon the ground. One may say that the figure is stronger than the ground, more resistant to influences that might tend to obliterate it. This resistant quality of the figure is the key to Wulf's study of memory. He showed his subjects simple drawings of forms, which he had them reproduce from memory after varied intervals of time. He found that the alterations which took place in the reproductions, as compared to the original drawings, could not be regarded simply as random lapses of memory, due to a weakening of associative bonds with time, but that they could be classified as falling into one of two groups: either they tend to accent or *sharpen* those features that enhance the figure which was originally seen, or they tend to deemphasize or *level* those features that would detract from it. In a sequence of recollections by the same subject, spaced at long intervals, such sharpening and leveling processes have a progressive character or cumulative trend.

Köhler showed that even where the situation seems to favor

the establishment of associative bonds to elements of the stimulus field, the organism's preference is to respond to relations. He trained hens to peck grains from the brighter of two cardboards. Then, in a critical test of what had been learned, he removed the negative stimulus, and paired the positive stimulus with another still brighter cardboard. The hens showed their preference for the brighter card of those exposed. There were other experiments of the same general plan in which children and chimpanzees served as the subjects. The essential point is very close to that of Wertheimer's experiment on illusory movement, but there is the great advantage that we are dealing here with the naive responses of hunger-motivated animals and children, and not with the introspections of theoretically minded psychologists. For these naive subjects, a *relation* is an immediately evident aspect of the stimulus field—not something which is perceived after training with many different pairs of stimuli, but something which is more readily grasped and responded to than an absolute size or an absolute brightness.

All the laws that govern the appearance of figures were summed up by Wertheimer (1923) in the single principle of *pregnancy.* This asserts that a figure always tends to be "as good as possible" for the given perceiver. That is to say, it will tend to a form which is as simple, as stable, and as broadly inclusive as possible under the given circumstances. The term pregnancy also conveys the thought that the issuance of meaning from the perceptual field depends primarily on the field's own dynamic organization. The productive thinker, says Wertheimer (1945), is one who is ready to accept what is pregnant in the field of his observation, and who does not introduce self-generated obstacles to the free development of its optimal figural structuring.

This point of view, which makes the thinker a vehicle of meaning rather than its discoverer, is quite consistent with the general viewpoint of Gestalt psychology, which has never given more than passing attention to problems of individuality. Even

Lewin, who emphasizes the importance of the individual case, still considers it from the standpoint of universality. He does not think of how two men might act differently in the same situation, but of how any man must act in a given situation, and of what the situational differences are that lead two men to behave differently under conditions that seem superficially the same. Therefore, when such concepts as leveling, sharpening, and response to figural instability are used—as we shall see later in this chapter—in the definition of personality types, the Gestaltist tends to look askance at these efforts and to question whether his basic principles are not being misapplied.

Association vs. Mental Set

Gestalt theory is concerned with the external or field determinants of perception. It tells us little or nothing about the individualizing factors which arise from experience. It is to these that we must now turn our attention, and we may begin by looking at a simple but rather ambiguous figure, in which different people may find different meanings.

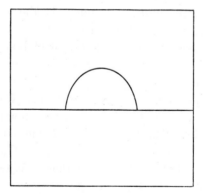

What is it? Most people will think first of the sun or the moon, rising or setting. We may therefore refer to these answers as "populars," a term we shall have occasion to use again in the discussion of projective tests. The minor differences among such answers may be unimportant, but it is possible that they do

reflect individual differences, as between dispositions to adventure and romance, or between optimism and pessimism.
What else may it be? The answers to this second question will
usually be more individualized. We may safely leave the reader
to provide his own. However, we can increase the likelihood of
similar answers by providing a hint: *It is a part of a person;
what is it?* A bald man seated in a sofa, seen from behind? A
baby standing close to a table? A woman in a bathtub, with only
one knee showing? Perhaps the reader can offer additional
interpretations. The longer the list of answers, gathered from
different persons, the more obvious it becomes that we cannot
afford to neglect the special experiences, interests, and attitudes
of the perceiver himself. The explanatory principles which we
may adduce to explain these individual differences, without
leaving the context of cognitive theory, are association, concept
formation, and mental set or determining tendency. We shall
discuss the first and last of these in the present section, leaving
concept formation aside until the next chapter.

The most obvious and most commonly accepted reason for
individuality in perceptual meanings is the content of the
person's past experience. A ditch digger and a paleontologist
do not see the same thing in a fragment of bone unearthed in
undisturbed subsoil; one sees a minor oddity, almost nothing at
all, where the other may see evidence of history-shaping proportions. This indisputable importance of the past in determining
the intellectual present has led to many attempts to explain
the whole of the thinking process as being no more than a
blend of present stimuli with the associations that they arouse,
because of coincidence in past experience. Without trying to
review the history of association theory, we can mention a
single crucial defect which keeps this type of explanation from
being adequate: the distinctive act of thought rests so often not
on the frequent or the vivid experience, but upon the rare and
fleeting experience which is recalled from a near oblivion when
it aptly fits the thinker's need. This is the type of event for

which we need explanation. The richness of associations, but not their strength, is a resource for the thinker. Memory is a valuable storehouse, but association theory does not explain how its treasures become available to us just when we need them. "Association by similarity" is not an acceptable answer, for this is not association at all, not an effect produced by past contiguities in experience, but a creative act of perception in the present, a phenomenon of the sort that we are trying to explain. To pursue this line of thought would lead us directly into the discussion of concept formation, which we have put off till the next chapter, because it has little direct bearing on the phenomena of perceptual selectivity and perceptual attitude, toward the definition of which we are moving.

The inadequacy of the principle of association to explain the content of perception and the progress of thinking was demonstrated most clearly in the experimentation of the Würzburg school. Again let us recall that even in the early years of the present century the liveliest issue in psychological discussion was still the question whether the content of thinking could be described solely in terms of conscious content composed of sensations and images. The negative answer to this question remains one of the great achievements in the history of scientific psychology, and we should not overlook the fact that it was an achievement of the introspective method. In a typical experiment on this problem, the observer would be given a series of fairly simple verbal problems, each of which would normally take just a few seconds for its solution. His main task, however, was not to find the answer, but to give the most detailed account possible of all the content of his mind during the interval between reading the stimulus word and recognizing the solution. Sometimes, using a technique which may be compared to the inspection of thin slices of brain tissue under a microscope in the effort to chart ascending and descending neural pathways, the process of thinking might be interrupted by a sudden signal, and the task of the observer was to describe the conscious content of his mind at the very instant of such interruption. Out of such experiments there came the realization that the progress of thought, from a problem to its solution, could not be described in terms of conscious content, for much of thought was imageless (Woodworth, 1906). The answer usually appeared suddenly, without conscious preparation by any sequence of images leading to it. It was characteristic, moreover, that the observer would report a sense of strain or tension, a vague awareness of problem setting and striving, from which all definable meaning was absent. This most important achievement of introspective psychology also signaled its demise, since it established the fact that the creative mental processes which were the chief object of its study were not accessible to introspection. At the same time, it opened the way to a more dynamic understanding of the thinking process, as something whose determination lies in the multiple depths of personality and not on the surface, where they might be open to easy inspection. The word *Einstellung,* translated as *mental set,* expresses the idea that the task which is assigned to the observer gives him an orientation which influences the associations that will follow, and does not merely guide him in selecting the correct association from those that appear. This is true regardless of whether the task orientation remains conscious or deteriorates into nothing more than a vague feeling of effort, as is usually the case. Ach (1905) provided a more expressive phrase, *determining tendency.* This carries the same general meaning, but it has less implication of transiency. A mental set is a condition that is induced by some short-term influence, such as an experimental instruction. A very good illustration is provided by Leeper's (1935) experiment, in which the subject can be led to interpret the same drawing as either a pretty young woman or an ugly old hag, depending on the expectation that has been set up by the immediately preceding experiences. Determining tendency, on the other hand, is a phrase which also embraces the more enduring dispositions which are the expressions of personality, although its experimental investigation will usually deal with temporary influences that are under the control of the experimenter. As one of his illustrations of determining tendency, Ach includes the post-hypnotic suggestion, which was, of course, also being used by Freud, at about this same time, in his efforts to demonstrate the reality of unconscious thinking.

The last important contribution in the tradition of the Würz-burg school was Selz's (1922) study of productive thinking, which opens with an analysis of the errors made by his observers. This also provides an interesting experimental parallel to Freud's use of similar material drawn from everyday experience, although in this case Freud has clear priority. In the *Psychopathology of Everyday Life* (1904, 1938a), Freud examined the determinants behind "slips of the tongue" and showed how they revealed unconscious motivations. The important point, however, was not merely to demonstrate the reality of unconscious thinking by still another example, but to show that the same kinds of determinants operate in logic and in error. This is what Selz also showed. For example, one of his observers was given the stimulus word *hour*, and the instruction to answer with a supraordinate concept. His answer was *day*. Although one day includes many hours, the concept day does not include the concept hour; it is a broader span of time, but not a broader concept. The subject, who had been upset by one or two immediately preceding errors, was seeking confusedly for something more inclusive than "hour." His error was not determined by a chance association, but by incomplete comprehension of the task. The product of his thought must still be understood as issuing out of his task orientation.

Mental set and determining tendency are the direct fore-runners of the Lewinian concept of tension systems, and Lewin's own early work was done in the atmosphere of controversy which still surrounded these issues in Germany during his student days. However, Lewin was emphatic in his insistence (1926, 1935) that it was not enough to recognize the need for such auxiliary mechanisms to explain the sequence of thoughts; in his opinion, the facts indicated that associative "and-connections"—the phrase is Wertheimer's—are completely ineffectual. He pointed to the subject's *need* as the sole source of the energy which brings about the movement or restructuring of the perceptual field.

The principles of cognition which we have been discussing in the preceding pages were established without regard for individual differences. However, some authors have suggested that significant individual differences exist with respect to one or another aspect of this total process. Thus, for example, Frenkel-Brunswik (1949) and Klein (1951) have spoken in somewhat similar terms of differences in tolerance for perceptual instability, and Klein has also spoken of differences in leveling and sharpening tendencies in perception. Many authors have tried to show how personal needs influence perception, and thus indirectly behavior. In the remainder of this chapter, we shall first review some of the more important studies of this nature, and we shall then describe some of the suggested dimensions of perceptual attitude.

Perceptual Selectivity

The experimental study of the influence of needs and interests on perception and memory has now reached the dimensions of a very lively movement, whose enthusiasts have sometimes claimed that perceptual selectivity is the central fact of personality. Although most of this work is quite recent, there is one important and influential contribution which stands as a bridge between the early work of the Gestalt school and the experiments that may be regarded as strictly of the present. In his work on *Remembering*, Bartlett (1932) showed that the conclusions which Wulf had reached in his study of the reproductions of content-free drawings from memory remain valid when they are applied to the meaningful materials of everyday life. He showed, for example, that the distortions which occur in the recollection of a story are not haphazard, but represent a shift of emphasis which makes the material as a whole conform better to the subject's original interpretation. There is not a simple dropping out of details, but a dynamic altering of the whole, in a direction that is subjectively determined. It is as if the subject takes advantage of the reduced potency of the absent stimulation, to recast it as he wishes.

Remembering . . . is an imaginative reconstruction, or construction, built out of the relation of our attitude toward a whole active mass of organized past reactions or experience, and to a little outstanding detail. . . . The outstanding detail is the result of that valuation of items in an organized mass which begins with the functioning of appetite and interest, and goes much further with the growth of interests and ideals.

Thus Bartlett goes beyond Wulf in demonstrating that the sharpening and leveling which occur in this reconstruction of details is in response to underlying motivations of the individual. He also shows in considerable detail how memory is influenced by expectations which have been derived from the social context in which the person lives.

This tendentious character of memory in both its errors and its selective retention has since been confirmed in a number of experimental studies. Levine and Murphy (1943) demonstrated the influence of motivation on the efficiency of memorizing. They compared two groups of students, one composed of known pro-Communist sympathizers and the other of known anti-Communists, on the efficiency with which they memorized and retained two lengthy prose passages about the Soviet Union. The passage which was pro-Soviet in its content was memorized more quickly and retained more effectively by the students who were sympathetic to the Soviet Union. For the passage which was anti-Soviet in its content, the reverse relationships obtained. Although the two groups of subjects were small, the differences were highly significant at every comparison, and they tended to increase in magnitude rather than to diminish in the course of the experiment.

Allport and Postman (1947), in a study of rumor, give attention to the nature of the distortions of recollection and the manner in which they accumulate as they pass from person to person. They utilized a technique which Bartlett had introduced, and which he called the method of serial reproduction. Many of us have played it as a parlor game. A short story is told to subject A; he repeats it privately to B; B passes it on to C, and so on. The story in its final form contains the accumulated distortions of many inexact reproductions. Despite the fact that under the conditions of the experiment the time intervals were quite short and the subjects were strongly motivated to be accurate, many tendentious errors occurred. For example, one such series starts with the description of a scene in a trolley car, in the center of which a rather properly dressed Negro man is talking to a white laborer who is holding an open razor in his hand. After the description has passed through half a dozen mouths, it is the Negro who holds the razor. Like Bartlett, Allport and Postman not only observe the phenomena of leveling and sharpening, but they also recognize that these tendencies are governed by the need to *assimilate* the perceived material in a form which is easily mastered and which is consistent with expectations developed from prior experience. They summarize the entire process in the following sentences, which deserve to be quoted at length, because they are a clear statement not only of the distortions which enter into the creation of rumors, but of almost everything that is positively known about the subject of perceptual selectivity.

Whenever a stimulus field is of potential importance to an individual, but at the same time unclear, or susceptible of divergent interpretations, a subjective structuring process is started. Although the process is complex (involving, as it does, leveling, sharpening, and assimilation), its essential nature can be characterized as an effort to reduce the stimulus to a simple and meaningful structure that has adaptive significance for the individual in terms of his own interests and experience. The process begins at the moment the ambiguous situation is perceived, but the effects are greatest if memory intervenes. The longer the time that elapses after the stimulus is perceived the greater the threefold change is likely to be. . . .

What seems to occur in all our experiments and in all related studies is that each subject finds the outer stimulus-world far too hard to grasp and retain in its objective character. For his own personal uses, it must be recast to fit not only his span of comprehension and his span of retention, but, likewise, his own personal needs and interests.

In this passage, there are two important restrictions placed on the generality of these conclusions. First, they are stated as applying only to the interpretation of stimulus fields which are unclear or ambiguous. Second, there is the observation that "the effects are greatest if memory intervenes." Many investigators have tried to demonstrate similar motivational effects in the phenomena of perceptual emphasis and selectivity, where forgetting is not a factor. Their purpose is to show that objectively similar experiences yield different meanings, as well as different memories, to persons of different interests. This emphasis on the subjective determinants of perception has been dubbed the "New Look" (Krech, 1949), and the phrase bids fair to survive in psychological discussion after it has been quite forgotten in the world of fashion, from which it was borrowed.

Schafer and Murphy (1943) divided each of two circles with a wavy line drawn so that either half, presented alone, would be perceived as a crudely drawn facial profile. (The ease with which this can be done is in itself a demonstration of how our universal social interest facilitates the recognition of faces in any visual material, where any conspicuous bump may be taken for a nose, and any recess beneath it for a mouth.) The subjects then learned names for these four faces, and, as they went through their practice trials, each subject received a small money reward whenever one of the faces from each disk was presented, and had a small sum taken away from him whenever the other face from that disk was shown. In the critical trials, the entire disk was shown, with its wavy middle line dividing it into two parts. Of course, this constituted an ambiguous figure, in which only one face could be seen at a time, the other being lost in the ground. Under these conditions, each subject saw the face that had been associated with satisfactions, rather than the one that had been a source of frustration. This result has been confirmed (Jackson, 1954), but it is unstable enough so that it may not appear when the same general design has been followed with some attendant conditions modified (Rock and Fleck, 1950).

Bruner, Postman, and their associates have contributed an important series of investigations and theoretical discussions on this problem. Several of these studies have been designed to demonstrate an enhancement of the apparent size of an object to which psychological importance is attached. Bruner and Goodman (1947) asked 10-year-olds to adjust the size of a disk of light, appearing on a glass screen, to equal the size of a coin. The adjustment was made by turning a dial with one hand, while viewing the coin held in the other. They did the same thing with cardboard disks instead of coins. They found that the children tended to overestimate the size of the coins but not of the cardboard disks; that this tendency was, in general, greater percentagewise as the coins increased in value; and— a circumstance which has led to extensive citing of this experiment in texts of social psychology—that children from poorer homes, who presumably placed greater value on the coins, overestimated their size more than did the children from wealthy homes. However, repetitions of this experiment by Carter and Schooler (1949) and by Rosenthal and Levi (1950) have thrown serious doubt on the validity of the last conclusion. Bruner and Postman (1948) found that college students judged disks inscribed with dollar signs and swastikas to be larger than those inscribed with a neutral design, indicating that negative value, as well as positive, could lead to a perceptual accentuation.

An experiment by Bruner, Postman, and McGinnies (1948) brought certain theoretical difficulties of the New Look into sharp relief. They selected six stimulus words to represent each of the major categories of the Allport-Vernon Scale of Values. These 36 words were tachistoscopically presented to their subjects, whose personal value systems also were appraised by the Allport-Vernon scale. Each word was repeatedly presented to each subject, with each successive exposure 1/100 second longer than the one preceding, until it was correctly perceived. In general, subjects required a shorter exposure to recognize words representative of their more highly esteemed values, and longer time for those representative of their disesteemed values. For example, one subject who scored highest on Esthetic value and lowest on Economic, required an exposure of only 8/100 second to recognize such words as *artist* and *elegant,* but approximately twice as long to recognize words like *useful* and *finance.* From a consideration of these results, and a study of the misreadings which preceded the correct recognitions, the authors concluded that the phenomenon of perceptual selectivity has at least three aspects: *selective sensitivity,* which lowers thresholds for higher-valued stimuli; *perceptual defense,* "which erects barriers against percepts and hypotheses incongruent with or threatening to the individual's values;" and *value resonance,* which directs perceptual guesses "in congruence with prevailing value orientations." The reader can readily see the parallel between these three aspects and the phenomena of sharpening, leveling, and assimilation.

The principle of perceptual defense became a source of embarrassment to the New Look. How does the subject know to "not recognize" the disesteemed word, if he does not first recognize it for one that he disesteems? Critics, and then the authors themselves, cast about for different explanations. Solomon and Howes (1951) contended that the effects could be explained by a more sophisticated recognition of the part played by differential familiarity with the various stimulus words used. Postman (1951) soon withdrew his support for the principle of perceptual defense. Both he and Bruner (1951) now prefer an explanation solely in terms of the differential strength of "perceptual hypotheses," which would result partly from differences in familiarity, and partly from the "motivational support" which

would be derived equally from positively weighted and negatively weighted experiences—that is, from the fear as well as
the wish.

This concept of perceptual hypothesis has much in common
with the behavioral "hypotheses," or individually preferred
methods of attack on problem situations, which Krechevsky
(1932) discovered in the behavior of rats, and with the derivative
concept of the "provisional try" which has been advanced by
Hilgard (1948). But whereas these learning theorists are thinking in terms of operations which are tested, if not in actual
practice, at least by an imaginal representation of their consequences, which requires a measurable space of time to run its
course, the perceptual hypothesis is confirmed or disconfirmed
almost instantaneously, perhaps in the very process of its forming, on the basis of its compatibility or incompatibility with other
cortical events. This sort of lightning acceptance or rejection of
an hypothesis is quite consistent with the idea, which we shall
examine in the next chapter, that the brain operates in essential
respects like a high-speed electronic computer. In describing the
provisional try, Hilgard says that it "is kept in suspension until
its consequences change its provisional status; if it is confirmed
it is an appropriate path of action to be followed under like
circumstances, if it is not confirmed it is inappropriate." The
theory of perceptual hypotheses implies that the brain can do
this at a subconscious level, making its multiple tests for
plausibility and acceptability before admitting the percept to
the full light of consciousness.

In judging the importance of the New Look, we must bear in
mind that the issue is not whether interests and needs are important determinants of behavior, but whether they exercise a
major part of their influence through the avenue of perception.
The effects which have been demonstrated are too slight and
unstable, and too difficult to reproduce, to be altogether convincing in this regard. Pastore (1949) contends that they can
be of little practical importance, because they occur only in

"marginal situations" where clear perception has purposely been made difficult. To this, the Murphy group replies (Chein et al., 1951) that *"marginal perceptual situations* are a major fact in everyday life." Indeed, the experiments only demonstrate in the laboratory a phenomenon that is already old in popular wisdom. We "see what we wish to see, hear what we wish to hear," and close eyes and ears to conflicting evidence. The mother may see an innocent child where the judge sees a hardened reprobate, and Murphy's phrase, that "needs push ahead of percepts" (1947) only echoes the adage that necessity is the mother of invention. The experiments add the important proof that such effects are involuntary, but they also leave us surprised that it should be so difficult to demonstrate this with any degree of consistency. As compared with the clinic, the laboratory still throws a feeble light into the shadows of the human mind. Still, it also has its advantages, and in these experiments we have a promising though still inadequate technique for analysis of the conditions which foster perceptual emphases and distortions.

The inconsistency of the experimental results inevitably raises the question whether individual differences, always the most refractory source of experimental error, are not being overlooked. Murphy (1947), who places considerable weight on the importance of perceptual autism, raises the question whether "proneness to autism is a generalized quality of individuals,"— that is, whether it should not be recognized that some individuals are strongly autistic even without provocation of any urgent need, while others are relatively free from such behavior. Klein, Schlessinger and Meister (1951) showed the need to take account of individual differences by comparing the size emphasis derived from the swastika symbol for a group of anti-Nazi German emigrés and control groups of native Americans. Contrary to expectations, group differences were not significant, although within each group there were individuals who showed consistent tendencies to over- or underestimation. This result led them (Klein and Shlessinger, 1949) to suggest that interest and autism provide too narrow a base for an adequate survey of individual differences in the perceptual process, regarded as a form of adaptive behavior. They suggest instead the search for "types" of persons who have "similarly organized perceptual systems." It is to this search that we now turn our attention.

PERCEPTUAL ATTITUDES

A perceptual attitude, as the term is used by Klein and his associates, represents a characteristic preference in the manner of perceiving external reality. Klein (1951) has defined several dimensions of attitudinal variation in perception. We find it convenient to begin with his definitions, because they can be readily related to aspects of the perceptual process as we have outlined it. In seeking for the dimensions of perceptual attitude, he and his co-workers looked first for striking individual differences in any one perceptual task, and then tried to predict correlated differences in other perceptual tasks, involving quite different materials. They were guided also by the clinically founded hypothesis that important differences in perceptual attitudes would correspond to distinctive ways of resolving the tension which, as Klein puts it, each person must feel between "inner strivings and the demands of reality." Thus, although these dimensions are defined in terms of cognitive function, they are assumed to have underlying motivational determinants.

The first of these dimensions is the contrasting emphasis on leveling and sharpening tendencies. Sharpening is described as "a tendency to be hypersensitive to minutiae, to respond excessively to fine nuances and small differences, to exaggerate change, and to keep adjacent or successive stimuli from fusing and losing identity." Opposed to this, there is a tendency "to reduce the saliency of figures against grounds, to level the differences between them." Both leveling and sharpening behavior are, as we have noted earlier, characteristic of perception and memory generally. Here the suggestion is made that some persons are more disposed than others to structure their experience in ways that emphasize difference. In making a series of size judgments, for example, "levelers" tend to continue using the same range of values after the original stimuli, unknown to them, have been gradually replaced by others that are much larger. "Sharpeners," on the other hand, are alert to such changes; their basic orientation is toward the detection of change and difference. At this point, we may call to mind the Bruner and Goodman experiment, in which size judgments were influenced by value judgments, presumably because bigness and value are so often associated in our experience. In that experiment, we may assume, a leveler would tend to equalize the coins in size, overestimating the small ones and underestimating the large ones. We may surmise that one reason for such behavior is reluctance to make any comparative judgment. Whatever the ostensible nature of the judgment that is called for, levelers recoil from making it, as a situation fraught with danger to themselves. On the other hand, there are some subjects who welcome the chance to make comparative judgments, and these become sharpeners. Levelers and sharpeners are the lambs and the lions of the perceptual arena.

Another of these dimensions of perceptual attitude is called "tolerance for perceptual instability." Again, we recall that instability is an aspect of all perception. However, some subjects are much more resistant to the figural shifts that result from such instability, such as the illusory movement experiences that are induced by the alternation of two figures in the visual field. For the "perceptually intolerant" person, Klein says, "things must appear as they are *known* to be: he desires stability above all." In taking the Rorschach test, such subjects show a very restricted use of fantasy. This dimension is one whose importance has also been stressed by Frenkel-Brunswik (1949). We must digress, before considering her provocative theory, to look first at the circumstances which gave rise to it.

In their widely branching study of *The Authoritarian Personality*, Adorno, Frenkel-Brunswik, Levinson, and Sanford (1949) explored the interrelatedness of motivational and cognitive structure in the behavior of bigoted persons. The design of their experiments and the nature of their conclusions sometimes suggests that they were motivated by an intolerance of intolerance which is possibly inconsistent with purely scientific endeavor, and which led them into some errors of methodology. (Cf. Christie and Jahoda, 1954.) However, the extent of their contribution will not be measured by the durability of their specific conclusions, but by the stimulus which they provided for the field of social psychology and the psychology of personality. Smith (1950) has aptly said that these investigators "set out to track a jackal and found themselves at grips with a behemoth." In their search for the personality correlates of anti-Semitic and anti-Negro attitudes, they were led to the conclusion that ethnic prejudice is but one expression of an authority-centered character structure, one which respects strength and disdains weakness, which is disposed to fawn before a tyrant and to act the bully toward an underdog. Associated with this character is a many-sided syndrome whose separate parts do not seem at first glance to be connected in any necessary way. The authoritarian personality is not only ethnocentric, but he also tends to be more rigid in other ways. The authors of *The Authoritarian Personality* postulate that the child's own experiences with authority, in his own family circle, influence his thinking about many different things in later life, because almost everything is seen as either sharing in the respect that is due to strength or as deserving only the contempt that is given to the weak.

As a direct extension of this study, Frenkel-Brunswik (1949) went on to study the formation of this character structure in childhood. She concluded that the syndrome of emotional and perceptual behavior is best explained as the expression of a general "intolerance of ambiguity," and she argued that tolerance for ambiguity should be regarded as a basic variable of personality. The cognitively intolerant person feels a need for definiteness in all his experiences, tends to view things as sharply black and white, is uneasy when confronted with a situation in which "yes-and-no" both seem appropriate. Social intolerance is but one expression of this disposition to divide the phenomenal world into sharply distinguished categories. She relates this need for definiteness to the psychoanalytic concept of ambivalent attitudes toward parents.

Synopsis of a variety of data suggests that the attempt to master aggression toward parental figures who are experienced as too threatening and powerful are among the important determinants of the tendency rigidly to avoid ambiguity of any sort. The requested submission and obedience to parental authority is only one of the rules which such a child learns. Dominance-submission, cleanliness-dirtiness, badness-goodness, virtue-vice, masculinity-femininity are some of the other dichotomies customarily upheld in the homes of such children. . . . Family relationships are based on roles clearly defined in terms of dominance and submission. Some of the children live in a situation comparable to permanent physical danger,[2] which leaves no time for finer discriminations and for attempts to get a fuller understanding of the factors involved but in which quick action leading to tangible and concrete results is the only appropriate behavior.

This discussion leaves no doubt that intolerance of ambiguity is presented as a basic variable of personality only in the sense that it is a far-reaching descriptive concept, not as an explanatory principle. That role is given to the parent-child relationship, which provides the mold in which all other experience is cast. The child's relation to his parents becomes the master analogy by which all other relationships are made meaningful. In this theoretical construction, Frenkel-Brunswik and her co-workers have been influenced simultaneously by the psychoanalytic concept of ambivalence and by the field-theoretical approach to problems of ambiguity, or instability, in perceptual fields. The description that she gives goes beyond a definition of intolerance of instability, in the sense intended by Klein, for she includes an intimation that a complex con-

---

[2] We should like to comment that such conditions of harsh discipline amounting to "permanent physical danger" also favor the acquisition of abnormal fixations, and may therefore be regarded as fostering rigidity in behavior altogether without regard to the specific value systems which are being taught and practiced in the home.

ceptual framework, as well as the simpler perceptual disposition, is involved in the determination of the observed behavior. This is an aspect of the problem to which we shall return in the next chapter.

The third major dimension of perceptual attitude which is defined by Klein is designated as the "physiognomic vs. literal" dimension, that is, the disposition to endow percepts with "an expressive or human-like aura," or, on the other hand, to perceive them in strictly objective terms. The tendency to animistic interpretation of inanimate forms has received considerable attention from psychologists of the Gestalt school. Werner (1926, 1940) has described such physiognomic interpretations as projections of our own feelings, and has emphasized their importance in children's perceptions. Arnheim (1949), expressing the usual emphasis of the Gestalt school on the inherent values of the stimulus field for *any* perceiver, has argued that physical forms often have a direct capacity to evoke specific emotional responses in us, because of a genuinely parallel structure (isomorphism) between the form and some physiological aspect of the response. It is generally accepted that the artist is particularly responsive to such influences, and able to accent them in his creations in ways that make them more meaningful to others. The rounded form of a woman sculptured by Maillol strikes us as solidly maternal and earthy, while an attenuated sculpture by Lehmbruck impresses us as spiritual and virtually sexless. Similar emotional impact may be achieved by abstract artists, whose sculptured forms may likewise seem "earthy" or "spiritual" while possessing no obvious resemblance to natural objects of any sort, animate or inanimate. It seems reasonable to suppose that people generally may be differentiated according to their sensitivity to such factors, not only in art works, but in casual experience.

Barron (1953a) has defined a dimension of "complexity-simplicity" which appears to be related to at least two of the perceptual attitudes which we have been discussing. His point of departure was the observation that, when subjects were asked to state their preferences in the pairs of abstract designs of the Welsh Figure Preference Test, some exhibited a fairly consistent tendency to prefer the more complex, and others to prefer the simpler and more symmetrical design in each pair. Subsequently, he found indications that the preference for complexity was associated positively with a good many other characteristics, including impulsiveness, sensuality, and independence of judgment—as measured in the situation devised by Asch, described on page 253. It was correlated negatively with rigidity, conservatism, and social conformity, and perhaps also with likability and lack of deceitfulness. It seems plausible that the liking for complexity should also be associated with a disposition toward sharpening rather than leveling responses, and with high tolerance for instability in the perceptual field.

Riggs (1952, 1953) has defined a series of three "new" personality dimensions which seem to correspond to Klein's attitudinal dimensions. The basis for her definitions is a simple test situation in which subjects are required to make sentences using certain words. The stimulus words are all homophones, that is, in their spoken form they are sounds which stand for several different meanings. The use to which each word is put, in the sentence constructed, is classified as either Literal, Indirect, or Exciting, and the relative frequency of these three modes of response is taken as a measure of the relative strength of the corresponding dispositions in behavior. The justification for considering that these are dimensions of personality is provided in the demonstration that marked individual differences appear, and tend to be consistent. In addition, Riggs showed that the scores of the sentence test could be used to predict behavior in many other kinds of test situations, as well as in personal relationships and leadership roles in a college dormitory group.

The *Literal* tendency is manifest as an orientation toward obvious physical reality, the *Indirect* tendency toward abstract or inner intangibles, the *Exciting* tendency toward intense exciting experience, e.g., of sex, aggression, power, and strong striving. In addition, the particular results indicated rejections characteristic of each tendency in this sample. People with *Literal* dominant avoid dynamic or abstract content, dislike irreality, and show little effort or originality in creative tasks. People with *Indirect* dominant avoid commonplace realism and overt expressions of affect. People with *Exciting* dominant avoid obvious conventional content, abstractions devoid of human reference, and ordinary colorless depictions of human activity.

The three variables of personality defined by Riggs may readily be paired with Klein's three dimensions of perceptual attitude. In each system, one of the dimensions is designated as Literal. Riggs' Indirect disposition clearly corresponds to Klein's tolerance for instability, since the preference for indirect and figurative meanings necessarily implies not only a readiness but even an eagerness to have things otherwise than "as they are *known* to be." This leaves Exciting disposition to be paired with the sharpening attitude, which is certainly not inappropriate.

The Literal, Indirect, and Exciting dispositions can likewise be readily paired with Sheldon's viscerotonic, cerebrotonic, and somatotonic components of temperament, which were conceived in a very different context. One may therefore question the justification for describing them as "new" variables, although it is not at all surprising that this parallel should escape attention, since most psychologists regard Sheldon's work as beneath notice. The most immediately convincing pairing, of course, is that between Exciting and the somatotonic temperament. The forcefulness of this parallel is accented by Fleishman's demonstration (in unpublished research) that delinquent boys make significantly higher Exciting scores on the sentence test than a random sampling of boys from the same social milieu.

From this discussion of perceptual selectivity and perceptual attitudes, it is quite evident that it is not possible to study individuality in the intellectual sphere, without becoming aware of motivational influences that have a noncognitive basis. Some of the reasons for this will become more apparent in the course of the next chapter.

CHAPTER 15

Cognitive Individuality, II

Concepts and Symbolism

$\mathcal{I}$n the preceding chapter, we looked at a number of examples of perceptual selectivity, in which the person's needs or interests influence the outcome of the perceptual process. Sometimes this process is *autistic,* that is, it results in distortions of reality that are wish-determined, and which tend to hinder effective adjustment rather than to assist it. If we give too much weight to such instances, there is a danger that we may think of selectivity as a limitation or even a pathology of perceptual function, by which the person needlessly narrows his outlook on the world. Actually, effective perception must always be selective. This can be seen in the fact that the adaptive nature of unlearned response tendencies is determined in large part by the inherited selectivity of sensory mechanisms, which insures that the organism shall be responsive to the right food, the right sex partner, or to some danger that had never been experienced before. Intelligent adaptation calls for a flexible selectivity, which enables the individual to attend now to one and now to another aspect of the environment. If perception is to serve the needs of the organism, these percepts, which can never include at any one time more than a fragment of the meaning of the environment to the individual, must faithfully transmit that fragment. The percept must somehow be a functional model of an essential aspect of the outer world. What the organism sees, or hears, or smells, must prepare it for the actual impact of environmental events of which these percepts are the signals. The percept need not correspond to the whole of reality, but it must faithfully correspond to some part of it. It must have meaning.

In the previous chapter, we have already considered some ways in which the choice of meaning is an expression of individuality. Now we wish to look more closely at the nature of meaning, in the effort to understand how the intellectual development of the person gives rise to a distinctive way of regarding the world.

THE PHYSICAL BASIS OF MEANING

To begin with, since meaning is a matter of figural structuring of the stimulus field, it seems reasonable to suppose that this configuration is achieved through the ordering of the afferent impulses in the sensory cortex. This consideration is the basis of Köhler's theory of isomorphism, which asserts that there structuring of the stimulus field, it seems reasonable to suppose that this configuration is achieved through the ordering of the afferent impulses in the sensory cortex. This consideration is the basis of Köhler's theory of isomorphism, which asserts that there is a direct correspondence between the spatial patterning of electrical phenomena in the cortex, and the figure as perceived. We see the figure thus, because it actually exists thus within our brain. Köhler's formulation of this theory was probably influenced by Wertheimer's speculation that the phi phenomenon, or pure movement experience, might have its basis in a nervous impulse which actually moves from one point of the visual cortex to another. Despite its attractive simplicity, this geometric analogy does not provide an adequate basis even for visual form recognition, where it is most directly applicable. Brain (1951) reminds us that "when we perceive a two-dimensional circle we do so by means of an activity of the brain which is halved, reduplicated, transposed, inverted, distorted, and three-dimensional." Furthermore, the theory of isomorphism, as Köhler has developed it (Köhler, 1940; Köhler and Wallach, 1944), is closely tied to his theory of electrocortical fields, which has been found inadequate in two recent experimental tests. Lashley, Chow, and Semmes (1951) taught rats to discriminate between simple visual forms, and then laid strips of gold foil on the cortex and inserted gold pins within it. There was no indication that visual perception had been disturbed, as it should have been if the patterning of electrical phenomena was essential to form recognition. Sperry and Miner (1955) made the complementary test of trying to disturb form recognition by inserting insulators, instead of conductors. They pushed mica plates into the brains of cats which had previously been taught visual discriminations. There was some loss, but it seemed to be directly related to the amount of tissue damage produced by the insertions. Both groups of investigators interpret their findings as definitely contradicting Köhler's electric field hypothesis.

Whether or not the cortical representation of an object resembles it in spatial extension, it must somehow constitute a physical analogy of the object, with similar functional characteristics, for it is only in this way that it can provide the basis for an imaginative elaboration of reality in planned behavior. It is not necessary, however, to follow Köhler in his supposition that a physical analogy of form must be a spatial analogy. He is correct in his basic assumption that the brain activity must be some understandable transformation of the field as perceived. If the relations between external reality and brain cells or processes were purely arbitrary, it would not be possible for human thinking to achieve its creativity, its capacity to predict external events. This position was convincingly stated by Craik (1943), whose insight introduced a new approach to the problem of the physiological nature of thinking, and sheds light at the same time on some crucial psychological problems.

Craik conceived of the brain as a physical mechanism, the outstanding characteristic of which is its flexibility in creating working models of reality. It does this, he says, "as a calculating machine can parallel the development of strains in a bridge." Its basic function is symbolism, which "is largely of the same kind as that which is familiar to us in mechanical devices which aid thought and calculation." It is a machine for making models, some of which are relatively simple—though apparently not so simple as the electrocortical patterns which Köhler postulates—while others are quite complex, like the mathematical models which we develop with the use of number concepts. Every thought is a model, an analogy, a symbol. This theory of thinking as symbolism goes beyond Köhler's theory of isomorphism in two respects. First, it is less limited in the range of its application, because there is not the same sort of expectation that shape will be modeled by shape, or tempo by tempo. As Craik envisages cortical activity, it does not copy reality but sets up analogies to it. The nature of these analogies is limited by the physical characteristics of the brain, and we must never expect them to yield a true picture of the universe, in all its "real" dimensions. They are working models of reality, good for our practical purposes, and we should expect no more. The second respect in which Craik's theory goes beyond Köhler's is in explaining how thought can take the shape of future reality, as well as why it corresponds to the present. Because the model has the necessary functional characteristics of reality, it can be given an operating trial. Thought permits us to run model trains over model bridges within our minds, and to make reliable judgments as to whether the real bridge will stand or fall.

Craik's suggestion that the whole process of thinking is a profusion of analogies provides a unifying concept which embraces all forms of perceptual and imaginal activity. Not only the recognition of pattern and form, but any act of memory or conceptualization, the seemingly aimless revery and the methodical mathematical formulation of a scientific problem, the incipient descriptive gesture and the studied verbal definition, the condensations of dreams and the teasing incongruities of wit, all have their basis in the brain's capacity to construct models of reality in its own activity. They are all instances of analogical symbolism, in a physical as well as a literary sense. It is therefore not surprising that we find basic temperamental dispositions expressing themselves, for example, through the symbolism of leveling and sharpening tendencies in perception. All behavior which involves higher thought processes is basically symbolic, and the little bits of symbolism which we detect as such or consciously employ are scarcely more than froth upon the waves. Analogical symbolism is not an oddity of poetic expression or religious ritual, but the very substance of perception, which is the foundation of thinking. Thus the richer development of perceptual capacity, which was achieved through the increased mass and the finer specialization of structure in the human brain, spontaneously gave rise to what Langer calls man's "need of symbolization" (cf. page 118). In addition to the broad implications which Craik, the neurologist, and Langer, the philosopher, saw in their discovery that human thinking is so completely saturated with symbolism, there is a special implication for the psychologist: that the dream and fantasy products and other symbolic activities which constitute an important source of information about the inner structure of the person are expressions of very basic functions, and not the results of a special symbolizing activity which is different from ordinary thinking. Later in this chapter, we shall pursue this implication. Now, let us consider some further speculation on the physiological nature of the thought process.

The Electronic Brain Analogy

Craik's early death prevented him from contributing to the fuller development of his views. Within the next few years, under the impetus of wartime needs, the development of the modern electronic computing machine gave new force to his argument. If the brain is a machine for making models, then the electronic computer, which resembles the animal brain in certain important physical respects as well as in this function, is the ideal model through which to study such a machine! This hypothesis has been carried forward in the work of Wiener (1948), von Neumann (1951), Ashby (1952), and others.

Electronic computers are of two principal kinds, called digital and analogy devices. Each of the elements of a digital machine has a finite number of states, usually two, and in this respect it is similar to the brain, each of whose neurons normally acts on the all-or-nothing principle. The design of a digital machine is such that in its progress from one state, which may be termed the problem, to another state, which may be termed the answer, it must pass through an exactly determinable sequence of intermediate steps, each of which may be precisely defined by assigning one of its possible states to each element in the machine. Many considerations make it appear unlikely that this type of computer can provide a satisfactory model for the activity of the human brain. As Lashley points out, the very efficiency of such devices in straightforward calculation, where the human brain with its ten billion operative units often stumbles and errs, suggests that the latter is operating on a different principle.

An analogical computer, on the other hand, is so constructed that it responds to some external influence by passing through a continuous series of states, reflecting the strength of that influence. Analogy computers are characteristically less accurate than digital computers. A thermometer is a simple example of an analogy device, and one may readily see how it is subject to error, depending, for example, on minute variations in the caliber of its tube. The continuous gradations of response which are characteristic of an analogy device can be achieved by a network of digital elements, whose combined operation must then be regarded as subject to statistical laws. McCulloch and Pitts (1947) have demonstrated that a network of this sort can achieve any distinction or description that can be attained through the use of language, and hence it is not unreasonable to think of such a machine as the vehicle of intelligent thought. In a purely anatomic sense, the brain presents the appearance of such a network, in which single digital elements have no measurable influence on the outcome of cortical activity. Thus Lashley (in Jeffress, 1951) states:

> The nervous activity underlying any bit of behavior must involve so many neurons that the action of any one cell can have little influence on the whole. . . . We must conceive of nervous activity as the interplay of impulses in a network of millions of active cells.

On the other hand, this does not imply that the network is homogeneous, as was once assumed by the proponents of mass-action theories. Weiss writes (*ibid.*):

> On the basis of all existing evidence, the nervous system must not be conceived of as a network of monotonic elements, but as a hierarchical system in which groups of neuronal complexes of different kinds are acting as units, the properties of which determine the configuration of the output pattern.

Each of these relatively isolated units may be conceived of as in itself an analogy device, which is so designed that it is better suited to one kind of symbolization than another.

In this connection, it is important to remember that the full sensory model for any experience is not located at any single point in the brain, since it must combine information whose proper evaluation involves the activity of different sensory areas. The complete physical model of an object, as it is represented in the brain, is therefore nothing like a shrunken image of the object, but consists instead of a multitude of separate symbolizations. Each of these may conceivably have a fairly definite locus, although in the aggregate the bits of information which must be reassembled to constitute a reasonably full imaginal representation of an object are scattered over extensive cortical areas. Such a theory conforms to the clinical data of aphasias, which show that old memories may often survive widespread organic damage, while on the other hand, a relatively circumscribed lesion may erase a categorically defined type of response capacity or recognition capacity (Nielsen, 1946). The model of a man is not a manikin, but a complex of many separate analogical processes, which may enter individually or in various combinations into behavioral interaction with the similarly multiple part models of other objects.

There are other respects, besides those that we have noted, in which the brain resembles an electronic computing machine. Both possess reverberating circuits, and whether or not these structures are the storehouse of all our memories, as has been suggested, it does seem likely that some of these circuits in the brain serve a purpose similar to that which they have in the machine: to provide temporary storage for the partial solutions which are reached in the course of working with a problem, and which must be put aside for later reference. Their extent, however, suggests a bigger role than this, and one may speculate that they may house the mental sets or problem settings which steer our operations, the tensions which continue until the task is done, and then disappear. Sweeping through wide areas and diverse structures of the brain, they seem ideally suited to perform that scanning function which brings into action any element of past experience which is relevant to the immediate problem. Perhaps it is through these that the "perceptual hypotheses" receive their initial, subconscious test.

Another respect in which the brain and the all-purpose electronic computer are similar is that both of them need to be "educated" before their potentialities can be converted into problem-solving abilities. However, they are not quite equal in this respect. Before the computer can solve any problem whatever, we must feed the necessary instructions into it. When we turn it to a fresh problem, the old instructions may be completely erased and a new set provided, and the machine then works at its new task without any prejudices derived from its past experience. However, as Ashby (1952) has demonstrated in his *Design for a Brain,* it would be theoretically possible to construct a computing machine which would start out with only a few built-in rules of operation, and which would organize itself in the course of its own experience to solve whatever new kinds of problems confront it. Such a machine is the brain: a living machine whose pattern and consequent behavior are predetermined in some respects, but one which takes on an increasing complexity of internal organization with every fresh operation in which it is involved. In this self-individuating process, the brain constantly acquires new modes of response to future problems, as well as to the situations already confronting it. The more specific rules of operation which are thus acquired are called habits; the more general ones are called *concepts*.

How Concepts Are Formed

The basis of all concept formation is the recognition of similar elements in different percepts. To avoid confusion, let it be remarked that the word concept, like most important words, has multiple meanings. Often, as in the phrase self-concept, it refers to the associative grouping of many traits that are attributed to a single object. That is quite different from the isolation of one trait which is observed in many objects. This process of generalization is always accompanied by a parallel process of differentiation, for it is not possible to delimit a class of objects, real or imagined, which are in any sense similar, without taking note also of how they differ from other objects. For this reason, concepts are often expressed as dichotomous relationships, like *large-small*.

Concepts are of course very unequal in difficulty. Similarity in certain salient physical characteristics will impress itself immediately upon any normal child, but there are other concepts so difficult that we can attain them only after long effort, if at all. In his discussion of the nature of scientific discovery, the mathematician Poincaré used an illustration taken from his own experience, which may serve as an example of a concept that must forever lie beyond the reach of most of us: namely, his discovery of the similarity between the arithmetic transformations of indefinite ternary quadratic forms, which he had used to define the class of Fuchsian functions, and certain transformations of non-Euclidean geometry. The concept of triangularity, on the other hand, is a rule of operation which most of us grasp quite readily, and which is not beyond the mental grasp of rats, although they attain it only after long training (Fields, 1932). In general, we form concepts most readily under conditions which provide the most concrete sensory support for the distinctions and similarities that are involved (Heidbreder, Bensley, and Ivy, 1948).

Concept formation at anything above a very rudimentary level requires a considerable flexibility in the figural structuring of stimulus fields. To achieve a concept means that we structure many different stimulus fields in such a way that each shows us the same figure, on a different ground. Let us illustrate this with an experimental example. A standard method for the investigation of concept formation is the controlled presentation of stimulus materials in which the subject, who may be unaware of the nature of the experiment, is expected to discover some initially obscure characteristics which will make it possible to organize them into conceptual groups. One such experiment was performed by Hull (1920), who used Chinese word characters as his materials. The written Chinese language consists of complex ideographs, which are built up of parts which are themselves ideographic symbols. For example, the symbol for "liquid" consists of several brush strokes which are apparently derived from an original representation of waves or ripples on the surface of water, and this is included in the more complex ideographs which are to be read as the words for harbor, ice, and delicious (mouth-watering), as well as many others. The subjects in this experiment were not told to look for these symbols within symbols, but they were required to memorize a name which applied to all the members of each set of characters that included the same minor ideographic element, and as they worked at this task they gradually became aware of the hidden cues. The formation of concepts often proceeds in this blind and fumbling manner. In this case, Hull showed, it could be greatly accelerated by drawing the crucial part of the ideograph in a different color, for a few trials. Obviously, this kind of emphasis reduces the ambiguity of the stimulus field. Much of the process of education consists in learning facts under conditions which give such preferential emphasis to certain conceptual configurations rather than to others, but we must all learn how to reorganize such preordered perceptual fields into new structures which are more meaningful for ourselves.

Concept formation is of course a continuing process, which goes on as long as our minds are flexible enough to gain new viewpoints on the world about us. There is reason to believe that the concepts which are formed in early childhood often play a decisive part in influencing the power and the nature of all our future thinking. To understand why this should be, it will be instructive once again to consider a physiological hypothesis concerning the manner in which concepts arise. Hebb (1949b) has advanced a theory which seeks to explain the dependence of our mature mental processes upon the early perceptual learning and concept formation. Although his line of thought is different from that of Craik, or the later work of Ashby on the brain as a self-organizing machine, he reaches conclusions which are consistent with theirs, and which supplement them in certain respects.

Hebb assumes that in a complex brain, in advance of experience, there would be a good deal of randomicity in the cortical response to external stimulation. The first stage of learning consists of the reduction of this randomicity, through the organization of cell assemblies or combinations of neurons which, because of their repeated simultaneous activation, come to operate together as integrated units, each of which is regularly responsive to some specific kind of sensory stimulation. This early perceptual learning provides the basis for the next stage, in which the cell assemblies are organized into larger groupings of somewhat less regular character, which tend to activate one another whenever they have some cell assemblies in common. This is the stage of early conceptual learning, in which things begin to hang together in thinking as they have been observed to do in experience. This activation of one brain activity cycle by another, because they have some cell assemblies in common, constitutes association by similarity. All this only lays the groundwork for the quick and sure learning of later life, which, as Hebb says, is no longer "an establishing of new connections but a selective reinforcement of connections already capable of functioning."

Hebb points out that animals with simpler brains are capable of faster learning in simple situations, because they do not have to go through as much of this primary process of integrating brain patterns. One line of evidence which he adduces to demonstrate the importance of early learning consists of the observations made of humans and animals who have regained their vision after early blindness. He cites the clinical observations of Senden (1932) on humans who, born blind, gained the power of vision through surgery, and Riesen's (1947) experimental observations of primates under similar conditions. Even when the visual apparatus is sound, such subjects have extreme difficulty in learning to interpret visual stimulation, and they are probably never able to make up in later life for the lack of primary visual learning in infancy. That is, their basic concepts have been formulated without respect to visual data, and therefore it is not possible for them to make the most effective use of such data in perception. Rats, under comparable conditions, show a similar difficulty in pattern discrimination during their first sight experiences, but usually within an hour the handicap is overcome.

To support his contention that concepts exist as neural integrations before they can be verbalized or have any clear relationship to any overt response, Hebb discusses the child's early confusions with respect to such positional concepts as up-down, in-out, front-back, and left-right. The meaning of such a dichotomous pair of categories is grasped before there is a definite meaning attached to either member of the pair taken by itself. This is shown, for example, by the fact that "the confusion of *up* is only with its opposite, and never with 'in' or 'back.' This means that the word has first acquired an association with a definite, limited set of conceptual coordinates." First one learns the concept, and later its name.

The child can very readily learn at the age of 3 that "right" and "left" each refers to a side of the body—but ah me, which one?

Here, in the discrimination of right and left, is the real paradigm of adult learning. What is first set up is a conceptual organization. By the age of 6 the word "right" clearly and immediately means sidedness to the child. A considerable conceptual elaboration has already occurred, and the stimulus effectively arouses that structure; but it arouses no prompt, specific response.

THE ABSTRACT ATTITUDE

Goldstein (1944) has described a dimension of abstractness vs. concreteness in behavior, depending on the extent to which use is made of concepts. In concrete behavior, we respond to the object which is immediately present, without regarding it as the member of a class or noting its resemblances to other objects. Even for a response of this sort, a good deal of integrative work must be performed by the brain, if the object is to be perceived as a clear figure. This integration results in part from the native organization of the brain, and in part from perceptual learning, which may conceivably have taken place in the manner hypothesized by Hebb. The extreme of concreteness consists in responding not to the object, but to the sensory qualities of the object, taken one at a time. Except in infancy, response of this sort is pathological—as we shall soon see in somewhat greater detail. In abstract or conceptual behavior, we see the object before us as a member of a class, and we are able voluntarily to select one aspect or another for our particular attention. "The healthy individual," says Goldstein, "combines both attitudes, and is able to shift voluntarily from one to the other, according to the demands of the situation."

The principal method which has been used in the investigation of this aspect of conceptual behavior is the sorting test (e.g., Hanfmann and Kasanin, 1942; Goldstein and Scherer, 1944). An assortment of objects is laid before the subject, and he is asked to arrange them in groups, in any way that he wishes. This procedure permits a good deal of individuality and spontaneity in response. After the subject's original preference is shown, he may be asked to make a new sorting, on some other basis. The objects to be sorted may be a set of blocks which vary in size, shape and color, or they may be a miscellaneous collection of common objects, including some real utensils and some toylike miniatures. Using such tests, Gelb and Goldstein (1925) had demonstrated that persons who had suffered severe brain injuries are incapable of assuming the abstract attitude, that is, they can deal with objects only on the basis of concrete qualities, and not as members of conceptual categories. Vigotsky (1934) showed that schizophrenic patients are also incapable of orderly conceptual thinking. Subsequently, Goldstein pointed out that the disturbances which result from schizophrenia and from organic brain lesions take different forms. In cases of brain injury, the conceptual system seems to disintegrate completely, to be replaced by simpler forms of response. In schizophrenia, on the other hand, the subject "develops his own pattern in grouping the blocks because his personal ideas enter into and influence the performance" (Goldstein, 1944). For example, a patient may place two blocks together because one has the color of bark and the other the color of leaves. Conceptual thinking in one type of patient is weak, while in the other it is bizarre. The organic patient is unable to form orderly figure-ground relationships, and he therefore seems to be at the mercy of the stimulating material, one or another aspect of which may catch his attention and dominate his response at a given instant. The schizophrenic patient creates arbitrary figures, often endowing the objects with a symbolism which escapes the understanding of others because it is attached to superficial features of the objects. The world of the organic is reduced and impoverished by his defective perception, whereas that of the schizophrenic patient undergoes an autistic dismemberment. The nature of this change is such that it could scarcely take place unless there were first a weakening of the conceptual structure. The superficial similarity with the behavior of the organic patient therefore tends to confirm the theory—for which there is much other evidence—that the basis of schizophrenia is in part organic.

There is room for a good deal of individual preference within the normal range of the abstract-concrete continuum. Purely conceptual thinking is difficult for all of us, and requires long training. We find geometry easier than algebra, because we can use the diagrams for concrete support. Concrete and abstract attitudes are usually blended in our activities. Hanfmann (1941) showed that in solving a difficult sorting problem, normal subjects who freely engage in trial-and-error manipulation of the materials are in general more successful, as measured by time scores, than others who first study the materials carefully, looking for a satisfactory principle of organization before they make a move. In a work of art, concrete and abstract attitudes may be blended, and it is not possible to say that the high development of one necessarily involves a slighting of the other. For example, the paintings of Van Eyck include an astonishing realism, while at the same time every object included in the composition has a carefully reasoned symbolic meaning, so that the cat, the book, the piece of fruit, the tower seen in the distance, must all be regarded as representatives of classes, not as concrete objects. The spectator may alternately take his delight in the artist's realism or in the artist's conception, or perhaps, like the artist, achieve a synthesis of both. When the canvas we survey is the world before us, rather than a picture, we still have the same alternatives.

The use of concepts leads to a more orderly and purposeful, and generally more efficient, process of association, as compared with the haphazard associations which arise in concrete thinking. The extreme of concrete association is the pathological word salad, where no thought can be carried to complete expression before it is displaced by another fragmentary thought, which has only the flimsiest connection to it. The abstract attitude, as Goldstein emphasizes, enables us to assume voluntarily a particular mental set, and thus to control the direction of our thinking. (We must therefore concede that Viki who spent five minutes looking for the toy dog, and who pretended to play with an imagined pulltoy, was capable of assuming the abstract attitude.) Concepts serve to fetch associations from memory, in the same way that a card-punch system selects just the cards we want out of a file. It takes but a moment to scan the immense resources of our knowledge, bringing into consciousness only those items which have the pattern for which we are seeking. The process is demonstrated with schematic clarity in the cross-word puzzle. A tall tree, native to Australia? A carnivorous African animal? Each item is generously cross-indexed, by every one of its qualities for which we have a concept available. The individual quality of each person's thinking therefore depends not only on the degree to which he can employ the abstract attitude, but also on the particular conceptual framework which he has developed, which comprises the set of rules of operation for his brain.

LEADING CONCEPTS

The system of concepts by which we organize our thinking is for the most part a social rather than an individual construction. In the course of intellectual development, one important phase of which is the acquisition of language, we gradually organize our brains to include more and more of the culturally elaborated system with which we are constantly in contact. Dennis (1951), in appraising the value of Hebb's theory, conjectures that the socialization of the child may consist largely in the process of primary learning which Hebb describes. Certainly a major part of socialization consists in learning to think with the concepts of our culture. However, this process does not follow an invariable pattern, and the individuality of the child consists in part in the special emphases that may have been attached to some concepts rather than to others.

Among the categorical concepts which we learn in early childhood, and which are capable of exercising a good deal of influence over later behavior, are such valuative dichotomies as good-bad, strong-weak, clever-stupid, safe-dangerous, exciting-dull, sick-healthy, living-dead. Each of these concepts is weighted with a substantial feeling content. For a given child, almost any such concept may become a touchstone by which he evaluates each new situation. Frenkel-Brunswik, we recall, believes that the strong-weak dichotomy plays this leading role in the authoritarian personality. When this effect is pronounced, many other concepts become distorted, so that they exist, as it were, almost as subcategories of strength and weakness, and not independently. Maslow (1948) suggests another such possibility when, in arguing for the need for a fresh approach to experience, and deploring the tendency to "rubricizing," he writes:

It would seem that a large proportion of our population responds with attention only to threatening experience. It is as if attention were to be regarded only as a response to danger and as a warning of the necessity for an emergency response. These people brush aside experiences which are nonthreatening and not dangerous, as therefore not being worthy of attention or any other response, cognitive or emotional. For them life is either a meeting of dangers or relaxation between dangers.

Although Maslow is thinking of persons who shun danger, and therefore never experience pleasurable excitements, there are also some persons who become addicts of danger, because no other kind of situation makes them feel so responsively alive.

With respect to the conceptual category of *living* and *dead,* there is evidence that different persons attach quite different meanings to these words. Dennis (1953) showed that even among college students, a substantial proportion will regard such objects as rivers and clouds as literally alive, which certainly represents a survival of childhood habits of thinking rather than the use of a logically defined concept. How very fundamental this particular concept can be is indicated further by Nielsen (1951), who has described instances of visual agnosia in which unilateral occipital lesions led to a complete loss of ability to recognize objects belonging to one of these categories, either the animate or the inanimate, while retaining the ability to recognize objects belonging to the complementary category. One patient was unable to see the doctor's finger held up before her nose, although she could see a pencil; another patient was blind to the pencil, although she could see the finger. The importance of this observation is in the evidence it provides that a logical or quasi-logical concept, which is formed early in childhood, can exercise such influence over the cortical traces of later experiences that it can lead, in some cases, to having at least the recognition knowledge of living things localized in the visual cortex of one hemisphere, while that for nonliving things is localized in the other hemisphere. If this were a universal kind of organization, the symptoms described by Nielsen would be observed more frequently, and would therefore have less significance for problems of individuality. Actually, there is other evidence to show that it is possible to have complete agnosia, for both animate and inanimate objects, when the lesion is limited to one hemisphere, indicating that the other hemisphere, although it continues to be perfectly healthy, has never been utilized in the recognition process. It is clear that the particular kind of aphasia or agnosia which a given patient exhibits depends on the distinctive pattern of his cortical development, as well as on the area which is involved in the lesion. It follows that the distinctive pattern of thinking by the intact brain must also depend on the pattern of organization, that is, on the conceptual structure. When college students taking an examination in biology soberly state that the ocean is alive—and even attribute consciousness to it—they betray a kind of individuality in thinking which must surely lead to inappropriate behavior in many other situations.

Exaggerated emphasis on a single concept may even lead to a breakdown of the conceptual system as such, that is, as a system of abstractions which enables us to deal with objects in a flexible manner, attending now to this aspect and now to that, according to need. When a single concept dominates all of a person's thinking so completely that every situation must be interpreted in terms of this one idea, inconsequential details will be stressed and important characteristics overlooked, leading to a general distortion of reality. When a certain young man said, in response to a question on the Wechsler-Bellevue Intelligence Scale, that wood and alcohol are alike because both are used in hospitals, his unusual answer betrayed the preoccupation with thoughts of sickness which had been interfering with his adjustment generally.

Osgood and Suci (1955) have recently published an article on the "factor analysis of meaning" which throws a very clear light on the relations that exist among common concepts, and which also holds out a promise of leading to a method of appraising the leading concepts for a given individual. Their subjects were asked to rate each of 20 common nouns, including such concrete nouns as lady, feather, and tornado and such abstract nouns as sin and fraud, on a set of 50 seven-step scales. Each of the scales was based upon a common bipolar concept, such as good-bad, wet-dry, and rough-smooth. The correlations among the scales were made the basis for a factor analysis. The results indicated that three common factors, which we may perhaps refer to as superconcepts, were together responsible for almost half of the total variance in the ratings. The first of these, which was responsible for 34 percent of total variance in judgments and for 69 percent of the common variance, is the superconcept of *value*. This has high loadings on such conceptual scales as good-bad and honest-dishonest, but negligible loadings on such other scales as hot-cold and large-small. The second superconcept, which is responsible for 15 percent of the common variance, is that of *power*, which has high loadings on strong-weak and rugged-delicate, but negligible loadings on fast-slow and sacred-profane. The third superconcept, which accounts for 13 percent of the common variance, is *activity*, which has high loadings on fast-slow and active-passive.

It is quite evident that all these scales would not have the same factor structure for every subject. If the same data were studied by other methods, including Stephenson's technique of inverse factor analysis, in which the correlations among persons rather than those among the rating-scales would be taken as the basis for analysis, it would certainly appear that the superconcepts of value, power, and activity have different relative importance for different individuals. For example, the results indicate that for the subjects as a group, the factor structure of healthy-sick is very much like that of rich-poor, but quite different from that of strong-weak. We would suspect that for many individual subjects, this relationship must be reversed. In general, one must assume that the superconcept of *power* would have greater and more pervasive influence in the ratings of those subjects who have an authoritarian personality, if there is any validity whatever in the picture of that personality as it has been presented. The demonstration of such individual differences in the factor structure of meanings would be an important step in the study of cognitive individuality.

SYMBOLISM IN DREAMS

The spontaneous analogical process which is involved in all conceptual thinking permits any object which is a member of a given category to serve as the symbol for any other object belonging to the same category. If this process were unchecked, this wealth of potential symbolism would introduce confusion into all our thinking. Under conditions of wakefulness, it is rather strictly controlled by problem-setting attitudes. During sleep, some control is being exercised, but it is evidently of a very different nature. Freud (**1900**, 1938b) thought of the conscious control as playing the part of a moral as well as a logical censor, and he interpreted the obviously symbolic character of the dream content as a disguise, which was necessary in order to smuggle these trespassing thoughts past the more relaxed but still not completely abrogated censorship. Hall (1953ab) has challenged this interpretation, declaring that dream symbols are nothing more than nonverbal representations of the dreamer's ideas, and that they constitute a kind of thinking which is less complex than that of waking life, and not, as Freud would have it, more complex. We must agree with the essential parts of Hall's analysis. The symbolism of dreams is only a part of the ever-present symbolism of thinking. It is less orderly, not because confusion has been introduced as a disguise, but because mental activity during sleep is less rigidly controlled. This does not make the dream any less valuable to the student of personality. It still represents, as Freud phrased it, "a royal road to the unconscious." It is at the same time a valuable demonstration that analogical symbolism does not require a foundation of verbal abstraction, but is the spontaneous expression of a high level of cortical organization.

At this point we shall present the synopses of several dreams, in order to illustrate the nature of analogical symbolism. For this purpose, we have selected a group of dreams in all of which coins appear, directly or indirectly, as important content. First, there are the two dreams which are recounted in Beck's fine instructional film, *Unconscious Motivation* (1950). In this film, whose action is unrehearsed, two college students, a young man and a young woman, are simultaneously hypnotized, and it is suggested to them that in childhood each had found a purse with a few pennies in it belonging to another child, then threw away the purse and used the money to buy candy. The subjects are awakened, then returned to the hypnotic state with the instruction to have a dream which will deal with the basis for the uneasy conflict which they both feel, without understanding why. (For some examples of the experimental study of dream symbolism under hypnosis, one may read translations of articles by Schrötter, Roffenstein, and Nachmansohn, in Rapaport, 1951.) The girl, in her dream, has a frightening ride on a merry-go-round which is a huge penny, and her efforts to escape are blocked by two men who are also made of pennies. The young man does not explicitly dream of money, but as he runs through a forest of threatening trees (which symbolize his mother rebuking him) he feels compelled to stop and pick up bright pebbles, and is aware of a sense of shame in doing so, which he attributes, in telling the dream, to the fact that it was "silly." The third dream is one told to me by a 14-year-old boy, who said that he is in a field where there are many coins scattered about. He fills his pockets with the coins, but to his despair they disappear, and he finds his pockets empty. The last dream is one I heard from a young woman, who had recently returned to her husband after a fairly long separation and much talk of divorce. She dreamed that she was eating pennies, which tasted unpleasant, but that she seemed to recall having eaten half-dollars, which had been much tastier. She interpreted this dream as an expression of resentment that while she was trying to prepare good meals on a limited budget, her husband had made a rather expensive purchase without consulting her.

In each of these dreams the coins, or the pebbles which in one instance replace them, serve as recondite symbols which are charged with feeling. The role which the coin plays is not determined by its reality function, but by a concept which is congruous to one of its meanings to the dreamer. For each dreamer it symbolizes something different, which can be understood only if we are sensitive to the feelings which suffuse it. For the girl, it is ineluctable danger, and as such it becomes the dangerous spinning platform and, giving us a further glimpse into her emotional life, a pair of threatening men. For the young man—who, by coincidence, had really lived through a similar petty theft experience in his childhood—it is temptation thrown in his path, irresistible yet demeaning. For the adolescent boy it is the envied status of adulthood, in which the power of money and masculine virility are intimately joined, so that the empty pockets are doubly expressive of his impotent despair. For the unhappy wife, the copper penny is the bitterness of marital discord, while the silver coin is the sweetness of remembered love. Each dreamer, directed by his own inner feelings, constructs a different yet meaningful analog. This profusion of creativity is evidence for the infinite wealth of analogical symbolism available to the human mind.

The great difficulty of dream interpretation lies in the fact that the dreamer has no direct access to the meaning of the symbol. He does not choose the symbol but merely experiences it, as the product of a kind of physiological resonance. It is of the greatest importance that feelings play a leading part in this process. Even though they remain unverbalized, our individualized feeling patterns—of luxuriating dependence, of arrogant dominance, of nurturant solicitude, of living under threat, of shame or fear or love or self-pity—also function as concepts, joining into a single class all the objects of one feeling attitude. These are the tension systems which, although they influence all our behavior, may be kept out of consciousness by mechanisms of defense, but find their symbolic expressions in the dream.

SYMBOLISM AND PROJECTIVE TESTING

The ease with which people invent symbols, without any awareness of this fact, is put to important use in the investigation of personality. We have already seen how, in the dream, a feeling may attach itself to any object and utilize it in a symbolic manner, without the dreamer being aware of the symbolism involved. When the therapist offers a child a family of dolls to play with, it is with the confident expectation that

these convenient symbols will soon become vehicles for the
transparent expression of feeling. How often the father doll is
mangled, and the baby brother crushed underfoot, in an act of
apparent negligence! However, the child will invent his own
symbols if they are not provided. Moustakas (1953) reports a
therapeutic interview with a boy of preschool age, who had a
still younger brother. A "big boat" and a "little boat" were
utilized in the child's play, with the big boat having many fine
qualities and the little boat seeming at first quite worthless.
Happily, in a later session, the little boat was allowed to dock
at the same pier, as a not unworthy companion to the larger
vessel, signaling a new attitude of tolerance toward the younger
brother. The child who engages in such play does not need to
understand that these are symbols for himself and his brother
in order to obtain the therapeutic benefit of expressing his feelings in an acceptant atmosphere. To the psychologist who observes the play, the child's previously hidden feelings are made
manifest, and in this sense they have been "projected." (The
meaning is quite different from when we speak of projection as
a mechanism of defense.)

A projective test always preserves some of the freedom of
such a play situation. The psychologist assigns a task to the
subject, with the expectation that the manner in which the task
is performed will reveal something about the subject's otherwise hidden feelings and impulses. In such a test, the success
of the performance is of little importance, except as it may be
a clue to such motivational factors as coöperativeness or self-
regard. The two outstanding tests of this type are the Rorschach
test, in which the subject is asked to tell what he sees in a
series of ink blots, and the Thematic Apperception Test, in
which he is asked to tell a fairly complete story about each of
a series of pictures. There are scores of others in common use,
and resourceful investigators create new ones to meet the
special needs of their research. The Draw-a-Person test (Machover, 1949) was discussed in Chapter 11. In the Blacky test

(Blum, 1949), the subject must interpret a series of cartoons in which a dog is the central figure. In MAPS (Schneidman, 1947), the subject is asked to make a picture story, having some freedom of choice to place his own cardboard actors on the sets provided. In Sentence Completions (e.g., Rotter and Willerman, 1947), the subject must complete such phrases as "He often wished he could . . ." or "When I meet a woman, I . . . ." In the World Test (Bühler and Kelly, 1941), a great many varied miniature objects are placed before a child, who may use them to construct whatever kind of "world" he fancies. The common feature of all these tests is the encouragement of fantasy. The technique of administration is always designed to facilitate maximum spontaneity on the part of the subject.

It is a surprising fact that in the theoretical discussion of projective tests, principal emphasis is usually placed on the ambiguity of the materials. Cattell (1951) carries this to the point of suggesting that these tests should more properly be called "misperception" tests. This frequent but by no means invariable ambiguity of the test materials is only one of the means used to stimulate fantasy. The essence of the projective test situation is not in the fact that it is relatively unstructured, so that the subject may make a highly individualized response, but in the fact that this response assumes symbolic character. It is the projective hypothesis that the subject's response will invariably have a symbolic meaning, and that this meaning is accessible to interpretation. This hypothesis offers a very promising approach to the problems of appraising human personality, especially when we are striving to understand aspects of the person which he is himself unaware of, or wishes to conceal. However, many frustrating experiences of research workers have shown that one man's symbol of meat may be another man's symbol of poison, and that careful validating studies must precede any pronouncement as to the meaningfulness of certain types of response. Because such studies are rare, the claims advanced for almost all projective tests must be studied with caution. Often indispensable in research, they rarely attain the reliability which is desirable in a clinical instrument.

Rorschach's inkblot test holds a unique position in the field of projective testing, despite the fact that there are other projective devices that are no whit inferior to it as instruments for the study of motivational dynamics and the self-concept. It holds its special position because Rorschach's work was distinguished by his systematic study of the purely formal characteristics of fantasy responses, apart from their content, and it is in this area that his test still holds unchallenged supremacy. His "apperceptive types" correspond to perceptual attitudes of far-reaching significance. For example, persons whose responses are predominantly based upon the larger and more readily isolated areas of the inkblots are said to be expressing a disposition to deal with "the immediate, essential characteristics of any problem," while those who tend predominantly to the use of small and less frequently isolated areas are regarded as expressing "the tendency to get lost in details." Without departing from the spirit of Rorschach's definitions, we may designate these perceptual dispositions as "practical" and "analytic" attitudes. He himself referred to the latter type of approach as "pedantic," thus showing his own distaste for the detail approach, but this academically oriented term is too limiting as a designation for a type of perceptual behavior which can be met on any educational level. Of particular interest to us is Rorschach's interpretation of the W (whole) response, which makes use of the entire stimulus blot. For reasons which shall presently appear, we shall call the perceptual disposition which expresses itself in an unusually large number of such responses the "integrative" attitude, but we shall defer discussion of it until the next chapter.

CHAPTER 16

Wisdom and Laughter

*I*n this chapter, we shall consider two aspects of that creative activity which man displays by virtue of his capacity to deal with symbols. He uses this capacity for work and for play—that is, it is not only a means by which he achieves greater mastery of the world, but also an activity in which he delights. One of these aspects is more prominent in the integrative, the other in the humorous attitude.

THE INTEGRATIVE ATTITUDE

Rorschach (1921, 1942) says that two conditions are necessary for a subject to produce an unusually large number of W responses. First, he must command an exceptional wealth of associative material—that is, he must be a person rich in experience, and usually someone of considerable education. In addition, however, he must have a special kind of orientation toward his task, and indeed toward tasks in general. This orientation is described in the following sentences:

> The production of a large number of W's requires a certain affective coloring, a special sort of volition, in addition to the wealth of engrams. This must be a "willing" attitude, its goal to conceive "the whole;" not infrequently, this attitude is combined with a strong antipathy for details. . . . The energy of this charge must not be confused with diligence in carrying out the test. . . . We deal with a "will to

produce," a disposition set toward producing. . . . Frequently the number of W's is an indicator of a conscious or unconscious "willing" in the direction of achieving complicated performances, such as abstraction or combination in the interpretations.

We should like to compare these remarks with Wertheimer's views on the personality of the productive thinker. Wertheimer (1945) presents the Gestalt view of productive thinking, according to which the stresses that lead to solution can be found in the problem itself, although, in accordance with the principle of isomorphism, they work themselves out in the brain of the thinker. The material of past experience also enters into this process, so that Rorschach's "engrams" are not completely unacceptable to Wertheimer, although he would attribute less importance to them. However, his insistence that the structural dynamics are inherent in the problem, and that ego stresses can only have disturbing consequences which may lead to false answers, causes the reader to wonder if the ideal thinker must be an impersonal machine. Anticipating this reaction, he writes:

When a picture is given here of the inner structural dynamics in the determination of processes, it does not mean that in this development man is merely passive. An attitude is implied on his part, a willingness to face problems straight, a readiness to follow them up courageously and sincerely. . . . To live in a fog, in an unsurveyable manifold of factors and forces that prevent a clear decision as to action, as to the main lines of the situation, is for many people an intolerable state of affairs. There is a tendency to structural clearness, surveyability, to truth as against petty views—the desire not to deceive oneself. If this desire to reach the true structure sincerely is weak, then structural simplification in a desired direction [i.e., autistic distortion] prevails.

Rorschach, the clinician, recognizes that "the will to produce" expresses itself in a "goal to conceive the whole." Wertheimer, not simply as the spokesman for Gestalt psychology but as personification of its dynamics, illustrates this when he speaks of the felt need for "structural clearness, surveyability,"—qualities of the good W. Rorschach says that often these subjects will have an antipathy for details, and Wertheimer concurs by setting "truth" in opposition to "*petty* views." Both men agree that high intelligence alone, without this integrative attitude, can never support productive thinking of a high order.

Validation for this viewpoint may be found in a comparison of the number of W responses in an average population, and the number given by persons whose intellectual achievement has been outstanding. The average W score for a large standardization group of employed adults has been reported as 5.5, with the bulk of this group falling below this figure in a markedly skewed distribution (Beck et al., 1950). In a series of investigations, Roe (1946, 1951ab, 1953) has examined 81 artists and scientists of national reputation, and her tables show that only four of these failed to give at least 6 W, with the mean at 12.3. Furthermore, this striking difference between the standardization group and these exceptionally creative men would doubtless be even more marked if the easy "popular" W's were excluded. (On the other hand, it should be noted that the artists and scientists showed no consistent tendency to excel in what are called "original" responses, which have been customarily regarded as providing the most direct evidence for creative capacity.)

The central importance of the integrative attitude for creativity arises from the fact that it is the attitudinal expression of the very process of analogical symbolism. It expresses the intensity of what Langer called "the need of symbolization," for it is only through a process of symbolization that integration of reality can be achieved. Other perceptual attitudes represent individually favored approaches to the task of symbolization, but in the consistently integrative attitude there must be, as Wertheimer wrote, the "willingness to face problems straight" rather than to sacrifice any of the wholeness, the "structural clearness," to fit an autistic preference. In the integrative attitude, the need of symbolization is paramount to every other need.

The most immediate expression of the integrative attitude, when it focuses upon a problem, is to formulate the solution in terms of an analogy. While Rorschach's "pedants" will decry this as a false method, there can be no question of its power and its necessity. Hebb (1949b) recognizes the inevitability of analogy in scientific thinking, because, as he puts it, "the new concept is only a modification of the old." Oppenheimer (1956), a distinguished physicist addressing an audience of psychologists, expressed the same idea: "Whether or not we talk of discovery or of invention, analogy is inevitable in human thought, because we come to new things in science with what equipment we have, which is how we have learned to think, and above all how we have learned to think about the relatedness of things." He describes the progress of science as a cyclical process of analogy and disanalogy—first the recognition of a gross similarity with something already known, then the recognition of the differentiating feature, which leads to the statement of a more universal principle. An imperfect analogy cannot long be tolerated by the integrative attitude, with its insistence on "structural clearness."

Although the integrative attitude attains its clearest contemporary expression in the field of science, it certainly shows itself in many other fields of cultural endeavor. The mythological picture of the world resting on the back of an elephant that stands on a turtle, and Dante's majestic *Inferno,* are both products of the same need to construct perceptual figures that encompass all our experience in one totality, and they both use the only tool that is available to us for this purpose—analogical symbolism. All the greater and lesser works of religion, philosophy, and art express the same need, and use the same method. They have other motivational sources as well, but, as Rorschach and Wertheimer both point out in their different ways, a strong development of the integrative attitude is essential for high intellectual achievement in any field.

Two research studies in the field of perceptual attitudes appear to be related to the general problem of the integrative attitude. Rokeach (1951ab) has classified subjects as tending to *compre-*

hensive or *isolated* or *narrow* cognitive structure, according to the kind of answer they give to a task which requires them to point out relationships among a large number of social concepts or movements. Bronfenbrenner (1953) has already pointed out the parallelism between these classifications and Rorschach's principal apperceptive modes, that is, the tendencies to pay principal attention to wholes, to major details, and to minor details. It seems possible that Rokeach's experimental procedure could be developed into a useful technique for appraisal of the integrative attitude. The other study which may be related is Barron's (1953a) research on "complexity" as a perceptual attitude, which was discussed in the preceding chapter. Perhaps the "complex" person is one who finds satisfaction in the labor of integration, and who therefore prefers the more complex experiences which challenge him in this area. The "simple" person prefers an obvious whole, which requires no labor on his part. Perhaps the puzzling fact that artists and scientists show a community of interest on the Strong Vocational Interest Test is to be explained by the fact that they both share this preference for complex, integration-demanding experiences.

THE HUMOROUS ATTITUDE

Human symbolizing activity also gives rise to another dimension of personality which we frequently prize very highly in our self-concepts and in our friends: the humorous attitude. Man is not only the sapient, but also the laughing animal. Of these two characteristics, it would seem that laughter is the more distinguishing, for the beginnings of rational intelligence can be found much lower in the animal scale than the beginnings of laughter. Perhaps the tremulous delight of a dog that greets its master, as shown especially in the expressive quiver of a stubby tail, has some physiological resemblance to the spasmodic outbursts of laughter. But nothing that is truly a smile or a laugh can be found below the level of the higher apes. In the chimpanzee, along with the occurrence of true laughter in response to tickling and the like, we also see clear instances of mischievous humor, a fact which confirms, rather than negates, the conclusion that the birth of humor is linked to the appearance of a fairly high order of intelligence.

There are many theories of humor. They all enjoy a good audience, for there are good jokes to support each of them and, as Freud pointed out, one of the effects of humor is to inhibit critical judgment. These theories fall into three groups, according to whether they stress the more obvious temperamental foundations of laughter, the less obvious "secondary gains" that we derive from wit and humor, or the intellectual component. They are classified, accordingly, as affective, conative, and cognitive theories. Our direct interest in the present chapter is in the cognitive aspect of humor, which we shall call the humorous attitude, but we shall not limit ourselves to this, for humor, like all other complex phenomena of personality, displays a close interaction of primary, nonprimary, and social influences.

We became acquainted with the laugh, and with its silent partner, the smile, in a double role, as the expression of physical well-being, and as the sign of maturing social behavior. The infant's early smile, and his later cooing delight, are charming bits of coquetry—that is, they are native releasers for positive social response by human adults. This leads not only to fondling, but to playful tickling, and to the still more stimulating experiences of being tossed overhead, or watching the peek-a-boo disappearances and reappearances of a friendly face. These are not tranquil, but exciting pleasures, which strangely border on the frightening experiences of falling and desertion, while they still contain the assurance of affectionate protection. The more vigorous laughter which they provoke no longer seems to be merely a buoyant satisfaction with the world, but an explosive expression of an excessive mobilization of energy, which takes this outlet because the strong element of trust colors the situation in a way to inhibit any aggressive discharge. There is the laughter of pat-a-cake, in which the child tests his strength and agility against the playfully moderated strength of the adult. Thus, through increasing stages of aggressiveness, we come to the exuberant laughter of victory, the boastful rejoicing in one's own power. Peek-a-boo and pat-a-cake may be cultural phenomena, but the disposition to laughter which they exploit is universal, and its expression in victory, as we saw in an earlier chapter, does not vary from the equator to the pole.

What unity exists in this spectrum of natural laughter? For one thing, the situations in which it appears are always of a social character. Solitary laughter is a learned accomplishment, and too much of it, like solitary drinking, is a malign addiction. Whenever we find humor, we are eager to share it. However, the social situations that are involved in unlearned laughter are quite diverse, and it seems at first a puzzling fact that basically the same expressive gestures and sounds should be involved in both dependent and aggressive satisfactions. Perhaps the key to this riddle can be found in the observation of Lorenz (p. 124), that if an aggressive species is to survive, there must be some native means of limiting the exercise of aggression between its own members. Laughter serves this function. Our own laughter disarms us, and makes us magnanimous to our victims.

When these events are viewed from a purely physiological standpoint, ignoring the part that they play in social relationships, they lead to the theory that laughter is the sudden release of pent-up energy. This is a widely held theory, which was advanced by Herbert Spencer, as well as by Kant, who described the comic as the result of "a strained expectation being suddenly reduced to nothing." There can be no doubt that this is one aspect of laughter, but the reader may test its extent for himself by engaging in an introspective exercise the next time he enjoys a good comedy program. When he catches himself in sudden laughter, let him ask if the sparkle of comedy is most immediately associated with a decrease or an increase of tension—whether the comedian's "build-up" prepares for a "letdown," or whether it does not rather first tranquilize us, then alert us for a sharp climactic experience of tension when the joke is sprung. In a recent experiment (Kenny, 1955), it was found that the funniest jokes were those whose endings could be successfully anticipated, and this supports the view that progressive build-up, not build-up and letdown, is the answer. The humor itself mobilizes the energy which finds release in laughter. The release is an important aspect of our pleasure, but it does not explain all of humor, any more than the pleasurable release of tension in a completed sexual act explains the need for sex and the pleasure in its excitement.

Our earlier theoretical considerations on the problem of temperament prompt us to ask the question, What kind of adjustive behavior does laughter facilitate? The answer, quite obviously, is that it encourages affectionate, affiliative behavior. It is the expression of "brotherly love"—not as an ethical command, but as a biological fact, as Ashley Montagu (1953) has striven to present it. How perfectly natural it is, then, that whenever we feel the stirring of a humorous thought, we also feel the warm need to impart it to someone else! When Mars, the mesomorph, shakes with laughter, he is ready to throw an arm over the shoulders of endomorphic Bacchus and begin the social revelry.

This laugh of victory, which serves to moderate aggression, has sometimes been regarded as the primary source of all humor. "The passion of laughter," wrote the authoritarian Hobbes, "is nothing but sudden glory arising in ourselves from sudden conception of some eminency in ourselves by comparison with the inferiority of others or with our own formerly." Laughter is so often gained at the expense of others that it seems plausible to believe that malice may be its principal motive. Goethe, whose view of humanity and enjoyment of life were both much broader than those of the dryly dogmatic Hobbes, recognized the importance of individual differences. "Nowhere," he said, "do men show their character more clearly than in the things they laugh at." The same implication lies in Freud's (**1905**, 1938d) statement, which has been strangely unexploited by the designers of tests for marital compatibility, that "every witticism demands its own public, and to laugh over the same witticisms is proof of absolute psychic agreement." In short, though laughter has a temperamental basis, it becomes canalized in ways that are determined by the formation and the preferred defenses of the self-concept.

A major part of Freud's theory of wit is that it provides a means for circumventing our repressions, and thus attaining the gratification of hidden desires by subterfuge. In this respect, he describes three main kinds of "tendency wit": exhibitionistic or obscene wit, aggressive or hostile wit, and cynical wit which is directed against authority and social dogma. Psychologists who have explored the possibility of using "humor tests" for the appraisal of personality characteristics have generally found that persons may indeed be distinguished according to their preferences among these and other types of humor. For example, Grziwok and Scodel (1956) found that subjects who include a good deal of aggressive content in the stories they tell on the TAT also prefer aggressive humor, while those who have relatively little aggressive content in their stories show a preference for social commentary humor. Cattell and Luborsky (1947) devised a humor test consisting of a collection of jokes which are to be rated by the subject as either funny or dull. Subsequently, Yarnold and Berkeley (1954) used the same material on a large population of Air Force officer candidates, and —in place of the 13 categories which Cattell and Luborsky had defined, and which have the abstruse subtlety that we have come to expect in Cattell's work—they developed seven humor scales. The themes of the jokes included in these seven scales are: sexual play, active self-assertion, scheming social manipulation, naïve lack of social aplomb, ridicule of authority, resigned acceptance of moral inferiority, and cynical realism.

Redlich, Levine, and Sohler (1951) describe the use of a test which consists of 20 selected cartoons, which are examined by the subject while the examiner notes his reaction on a six-point scale: negative response, no response, half-smile, smile, chuckle, and laugh. The subject is then asked to sort the cartoons into piles of those he likes, those he dislikes, and those toward which he feels indifferent, and he is asked to explain the point of each cartoon and any associations that it may arouse. In particular, Levine points out that one must take note not only of the kinds of jokes at which people laugh most readily but also of the jokes they fail to understand, because they touch upon areas of excessive inhibition, which cannot be relaxed even under the influence of humor. He offers the example of "an aggressive professional woman" who simply could not see the point of a Thurber cartoon which depicted "a very small and frightened man coming home to a house which takes the form of the large, angry face of a woman."

Freud did not intend to have his interpretation of wit applied to all forms of the comic. His famous summary statement, that "the pleasure of wit originates from an economy of expenditure in inhibition, of the comic from an economy of expenditure in thought, and of humor from an economy of expenditure in feeling" has no meaning for us unless we carefully follow his distinctions between these forms. It is only *wit* which arises from the unconscious, and the economy of inhibition is not so much in the momentary release from inhibitory restraint of desire, as in the fact that in wit—which may be defined as the sudden revelation of similarities between things that are apparently quite dissimilar—we permit ourselves to speak in the absurd juxtapositions in which the unconscious always deals. To paraphrase Pirandello, "Logic takes a holiday," and we rejoice as schoolboys do when the teacher is absent. The *comic* is typically clownish or awkward, and the pleasure in "economy of thought" arises from a comparison of this wastefulness with our own more efficient handling of a similar situation. *Humor,* in Freud's sense, deals with situations which seem at first to involve our deepest sympathies, but are then revealed as trivial, so that we find it possible to conserve the deep feeling which we had been preparing to expend. In a later essay, Freud (**1928**, 1950a) returned to the subject of humor, and stated that just as wit is a contribution of the unconscious, so humor is a contribution of the superego. This relationship is shown most clearly when we take a humorous attitude toward our own troubles or short-comings, and thus at once play the part of the helpless child and the understanding parent. The pleasure of humor, says Freud, is less intense than that of wit or the comic, yet we prize it more highly. "It is not everyone who is capable of the humorous attitude; it is a rare and precious gift, and there are many people who have not even the capacity for deriving pleasure from humor when it is presented to them by others." In humor, the ego shows itself strong in the face of adversity, since it finds a cause for pleasure even in misfortune, and it must therefore be regarded as one of the mechanisms of defense.

These last two characteristics, the denial of the claim of reality and the triumph of the pleasure principle, cause humor to approximate to the regressive or reactionary processes which engage our attention so largely in psychopathology. By its repudiation of the possibility of suffering, it takes its place in the great series of methods devised by the mind of man for evading the compulsion to suffer—a series which begins with neurosis and culminates in delusions, and includes intoxication, self-induced states of abstraction and ecstasy.

Let us now turn to the analysis of the cognitive aspect of humor, using the word again in its more inclusive sense, to cover the whole range from unlearned laughter to our most sophisticated pleasures. In defining the cognitive basis of the humorous attitude, we shall see a strong parallel to Freud's discussion of the techniques of wit, and his emphasis on the role of "economy" in every form of the comic.

Wherever we find humor, we find analogy, and also an awareness that the analogy is imperfect. If we laugh at the man who almost breaks a leg, it is because we perceive the parallel to a more tragic outcome, on the one hand, and to a "victory" for ourselves, on the other. If the secure and healthy infant can laugh unrestrainedly as he is tossed overhead by an adult whom he trusts, it is only because the mock danger is recognized as a sport. The game of peek-a-boo cannot delight the child before his intelligence can grasp the pretense of "as if I were not really here all the time," and it loses its charm as soon as the hidden presence becomes too obvious. The girl who hides behind her fan may play a maturer form of the same game, but now she offers her suitor a subtler misanalogy, between the retreat of modesty and the provocative retreat to a more permissive privacy.

The humorous attitude does not merely tolerate instability, but actively seeks it and delights in mastering it. It constitutes an intellectual adventurism, which gains satisfaction from simultaneously experiencing the same field as structured in two, even three or more, different ways. The objection might be raised that the humorous attitude is not basic enough to qualify as a perceptual attitude, that it does not manifest itself in relation to simple figure-ground relationships. Yet humor can be conveyed by an added flourish to a decorative design, or an added repetitious phrase in music, which hints at another, subtler meaning besides the obvious one, even though there is no definable meaning at all in the design or the music as such. The root of humor is in our readiness to perceive multiple meanings, not in the meanings themselves. It is a nonprimary drive.

One is tempted to quote whole pages of Freud's treatise on wit in defense of this position. The ambiguities, the condensations, the displacements, all the technical devices which Freud recognized as common to wit and the dream, are forms of analogy. And Freud himself explicitly recognizes that it is "the technical means of wit (which) produce a feeling of pleasure in the hearer." We take direct satisfaction from the exercise of this faculty, quite apart from the use we make of it for the indirect gratification of other needs.

When we do not use our psychic apparatus for the fulfillment of one of our indispensable gratifications, we let it work for pleasure, and we seek to derive pleasure from its own activity. I suspect that this is really the condition which underlies all esthetic thinking, but I know too little about esthetics to be willing to support this theory. About wit, however, I can assert . . . that it is an activity whose purpose is to derive pleasure—be it intellectual or otherwise—from the psychic processes.

Although Freud goes at great length into the word plays that are commonly employed in wit, he recognizes that "good wit" always reveals some true conceptual likeness between the objects that are being compared. In the comic and in humor, using these words now in Freud's narrower sense, situational analogies and teasing situational discrepancies are always present. Thus Freud writes, "It is a condition for the origin of the comic that we are induced to apply—either *simultaneously or in rapid succession*—to the same thought function two different modes of ideas, between which the 'comparison' then takes place and the comic difference results." The analogy aspect of humor was not so explicitly stated by Freud in his earlier treatise, although it is evident enough in each of his examples. Two of these are instances of gallows humor. In one, the criminal who is being led to his execution early on a Monday morning remarks, "Yes, this week is beginning well." In the other, a criminal in the same situation asks for a scarf, so that he shall not catch cold. In his later essay (1928), Freud sums it all up in one grand analogy: "Look here! This is all that this seemingly dangerous world amounts to. Child's play—the very thing to jest about!"

However, it is not analogy, but misanalogy which creates wit or humor. It is the pretended danger that is recognized as not dangerous; the grimace that fails to frighten, like an architectural gargoyle; the execution that is dismissed as lightly as a morning constitutional; it is *La Grande Dame Malaprope.* The secret of the enormous significance which humor can have in our lives, and the tremendous satisfactions which we can derive from it, lies in great part in that fact of which Freud was aware, but which he unaccountably limited to the realm of wit alone: that humor is not strained, but is the spontaneous expression of our unconscious mentations. It is a thrifty pleasure indeed, for it salvages what orderly inhibition would suppress, and thus turn to waste. But it is far from being, as Freud described it, a "euphoria which . . . is nothing but the state of a bygone time, in which we were wont to defray our psychic work with slight expenditure." The pleasure that we find in it comes from the flexing of our conceptual muscles, as we achieve the harmony of a meaningful discordance.

CHAPTER 17

Control: Anxiety and Integration

THE PROBLEM OF CONTROL

*M*an's ability to plan his behavior is not wholly explained by his ability to construct such brain analogies as we discussed in the preceding chapters. He must have in addition the power to refrain from action until he has judged the consequences. Without self-restraint, wisdom would be indistinguishable from folly. The need for inhibitory controls is incessant: to stay awake on sentry duty, study on a hot night, refrain from unkind criticism, forego a forbidden sweet, suppress an inopportune cough, obey the speed limit on the open highway, he restrained in laughter at one's own jokes, count ten before speaking in anger, etc., etc. The importance of control as an aspect of behavior may also be indicated by calling to mind some of the terms that are used to describe individuals who lack adequate control. They may be called thoughtless, week-willed, impetuous, suggestible, distractible, imprudent, absent-minded, fickle, criminal, or bad losers. This incomplete listing is enough to show that many kinds of control are needed, in different situations. Furthermore, excess of control can be as damaging as its deficit. One must be quick in emergency, spontaneous in conversation, and relaxed in play. The individual who suffers from excess of control may be described as in-decisive, compulsive, stubborn, rigid, overinhibited, suffering from choice anxiety, or, at the extreme, as catatonic—that is, suffering from an exaggeration of control so great as to present the appearance of organic paralysis. For one individual, to choose between two motion picture programs, neither of which has any-thing very special to recommend it, may be a difficult decision. For another, a decision in favor of one course of action is instantly forgotten the moment another is suggested, even before there has been a chance to weigh one against the other. Both are equally suffering from defects of control.

This problem of choice, or the suppression of one possible response in favor of another, exists wherever there is flexibility in behavior. Years ago, the biologist von Uexküll described the starfish as a "republic of reflexes," which resolved the conflict of its impulses by permitting the arm which was most strongly stimulated to take the lead in establishing the pattern of action. This resolution of conflict takes place within the nerve net, so that a single integrated pattern of movement quickly arises even in the face of multiple stimulation which would otherwise pro-voke different responses. Higher animals meet the same problem by means of a hierarchic organization of the central nervous system, which includes successive stages of inhibitory control by higher over lower centers, and many stages of feedback to the controlling centers, both from the periphery and from within the nervous system.

The development of these inhibitory powers takes place within the general framework of what has already been described as the principle of anterior dominance, and is frequently called the principle of encephalization, a concept which was introduced by the pioneer neurologist Jackson. According to this principle, the evolutionary development of the brain has given rise to a hierarchic relationship among the parts, with the newer, anterior portions dominating the older, more caudal portions. This relationship has been studied in some detail as it concerns the hypothalamic centers which integrate various aspects of unlearned behavior. In particular, it has been noted that the patterns of fear and anger are normally held in check by the steady inhibitory action of higher nervous levels, and they come into play when these checks are removed through the intervention of still higher centers, in an act of disinhibition. This is a specific instance of the general principle that natively organized patterns of response are "constantly primed and ready for action," but need the trigger release of disinhibition. The constant interplay of emotional excitation from below, and cortical inhibition from above, leads to various degrees of partial exercise of the response pattern.

The hierarchic organization of the nervous system is fortunately incomplete. It is not so rigidly organized that conflict and decision do not have a place. The brain can hatch more than one plan at a time, give attention to more than one stimulus, or view the same situation in a fluctuating and unstable configuration. Any given situation includes aspects which are analogous to more than one past experience, and hence may arouse impulses to more than one kind of action. Such fluctuation and such multiple parallel processes are the necessary basis for flexibility in our adjustments. If the brain were completely hierarchic, we would be single-purposed machines, without conflict or confusion. As it is, plans and motives compete for satisfaction, because there is no clear channel of authority.

As a result of this neural interplay, the faint record of experience may be able to dominate a far stronger immediate stimulation from the environment. In man, the prolonged inhibition of overt motor response permits long sequences of intracortical activity for the thoughtful planning of behavior. Nearly a century has passed since Sechenov (1863), the forerunner and teacher of Pavlov, defined thought as "a mental reflex reduced to its first two-thirds," that is, one in which the effector component has been inhibited. What we have learned since further emphasizes that a high development of cortical inhibitory control is the necessary condition for escape from the stimulus-bound life of the animal, or the very young child, to the largely intellectual life of man.

CONTROL AS A TEMPERAMENTAL VARIABLE

In view of this evident continuity, it may be questioned whether control is anything more than an aspect of impulsiveness. It is possible to point to many parallels between human and animal behavior in this area. The contrast of excitable and inhibited individuals has been noted among dogs (Pavlov) as well as among human infants (Fries). The paralysis of total inhibition is an unlearned defense pattern of many animals. The hierarchic organization of inhibiting mechanisms has been shown most clearly in Bard and Mountcastle's (1947) experiments on cats, with whom frontal ablation was shown to result in placid behavior—not unlike that of some lobectomized human patients! —while more thorough decortication produced an animal that would show rage at the slightest provocation or none at all—a symptom which appears clinically in humans with brain tumors.

Electroencephalographic studies provide mounting evidence that childhood behavior disorders in which impulsiveness and suggestibility are prominent symptoms are frequently the result of abnormalities of brain function, which may have their basis in heredity, injury, or illness. The voltage changes in EEG records are studied by a form of harmonic analysis, and are classified in certain frequency ranges. Alpha waves, which are most prominent in records taken from normal adults in a restful waking state, have a frequency of about 10 per second. Beta waves are much faster, and theta waves slower. The latter may be provoked in a normal adult by annoying stimulation (Walter, 1953). Delta waves are slower still, and their occurrence in waking adults often betrays the presence of a brain tumor. Jenkins and Pacella (1943) studied the EEG responses of delinquent boys in a training school. Most of these boys had been involved in stealing or gang offenses, but a considerable number had gotten into their difficulties because of impulsivity, irritability, and poor control. Only 30 percent of the first group, but more than 70 percent of the second group, had abnormal EEG records, and many of the abnormalities in the second group were apparently the aftermaths of head injuries or encephalitic illness. Kennard (1949) states that 60 percent of children with behavior disorders, and 40 percent of their normal relatives, show abnormal dysrhythmia such as occurs in only 10 to 15 percent of the normal population. Hill (1950) summarizes many similar studies, all tending to support the conclusion that abnormal EEG's are characteristic also of psychopathic adults. He emphasizes, however, that this is apparently "the expression of a failure in maturation processes," since "many of the records of young psychopaths would pass for normal in children. The excess of the theta rhythm observed by many workers in behavior problem children is the same type of abnormality as that seen in the adult psychopath, yet all children with such disorders do not become psychopathic adults."

The maturational development of inhibitory capacity in childhood has already been discussed as an aspect of normal growth, and particularly in relation to the child's acquisition of control over the processes of bodily evacuation. Although mastery of this problem signalizes the attainment of a fair degree of cortical inhibitory control, it does not by any means indicate that the maturational process is even nearly complete. Bousfield and Orbison (1952) point out that it continues through adolescence and into early maturity, as shown by the fact that EEG records do not show a fully adult pattern before the age of 19 years. Hence, they declare, we must credit physiological maturation—glandular as well as neural—as the basis for those characteristic changes in emotional behavior which we have been prone to regard as the results of disciplinary training.

CONDITIONED INHIBITION, AND INHIBITION BY INTERFERENCE

Training also plays an important part in the development of

inhibitory control. Whenever we learn a new way to respond to any situation, the complete process of learning involves not only the acquisition of a new response, but also the suppression of the old. Often our attention is fixed primarily on this learning of inhibition, rather than on the acquisition of any new overt response. We learn to "not do" something, to replace it by inaction. To explain such conditioned inhibition in his dogs, Pavlov (1927) postulated that every stimulation of the sensory cortex has both excitatory and inhibitory aspects, and he assumed further that the basis for excitable and inhibited types was the predominance of one or the other of these processes in individual animals. The authors of *Frustration and Aggression* (Dollard, Doob, Miller, Mowrer, and Sears, 1939) were content to ascribe such learning to "the law of effect: those actions cease to occur which, in the past, have been followed by punishment." However, the original legislator, Thorndike, had already (1932) amended this "law" after discovering that punishment has no demonstrable "stamping-out" effect. One of the group, Mowrer (1939), provided a possible key to the riddle, with his observation that even when a response does not attain its objective, the fact that it brings about a reduction of anxiety may be regarded as a positive reinforcement. This solution, which fits neatly into Hull's monolithic scheme that all learning is brought about by reduction of need tensions, soon received wide acceptance. In a later work, Dollard and Miller (1950) illustrate conditioned inhibition with the hypothetical case of a soldier who "learns the habits of not thinking about his combat experience"—that is, represses these experiences and develops amnesia for them—because the cessation of such thoughts, on the occasions when he did entertain them, brought about a reduction of the anxiety which they aroused. Despite the ingenuity of this suggestion, and the enthusiasm with which it was received by others, Mowrer himself was soon (1947) to diminish its importance by the formulation of his two-factor theory of learning. (See page 192.) Departing from the position that no

therefore serves a restrictive, controlling function, rather than the creative function which is commonly attributed to it.

In an earlier chapter, we have already seen how the Würzburg school produced experimental evidence that consciousness plays no essential part in creative thinking. There are many everyday experiences which serve to demonstrate the same fact. A solution to the problem that tormented us yesterday, or the name that we could not recall half an hour earlier, suddenly occurs to us in a relaxed and inattentive moment, that is, when inhibitory processes are at a minimum. Then the creative process, which was hampered by an excess of effort, produces an answer. The distinguished mathematician Poincaré (1915), as well as many other creative thinkers of the first order, have attested to the importance of this phenomenon as almost a regular rule of scientific discovery, where the days, weeks, or years of strenuous coping with a problem seem but to prepare the way for that sudden, seemingly effortless flash of integrating insight which may come, as it did to Poincaré, while he was climbing into a bus and carrying on a conversation about a totally different matter, on a day when his mathematical problems had been completely put aside in favor of a geological excursion. We must not, however, diminish the importance of the fact that the correctness of his insight was recognized by Poincaré in a conscious process.

We all have similar experiences of a lesser order. When we feel at ease in talking about some subject with which we are familiar, the spontaneity of our speech often precludes any foreknowledge of the words that we will speak a moment later, and which are largely determined by the syntax of the sentence that is already half-spoken. We become aware of our intellectual product simultaneously with its utterance, and may be pleasantly surprised by some apt illustration as it flows from our lips. At other times, we become aware of a block in the creative process, or of a logical fault in the shaping thought, our speech slows down, and we make the conscious, hesitant review of what we *might* say, judge before we speak, say the acceptable and reject the unacceptable.

This process of conscious critical review is only the highest of three levels of "censorship" which Freud (1915, 1925b) defined. In our discussion, we have spoken of the difference between conscious and not-conscious processes, reserving the word unconscious for use in the meaning which Freud gave to it, as designating processes that are *inadmissible* into consciousness. (Freud met this problem of ambiguity by using unconscious, as an adjective, in the sense of not-conscious, and designating "the unconscious," as a system, with the symbol Ucs.) The most basic level of censorship, as he conceived it, is that which stands between the unconscious and the preconscious, and which is called repression. It is within the preconscious that the greater part of the not-conscious activity takes place, under the direction of problem settings, attitudes, and evaluative dispositions whose combined operation represents a second level of selection or censorship. Freud spoke of this as a censorship which stands between the preconscious and the conscious, but he gave it comparatively little attention. It includes most of the processes that we have dealt with in the chapters on cognitive individuality. Finally, as if at the end of the assembly line, there sits the conscious censor, who makes the final inspection of the product, in the crucial stage of quality control. This evaluative review is one of the functions of cortical inhibitory control, by means of which the not-conscious productive processes of thinking are kept channeled toward the conscious goal.

However, we must now ask whether the concept of the unconscious, as a realm of thoughts inadmissible to consciousness, may not be superfluous, once it is recognized that the determination of conscious content always involves processes of negative as well as positive selection among the available not-conscious processes. The Freudian scheme of unconscious, preconscious, and conscious mental processes is like a naïve typology, in which certain "typical" cases have been set up as the representatives of classes, and the continuity of the distribution has been dis-

reinforcement can take place without tension reduction, he stated that it is characteristic of emotional responses that they can be readily conditioned by contiguity alone. Shoben (1949) recognizes the practical importance of this theory in his discussion of the relation between learning theory and psychotherapy. The doctrine that anxiety, and other emotional states, can be conditioned by events that do not include any element of tension reduction also facilitates our understanding of the commonly observed deleterious effects of conditioned inhibition. When, under the threat of punishment or the force of admonition, we learn to "not do" or inhibit a response, we are at the same time attaching anxiety to the situation, and indeed to many of its separate aspects. In consequence, there is a danger of generalized inhibitory effects, which reduce the flexibility of behavior, and hence the ability of the individual to acquire any new adjustive response in place of the one that is inhibited. Tolman (1948) has described this situation as one which favors the acquisition of "narrow" rather than broad "cognitive maps." It may be illustrated by the behavior of a rat which, having failed to form any consistent habit in a free-choice situation, quickly develops a rigid "fixation" when the element of punishment is introduced at the point of choice (Diamond, 1934). This is the type of behavior which appears in the abnormal fixations described by Maier (1949), although Mowrer (1950) himself prefers to explain Maier's results as an instance of learning by anxiety reduction.

Under happier circumstances, from a pedagogic viewpoint, the attention of the learner is focused primarily on the acquisition of the new response, and the suppression of the old takes place as a matter of course. This is an instance of inhibition by interference, due to the incompatibility of the new and the old responses. Such learning involves no necessary forgetting or erasing of the old response, but only an enrichment of the individual's repertoire of behavior by the addition of a new response of higher probability in the given situation. If the new response proves impossible or inadvisable under some special condition, the old response is still available. The range of behavior has been increased, rather than narrowed, as in the case of conditioned inhibition.

The repeated experience of learning by one or the other of these methods has widespread effects on the general style of behavior. When emphasis is placed on the rewarding of successful responses, the individual remains ever ready for new learning. Harlow (1949) has shown how it is possible even to establish "learning sets" in monkeys, so that they become capable of guiding their behavior in a choice situation on the basis of their experience, whether successful or unsuccessful, in a single trial. If, instead, emphasis is placed on the conditioned inhibition of the unwanted response, the likely result is a generalization of inhibitory effects which constitutes an important and harmful modification of temperament, such as we noticed in many fearful animals.

THE SCHEMATIC REPRESENTATION OF CONFLICT

A conflict situation is one in which the rivalry of incompatible behaviors is not resolved without a noticeable reduction in the efficiency of performance of the dominant response. Some of the ways in which this may show itself are in hesitation, in incipient movements toward the performance of the suppressed response, in an unnecessary expenditure of effort for the response performed, in lapses into daydreaming or idleness despite the need for planned behavior, and in a feeling of guiltiness which accompanies the response. The application of Lewin's method of topological and vector analysis to such conflict situations serves to show that we cannot adequately represent them in terms of balancing and interacting motive forces, but that we must explicitly recognize the part played by the inhibitory process. Lewin (1935) states that there are three types of conflict: approach-approach, avoidance-avoidance, and approach-avoidance. The first calls for an exercise of preference between goals both of which carry positive valence, the second for choice of a lesser evil where each possibility carries a negative valence, and the third for acceptance or rejection of a course of conduct which, because of its mixed consequences, has both negative and positive valence. It is not difficult to translate into such terms the problem, for example, of choice between two professions, of which the more prestigeful also requires a longer and harder course of preparation, or whether to pick a mystery or a textbook for an evening's reading. Lewin depicted such situations by representing the various possibilities for action by vectors, but he recognized that analysis in these terms alone is inadequate. In particular, in the case of avoidance-avoidance conflicts the subject would "leave the field" if there were no constraining force which prevents this. He therefore introduces the concept of the barrier, which is in effect a representation of direct inhibition. He writes: "One must distinguish between *driving* forces, which correspond to positive or negative valence, and *restraining* forces, which correspond to barriers." When barriers become too strong, as under conditions of "hopelessness and fear," the result is reduced flexibility of behavior, or *rigidity* of personality structure. Sometimes an excessively strong motivation for the task may give rise to a similar rigidity, for it may make the individual incapable of adopting a detour solution which would make the goal temporarily more remote. When the real barriers seem insuperable, the individual may nevertheless "leave the field" by escaping to the "level of irreality," in which it is possible to approach the goal in fantasy while evading the obstacles of the real situation.

Another kind of analysis of conflict situations is given by Miller (1944). He points out that as one comes closer to the realization of any goal, both the strength of attraction and the strength of repulsion—what Lewin calls the positive and negative valence—increase, but that this effect is usually more pronounced for repulsion than for attraction. Hence, he says, "the avoidance gradient is steeper than the approach gradient." It follows that in an approach-avoidance conflict, there will often be a point short of the goal where the two gradients cross, where the rapidly increasing fear or avoidance begins to exceed the slower increasing attraction in motivational strength. The individual will approach rather readily until this point, but be unable to push beyond it, like a suitor who resolves each week that he is going to "pop the question" on his next date, but always backs away from it when the opportunity is offered. Another deduction from the principle of gradients is that the solution of any true approach-approach conflict must be a quite simple matter, because as soon as one has brought one of the alternatives a little nearer to realization, its motivational force is likewise increased. Therefore, if the young man cannot make up his mind between being a doctor and a lawyer, we must suspect that it is not that these are so equal in attractiveness, but perhaps that he fears the responsibility of either. The normally hungry donkey cannot starve between two equally attractive stacks of hay, although it is possible for a dog to acquire a conditioned fear response so strong that it will starve to death before he can overcome his fear.

ANXIETY AND CONTROL

Anxiety is a frequent accompaniment of what we have been calling overcontrolled behavior, that is, behavior which is rendered ineffectual by the disturbing influence of overgeneralized inhibitory controls. There is general agreement that anxiety is (1) a distressing experience akin to fear, (2) which lacks any basis in a genuine external threat to the organism, and (3) which is in some way related to the defense of the self-concept. To understand anxiety, we must explain why it takes the appearance of fear, which is an expression of temperamental characteristics which man holds in common with other mammals, and also what is the nature of its dependence on the higher mental processes.

One explanation of anxiety is that it is not fear at all, but

regarded. It might be better to say only that mental processes, which can influence our behavior without acquiring the quality of being conscious, differ with respect to the probability that they may acquire that quality, that is, the probability that they may pass through the lower levels of selection or censorship in a form which subjects them to the test of the higher. Such a reformulation takes away nothing from the effectiveness of the distinction which Freud made. He stated that unconscious processes ignore contradictions of time and logic, and other realistic conditions, and that their energy is readily deflected into substitutive channels, a characteristic which he called primary process. Preconscious processes, on the other hand, obey the rules of logical negation, of orderly time relationships, and reality testing, and they exhibit a relative constancy of goal directedness which he called secondary process. The two realms are not distinct, for—as Freud pointed out in his analysis of wit—these restraints may sometimes be relaxed even in consciousness. Differences in susceptibility to reality controls, as well as variations in the vigor of these controls at different times, provide an adequate and more parsimonious explanation for the phenomena which Freud sought to explain by his hypothesis of unconscious, preconscious, and conscious mental strata.

One of the distinguishing marks of conscious control is the fact that its criteria, unlike those of the not-conscious, are themselves open to examination and review. Accordingly, conscious controls have a greater likelihood of being realistic, logical, and socially integrated.

The Role of Language in Control

A large part of conscious control is exercised in language, or at least takes forms which are dependent on language for their development. Legal and ethical systems, moral prohibitions and exhortations, formal logical and scientific criteria for validity of our thinking are all expressed in language. Language is the socialized tool of symbolism, whose existence makes symbolism easier for each of us, just as saws, hammers, and nails make it easier to erect a shelter. As such, it creates many new possibilities for the control of behavior. A word or phrase may symbolize whole classes of actions which are desirable or undesirable, and thus provide an effective means for generalizing inhibitory controls which may first be learned in a circumscribed situation. "Thou shalt not kill" may be taught without the need for a practical demonstration of the prohibited conduct. Language provides cues for self-stimulation, helping to keep in mind long-term goals which might otherwise be forgotten, as well as to formulate the long behavior sequences which may lead to their realization. It brings into our present awareness the experience of past generations, which would otherwise be inaccessible. It makes possible the construction of logical systems, by which we may test the validity of our deductions and inferences. Its extension in mathematics makes it possible for our thought to transcend the limits of time and space to which our senses are bound. By means of its varied symbolic manipulations, man gains tremendously in control over himself and his environment.

However, these processes also open up corresponding dangers. In the eighteenth century, the philosopher Helvetius wrote: "Man is born ignorant, but not stupid, and it requires much education to make him so." Before him, Hobbes had wisely though less wittily observed (in the *Leviathan*) that although man "can by words reduce the consequences he finds to general rules . . . this privilege is allayed by another; and that is, by the privilege of absurdity; to which no living creature is subject, but man only. And of men, those are of all most subject to it, that profess philosophy." The rules which Hobbes gives to avoid such absurdity are essentially those that have been amplified by the modern semanticists (e.g., Korzybski, 1933), who warn us of the dangers of too facile generalization, of pseudological constructions, of reification of concepts, which are inherent in the uncritical use of language. When man permits the artificial, symbolic world which he creates in language (or in the pictorial symbolism of comics, motion pictures, and television) to take precedence over the real world, he becomes capable of committing error on a scale which is impossible for less intelligent beings. The lie, the wishful fantasy, the unreal abstraction, the nonexistent hazard, the fear of one word and the false confidence in another, when neither has substance, are all used to deceive ourselves as well as others. Properly used, language helps us to achieve the goal of conscious control: behavior that is realistic, logical, and socially integrated. Improperly used, it can match the unconscious in the production of behavior that is unrealistic, illogical, and autistic.

THE APPRAISAL OF CONTROL

In the equation of adjustment, intensity of conflict is not more important than efficiency of control. Under the very best of conditions, the conflict of decision is a natural part of our lives, and the integrated person is not one who is without conflict, but one whose conflicts are resolved without noticeable impairment of efficiency in adjustment. However, it is only recently that this fact has received adequate recognition, in efforts to develop instruments of appraisal for those positive aspects of personality organization which protect the individual from the adverse effects of stress. Clinicians have ordinarily been called upon to discover the reason for breakdown, after it has occurred. They have been ingenious in devising methods of doing this, but, when the same methods are applied to persons who are functioning satisfactorily in the community, the results usually raise the startling question, Why are not the rest of us also institutionalized?

There are many practical situations in which the appraisal of control, rather than the appraisal of conflict, is of primary importance. During wartime, psychologists were asked to help make the preventive detection of individuals who would be unable to withstand the exceptional stresses of battle or of tours of duty in isolated places. Especially crucial was the selection of men for the "cloak and dagger" activities of the Office of Strategic Services. This assessment program was under the direction of Murray, the originator of the TAT, and in it considerable reliance was placed on contrived "life situations" in which the psychologists played the part of participant-observers, to borrow Sullivan's term for the role of the psychotherapist. The resort to this method, which had been introduced by German psychologists for the selection of army officers, may be taken as an indication of distrust in the more conventional psychodiagnostic instruments, at least for the purpose of assessing high levels of control and the qualities of leadership and resourcefulness. However, experience with it did not support the conclusion that test situations could be made more valid simply by making them more lifelike. (O.S.S. Assessment Staff, 1948.) Very similar problems arise in the selection of policemen, and a number of progressive police departments throughout the country now employ psychologists to help detect "bad risks" among their candidates. In industry, the traditional function of psychologists in personnel selection has been expanded, in many large firms, by engaging consulting clinical psychologists to advise on the selection of personnel for advancement to executive positions. In all such jobs, the problem is to appraise control rather than abilities, and the job is only half done if we do no more than search for signs of weakness in the structure; what is at least equally important is to determine its strengths. The cracks in a concrete wall are not too important, if we know that it contains adequate reinforcing steel.

The Rorschach inkblot test is one of the tests which is most commonly used for the appraisal of control. The complexity of the problems of interpretation of this test forbids any attempt to describe the manner of its use for this purpose in a short space. Such varied factors are considered as the accuracy of reported percepts (form level), relative productiveness on achromatic and chromatic cards, and ability to see "populars," that is, to take the point of view that most other persons take, in situations which do not call for originality. Many of the factors in a Rorschach record which enter into the appraisal of control have been brought together by Klopfer and his associates (Klopfer et al., 1954) in a Prognostic Rating Scale. This scale consists of a fairly arbitrary weighting of many different aspects of test performance, leading to a composite score for "ego strength," which is supposed to discriminate between clinical patients who might be expected to profit from therapy and those who lack the inner resources needed for successful participation in a therapeutic program. However, this scale is offered only as "a preliminary attempt," and there is as yet inadequate evidence to show that it can do the task for which it is designed.

Another "ego strength" scale, intended to serve the same prognostic function, has been devised by Barron (1953b). This scale is constructed from items of the MMPI, following the same empirical procedures that were used in establishing the original MMPI scales. Two groups of psychoneurotic patients were compared, one consisting of those who were judged to have made considerable progress during six months of clinic treatment, the other consisting of those who had apparently made no progress. All had taken the MMPI before the beginning of treatment, and examination of the records showed that there were 68 items on which the two groups differed significantly. Barron has since reported success in using this scale among army officers and other normal groups, where he has found that it shows positive relationship with a number of desirable personality characteristics.

Uneven performance on any of the more widely used, individually administered intelligence tests is frequently interpreted as a sign of poor control. The Wechsler-Bellevue Intelligence Scales have been the object of much research in this regard. Rapaport (1945) pointed particularly to "temporary inefficiencies," especially in the course of the Digit Span subtest, as indicative of the disruptive effects of unmastered anxiety. Another subtest which deserves attention at this point is Comprehension, which includes a number of hypothetical practical problem situations, some of which have an emergency nature. Panicky response to these problems, even without the stress of the real situation, often betrays the individual's own judgment that he would fail to meet the situation adequately. Poor reality contact may be revealed by ridiculously inappropriate answers to such questions of Information as the population of the United States or the distance from New York to Paris. Most clinicians regard such answers as symptomatic of far more than poor intelligence, but published proof of the validity of such interpretation is lacking.

One of the essential elements of control is the capacity to work for a deferred goal, and it was long ago suggested that the Porteus Maze Test can be used to measure this capacity. This test consists of a series of paper-and-pencil labyrinths like those sometimes found in newspaper puzzle corners, graded in difficulty from very simple to fairly complex patterns. Porteus (1924) claimed that its value lay in the fact that it required prudence and planning, while it penalized "impulsiveness, irresolution, suggestibility, nervousness, and excitability." At that time, he was thinking primarily in terms of a diagnostic instrument which could differentiate between feeble-minded persons who required institutionalization and others who might perform no better on a standard intelligence test, but still could adjust satisfactorily to the requirements of a simple occupation and live in the community without constant close supervision. Recently, Porteus, and Peters (1947) found that patients who have undergone frontal brain surgery also showed a decline in performance on the maze test, although mental deterioration could not be shown in a Binet score. This supports the contention that the maze test helps to assess foresight, planning, and freedom from impulsiveness.

Another essential element of control is frustration tolerance. Rosenzweig's P-F Study, or Picture-Frustration Test (1945), is designed not so much to measure the strength of frustration tolerance as to reveal the individual's characteristic manner of response to frustrating situations. There are separate forms for children and adults, each consisting of a series of cartoons presenting incidents in which one of the participants undergoes a frustrating experience. The subject is asked to imagine the victim's verbal response to the situation. This is scored on two dimensions: first, as to whether the hostility aroused is directed outwardly, inwardly, or is altogether denied; second, as to whether the content of the answer indicates a focus of attention on the frustrating circumstance, on the assignment of blame, or on the individual's own continuing need. Categories on the first dimension are designated as extrapunitive, intropunitive, and impunitive; those on the second dimension are called obstacle-dominant, ego-defensive, or need-persistive.

Techniques such as those that we have been discussing have sufficient success in clinical application to justify the time spent upon them, but they still fall far short of a desired level of efficiency. When the problem is one of selecting poor risks in an already select population of normal subjects, it is doubtful whether they can offer anything of value. Holtzman and Sells (1054) found that the judgments of skilled clinicians, based on a battery of personality tests—which, however, had been modified so as to permit group administration—were of no demonstrable value in predicting which of a population of aviation cadets would be eliminated from flight training because of personality disturbance. Kelly and Fiske (1951) found that clinical judgments on the future success of student clinical psychologists were also of very limited value, and that the scores of single objective tests were sometimes more valid than the opinions of experts based on a global consideration of an extensive battery. These are disturbing results, which show us how little progress has been made toward the objective of appraising the factor of control in personality.

THE WHOLE PERSON

It is customary to speak of the well-adjusted person as

"integrated." This may be taken to mean that the parts of the person fit harmoniously together, that the activity of one part does not disrupt the activity of another, and that each part seems even to foster the development of all the rest. However, integration is sometimes understood in the sense of unity, as implying that there is a necessary close interaction among all the parts, and that the true understanding of any segment of this total pattern would enable a wise observer to reconstruct the whole, somewhat as the whole of some simple animal might be regenerated from a part. However, one may easily overstate the case for the organic unity of the individual. Just as the scope of regeneration becomes more limited as the animal grows in complexity, so too the possibility of prediction from one bit of behavior to another becomes less sure.

Lewin, who emphasized the importance of differentiation, clearly underlined the danger of assuming too much unity in behavior. He wrote (1926, 1935):

> The relations of psychical events to each other and the breadth of influence of each single experience upon the other psychical processes depend not simply upon their strength, indeed not even upon their real importance. The individual psychcial experiences, the actions and emotion, purposes, wishes, and hopes are rather *imbedded in quite definite psychical structures, spheres of the personality, and whole processes.* . . .
> If there were not this sometimes astoundingly complete segregation of different psychical systems from each other, if there were instead a permanently real unity of the mind of such kind that all the phychical tensions present at a given time had to be regarded as tensions in a uniform, unitary, closed system, no ordered action would be possible. . . .
> . . . Doubtless there exist in certain spheres,, for example in the motorium, a relatively high degree of unity. But however high one may estimate the degree of unity in a psychical totality, the recognition that within the mind there are regions of extremely various degrees of coherence remains an exceedingly important condition of more penetrating psychological research.

As a matter of fact, the appearance of unity is often a symptom of maladjustment. What is rigidity—which Lewin defined as a quality of mind which hinders differentiation of mental structure —but a kind of obtuse unity in the face of the diversity of circumstance? Who is more unified than the paranoiac, who relates every event to one delusional system? Who is less mature than the adult whose self-concept cannot tolerate the invasion of one little white lie? The most consistent unity to which we have appealed, in our account of the person, is that central feeling habit which is not the expression of the total personality, but the resurgence of a part in the face of difficulties. For the adjusted individual, as for the professional actor, it is a cardinal principle that "the play must go on," and we perform our many roles, in business, home, and club, with surprisingly little mutual interference. We carry our cathexes in many baskets, and are thus insured against the calamity that may befall a too unitary investment. As we move from situation to situation, we change our roles—the social selves whose multiplicity was recognized by William James—as we might change our garments, and each such change brings about the selective disinhibition of an appropriate action system, and the simultaneous inhibition of all its rivals.

The work of Witkin and his collaborators (Witkin et al., 1954) points up the relation between mature control and successful differentiation. Witkin's subjects were confronted with the task of finding the true vertical, while they sat in a tilted chair within a tilted room. The only useful cues for the solution of this problem are the sensations which arise from the action of gravity on one's own body, especially the body pressure against the chair. The visual cues, which are ordinarily more reliable and upon which we are accustomed to place maximum reliance, have been subverted in the tilted room, and they must therefore be disregarded. Many subjects found it utterly impossible to do this. They did not feel comfortably vertical unless they aligned themselves with the tilted room, even though they might then themselves be tilted at an angle of 30 degrees. Witkin calls such behavior *field-dependent,* and his clinical collaborators provided evidence that it was linked with poor personal control, low self-esteem, and general psychological immaturity. Field dependency should not be regarded as a perceptual attitude. Actually, the field-dependent person is suffering from an inability to abandon some of his accustomed unity, in order to achieve a differentiation which the situation demands. The subject in the tilted room must be able to set aside one part of himself, that is, his habitual manner of reacting to the seen world. In the same way, when one of Asch's subjects is confronted with a solid front of unreasonable opinion, he must be able to put aside a part of himself, that part which has learned to respect unanimity of opinion and to conform to the social pressure of his companions. These experimental situations test a capacity for partial self-alienation which is an essential aspect of inhibitory control, and which is exercised in less unusual ways whenever we find that the familiar way of dealing with a situation is no longer adequate.

In many of his writings, Allport has stressed the uniqueness of each individual, but he does not mean to imply thereby that the personality is unified. He writes (1937):

As a rule we stereotype our judgments even of our most intimate friends, and see greater consistency in their behavior than we should. The reason for this over-simplification, of course, is the reason for all time-saving clichés: we cannot afford to think or to deal with objects in all their intricate and confusing aspects. Hence we seek the "essence," and in so doing often arrive no further than a pigeon-hole. It is for this reason that psychology with its corrective patience may improve upon the too simple perceptions of common sense.

Even when Allport (1955) selects an example to illustrate the point that "a few leading characteristics do in fact depict the course of growth," the instance is one in which the conflict of personal disunity is evident: the autobiographic statement of H. G. Wells, "that two dominant themes cover almost all of his life history. These, he says, are first his interest in the achievement of an ordered world; and second, sex."

Such unity as we discover in the world is, as Allport hints, only the expression of our own perceptual need. Still, the psychologist's search for unity in the person does have one solid justification in fact: the object of his study is also a perceiving person, who has felt the need to see *his self* as integral. Nevertheless, we must recognize that the self-concept is not the whole person, and really effective harmony is rarely achieved even within the self-concept.

It is for this reason that we must study the person in many ways, and that we can never hope to reach the end of our study. The psychologist's task is like what is called by mathematicians the impasse of the mapmaker: it is impossible to draw a map of a territory within which the map lies, and make it contain all the detail of the map itself. It is impossible for all the fullness of a person to be included, capsule form, within the intellectual grasp of another person, or of that person himself. This inevitable skimpiness of understanding has the paradoxical consequence that a greater appearance of wholeness may be gained by a highly simplified, and hence more readily unified account than by one which makes greater effort at thoroughness. Just as the artist gains esthetic unity by the selection of detail, so the psychologist may create (for himself as well as others) an illusion of fuller understanding than he really possesses, by more or less successfully relating many different aspects of the personality to some central theme, while neglecting areas within which this "red thread" is a less effective unifying concept. Viewing the personality consistently from some central reference point, such as the psychosexual level or the self-concept, one may succeed in creating the illusion that the personality is being seen "as a whole," but this quality of unity resides only in the consistency of representation, and gives no assurance that the representation is complete. At another time, to meet another purpose, we may need to see the person in a different configuration. Thus we knew at the outset that our effort must be aimed at condensation, having as its goal a pragmatic selectivity, with no pretense at exhaustiveness. The schema which we have followed was intended only to embrace the most important aspects of personality, and it is avowedly a compromise with reality, dictated by our own needs for relative simplicity. Life is less simple in fact than we should like to picture it in theory. To "see the whole person" must always remain the unapproachable limit of psychological science, a goal beyond attainment.

References

Abraham, K., 1927. *Selected papers*, ed. by E. Jones, London, Hogarth.

Ach, N., 1905. *Ueber die Willenstätigkeit und das Denken*, Göttingen, Vandenhoeck and Ruprecht.

Adcock, C., 1948. A factorial examination of Sheldon's types, *J. Pers.*, 16:312-319.

Adler, A., 1917. *The neurotic constitution*, New York, Moffat, Yard & Co.

Adler, A., 1929. *The science of living*, New York, Greenberg.

Adler, A., 1933. *Social interest*, London, Faber.

Adorno, T. W., Frenkel-Brunswik, Elsa, Levinson, D. J., and Sanford, R. N., 1950. *The authoritarian personality*, New York, Harper.

Adrian, E. D., 1947. *The physical background of perception*, London, Oxford University Press.

Aldrich, C. A., Sung, C., and Knop, Catherine, 1945. The crying of newly born babies: I. Community phase. *J. Pediat.*, 26:313-326.

Alexander, F., 1934. The influence of psychologic factors upon gastrointestinal disturbances: a symposium. I. General principles, objectives, and preliminary results. *Psychoanalyt. Quart.*, 3:501-539.

Alexander, F., 1952. Development of the fundamental concepts of psychoanalysis, in *Dynamic psychiatry*, ed. by F. Alexander and Helen Ross, Chicago, University of Chicago. Pp. 3-34.

Allport, F., 1934. The J-curve hypothesis of conforming behavior, *J. social Psychol.*, 5:141-183.

Allport, G. W., 1928. A test for ascendance-submission, *J. abn. social Psychol.*, 23:118-136.

Allport, G. W., 1937. *Personality: a psychological interpretation*, New York, Holt.

Allport, G. W., 1946. Effect: a secondary principle of learning, *Psychol. Rev.*, 53:335-347.

Allport, G. W., 1950. *The nature of personality*, Cambridge, Mass., Addison-Wesley.

Allport, G. W., 1954. *The nature of prejudice*, Cambridge, Mass., Addison-Wesley.

Allport, G. W., 1955. *Becoming*, New Haven, Yale University Press.

Allport, G. W., and Odbert, H. S., 1936. Trait-names: a psycholexical study, *Psychol. Monographs*, 47, No. 211.

427

Allport, G. W., and Postman, L. J., 1947. The basic psychology of rumor, in *Readings in social psychology*, ed. by E. L. Hartley et al., New York, Holt. Pp. 547-558.

Allport, G. W., and Vernon, P. E., 1931. A test of personal values, *J. abn. social Psychol.*, 26:231-248.

Ansbacher, H. L., 1953. "Neo-Freudian" of "Neo-Adlerian"? *Am. Psychologist*, 8:165-166.

Arnheim, R., 1949. The gestalt theory of expression, *Psychol. Rev.*, 56:156-171.

Asch, S., 1951. Effects of group pressure upon the modification and distortion of judgments, in *Groups, leadership, and men*, ed. by H. Guetzkow, Pittsburgh, Carnegie Press. Pp. 177-190.

Ashby, W. R., 1952. *Design for a brain*, New York, Wiley.

Atkinson, J. W., 1953. The achievement motive and recall of interrupted and completed tasks, *J. exptl. Psychol.*, 46:381-390.

Baas, M. L., 1950. Kuder interest patterns of psychologists, *J. appl. Psychol.*, 34:115-117.

Balinsky, B., 1941. An analysis of the mental factors of various age groups from nine to sixty, *Genet. Psychol. Monographs*, 23:191-234.

Balint, M., 1948. Individual differences of behavior in early infancy, and an objective method of recording them, *J. genet. Psychol.*, 73:57-117.

Bard, P., 1934. The neuro-humoral basis of emotional reactions, in *Handbook of general experimental psychology*, ed. by C. Murchison, Worcester, Mass., Clark University Press. Pp. 264-311.

Bard, P., 1950. Central nervous mechanisms for the expression of anger in animals, in *Feelings and emotions*, ed. by M. L. Reymert, New York, McGraw-Hill. Pp. 211-237.

Bard, P., and Mountcastle, V. B., 1947. Some forebrain mechanisms involved in expression of rage with special reference to suppression of angry behavior, *Research Publ. Assoc. Nervous Mental Disease*, 27:362-404.

Barker, R. G., Dembo, Tamara, and Lewin, K., 1941. Frustration and regression, *Univ. Iowa Studies Child Welf.*, No. 18. (Condensed, in *Child behavior and development*, ed. by R. G. Barker, J. S. Kounin, and H. F. Wright, New York, McGraw-Hill, 1943. Pp. 441-458.)

Barron, F., 1953a. Complexity-simplicity as a personality dimension, *J. abn. social Psychol.*, 48:163-172.

Barron, F., 1953b. An ego-strength scale which predicts response to psychotherapy, *J. consult. Psychol.*, 17:328-333.

Bartlett, F. C., 1932. *Remembering*, New York, Macmillan.

Bayley, Nancy, 1932. A study of the crying of infants during mental and physical tests, *J. genet. Psychol.*, 40:306-329.

Beach, F. A., 1948. *Hormones and behavior,* New York, Hoeber.

Beach, F. A., 1951. Instinctive behavior: reproductive activities, in *Handbook of experimental psychology,* ed. by S. S. Stevens, New York, Wiley. Pp. 387-434.

Beck, L., 1950. *Unconscious motivation,* 16 mm film, San Francisco, Association Films.

Beck, S. J., Rabin, A. I., Thiesen, W. C., Molish, H., and Thetford, W. N., 1950. The normal personality as projected in the Rorschach test, *J. Psychol.,* 30:241-298.

Beeman, Eliz. A., 1947. The effect of male hormone on aggressive behavior in mice, *Physiol. Zool.,* 20:373-405.

Bernreuter, R. G., 1933a. The measurement of self-sufficiency, *J. abn. social Psychol.,* 28:291-300.

Bernreuter, R. G., 1933b. The theory and construction of the personality inventory, *J. social Psychol.,* 4:387-405.

Binet, A., and Simon, Th., 1905. Méthodes nouvelles pour le diagnostique du niveau intellectuel des anormaux, *Année psychol.,* 11:191-244. (Excerpts in *Readings in the history of psychology,* ed. by W. Dennis, New York, Appleton-Century-Crofts, 1948. Pp. 412-419.)

Blos, P., 1941. *The adolescent personality,* New York, Appleton-Century-Crofts.

Blum, G. S., 1949. A study of the psychoanalytic theory of psychosexual development, *Genet. Psychol. Monographs,* 30:3-99.

Bonin, G. von., 1950. *Essay on the cerebral cortex,* Springfield, Ill., Thomas.

Bousefield, W. A., and Orbison, W. L., 1952. Ontogenesis of emotional behavior, *Psychol. Rev.,* 59:1-7.

Bowlby, J., 1953. Critical phases in the development of social responses in men and other animals, in *Prospects in psychiatric research,* ed. by J. M. Tanner, Springfield, Ill., Thomas. Pp. 25-32.

Brain, W. R., 1951. *Mind, perception, and science,* Springfield, Ill., Thomas.

Bridges, K. M. B., 1932. Emotional development in early infancy, *Child Develop.,* 3:324-334.

Bronfenbrenner,U., 1953. Personality, in *Ann. Rev. Psychol.,* 4:157-182. Stanford, Calif.

Bruner, J. S., 1951. Personality dynamics and the process of perceiving, in *Perception: an approach to personality,* ed. by R. R. Blake and G. V. Ramsey, New York, Ronald. Pp. 121-147.

Bruner, J. S., and Goodman, C. G., 1947. Value and need as organizing factors in perception, *J. abn. social Psychol.,* 42:33-44.

Bruner, J. S., and Postman, L., 1948. Symbolic value as an organizing factor in perception, *J. social Psychol.,* 27:203-208.

Bruner, J. S., Postman, L., and McGinnies, E., 1948. Personal values as selective factors in perception, *J. abn. social Psychol.*, 43:142-154.

Buck, J. N., 1948. The H-T-P technique, *J. clin. Psychol.*, 4:317-396.

Bugental, J. F. T., and Zelen, S. L., 1950. Investigations into the self-concept: I. The W-A-Y technique, *J. Personality*, 18:483-498.

Bühler, Charlotte, and Kelly, G., 1941. *The World Test, a measurement of emotional disturbance*, New York, Psychological Corporation.

Cannon, W. B., 1927. *Bodily changes in hunger, pain, fear and rage*, New York, Appleton-Century-Crofts.

Cannon, W. B., 1932. *The wisdom of the body*, New York, Norton.

Cantarow, A., and Trumper, M., 1949. *Clinical biochemistry*, Philadelphia, Saunders.

Carmichael, L., 1941. The experimental embryology of mind, *Psychol. Bull.*, 38:1-28.

Carter, L. F., and Schooler, K., 1949. Value, need, and other factors in perception, *Psychol. Rev.*, 56:200-207.

Cattell, R. B., 1945. The diagnosis and classification of neurotic states: a reinterpretation of Eysenck's factors, *J. nervous mental Disease*, 102:576-589.

Cattell, R. B., 1946. *Description and measurement of personality*, Yonkers, World Book.

Cattell, R. B., 1951. Principles of design in "projective" or misperceptive tests of personality, in *An introduction to projective tests*, ed. by H. H. Anderson and Gladys L. Anderson, Englewood Cliffs, N. J., Prentice-Hall. Pp. 55-98.

Cattell, R. B., and Luborsky, L. B., 1947. Personality factors in response to humor, *J. abn. social Psychol.*, 42:402-421.

Chein, I., Lane, R., Murphy, G., Proshansky, H., and Schaefer, R., 1951. Need as a determinant of perception: a reply to Pastore, *J. Psychol.*, 31:129-136.

Child, C. M., 1924. *Physiological foundations of behavior*, New York, Holt.

Child, I. L., 1950. The relation of somatotype to self-ratings on Sheldon's temperamental traits, *J. Personality*, 18:440-453.

Christie, R., and Jahoda, Marie (eds.), 1954. *Studies in the scope and method of "The Authoritarian Personality,"* Glencoe, Ill., Free Press.

Clark, K. B., and Clark, Mamie K., 1940. Skin color as a factor in racial identification of Negro pre-school children, *J. social Psychol.*, 11:159-169.

Cohen, L. D., 1950. Patterns of response in level of aspiration tasks, *Educ. psychol. Measmt.*, 10:664-684.

Cook, S. W., 1939. The production of "experimental neurosis" in the rat, *Psychosom. Med.*, 1:293-308.

Cooley, C. H., 1902. *Human nature and the social order,* New York, Scribner.

Craik, K. J. W., 1943. *On the nature of explanation,* London, Cambridge University Press.

Darwin, C., 1872. *The expression of the emotions in man and animals,* London, Murray.

Davis, A., and Havighurst, R. J., 1946. Social class and color differences in child-rearing, *Am. sociological Rev.,* 11:698-710.

Dempsey, E. W., 1951. Homeostasis, in *Handbook of experimental psychology,* ed. by S. S. Stevens, New York, Wiley. Pp. 209-235.

Dennis, W., 1951. Developmental theories, in *Current trends in psychological theory,* ed. by W. Dennis, Pittsburgh, University of Pittsburgh Press. Pp. 1-20.

Dennis, W., 1953. Animistic thinking among college and university students, *Sci. Monthly,* 76:247-249.

Diamond, S., 1934. Habit-formation under non-selective conditions, *J. comp. physiol. Psychol.,* 17:109-122.

Diamond, S., 1939. A neglected aspect of motivation, *Sociometry,* 2:77-85.

Diamond, S., 1948. The interpretation of interest profiles, *J. appl. Psychol.,* 35:512-520.

Diamond, S., 1954. The house and tree in verbal fantasy: I. Sex differences in themes and content; II. Their different roles, *J. proj. Tech.,* 18:316-325, 414-417.

Diamond, S., 1955. Sex stereotypes and acceptance of sex role, *J. Psychol.,* 39:385-388.

Doll, E. A., 1953. *The measurement of social competence,* Minneapolis, Educational Publishers.

Dollard, J., Doob, L. W., Miller, N. E., Mowrer, O. H., and Sears, R. R., 1939. *Frustration and aggression,* New Haven, Yale University Press.

Dollard, J., and Miller, N. E., 1950. *Personality and psychotherapy,* New York, McGraw-Hill.

Downey, June E., 1926. How the psychologist reacts to the distinction "extravert-introvert," *J. abn. social Psychol.,* 20:407-415.

Duffy, Eliz., 1949. A systematic framework for the description of personality, *J. abn. social Psychol.,* 44:175-190.

Dworkin, S., 1939. Conditioning neuroses in dog and cat, *Psychosom. Med.,* 1:388-396.

Eppinger, H., and Hess, L., 1915. Vagotonia, *Nerv. ment. Dis. Monographs,* No. 20.

Erikson, E., 1950. *Childhood and society,* New York, Norton.

Escalona, Sibylle, 1943. Play and substitute satisfactions, in *Child behavior and development,* ed. by R. G. Barker, J. S. Kounin, and H. F. Wright, New York, McGraw-Hill. Pp. 363-378.

Escalona, Sibylle, 1948. Some considerations regarding psychotherapy with psychotic children, *Bull. Menninger Clin.*, **12**:126-134.

Escalona, Sibylle, 1953. Emotional development in the first year of life, in *Sixth conference on problems of infancy and childhood*, ed. by M. Senn, New York, Josiah Macy, Jr. Foundation. Pp. 11-92.

Eysenck, H. J., 1947. *Dimensions of personality*, London, Routledge and Kegan Paul.

Eysenck, H. J., 1952. *The scientific study of personality*, New York, Macmillan.

Eysenck, H. J., 1953. *The structure of human personality*, New York, Wiley.

Farris, E. J., Yeakel, E. H., and Medoff, H. S., 1945. Development of hypertension in emotional gray Norway rats after air blasting. *Am. J. Physiol.*, **144**:331-333.

Fenichel, O., 1945. *The psychoanalytic theory of neurosis*, New York, Norton.

Fields, P. E., 1932. Studies in concept formation: I. The development of the concept of triangularity by the white rat, *Comp. Psychol. Monographs*, 9, No. 2.

Fiske, D. W., 1949. Consistency of the factorial structures of personality ratings from different sources, *J. abn. social Psychol.*, **44**:329-344.

Flanagan, J. C., 1935. *Factor analysis in the study of personality*, Palo Alto, Stanford University Press.

Fleischmann, Barney, 1954. *Unpublished manuscript.*

Flugel, J. C., 1954. Humor and laughter, in *Handbook of social psychology*, ed. by G. Lindzey, Cambridge, Mass., Addison-Wesley. Pp. 709-734.

Ford, C. F., and Tyler, Leona E., 1952. A factor analysis of Terman and Miles' M-F test, *J. appl. Psychol.*, **36**:251-253.

Forer, B., 1953. Personality factors in occupational choice, *Educ. psychol. Measmt.*, **13**:361-366.

Franck, Kate, and Rosen, E., 1949. A projective test of masculinity-femininity, *J. consult. Psychol.*, **13**:247-256.

Frank, J. D., 1935. Some psychological determinants of level of aspiration, *Am. J. Psychol.*, **47**:285-293.

Fredericson, E., 1950. The effects of food-deprivation upon competitive and spontaneous combat in C57 black mice, *J. Psychol.*, **29**:89-100.

Fredericson, E., 1952a. Reciprocal fostering of two inbred strains and its effect on the modification of inherited aggressive behavior, *Am. Psychologist*, **7**:241-242 (abstract).

Fredericson, E., 1952b. Aggressiveness in female mice, *J. comp. physiol. Psychol.*, **45**:254-257.

Freeman, G. L., 1948a. *The energetics of human behavior,* Ithaca, Cornell University Press.

Freeman, G. L., 1948b. *Physiological psychology,* New York, Van Nostrand.

Frenkel-Brunswick, Else, 1949. Intolerance of ambiguity as an emotional and perceptual personality variable, *J. Personality,* 18:108-143.

Frenkel-Brunswik, Else, 1951. Personality theory and perception, in *Perception: an approach to personality,* ed. by R. R. Blake and G. V. Ramsey, New York, Ronald. Pp. 356-419.

Freud, Anna, 1936. *The ego and the mechanisms of defense,* London, Hogarth.

Freud, S., 1924a. Character and anal erotism, in *Collected papers, vol. II,* London, Hogarth. Pp. 45-50.

Freud, S., 1924b. "Civilized" sexual morality and modern nervousness, *ibid.,* 76-99.

Freud, S., 1925a. On narcissism: an introduction, in *Collected papers, vol. IV,* London, Hogarth. Pp. 30-59.

Freud, S., 1925b. The unconscious, *ibid.,* 98-136.

Freud, S., 1927. *The ego and the id,* London, Hogarth.

Freud, S., 1936. *The problem of anxiety,* New York, Norton.

Freud, S., 1938a. Psychopathology of everyday life, in *Basic writings of Sigmund Freud,* ed. by A. A. Brill, New York, Modern Library. Pp. 33-178.

Freud, S., 1938b. The interpretation of dreams, *ibid.,* 179-549.

Freud, S., 1938c. Three contributions to the theory of sex, *ibid.,* 551-629.

Freud, S., 1938d. Wit and its relation to the unconscious, *ibid.,* 631-803.

Freud, S., 1950a. Humor, in *Collected papers, vol. V,* London, Hogarth. Pp. 215-221.

Freud, S., 1950b. Why war? *ibid.,* 273-279.

Fromm, E., 1941. *Escape from freedom,* New York, Rinehart.

Fromm, E., 1947. *Man for himself,* New York, Rinehart.

Friedman, I., 1955. Phenomenal, ideal, and projected conceptions of self, *J. abn. social Psychol.,* 51:611-615.

Fries, Margaret E., 1944. Psychosomatic relations between mother and infant, *Psychosom. Med.,* 6:159-162.

Fuller, J. L., 1946. Activity, heart rate, and pneumograms of normal dogs during excitement, *Anat. Record,* 96:94-95.

Fuller, J. L., 1948. Individual differences in the reactivity of dogs, *J. comp. physiol. Psychol.,* 41:339-347.

Fuller, J. L., and Gillum, E., 1950. A study of factors influencing performance of dogs on a delayed response test, *J. genet. Psychol.,* 76:241-252.

Funkenstein, D. H., 1955. The physiology of fear and anger, *Sci. American*, 192:74-81.

Garrett, H. E., 1946. A developmental theory of intelligence, *Am. Psychologist*, 1:372-378.

Gates, Georgina A., 1928. *The modern cat: her mind and manners*, New York, Macmillan.

Geldard, F. A., 1953. *The human senses*, New York, Wiley.

Gesell, A., Amatruda, Catherine S., Gastner, B. M., and Thompson, Helen, 1939. *Biographies of child development*, New York, Hoeber.

Gesell, A., with Ames, Louise, 1937. Early evidences of individuality in the human infant, *J. genet. Psychol.*, 47:339-361.

Gesell, A., and Ilg, Frances L., 1943. *Infant and child in the culture of today*, New York, Harper.

Gesell, A., and Ilg, Frances L., 1946. *The child from five to ten*, New York, Harper.

Gesell, A., and Thompson, Helen, 1929. Learning and growth in identical infant twins, *Genet. Psychol. Monographs*, 6:1-124.

Gesell, A., and Thompson, Helen, 1941. Twins T and C from infancy to adolescence, *Genet. Psychol. Monographs*, 24:3-121.

Ginsburg, B., and Allee, W. C., 1942. Some effects of conditioning on social dominance and subordination in inbred strains of mice, *Physiol. Zool.*, 15:585-606.

Glueck, S., and Glueck, Eleanor, 1950. *Unraveling juvenile delinquency*, New York, Commonwealth Fund.

Goldfarb, W., 1943. The effects of early institutional care on adolescent personality, *J. educ. Research*, 12:106-129.

Goldfarb, W., 1947. Variations in adolescent adjustment of institutionally-reared children, *Am. J. Orthopsychiat.*, 17:449-457.

Goldstein, K., 1935. *The organism*, New York, American Book Co.

Goldstein, K., 1944. The significance of psychological research in schizophrenia, in *Contemporary psychopathology*, ed. by S. Tomkins, Cambridge, Mass., Harvard University Press. Pp. 302-318.

Goldstein, K., and Scheerer, M., 1944. Abstract and concrete behavior: an experimental study with special tests, *Psychol. Monographs*, 53, No. 239.

Goodenough, Florence L., 1926. *Measurement of intelligence by drawings*, Yonkers, World Book.

Goodenough, Florence L., 1932. Expression of the emotion in a blind-deaf child, *J. abn. social Psychol.*, 27:328-333.

Gordon, K., 1943. The natural history and behavior of the Western chipmunk and the mantled ground squirrel, *Oregon State Monographs, Stud. Zool.*, No. 15.

Gorer, G., and Rickman, J., 1950. *The people of Great Russia*, New York, Chanticleer Press.

Gough, H. G., 1950. *Predicting success in graduate training: a progress report*, Berkeley, Calif., University of California Institute of Personality Assessment and Research. (Mimeograph.)

Gould, Rosalind, 1939. An experimental analysis of "level of aspiration," *Genet. Psychol. Monographs*, 21:3-115.

Greenacre, Phyllis, 1945. The biological economy of birth, *Psychoanalyt. Stud. Child*, 1:31-51.

Griffiths, W. J., and Stringer, W. F., 1952. The effects of intense stimulation experience during infancy on adult behavior in the rat, *J. comp. physiol. Psychol.*, 45:301-306.

Grinker, R. R., 1939. Hypothalamic functions in psychosomatic interrelations, *Psychosom. Med.*, 1:19-47.

Grosslight, J. H., and Child, I. L., 1947. Persistence as a function of previous experience of failure followed by success, *Am. J. Psychol.*, 60:378-387.

Grziwok, R., and Scodel, A., 1956. Some psychological correlates of humor preferences, *J. consult. Psychol.*, 20:42.

Guilford, J. P., 1948. The Guilford personality inventories, in *Encyclopedia of vocational guidance*, ed. by O. Kaplan, New York, Philosophical Library. Pp. 1007-1010.

Guilford, J. P., 1950. Creativity, *Am. Psychologist*, 5:444-454.

Guilford, J. P., and Guilford, R., 1934. An analysis of the factors in a typical test of introversion-extraversion, *J. abn. social Psychol.*, 28:377-399.

Guilford, J. P., and Zimmerman, W. S., 1947. Some AAF findings concerning aptitude factors, *Occupations*, 26:154-159.

Guthrie, E. R., 1938. *The psychology of human conflict*, New York, Harper.

Guthrie, E. R., and Horton, G. P., 1946. *Cats in a problem box*, New York, Rinehart.

Hall, C. S., 1934. Emotional behavior in the rat. I. Defecation and urination as measures of individual differences in emotionality, *J. comp. Psychol.*, 18:385-403.

Hall, C. S., 1951. The genetics of behavior, in *Handbook of experimental psychology*, ed. by S. S. Stevens, New York, Wiley. Pp. 304-329.

Hall, C. S., 1953a. A cognitive theory of dream symbols, *J. genet. Psychol.*, 48:169-186.

Hall, C. S., 1953b. A cognitive theory of dreams, *J. genet. Psychol.*, 49:273-282.

Hall, C. S., and Klein, S. J., 1942. Individual differences in aggressiveness in rats. *J. comp. Psychol.*, 33:371-383.

Hall, C. S., and Whiteman, P. H., 1951. The effects of infantile stimulation upon later emotional stability in the mouse, *J. comp. physiol. Psychol.*, 44:61-66.

Hanfmann, Eugenia, 1941. A study of personal patterns in an intellectual performance, *Character and Personality*, 9:315-325.

Hanfmann, Eugenia, and Kasanin, J., 1942. Conceptual thinking in schizophrenia, *Nervous mental Disease Monographs Ser.*, No. 67.

Harlow, H. F., 1949. The formation of learning sets, *Psychol. Rev.*, 56:51-65.

Harlow, H. F., Harlow, Margaret K., and Meyer, D. R., 1950. Learning motivated by a manipulation drive, *J. expertl. Psychol.*, 40:228-234.

Hathaway, S. R., and McKinley, J. C., 1943. *The Minnesota Multiphasic Personality Inventory*, Minneapolis, University of Minnesota Press.

Hayes, K. J., 1950. Vocalization and speech in chimpanzees, *Am. Psychologist*, 5:275-276 (abstract).

Hayes, Cathy, 1951. *The ape in our house*, New York, Harper.

Hebb, D. O., 1946a. Emotion in man and animal: an analysis of the intuitive process of recognition, *Psychol. Rev.*, 53:88-106.

Hebb, D. O., 1946b. On the nature of fear, *Psychol. Rev.*, 53:259-276.

Hebb, D. O., 1947. Spontaneous neurosis in chimpanzees: theoretical relations with clinical and experimental phenomena, *Psychosom. Med.*, 9:3-16.

Hebb, D. O., 1949a. Temperament in chimpanzees: I. Method of analysis, *J. comp. physiol. Psychol.*, 42:192-206.

Hebb, D. O., 1949b. *The organization of behavior*, New York, Wiley.

Heidbreder, Edna, 1930. Self-rating and preferences, *J. abn. social Psychol.*, 25:62-74.

Heidbreder, Edna, Bensley, Mary Louise, and Ivy, Margaret, 1948. The attainment of concepts: IV. Regularities and levels. *J. Psychol.*, 25:299-329.

Heston, J. C., 1948. A comparison of four masculinity-femininity scales, *Educ. psychol. Measmt.*, 8:375-388.

Hilgard, E. R., 1948. *Theories of learning*, New York, Appleton-Century-Crofts.

Hilgard, E. R., 1949. Human motives and the concept of the self, *Am. Psychologist*, 4:374-382.

Hill, D., 1950. Psychiatry, in *Electroencephalography*, ed. by D. Hill and G. Parr, New York, Macmillan. Pp. 319-364.

Holt, E. B., 1931. *Animal drive and the learning process*, New York, Holt.

Holtzman, W. H., and Sells, S. B., 1954. Prediction of flying success by clinical analysis of test protocols, *J. abn. social Psychol.*, 49:485-490.

Hooker, D., 1943. Reflex activities in the human foetus, in *Child behavior and development*, ed. by R. G. Barker, J. S. Kounin, and H. F. Wright, New York, McGraw-Hill. Pp. 17-28.

Hoppe, F., 1930. Erfolg und Miserfolg, *Psychol. Forsch.*, 14:1-62. (Abstracted in Lewin, 1935.)

Horney, Karen, 1937. *The neurotic personality of our time*, New York, Norton.

Horney, Karen, 1939. *New ways in psychoanalysis*, New York, Norton.

Horney, Karen, 1945. *Our inner conflicts*, New York, Norton.

Horowitz, E., 1935. Spatial localization of the self, *J. social Psychol.*, 6:379-387.

Hull, C. L., 1920. Quantitative aspects of the evolution of concepts, *Psychol. Monographs*, 28, No. 123.

Hull, C. L., 1943. *Principles of behavior*, New York, Appleton-Century-Crofts.

Hunt, J. McV., 1941. Effects of infantile feeding frustration upon adult hoarding behavior in the albino rat, *J. abn. social Psychol.*, 36:338-360.

Hunt, J. McV., Schlossberg, H., Solomon, R., and Stellar, E., 1947. Studies in the effects of infantile experience on adult behavior in rats. I. Effects of infantile feeding frustration on adult hoarding, *J. comp. physiol. Psychol.*, 40:291-304.

Irwin, F. W., 1953. Stated expectations as functions of probability and desirability of outcomes, *J. Personality*, 21:329-335.

Irwin, J. R., 1947. Galen on the temperaments, *J. gen. Psychol.*, 36:45-64.

Jackson, D. N., 1954. A further examination of the role of autism in a visual figure-ground relationship, *J. Psychol.*, 38:339-357.

James, W., 1890. *Principles of psychology*, New York, Holt.

James, W. T., 1941. Morphologic form and its relation to behavior, in Stockard, C., *Genetic and endocrine basis for differences in form and behavior*, Philadelphia, Wistar Institute.

James, W. T., 1949. Dominant and submissive behavior in puppies as indicated by food-intake, *J. genet. Psychol.*, 75:33-43.

James, W. T., 1951. Social organization among dogs of different temperaments, terriers and beagles, reared together, *J. comp. physiol. Psychol.*, 44:71-77.

Jaynes, J., 1956. Imprinting: the interaction of learned and innate behavior: I. Development and generalization, *J. comp. physiol. Psychol.*, 49:201-206.

Jenkins, R. L., and Pacella, B. L., 1943. Electroencephalographic studies of delinquent boys, *Am. J. Orthopsychiat.*, 13:107-120.

Jones, H. E., 1930. The galvanic skin reflex in infancy, *Child Develop.*, 1:106-110.

Jones, H. E., 1943. *Development in adolescence*, New York, Appleton-Century.

Jones, H. E., 1949. *Motor performance and growth*, Berkeley, Calif., University of California Press.

Jones, H. E., and Jones, Mary C., 1928. Fear, *Childhood Educ.*, 5:136-143.

Jost, H., and Sontag, L. W., 1944. The genetic factor in autonomic nervous system function, *Psychosom. Med.*, 6:308-310.

Jung, C. G., 1923. *Psychological types*, London, Routledge and Kegan Paul.

Jung, C. G., 1933. *Modern man in search of a soul*, London, Kegan Paul.

Kahn, K. W., 1951. The effect of severe defeat at various age levels on the aggressive behavior of mice, *J. genet. Psychol.*, 79:117-130.

Kardiner, A., 1939. *The individual and his society*, New York, Columbia Univ. Press.

Kardiner, A., 1945. (With collaboration of R. Linton, Cora DuBois, and J. West) *The psychological frontiers of society*, New York, Columbia Univ. Press.

Kardiner, A., and Ovesey, L., 1951. *The mark of oppression: a psychosocial study of the American Negro*, New York, Norton.

Kelemen, G., 1949. Structure and performance in animal language, *Arch. Otolaryng.*, 50:740-744.

Kelly, E. L., and Fiske, D. W., 1951. *The prediction of performance in clinical psychology*, Ann Arbor, Univ. of Michigan Press.

Kellogg, W. N., and Kellogg, L. A., 1933. *The ape and the child*, New York, McGraw-Hill.

Kempf, E. J., 1918. The autonomic functions and the personality, *Nerv. ment. Dis. Monographs*, No. 28.

Kennard, Margaret A., 1949. Inheritance of electroencephalogram patterns in children with behavior disorders, *Psychosom. Med.*, 11:151-157.

Kenny, D. T., 1955. The contingency of humor appreciation on the stimulus-confirmation of joke-ending expectations, *J. abn. social Psychol.*, 51:644-648.

Kinder, Elaine F., 1947. Development of personality characteristics, *Am. Psychologist*, 2:267 (abstract).

Kinsey, A. C., Pomeroy, W. B., and Martine, C. E., 1948. *Sexual behavior in the human male*, Philadelphia, Saunders.

Klein, G. S., 1951. The personal world through perception, 328-355, in Blake, R. R., and Ramsey, G. V. (eds.), *Perception: an approach to personality*, New York, Ronald.

Klein, G. S., and Schlessinger, H., 1949. Where is the perceiver in perceptual theory? *J. Personality*, 18:32-47.

Klein, G. S., Schlessinger, H., and Meister, D. E., 1951. The effect of personal values on perception: an experimental critique, *Psychol. Rev.*, **58**:96-112.

Klineberg, O., 1940. *Social psychology*, New York, Holt.

Klopfer, B., Ainsworth, Mary D., Klopfer, W. G., and Holt, R. R., 1954. *Developments in the Rorschach technique, vol. I*, Yonkers, World Book.

Koffka, K., 1924. *The growth of the mind*, New York, Harcourt, Brace.

Köhler, W., 1918. Nachweis einfacher Strukturfunktionen beim Schimpansen und beim Haushuhn, *Abh. königl. preuss. Akad. Wiss., Phys. Math. Klasse*, Nr. 2, 1-101. (Condensed transl. in *Source book of gestalt psychology*, ed. by W. D. Ellis, New York, Harcourt, Brace, 1938. Pp. 217-227.)

Köhler, W., 1925. *The mentality of apes*, New York, Harcourt, Brace.

Köhler, W., 1940. *Dynamics in psychology*, New York, Liveright.

Köhler, W., and Wallach, H., 1944. Figural after-effects: an investigation of visual processes, *Proc. Am. Phil. Soc.*, **88**:269-357.

Kohn, N., 1948. Kuder Preference Record masculinity-femininity scale, *J. social Psychol.*, **27**:127-128.

Korzybski, A., 1933. *Science and sanity*, Lakeville, Conn., International Non-Aristotelian Library.

Koster, R., 1943. Hormone factors in male behavior of the female rat, *Endocrinology*, **33**:337-348.

Krech, D., 1949. Notes toward a psychological theory, *J. Personality*, **18**:66-87.

Krechevsky, I., 1932. "Hypotheses" in rats, *Psychol. Rev.*, **39**:516-532.

Kretschmer, E., 1925. *Physique and character*, London, Kegan Paul.

Kriedt, P. H., 1949. Vocational interests of psychologists, *J. appl. Psychol.*, **33**:482-488.

Kuder, G. F., 1946. *Manual to the Kuder Preference Record*, Chicago, Science Research Associates.

Lacey, J. I., 1950. Individual differences in somatic response patterns, *J. comp. physiol. Psychol.*, **43**:338-350.

Laird, D. A., 1925. Detecting abnormal behavior, *J. abn. social Psychol.*, **20**:128-141.

Landis, C., 1934. The expressions of emotion, in *Handbook of general experimental psychology*, ed. by C. Murchison, Worcester, Mass., Clark University Press. Pp. 312-351.

Langer, Suzanne, 1942. *Philosophy in a new key*, Cambridge, Mass., Harvard University Press.

Lashley, K. S., 1947. Structural relation in the nervous system in relation to behavior, *Psychol. Rev.*, **54**:325-334.

Lashley, K. S., 1951. The problem of serial order in behavior, in *Cerebral mechanisms in behavior*, ed. by L. A. Jeffress, New York, Wiley. Pp. 112-146.

Lashley, K. S., Chow, K. L., and Semmes, Josephine, 1951. An examination of the electrical field theory of cerebral integration, *Psychol. Rev.*, 58:123-136.

Lecky, P., 1945. *Self-consistency; a theory of personality*, New York, Island Press.

Leeper, R., 1935. Study of a neglected portion of the field of learning—the development of sensory organization, *J. genet. Psychol.*, 46:41-75.

Leeper, R., 1948. A motivational theory of emotion to replace "emotion as a disorganized response," *Psychol. Rev.*, 55:5-21.

Levine, J. M., and Murphy, G., 1943. The learning and forgetting of controversial material, *J. abn. social Psychol.*, 38:507-517.

Levy, D., 1934. Experiments on the sucking reflex and social behavior of dogs, *Am. J. Orthpsychiat.*, 4:203-224.

Levy, D., 1943. *Maternal overprotection*, New York, Columbia University Press.

Lewin, K., 1935. *Dynamic theory of personality*, New York, McGraw-Hill.

Lewin, K., 1948. *Resolving social conflicts*, New York, Harper.

Licklider, L. L., and Licklider, J. C. R., 1950. Observations on the hoarding behavior of rats, *J. comp. physiol. Psychol.*, 43:129-134.

Loomis, S. D., and Green, A. W., 1947. The pattern of conflict in a typical state university, *J. abn. social Psychol.*, 42:342-355.

Lorenz, K., 1937. The companion in the bird's world, *Auk*, 54:245-273.

Lorenz, K., 1952. *King Solomon's Ring*, New York, Crowell.

Lovell, Constance, 1945. A study of the factor structure of thirteen personality variables, *Educ. psychol. Measmt.*, 5:335-350.

Luchins, A. S., 1951. On recent usage of the Einstellungs-effect as a test of rigidity, *J. consult. Psychol.*, 4:89-94.

Luria, A. R., 1932. *The nature of human conflicts*, New York, Liveright.

Lurie, L. A., 1953. The role of endocrine factors in delinquency, *Am. J. Orthopsychiat.*, 33:21-30.

Machover, Karen, 1949. *Personality projection in the drawing of the human figure*, Springfield, Ill., Thomas.

Mahler, Margaret S., 1952. On child psychosis and schizophrenia: autistic and symbiotic infantile psychoses, *Psychoanal. Stud. Child*, 7:286-305.

Maier, N. R. F., 1949. *Frustration*, New York, McGraw-Hill.

Marks, R. W., 1951. The effect of probability, desirability, and "privilege" on the stated expectations of children, *J. Personality,* 19:332-351.

Martins, T., and Valle, J. R., 1948. Hormonal regulation of the micturitional behavior of the dog, *J. comp. physiol. Psychol.,* 41:301-311.

Maslow, A. H., 1936. The role of dominance in the social and sexual behavior of infrahuman primates. III. A theory of sexual behavior of infrahuman primates, *J. genet. Psychol.,* 48:310-338.

Maslow, A. H., 1939. Dominance, personality, and social behavior in women, *J. social Psychol.,* 10:3-39.

Maslow, A. H., 1943. A theory of human motivation, *Psychol. Rev.,* 50:370-396.

Maslow, A. H., 1948. Cognition of the particular and the general, *Psychol. Rev.,* 55:22-40.

Masserman, J. H., 1943. *Behavior and neurosis,* Chicago, University of Chicago Press.

May, R., 1950. *The meaning of anxiety,* New York, Ronald.

McClelland, D. C., Atkinson, J. W., Clark, R. A., and Lowell, E. L., 1953. *The achievement motive,* New York, Appleton-Century-Crofts.

McCulloch, W. S., and Pitts, W., 1947. How we know universals, *Bull. math. Biophys.,* 9:127-147.

McKelvey, R. K., and Marx, M. H., 1951. Effects of infantile food and water deprivation on adult hoarding in the rat, *J. comp. physiol. Psychol.,* 44:423-430.

Mead, Margaret, 1947. On the implications for anthropology of the Gessell-Ilg approach to maturation, *Am. Anthrop.,* 49:69-77.

Mead, Margaret, 1949. *Male and female,* New York, Morrow.

Miller, N. E., 1944. Experimental studies of conflict, in *Personality and the behavior disorders,* ed. by J. McV. Hunt, New York, Ronald. Pp. 431-465.

Miller, N. E., 1948. Theory and experiment relating psychoanalytic displacement to stimulus response generalization, *J. abn. social Psychol.,* 43:155-178.

Miller, N. E., 1951. Learnable drives and rewards, in *Handbook of experimental psychology,* ed. by S. S. Stevens, New York, Wiley. Pp. 435-472.

Miller, N. E., and Dollard, J., 1941. *Social learning and imitation,* New Haven, Yale University Press.

Montagu, A., 1953. *The meaning of love,* New York, Julian Press.

Moreno, J. F., 1946. *Psychodrama,* New York, Beacon House.

Morgan, C. L., 1901. *Introduction to comparative psychology,* New York, Scribner.

Morgan, C. T., and Stellar, E., 1950. *Physiological psychology,* New York, McGraw-Hill.

Moustakas, C. E., 1953. *Children in play therapy*, New York, McGraw-Hill.

Mowrer, O. H., 1939. A stimulus-response analysis of anxiety and its role as a reinforcing agent, *Psychol. Rev.*, **46**:553-565.

Mowrer, O. H., 1941. Animal studies in the genesis of personality, *Trans. N. Y. Acad. Sci.*, Series II, **3**:1-4.

Mowrer, O. H., 1946. The law of effect and ego psychology, *Psychol. Rev.*, **53**:321-334.

Mowrer, O. H., 1947. On the dual nature of learning—a reinterpretation of "conditioning" and "problem solving," *Harv. Educ. Rev.*, **17**:102-148. (Also in Mowrer, 1950.)

Mowrer, O. H., 1950. *Learning theory and personality dynamics*, New York, Ronald.

Murphy, G., 1947. *Personality: a bio-social approach*, New York, Harper.

Murray, H. A., et al., 1938. *Explorations in personality*, New York, Oxford University Press.

Murray, H. A., and Staff of the Harvard Psychological Clinic, 1943. *Thematic Apperception Test*, Cambridge, Mass., Harvard University Press.

Neilon, Patricia, 1948. Shirley's babies after 15 years, *J. genet. Psychol.*, **73**:175-186.

Neumann, J. von, 1951. The general analogical theory of automata, in *Cerebral mechanisms in behavior*, ed. by L. A. Jeffress, New York, Wiley. Pp. 1-41.

Newcomb, T. M., 1943. *Personality and social change*, New York, Dryden.

Newcomb, T. M., 1950. *Social psychology*, New York, Dryden.

Nielsen, J. M., 1946. *Agnosia, apraxia, aphasia*, New York, Hoeber.

Nielsen, J. M., 1951. Discussant, in *Cerebral mechanisms in behavior*, ed. by L. A. Jeffress, New York, Wiley. Pp. 183-191.

Nissen, H. W., 1931. A field study of the chimpanzee, *Comp. Psychol. Monographs*, 8, No. 36.

Nissen, H. W., 1951. Social behavior in primates, in *Comparative psychology*, 3rd edition, ed. by C. P. Stone, Englewood Cliffs, N. J., Prentice-Hall. Pp. 423-457.

Norman, R. D., 1953. The interrelationships among acceptance-rejection, self-other identity, insight into self, and realistic perception of others, *J. social Psychol.*, **37**:205-235.

Oppenheimer, R., 1956. Analogy in science, *Am. Psychologist*, **11**:127-135.

Orlansky, H., 1949. Infant care and personality, *Psychol. Bull.*, **46**:1-48.

Osgood, C. E., and Suci, G. J., 1955. Factor analysis of meaning, *J. exptl. Psychol.*, **50**:325-338.

O.S.S. Assessment Staff, 1948. *The assessment of men,* New York, Rinehart.

Ovsiankina, M., 1928. Die Wideraufnahme unterbrochener Handlungen, *Psychol. Forsch.,* 11:302-372. (Abstracted in Lewin, 1935, and Escalona, 1943.)

Pastore, N., 1949. Need as a determinant of perception, *J. Psychol.,* 28:457-475.

Pavlov, I., 1927. *Conditioned reflexes,* London, Oxford University Press.

Phillips, E. L., 1951. Attitudes toward self and others: a brief questionnaire report, *J. consult. Psychol.,* 15:79-81.

Piaget, J., 1929. *The child's conception of the world,* New York, Harcourt, Brace.

Piaget, J., 1932. *The language and thought of the child,* New York, Harcourt, Brace.

Poincaré, H., 1915. The foundations of science, Lancaster, Pa., Science Press.

Porteus, S. D., 1924. *Guide to the Porteus Maze Test,* Vineland, N. J., The Training School.

Porteus, S. D., and Peters, H. N., 1947. Maze test validation and psychosurgery, *Genet. Psychol. Monographs,* 36:3-86.

Postman, L., 1951. Toward a general theory of cognition, in *Social psychology at the crossroads,* ed. by J. H. Rohrer and M. Sherif, New York, Harper. Pp. 242-272.

Postman, L., and Bruner, J. S., 1948. Perception under stress, *Psychol. Rev.,* 55:314-323.

Postman, L., Bruner, J. S., and McGinnies, E., 1948. Personal values as selective factors in perception, *J. abn. social Psychol.,* 43:142-154.

Pratt, K. C., Nelson, A. C., and Sun, K. H., 1930. The behavior of the newborn infant, *Ohio State Univ. Contrib. Psychol.,* No. 10.

Rabban, M., 1950. Sex-role identification in young children in two diverse social groups, *Genet. Psychol. Monographs,* 42:81-158.

Raimy, V. C., 1948. Self-reference in counseling interviews, *J. consult. Psychol.,* 12:153-163.

Rapaport, D., 1945. *Diagnostic psychological testing,* Chicago, Year Book Publishers.

Rapaport, D., 1951. *Organization and pathology of thought,* New York, Columbia University Press.

Redl, F., and Wineman, D., 1951. *Children who hate,* Glencoe, Ill., Free Press.

Redlich, F. C., Levine, J., and Sohler, T. P., 1951. A mirth response test, *Am. J. Orthopsychiat.,* 21:717-733.

Reich, W., 1949. *Character analysis,* New York, Orgone Institute.

Ribble, Margaret, 1943. *The rights of infants,* New York, Columbia University Press.

Ribble, Margaret, 1944. Infantile experience in relation to personality development, in *Personality and the behavior disorders*, ed. by J. McV. Hunt, New York, Ronald. Pp. 621-651.

Riesen, A. H., 1947. The development of visual perception in man and the chimpanzee, *Science,* 106:107-108.

Riess, B. F., 1946. "Freezing" behavior in rats and its social causation, *J. social Psychol.,* 24:249-251.

Riggs, Margaret M., 1952. An investigation of the nature and generality of three new personality variables. I. The sentence test; II. Related behavior. *J. Personality,* 20:322-344; 21:411-440.

Rock, I., and Fleck, F. S., 1950. A re-examination of the effect of monetary reward and punishment in figure-ground perception, *J. exptl. Psychol.,* 40:766-776.

Roe, Anne, 1946. Painting and personality, *Rorsch. Research Exch.,* 10:86-100.

Roe, Anne, 1951a. A psychological study of eminent biologists, *Psychol. Monographs,* 65, No. 331.

Roe, Anne, 1951b. A psychological study of physical scientists, *Genet. Psychol. Monographs,* 43:121-235.

Roe, Anne, 1953. A psychological study of eminent psychologists and anthropologists, and a comparison with biological and physical scientists, *Psychol. Monographs,* 67, No. 352.

Rogers, C. R., 1942. *Counseling and psychotherapy,* Boston, Houghton Mifflin.

Rogers, C. R., 1951a. *Client-centered therapy,* Boston, Houghton Mifflin.

Rogers, C. R., 1951b. Perceptual reorganization in client-centered therapy, in *Perception: an approach to personality,* ed. by R. R. Blake and G. V. Ramsey, New York, Ronald. Pp. 307-327.

Rogers, C. R., and Dymond, Rosalind, 1954. *Psychotherapy and Personality change,* Chicago, University of Chicago Press.

Roheim, G., 1933. Psychoanalysis and anthropology, in *Psychoanalysis today,* ed. by S. Lorand, New York, Covici.

Rokeach, M., 1951a. A method for studying individual differences in "narrowmindedness," *J. Personality,* 20:219-233.

Rokeach, M., 1951b. "Narrowmindedness" and personality, *J. Personality,* 20:234-251.

Rorschach, H., 1942. *Psychodiagnostics* (Engl. transl.), Bern, Switzerland, Huber.

Rosenthal, B. G., and Levi, J. H., 1950. Value, need, and attitude towards money as determinants of perception, *Am. Psychologist,* 5:213 (abstract).

Rosenzweig, S., 1945. The picture-association method and its application in a study of reactions to frustration, *J. Personality,* 14:3-23.

Rotter, J. B., 1942. Level of aspiration as a method in the study of personality. II. Development and evaluation of a controlled method, *J. exptl. Psychol.*, 31:410-422.

Rotter, J. B., and Willerman, B., 1947. The incomplete sentences test as a method of studying personality, *J. consult. Psychol.*, 11:43-48.

Rubin, E., 1921. *Visuell wahrgenommene Figuren*, Copenhagen, Gyldendalska Boghandel.

Sarbin, T. R., and Berdie, R. F., 1940. Relation of measured interests to the Allport-Vernon Study of Values, *J. appl. Psychol.*, 24:287-296.

Saul, L. J., 1947. *Emotional maturity*, Philadelphia, Lippincott.

Schafer, R., and Murphy, G., 1943. The role of autism in a visual figure-ground relationship, *J. exptl. Psychol.*, 3:335-343.

Schilder, P., 1935. *The image and appearance of the human body*, London, Kegan Paul.

Schjelderup-Ebbe, T., 1935. Social behavior of birds, in *Handbook of social psychology*, ed. by C. Murchison, Worcester, Mass., Clark University Press. Pp. 947-972.

Schlossberg, H., 1937. The relationship between success and the laws of conditioning, *Psychol. Rev.*, 44:379-394.

Schneidman, E. S., 1947. The make-a-picture-story (MAPS) personality test: a preliminary report, *J. consult. Psychol.*, 11:315-325.

Scott, J. P., 1947. Emotional behavior of fighting mice caused by conflict between weak stimulatory and weak inhibitory training, *J. comp. physiol. Psychol.*, 40:275-282.

Scott, J. P., and Marston, Mary-'Vesta, 1950. Critical periods affecting the development of normal and maladjustive behavior of puppies, *J. genet. Psychol.*, 77:25-60.

Sears, Pauline S., 1940. Level of aspiration in academically successful and unsuccessful children, *J. abn. social Psychol.*, 35:498-536.

Sears, R. R., and Wise, G. W., 1950. Relation of cup feeding in infancy to thumb-sucking and the oral drive, *Am. J. Orthopsychiat.*, 20:123-138.

Seashore, H. G., 1947. Validation of the Study of Values for two vocational groups at the college level, *Educ. psychol. Measmt.*, 7:757-764.

Seltzer, C. C., 1945. The relationship between the masculine component and personality, *Am. J. phys. Anthrop.*, 3:33-47.

Seltzer, C. C., 1950. A comparative study of the morphological characteristics of delinquents and non-delinquents, in S. and Eleanor Glueck, *Unraveling Juvenile Delinquency*, New York, Commonwealth Fund. Pp. 307-350.

Selye, H., 1956. *The stress of life*, New York, McGraw-Hill.

Selz, O., 1922. *Psychologie des Irrtums und des produktiven Denkens*, Bonn, Friedrich Cohen.

Senden, M. von, 1932. *Raum- und Gestaltauffassung bei operierten Blindgeborenen vor und nach der Operation*, Leipzig, Barth.

Seward, J. P., 1953. How are motives learned? *Psychol. Rev.*, 60:99-110.

Sheerer, Eliz. T., 1949. An analysis of the relationship between acceptance of and respect for self and acceptance of and respect for others in ten counseling cases, *J. consult. Psychol.*, 13:169-175.

Sheldon, W. H., 1940. *The varieties of human physique*, New York, Harper.

Sheldon, W. H., 1942. *The varieties of temperament*, New York, Harper.

Sheldon, W. H., 1944. Constitutional factors in personality, in *Personality and the behavior disorders*, ed. by J. McV. Hunt, New York, Ronald. Pp. 526-549.

Sheldon, W. H., 1949. *Varieties of delinquent youth*, New York, Harper.

Shepler, B. F., 1951. A comparison of masculinity-femininity measures, *J. consult. Psychol.*, 15:484-486.

Sherif, M., 1936. *The psychology of social norms*, New York, Harper.

Sherif, M., 1948. *An outline of social psychology*, New York, Harper.

Sherrington, C. S., 1906. *The integrative action of the nervous system*, New Haven, Yale University Press.

Shirley, Mary, 1931. *The first two years, vol. I. Postural and locomotor development*, Minneapolis, University of Minnesota Press.

Shirley, Mary, 1933. *The first two years, vol. III. Personality manifestations*, Minneapolis, University of Minnesota Press.

Shirley, Mary, 1939. A behavior syndrome characterizing prematurely born children, *Child Develop.*, 10:115-128.

Shoben, E. J., 1949. Psychotherapy as a problem in learning theory, *Psychol. Bull.*, 46:366-392.

Skinner, B. F., 1938. *The behavior of organisms*, New York, Appleton-Century.

Skinner, B. F., 1953. *Science and behavior*, New York, Macmillan.

Smith, M. B., 1950. Review of "The authoritarian personality," *J. abn. social Psychol.*, 45:775-779.

Sollenberger, R. T., 1940. Some relationships between the urinary excretion of male hormone by maturing boys and their expressed interests and attitudes, *J. Psychol.*, 9:179-190.

Solomon, R. L., and Howes, D. H., 1951. Word frequency, personal values, and visual duration thresholds, *Psychol. Rev.*, 58:256-270.

Spearman, C. E., 1904. "Generalized intelligence" objectively determined and measured, *Am. J. Psychol.*, 15:201-292.

Spearman, C. E., 1927. *The abilities of man*, New York, Macmillan.

Sperry, R. W., and Miner, Nancy, 1955. Pattern perception following insertion of mica plates into visual cortex, *J. comp. physiol. Psychol.* 48:463-469.

Spitz, R., 1945. Hospitalism, *Psychoanalyt. Stud. Child,* 1:53-74.

Spitz, R., with Wolf, Rose, 1946. The smiling response, *Genet. Psychol. Monographs,* 34:57-125.

Spranger, E., 1928. *Types of men,* Halle, Niemyer.

Stagner, R., 1948. *Psychology of personality* (rev. ed.), New York, McGraw-Hill.

Stagner, R., and Karwoski, T. F., 1952. *Psychology,* New York, McGraw-Hill.

Stanley, W. C., and Jaynes, J., 1949. The function of the frontal cortex, *Psychol. Rev.,* 56:18-32.

Stephenson, W., 1935. Correlating persons instead of tests, *Character and Personality,* 4:17-24.

Stephenson, W., 1953. *The study of behavior,* Chicago, University of Chicago Press.

Stewart, Ann, 1953. Excessive crying in infants—a family disease, in *Sixth conference on problems of infancy and childhood,* ed. by M. Senn, New York, Josiah Macy, Jr. Foundation. Pp. 138-160.

Stockard, C., 1931. *The physical basis of personality,* New York, Norton.

Stockard, C., 1941. *Genetic and endocrine basis for differences in form and behavior,* Philadelphia, Wistar Institute.

Stoke, S. M., 1950. An inquiry into the concept of identification, *J. genet. Psychol.,* 76:163-189.

Strong, E. K., 1943. *Vocational interests of men and women,* Palo Alto, Stanford University Press.

Sullivan, H. S., 1953. *The interpersonal theory of psychiatry,* New York, Norton.

Sumner, F. C., and Johnson, E. E., 1949. Sex differences in level of aspiration and in self-estimates of performance in a classroom situation, *J. Psychol.* 27:483-490.

Super, D. E., 1949. *Appraising vocational fitness,* New York, Harper.

Symonds, P., 1946. *The dynamics of human adjustment,* New York, Appleton-Century-Crofts.

Taylor, Janet A., 1953. A personality scale of manifest anxiety, *J. abn. social Psychol.,* 48:285-290.

Taylor, C., and Combs, A., 1952. Self-acceptance and adjustment, *J. consult. Psychol.,* 16:89-91.

Terman, L. M., 1916. *The measurement of intelligence,* Boston, Houghton Mifflin.

Terman, L. M., and Miles, Catherine C., 1936. *Sex and personality,* New York, McGraw-Hill.

Thorndike, E. L., 1911. *Animal intelligence,* New York, Macmillan.

Thorndike, E. L., 1932. *Fundamentals of learning,* New York, Teachers College, Columbia University.

Thorndike, E. L., 1935. *Psychology of wants, interests, and attitudes,* New York, Appleton-Century.

Thorndike, E. L., 1940. *Human nature and the social order,* New York, Macmillan.

Thurstone, L. L., 1931. A multiple factor study of vocational interests, *Personnel J.,* 10:198-205.

Thurstone, L. L., 1938. Primary mental abilities, *Psychometric Monographs,* No. 1.

Thurstone, L. L., 1947. *Multiple factor analysis,* Chicago, University of Chicago Press.

Thurstone, L. L., 1951. The dimensions of temperament, *Psychometrika,* 16:11-20.

Thurstone, L. L., and Thurstone, Thelma G., 1930. A neurotic inventory, *J. social Psychol.,* 1:3-30.

Thurstone, L. L., and Thurstone, Thelma G., 1946. *Tests of primary mental abilities for ages 5 and 6.* Chicago, Science Research Associates.

Tinbergen, N., 1951. *The study of instinct,* Oxford, Clarendon Press.

Tolman, E. C., 1932. *Purposive behavior in animals and men,* New York, Appleton-Century.

Tolman, E. C., 1948. Cognitive maps of rats and men, *Psychol. Rev.,* 55:189-208.

Tolman, E. C., 1949. There is more than one kind of learning, *Psychol. Rev.,* 56:144-155.

Triggs, F. O., 1947. A study of the relationship of measured interests to measured mechanical aptitudes, personality, and vocabulary, *Am. Psychologist,* 2:296 (abstract).

Tyler, F. T., 1951. A factorial analysis of fifteen MMPI scales, *J. consult. Psychol.,* 15:451-456.

Vigotsky, I. S., 1934. Thought in schizophrenia, *Arch. Neurol. Psychiat.,* 31:1063-1077.

Walter, W. G., 1953. *The living brain,* New York, Norton.

Washburn Ruth W., 1929. A study of the smiling and laughing of infants in the first year of life, *Genet. Psychol. Monographs,* 6:397-539.

Watson, J. B., 1924. *Psychology from the standpoint of a behaviorist,* Philadelphia, Lippincott.

Watson, J. B., and Rayner, Rosalie, 1920. Conditioned emotional reactions, *J. exptl. Psychol.,* 3:1-14.

Wechsler, D., 1941. *The measurement of adult intelligence,* Baltimore, Williams & Wilkins.

Wechsler, D., 1950. Cognitive, conative, and nonintellective intelligence, *Am. Psychologist*, **5**:78-83.

Weiss, P., 1951. Discussant, in *Cerebral mechanisms in behavior*, ed. by L. A. Jeffress, New York, Wiley. Pp. 72-77.

Wells, F. L., 1947. Verbal facility: positive and negative associations, *J. Psychol.*, **23**:3-14.

Wenger, M. A., 1938. Some relationships between muscular processes and personality and their factorial analysis, *Child Develop.*, **9**:261-276.

Wenger, M. A., 1941. The measurement of individual differences in autonomic balance, *Psychosom. Med.*, **3**:427-434.

Wenger, M. A., 1947. Preliminary study of the significance of measures of autonomic balance, *Psychosom. Med.*, **9**:301-309.

Wenger, M. A., and Wellington, Margaret, 1943. The measurement of autonomic balance in children: method and normative data, *Psychosom. Med.*, **5**:241-253.

Werner, H., 1940. *The comparative psychology of mental development*, New York, Harper.

Wertheimer, M., 1912. Experimentelle Studien über das Sehen von Bewegungen, *Z. Psychol.*, **61**:161-265.

Wertheimer, M., 1923. Untersuchungen zur Lehre von der Gestalt, II. *Psychol. Forsch.*, **4**:301-350. (Condensed transl. in *Source book of gestalt psychology*, ed. by W. D. Ellis, New York, Harcourt, Brace, 1938. Pp. 274-282.)

Wertheimer, M., 1945. *Productive thinking*, New York, Harper.

Wheeler, W. M., Little, K. B., and Lehner, G. F. J., 1951. The internal structure of the MMPI, *J. consult. Psychol.*, **15**:134-141.

Whiting, J. W. M., 1954. The cross-cultural method, in *Handbook of social psychology*, ed. by G. Lindzey, Cambridge, Mass., Addison-Wesley. Pp. 523-531.

Whiting, J. W. M., and Child, I. L., 1953. *Child training and personality*, New Haven, Yale University Press.

Whitney, L. F., 1947. *How to breed dogs*, New York, Orange Judd.

Wiener, N., 1948. *Cybernetics*, New York, Wiley.

Wilson, R. C., Guilford, J. P., and Christensen, P. R., 1953. The measurement of individual differences in originality, *Psychol. Bull.*, **50**:362-370.

Witkin, H. A., Lewis, Helen B., Hertzman, M., Machover, Karen, Meissner, P., and Wapner, S., 1954. *Personality through perception: an experimental and clinical study*, New York, Harper.

Wolf, A., 1943. The dynamics of the selective inhibition of specific functions in neurosis: a preliminary report, *Psychsom. Med.*, **5**:27-38.

Wolfe, J. B., 1936. Effectiveness of token rewards for chimpanzees, *Comp. Psychol. Monographs*, **13**, No. 60.

Wolff, W., 1947. *The personality of the preschool child*, New York, Grune and Stratton.

Woodcock, Louise P., 1941. *Life and ways of the two-year-old*, New York, Dutton.

Woodworth, R. S., 1906. Imageless thought, *J. Phil. Psychol. sci. Meth.*, 3:701-708.

Wright, J. C., 1944. *A study of high school students' insight into their problems and resources*, unpublished Master's thesis, Ohio State University. (Cited by Robinson, F. P., *Principles and procedures in student counseling*, New York, Harper, 1950.

Wulf, F., 1922. Ueber die Veränderung der Vorstellungen (Gedächtnis und Gestalt), *Psychol. Forsch.*, 1:333-373. (Condensed transl. in *Source book of gestalt psychology*, ed. by W. D. Ellis, New York, Harcourt, Brace, 1938. Pp. 136-148.)

Yarnold, J. K., and Berkeley, M. H., 1954. An analysis of the Cattell-Luborsky humor test into homogeneous scales, *J. abn. social Psychol.*, 49:543-546.

Yeakel, E. H., and Rhoades, R. P., 1941. Comparison of body and endocrine gland weights of emotional and non-emotional rats, *Endocrinology*, 28:337-340.

Yerkes, R. M., 1943. *Chimpanzees*, New Haven, Yale University Press.

Yerkes, R. M., and Yerkes, Ada W., 1935. Social behavior in infrahuman primates, in *Handbook of social psychology*, ed. by C. Murchison, Worcester, Clark University Press. Pp. 973-1033.

Yerkes, R. M., and Yerkes, Ada W., 1936. Nature and conditions of avoidance (fear) response in the chimpanzees, *J. comp. Psychol.*, 21:53-66.

Young, P. T., 1936. *Motivation of behavior*, New York, Wiley.

Young, P. T., 1949. Emotion as disorganized response—a reply to Professor Leeper, *Psychol. Rev.* 56:184-191.

Zeigarnik, B., 1927. Ueber das Behalten erledigter und unerledigter Handlungen, *Psychol. Forsch.*, 9:1-85. (Condensed transl. in *Source book of gestalt psychology*, ed. by W. D. Ellis, New York, Harcourt, Brace, 1938. Pp. 300-314.)

Zuk, G. H., 1956. *The plasticity of physique*, Paper read at Western Psychol. Assoc., San Francisco, March 1956.

Index of Names

Abraham, K., 213
Ach, N., 338f.
Adcock, C., 143
Adler, A., 197, 232, 258f., 266, 268, 290f.
Adorno, T. W., 349
Adrian, E. D., 118
Aldrich, C. A., 99
Alexander, F., 197, 217, 260
Allee, W. C., 31, 36
Allport, F., 311
Allport, G. W., 2, 95, 161, 164, 192, 198, 270, 297, 305, 342, 424
Ames, L., 186
Ansbacher, H. L., 258
Arnheim, R., 352
Asch, S., 253, 353, 424
Ashby, W. R., 360, 362, 365
Atkinson, J. W., 284

Baas, M. L., 307
Balinsky, B., 327
Balint, M., 100
Bard, P., 66f., 398
Barker, R. G., 224, 227
Barron, F., 352, 385, 419
Bartlett, F. C., 340-342
Bayley, N., 99f., 154
Beach, F. A., 18, 49
Beck, L., 375
Beck, S. J., 383
Beeman, E. A., 32
Bensley, M. L., 364
Berdie, R. F., 305
Berkeley, M. H., 389
Bernard, C., 12
Bernreuter, R. G., 160f., 163
Binet, A., 322
Blos, P., 247
Blum, G. S., 379
Bonin, G. von, 118

Bousefield, W. A., 399
Bowlby, J., 56
Brain, W. R., 356
Bridges, K. M. B., 95
Bronfenbrenner, U., 385
Bruner, J. S., 344f., 349
Buck, J. N., 239
Bugental, J. F. T., 256
Bühler, C., 379

Cannon, W. B., 11, 29, 132, 149
Cantarow, A., 319
Carmichael, L., 13
Carter, L. F., 344
Cattell, R. B., 151, 163-171, 322, 379, 389
Chein, I., 347
Child, C. M., 25
Child, I. L., 109, 143-145, 194, 200, 202, 220, 250
Chow, K. L., 357
Christensen, P. R., 329
Christie, R., 350
Clark, K. B., 271
Clark, M. K., 271
Cohen, L. D., 281
Combs, A., 277
Cook, S. W., 46f.
Cooley, C. H., 252
Craik, K. J. W., 118, 357-360, 365

Dante Alighieri, 384
Darwin, C., 94
Davis, A., 202
Dembo, T., 224, 227
Dempsey, E. W., 12
Dennis, W., 370, 372
Diamond, S., 20, 45, 193, 245, 307, 313, 401
Doll, E. A., 208
Dollard, J., 215, 249, 297, 400

451